Heaven's Purge

Heaven's Purge

Purgatory in Late Antiquity

ISABEL MOREIRA

UNIVERSITY PRESS

Oxford University Press is a department of the University of Oxford.
It furthers the University's objective of excellence in research, scholarship,
and education by publishing worldwide.

Oxford   New York
Auckland   Cape Town   Dar es Salaam   Hong Kong   Karachi
Kuala Lumpur   Madrid   Melbourne   Mexico City   Nairobi
New Delhi   Shanghai   Taipei   Toronto

With offices in
Argentina   Austria   Brazil   Chile   Czech Republic   France   Greece
Guatemala   Hungary   Italy   Japan   Poland   Portugal   Singapore
South Korea   Switzerland   Thailand   Turkey   Ukraine   Vietnam

Oxford is a registered trade mark of Oxford University Press
in the UK and certain other countries.

Published in the United States of America by
Oxford University Press
198 Madison Avenue, New York, NY 10016

© Oxford University Press 2010

First issued as an Oxford University Press paperback, 2014.

All rights reserved. No part of this publication may be reproduced, stored in a retrieval system, or transmitted, in any form or by any means, without the prior permission in writing of Oxford University Press, or as expressly permitted by law, by license, or under terms agreed with the appropriate reproduction rights organization. Inquiries concerning reproduction outside the scope of the above should be sent to the Rights Department, Oxford University Press, at the address above.

You must not circulate this work in any other form
and you must impose this same condition on any acquirer.

Library of Congress Cataloging-in-Publication Data
Moreira, Isabel.
Heaven's purge : purgatory in late antiquity / Isabel Moreira.
p. cm.
ISBN 978-0-19-973604-1 (hardcover); 978-0-19-937501-1 (paperback)
1. Purgatory—History of doctrines—Early church, ca. 30–600. I. Title.
BT843.M67   2010
236'.509015—dc22   2009046032

For Robert, Laura, and Julia

Acknowledgments

It has been a daunting task to write this book at a time when professional and personal obligations have been high. It is a pleasure, therefore, to be able to thank those who have provided me with the time and support I needed to complete this book. First, I thank the University of Utah for supporting my research. A faculty fellowship in fall 2008 and a sabbatical leave in spring 2009 allowed me to complete this book to schedule. I am also enormously grateful to the Tanner Center for the Humanities at the University of Utah for a Virgil C. Aldrich Fellowship for a semester in which I hammered out preliminary ideas and benefited from the thoughtful suggestions and guidance of Vincent Cheng, its director, and the other fellows.

The interlibrary loan staff at the University of Utah's Marriott Library have been efficient and helpful, and I have benefited for many years from the expertise of Ceres Birkhead, an impressive professional librarian. Additionally, I thank the library staff at the Pontifical Institute for Mediaeval Studies in Toronto, who have provided help and access to their enviable collection.

It has been greatly to the benefit of this project that some generous scholars and friends have read chapters and made suggestions for improvement. Alan Bernstein, Bonnie Effros, Lisa Bitel, Jill Harries, George H. Brown, and Eric Hinderaker read individual chapters. Margaret Toscano, a dear friend and colleague, has listened to my ideas for a number of years, and always helped when a Latin query arose. To Alan Bernstein, with whom I have been involved in deep debates about purgatory, I acknowledge a special debt of gratitude and appreciation. Over the past few years we have discovered common interests and occasional exhilarating disagreements. The book has benefitted from his sage commentary even while it is apparent that often I ultimately went my own way. It has been a privilege to have benefitted from his generous advice. All errors are, of course, entirely my own. I would also like to thank the anonymous reviewers for Oxford University Press who offered specific suggestions at an earlier stage in the project, and Cynthia Reed and the editorial staff of the press for their interest in the book and friendly help.

Dear friends and family have lived with me through my obsession with purgatory—no easy task. I thank Kay and Mike Ringwood, Rebecca Horn, Jim Lehning, Megan Armstrong, Isabelle Cochelin, Emily Michelson, Marilyn Davies, and Fiona Webster. They have had to hear more about purgatory than they ever would have imagined. Last, but always foremost, I thank my closest family. With deepest love I thank my father, my mother (always), and my sister. My greatest debt, however, is to my husband, Robert Summerfield, who has supported me through this entire process with love and humour. He read and commented on the entire manuscript in multiple drafts, offered great suggestions, and kept all our priorities in perspective. He is incomparable—the companion of my heart. My daughters Laura and Julia were born during the time this book was first taking shape. Almost as soon as they could formulate such thoughts, they asked questions about life and death that challenge the capacity of any person to provide answers. From Laura, who is 7, who continues to grapple seriously with questions of mortality, and Julia who is 4 and who has just begun, I have found inspiration and resolve.

Contents

Introduction: Purgatory in Late Antiquity, 3

1. Purgatory in Early Christian and Patristic Thought, 15
2. Of Sons and Slaves: Violence and Correction in the Afterlife, 39
3. *O Purgatorium Caeleste!*: Purging Body and Soul at St. Martin's Shrine, 63
4. Purgation in the Sixth and Seventh Centuries, 81
5. Purgatory, Penitentials, and the Irish Question, 113
6. Purgatory in Bede and Boniface, 147
7. Missionary Eschatology and the Politics of Certainty, 177
8. Barbarians, Law Codes, and Purgatory, 193

Conclusion, 207

Notes, 213

Abbreviations, 279

Bibliography, 281

Index, 305

Heaven's Purge

Introduction

Purgatory in Late Antiquity

When addressing the subject of the future life, Julianus Pomerius, a late fifth-century African rhetor and priest living in exile in Gaul, expressed a caution that the historian does well to heed: "more is believed than is put down in writing." How does one write a history of purgatory? How does one write the history of an idea whose very authors were often reluctant to speak about it? When Julianus wrote of "the nature of that future life which one ought rather to believe in than to speak of" or indeed when Augustine, that most prolix of authorities, cautioned that the existence of a postmortem fire of purification "may yield to a solution or remain in doubt," we are clearly in a field of inquiry in which few certainties are to be found.[1] The idea of purgatory has been investigated many times, over many centuries, and in various ways; as religious tenet, as confessional belief, as theology and eschatology, as social and intellectual history, as literature, art, and folklore. All perspectives must inform our view when the scraps of textual "evidence" that undergird the notion fall so drastically short of the concepts they spawned. That more is believed than is put down in writing may be the albatross of historical inquiry generally, but it is a problem that particularly besets the earliest history of purgatory.

This book has no claims to comprehensiveness. It takes its own path. The intellectual traditions of purgatory have their place in this study, of course, but so too do some of the ways Christian writers thought and wrote about the subject of purification and purgation in other contexts. The subject was deeply personal for them. The great Christian figures of late antiquity inquired into purgatory's fires because they were taught to train their eyes daily upon death. In writing about what awaited them beyond the grave, Christians revealed their hopes for perfection and their fears of rejection; their fear of violence and captivity and their desire for love and autonomy; their preoccupations with status, entitlement, and hierarchy; and ultimately, their quest to discover doctrinal certainty and to be able to preach it.

The notion of purgatory as a theological and cultural belief in these early centuries is gradually being fleshed out. Fine individual studies of texts, cultural attitudes, and the nature of sacramental relationships, now shed light on the centuries at the "end of late antiquity." Furthermore, the importance of seventh- and eighth-century writings and institutions in the formation of characteristically western ideas about purgatory is now much more widely recognized than it was twenty years ago. How the evidence of those two vital centuries should be interpreted, however, is very much up for grabs. The debates and consequences of competing perspectives on that era promise lively disagreement for some time to come.

It is surely significant that the seventh and eighth centuries saw the emergence of literature concerned with purgatory, sin, and penance. Suddenly we have texts that describe postmortem purgation and that give us information on who must undergo it, suggestions on how to avoid it, and explanations of how it must work. Why was this so? Why was there suddenly so much interest at that time in extending a biblical metaphor of spiritual cleansing into a place or stage in the afterlife with defined dimensions, geography, time, and inhabitants? It may not be possible to answer every question one would like for this early period, but there is every reason to try. In the early Christian centuries the educated elite lived, wrote, and preached with the belief that they would be held accountable in the afterlife for their actions and words, and they hoped that they would be found sufficiently pure to be able to encounter their maker. The degree to which they imagined such preparations for heavenly existence as painful, violent, merciful, and compassionate says a lot about who they were and how they viewed their neighbours. It is not possible, for example, to fully understand notions of violence in the early middle ages without acknowledging that not only did they live their lives with violence and the fear of it, but also when they read a book or heard a preacher, they had the image and threat of otherworldly violence lobbed at them too.[2]

The precise moment during which purgatory became a "real" place in the imagined otherworld may never be recovered. Indeed, such an investigation is of limited value. Purgatory appears to have functioned both as imagined place and as metaphor simultaneously. However, the idea of purgatory as a staging post in the afterlife, with recognizable features, descriptive energy, theological justification, and political use, burst on to the eschatological landscape in the eighth century. In the works of Bede, Boniface, and their successors, notwithstanding their respective abilities to understand afterlife matters metaphorically, purgatory assumed physical features: valleys, rivers, and chasms; it operated in tune with human perceptions of time, emotion, hope, and justice. Although it was imagined to be part of God's domain, it was a realm in which fires fed on human sin like dry kindling.

In the later middle ages, writers embellished the notion of purgatory with all the novel punishments and environments that rich imaginations could devise. Yet, for all its centrality to the work of the high medieval church, purgatory's theological existence was always somewhat marginal before the thirteenth century. At the First Council at Lyons in 1245, the existence of a place called purgatory was identified as a Latin belief distinct from that of the Greeks; only at the Second Council of Lyons in 1274 was purgatory given formal definition by a papal council.[3] Yet before these conciliar pronouncements, purgatory's existence was hardly doubted. For centuries purgatory's features and purpose were fleshed out by religious groups, political players, writers, poets, visionaries, and by clerics and ordinary people telling ghost stories.[4] At some level, popular interest in purgatory drove its importance and utility.[5] For centuries, purgatory did not need an official stamp, because it had gradually seeped into a common Christian understanding of where dead Christians went.

This study seeks to examine the ideas and culture that supported such a belief. The purgatorial ideas expressed in the "long" late antiquity discussed here, up to the eighth century, must be viewed as a distinct phase in a much longer history of the idea, an idea of purgation that has stretched from biblical times to the modern era. It is a distortion to view earlier ideas about purgation simply as a prelude to a later high medieval ideology. Purgatory in late antiquity arose from late antique culture and its understanding of the Bible, patristic writings, visionary literature, and the history and authority of the church. As such, Christian purgatory was a late antique idea and, to some extent, a late antique invention. Much of the substance and language of the idea was inherited from antiquity, but early medieval ideas about purgatory and purgation did not entirely depend on them.

Writers of the early middle ages would not have agreed with this view. For them, evidence of purgatory's existence as early Christian belief was to be found in the scriptures. A favoured text was 1 Corinthians 3:13–15 that described how the Christian's good works would be tested by fire "for the Day will disclose it, because it will be revealed with fire, and the fire will test what sort of work each one has done . . . though he himself will be saved, but only as through fire."[6] Once a purgatorial place appeared in visions of the afterlife, its scriptural justification seemed clear. In fidelity to biblical tradition and patristic opinion, writers such as Bede and Boniface were probably unaware that they were legitimizing theological speculation, by the simple act of consolidating and affirming connections among ancient practices such as prayer for the dead, masses for the dead, offerings for the dead, and the hope for divine intervention. This is a book about their world—the world of late antique and early medieval clerics and their flock. Late antique purgatory was often a loose system of compatible ideas about prayer, intercession, afterlife belief, and theology concerning infernal realms that somehow coalesced and gelled by the turn of the eighth century to become a place, or prolonged stage, that was given an existence in the afterlife. Purgatory at this time was only just becoming imagined as a place in the afterlife; purgatory, purgation, and punishment continued to be processes that could be imagined in multiple ways, even by the same author. Furthermore, purgation in this life and the next was fertile ground for metaphor, theory, and real-life observation. In this book I can only begin to scratch the surface of purgatory's meaning in late antiquity and the early Middle Ages. However, I hope to raise some issues relating to the way early purgatory and purgation have been discussed and to suggest that the texts from these centuries have the potential to offer much to our understanding of the way purgatory was able to thrive as a theological idea.

Modern historians, however, cannot neglect the long and contentious history of purgatory, especially Reformation criticism of the institution of purgatory. Historically, confessional divides have played a major role in the presentation and interpretation of the early history of purgatory, and modern scholars, too, advance their particular perspectives arising from religious, secular, and—dare one say it—national biases. In some respects, the historical appraisal of purgatory's origins advanced by Protestant reformers continues to define the field because Protestant attacks focused on the notion that purgatory was invented in late antiquity and was a symptom of religious and cultural decline in those centuries. Their views made purgatory not just a religious idea but an ideological marker. Most Christians have traditionally accepted the existence of a purificatory fire after death, but not all have accepted purgatory. The views of sixteenth-century reformers are worth prefacing here since in many ways they set the agenda for subsequent inquiry.

Responses to the later medieval version of purgatory have cast a long shadow on the historiography. The first critical inquiries into purgatory's history were penned by purgatory's most vociferous detractors: the Protestant reformers of the sixteenth century.[7] (Cathars, Waldenses, Lollards, and Hussites had denied purgatory's existence before, but they were not writing history.[8]) It was the Protestant reformers who first identified purgatory's beginnings in the early middle ages: for them, purgatory was a fabrication forged in the political melee of late antiquity. However, in the manner of conspiracy hunters, they saw enemies everywhere: the barbarians, the papacy, and the priests. Thus there were differences of opinion as to what aspect of late antique society was responsible for purgatory's rise. One view that obtained some currency was that the barbarian invasions, and the infusion of barbarian culture, explained a shift in Christian belief from the civilized time of Augustine (to whom they attributed a subtle theology of the afterlife), to the barbarian era of Gregory the Great, with his dialogic discussion of purgatory and his vivid descriptions of afterlife visions. According to this interpretation, a "dark age" had fallen over Europe, during which time proponents of Christian culture struggled, not always successfully, to maintain their purity in the face of barbarian assault.[9] Furthermore, it was thought that some clerics connived in purgatory's "creation" as a means to accommodate pagan beliefs about the afterlife during the stressful era of European conversion. Thus Protestant detractors of the theology of purgatory forcefully depicted purgatory as a degenerate creation of a society debased of culture and true Christian understanding.[10]

Another critical view focused on the clergy, particularly the papacy. Some Protestant reformers viewed purgatory as a "papist" plot—a papacy-sanctioned conspiracy against true Christianity— the bastard progeny of a superstitious age. In fact, as already noted, purgatory achieved theological legitimacy in the thirteenth century and even more prominently at the Council of Florence in 1439. That long-overdue legitimation may have heralded its ultimate demise in the Protestant world because it had finally become for them what Protestants had always suspected: a papal abomination. Viewed from the perspective of the end of the middle ages, when purgatory had developed into a major social and financial institution, the papacy's role in promoting purgatory was portrayed cynically as self-serving from its earliest beginnings. The immediate context for Protestant views of the papacy's involvement in purgatory was contemporary outrage at two papal positions: the papacy's claim to control entry into afterlife destinations and its refusal to "spring forth" all souls from torment through an act of charity. Protestant reformers attacked both these contingent aspects of papal control.

The charge that purgatory was a papal conspiracy against true Christians was probably more damaging than the assertion that it was a symptom of barbarism. Essentially, purgatory did not survive in Protestant countries because of its papal associations. But what appeared to some in the sixteenth century to be the firm association of the papacy with purgatory must not overshadow our understanding of papal influence in the earliest years of purgatory's formation. The role of Gregory the Great's writings, for instance, must be evaluated without anticipating the papal ambitions of a later age. Likewise the connection of clerical masses and the liturgy to purgatory must be examined without recourse to the subsequent associations that those connections appeared to have in a later age.

Catholic responses to these criticisms invoked biblical "proofs" for purgatory, argued that purgatory had always been present as an implicit underpinning of Christianity, and dismissed the paucity of written evidence as unimportant; in other words, the absence of evidence was not evidence of its absence. Catholic reformers of the sixteenth and seventeenth centuries worked to salvage the theology of purgatory from the wreckage of its history of clerical abuse, without removing papal authority over it. They were successful in this so that purgatory became even more deeply imbedded in Catholic *cultus* in the seventeenth century than before.[11]

Modern scholars have proposed variations on many of these themes in order to explain the origins of medieval purgatory. For example, "barbarian" ideas and culture are still touted as being instrumental in shaping purgatory. In 1990, Jacques Le Goff suggested that early penitentials, with their complex registers of infractions and remedies, were modeled after barbarian laws.[12] Since penitential literature is often connected with purgatory, we have in Le Goff an indirect connection of purgatory with barbarian law. (I examine the assumptions underlying this connection in chapter 8.) In a different tack on the barbarian provenance of purgatory, Peter Brown has imputed purgatory's implicit values to the deeply introspective world of an Irish, Celtic belief system as revealed in the tariffed penances of insular penitential literature, a worldview in tension with the "sunnier, more optimistic" Mediterranean Christianity of late antiquity.[13]

Whether purgatory's features are attributed to the influence of penitential tariffs, or to the compensation ideology of "barbarian" law codes, the implicit assumption of this approach is the same: purgatory is viewed as having arisen directly from late antique political and social customs and institutions. While it is clear that a biblical scholar such as Bede would interpret his patristic reading in the light of present as well as past institutions, I disagree with the way some of the later documentation (penitentials and law codes) has been easily pinned to the developing views of the afterlife in these works. As I hope to show, it is problematic to suppose that there were necessarily tight connections between the world of secular governance and an afterlife that was perceived as divinely ordered. For example, when Jacques Le Goff argued that purgatory was "born" in the twelfth century, it led him to harness purgatory's heyday to medieval feudalism: feudalism's three estates being a mirror of the tripartite ordering of the Christian otherworld.[14] Now that purgatory's existence is often backdated to the early middle ages, its inception is argued by some historians to coincide with barbarian laws and Irish penitentialism.

In recent years purgatory has attracted growing scholarly attention. The broadest treatment of the intellectual history of purgatory in the middle ages has already been mentioned: Jacques Le Goff's *The Birth of Purgatory*, first published in 1981 as *La naissance du purgatoire*. It has its idiosyncracies, but it is a work of enormous erudition and remains an essential starting point for investigations of medieval purgatory.[15] Its most notable claim was that medieval purgatory only came into existence when "purgatory" first appeared as a noun, in the decade from 1170 to 1180, and that its "birth" reflected the society and intellectual vigour of the twelfth century.[16] This rigid categorization remains unsatisfactory to most historians, and it undervalued Le Goff's own investigation into the rich texts of the early middle ages.[17] Indeed, while Anglophone historians tend to have few qualms about calling the earliest descriptions of postmortem cleansing "purgatory," there is still considerable resistance to using that term before the high middle ages in scholarship influenced by Le Goff. Other works by Le Goff have fleshed out further aspects of purgatorial culture in accessible ways, such as the importance of concepts of time and money in the high middle ages. His work remains an important entry point for the study of purgatory even if his larger thesis concerning purgatory's "birth" in the urban and scholastic milieu of the twelfth century has been widely challenged.

More recently, Claude Carozzi has deepened our knowledge of the early medieval afterlife in numerous articles and in his massive *Le voyage de l'âme dans l'au-delà*.[18] More than any other scholar, Carozzi has drawn our attention to the deep literary and cultural underpinnings of visionary literature. Drawing on his expertise on the *Vision of Paul*, Carozzi's analysis of the visions of Fursey and Drythelm, and the *Vision of the Monk of Wenlock*, the earliest visions to depict purgatory, is groundbreaking. While I disagree with him on some aspects of his analysis, his study of the classification of sins in the visions and in the penitentials is the most serious and detailed investigation to date.

Peter Brown's articles on amnesty and purgation have given enormous impetus to the study of purgatory in the English language. Importantly, his work has done much to focus attention on late antiquity as a key moment in the formation of purgatory. The question as to when and why purgatory arose in the West at this time has been addressed by a number of recent scholars, including Brown, and they have seen a dynamic process at work. For historians tend to approach the history of eschatology, like the history of other subjects, with an eagerness to discover moments of change. Recent scholarship has come to focus on the seventh century as a significant juncture in the history of the afterlife in the Latin West. The appearance in that century of newly penned literary tales of visionary travel has borne much of the burden of such arguments.[19] The seventh-century visions of Barontus and Fursey, in particular, have been invoked as evidence for both the emergence of the individual (Claude Carozzi and Peter Brown[20]) and the emergence of visionary literature in the West (J. N. Hillgarth, Maria Pia Ciccarese, and many others).[21] More recently, Brown has termed the seventh century as the "end of the ancient other world."

Peter Brown is a trenchant proponent of a seventh-century watershed in the history of the afterlife.[22] He argues that Christian expectations of the afterlife were rooted in two important concepts: ideas of "amnesty" and "purgation." For Brown, the seventh century marks the period when the balance between these two concepts changed, when Irish ideas of individual recompense jarred against an older world of community-wide hopes of amnesty. This clash of imaginative structures, according to Brown, signaled the true end of the ancient otherworld and the beginning of the more "familiar" medieval representation of the afterlife in which purgation of sins dominates. In his words: "Our own notions of the other world go back, effectively, to the seventh century and no further."[23] His view of the influence of penitential ideas and in particular the *Vision of Fursey* has found support in a recent article by Marilyn Dunn who has gone further to suggest that Gregory the Great's *Dialogues*, so vital a source for medieval justifications of purgatory, was authored in the late seventh century in a Northumbrian context.[24] The importance of Irish sources on ideas about the afterlife has found recent voice also in the work of Marina Smyth.[25]

These apparent watersheds in the history of the afterlife often warrant greater scrutiny, and they are clearly identified and addressed in their appropriate places in this book. Specialized studies on the afterlife and related fields have contributed enormously to our view of the afterlife in these critical early centuries. I can mention only a few. Alan Bernstein's foundational work on hell and Jeffrey Trumbower's elegant study *Rescue for the Dead* have set the course on which future studies must build.[26] Textual studies by Maria Pia Ciccarese, Claude Carozzi, and Lenka Jiroušková invite deeper analysis into transmission of texts and ideas.[27] The work of Éric Rebillard has allowed for a more subtle understanding of the penitential changes occurring in the early fifth century and thus provides a different view on what was going on in the seventh century.[28] Bonnie Effros's work on the archaeology and culture of death in the

Merovingian realms has enriched and complicated our picture of the diverse ways in which people reacted to death and memorialized it.[29] Arnold Angenendt's work on the liturgy, Damien Sicard's study of funerary liturgies prior to the Carolingian reforms, and Frederick Paxton's investigation of the rituals that surrounded the dying and the dead have greatly refined our view of changing attitudes toward death and dying.[30]

There is no clear, linear trajectory of belief in purgation in our sources. Yet, as I will argue in this book, I see Bede's theological justification of purgatory at the turn of the eighth century as being a crucial moment in the formation and acceptance of purgatory by later Christian thinkers.[31] Bede, a Northumbrian monk, provides the first technical description of purgatory as a place with specific functions in his *Homilies* and in the *Commentary on Proverbs*.[32] He provides a theological justification in his *Commentary on Proverbs*. Together with his description of the vision of a layman, Drythelm, in his *Ecclesiastical History*, Bede secures a vital intellectual link between the theological commonplaces about "purgatorial fires" derived from Augustine, Gregory the Great, and other early medieval writers, and a clear visionary description of a place of tortuous, extended purgation. Yet Bede's contribution to the history of purgatory has received uneven attention in previous works. While Bede was the "worshipful" "Saint" Bede for sixteenth-century Catholics who saw support in his writings for the antiquity of purgatorial teachings, Protestants were apt either to dismiss his writings as evidence of primitive practice or to attack him for repeating popish error. The 1567 translation of Bede's *Ecclesiastical History* into English by the Catholic Thomas Stapleton spurred much of the contention since the work could now be read more widely. In particular, Bede's reputation received a concerted drubbing in the prolific publications of the sixteenth-century Cambridge divine, William Fulke, who even went so far as to claim that Bede's proximity to the time of the Antichrist (the papacy after Gregory I's time) occluded his judgement.[33] Eventually, much of the confessional rancor subsided, replaced by intellectual and nationalistic snobbery. Still, scholarly works of the nineteenth century generally acknowledged Bede's contribution. For example, Thomas Wright's pitying account of Irish beliefs in *St. Patrick's Purgatory*, published in 1844, discussed Bede's epitome of the *Vision of Fursey* and Bede's account of the *Vision of Drythelm* as certain pre-Conquest witnesses to purgatory in the British Isles.[34] At the end of the century, on the sole basis of Bede's *Vision of Drythelm*, Ernest J. Becker identified Bede as "the first to promulgate a definite doctrine on purgatory on English soil."[35] Bede's homilies and commentaries were not mentioned by him. Meanwhile, Bede's importance to purgatory's inception was completely ignored by

Protestant and Catholic religious polemicists alike.[36] Since Bede has caught the attention of writers intermittently, my own focus on Bede cannot be viewed as new from a longer historiographical perspective. Le Goff's *Birth of Purgatory*, however, pointed scholarly attention away from the early middle ages generally and away from Bede in particular.[37] While the pendulum is swinging back to the North in the studies of Carozzi and Brown, my emphasis on Bede leads me to different conclusions about the milieu of early purgatory as compared to those advanced in recent works. In placing Bede's theological response to Origen at the forefront of the formation of an accepted theology of purgatory in the West, I am necessarily led to different conclusions about purgatory's history and meaning.

My use of the term "purgatory" for this early period requires some explanation. The importance of the terminology of purgatory was given great emphasis by Le Goff, who argued that "until the twelfth century the noun *purgatorium* did not exist; *the* purgatory had not yet been born," and for whom the appearance of the noun in the twelfth century was a crucial indicator that purgatory had achieved some notional reality in peoples' minds that hitherto eluded them. This distinction is still important for many scholars who work in this field, although it should be noted that earlier instances of the noun have been adduced, possibly even as early as Bede. In order to maintain a distinction between the myriad purgatorial beliefs of late antiquity and those ideas that governed purgatory's acceptance as Catholic doctrine later in the middle ages, I refer to "purgatory" in these centuries in the lower case. In fact, the early terminology of purgation, of spiritual cleansing, was so fluid that a simple search for examples of the verb form *purgare* (to cleanse) does not come close to identifying key texts. Verbs of cleansing *(mundare)* and purging *(purgare)* were commonplace, and importantly they were used to denote cleansing that was both bodily and spiritual, as part of a process that spanned both the present life and the afterlife. Most common, when writers in this period referred to postmortem purgation they referenced the fire of purgation in some way, usually *ignis purgatorius* or some variant. My use of the lowercase "purgatory" is dictated by two concerns: to acknowledge that there were crucial differences between early Christian conceptions of purgatory and what came later to be accepted as Catholic doctrine, and a desire to avoid the teleology inherent in labeling later doctrine as necessarily normative.

This book approaches the subject of purgatory's early history from a number of angles. First, I emphasize that in late antiquity purgatory became a place of violence against Christian bodies, both in visions of the afterlife and in theology. Images of violence are not conventionally understood as images of purification and cleansing. However, as I outline in the first two chapters, purgation came to be viewed, in late antiquity, as a goal achieved by punishment—as correction achieved through punishment in life and as salvation *after* punishment in the afterlife. The juxtaposition of metaphors concerning slavery with those of parental correction of sons was a powerful vehicle for understanding how images of violence could be comprehended as God's just treatment of the Christian soul.

Second, purgation was a powerful cultural metaphor. Metaphors of purgation were diffuse in the culture of late antiquity and the early middle ages, and they drew on a variety of images and verbal expressions. For example, bodily torment could be observed in medical contexts and in the contortions of suppliants at the shrines of the saints; purgation was readily viewed as a form of bodily violence that was ultimately beneficial to physical and spiritual health. Furthermore, while bodily purging was temporary and beneficial, it also placed the sufferer in an interim state between sickness and health. Whether seen as punishment for transgressive behaviour or as the body's autonomous rejection of what was noxious, the experience of purging as being between states was important for the early medieval understanding of purgatory.

The intellectual tradition of purgatory proves to be a fascinating story: the theological thread that led from scripture and patristic thought to Bede's crucial formulation of purgatory's theology is long and contorted. The difficulties in identifying the impact of a theology of purgatory when put to "use" in the missionary field are part of this story. I have also examined the claims that have been made for certain kinds of literature in influencing the nature and under standing of purgatory: visions and the liturgy, penitentials, and barbarian law codes.

While the emergence of purgatory has traditionally been explained by citing subsequent anxieties about political motivation and abuse, the ideas and institutions that promoted belief in purgatory need to be considered in their own time and context. In order to find the impetus that gave birth to early ideas about purgatory, we must ask less cynical questions. When and in what contexts did purgatory arise as acceptable Christian belief? In what milieu did the sources appear that advanced the notion that a purgatorial place existed? In which sources could a shift in expectations of the afterlife simply slip in without need for radical change? What was new, timely, exciting, and successful in the idea of purgatory that made it appealing to those who wrote about it and to those who read about it? In what arenas was purgatory a successful idea, and in what contexts was purgatory's emergence an inadequate social and religious tool? To what extent was it a stumbling block to the promotion of Christian ideology? My intention in this work is to direct a few chosen spotlights on areas where sources, ideas, and contemporary scholarship on purgatory and purgation intersect.

I

Purgatory in Early Christian and Patristic Thought

Medieval writers did not view purgatory as a novelty. For them, the images of purgation that they read about in visions, and the intercessions that mitigated its horrors, must always have existed, and they looked to scriptures and patristic opinion to support that view. They were probably little aware of how much of the theology of purgatory was an imaginative feat of intellectual engineering and how much their own belief in the idea of purgatory served to enlarge and solidify a notion that was only hinted at in the scriptures.

This chapter is the first of three to examine the idea of purgatory in authoritative Christian writings and the stages by which that idea became increasingly central to Christian thought (chapters 4 and 6 continue the story). These chapters do not attempt to provide an exhaustive survey of the intellectual and doctrinal history of purgatory prior to the eighth century.[1] Rather, these chapters explore how ideas about purgatory developed in late antiquity so that by the time Bede and Boniface were writing, the existence of a place of purgation in the afterlife could be described by them without a sense that what they were writing was in any way new.

This chapter will identify some of the earliest texts to describe important elements in purgatorial thinking and, ultimately, a purgatorial place in the afterlife. These texts present us with a complex picture of what ancients believed about afterlife purgation. They reveal that some concerns about postmortem purification were fairly consistent in late antiquity: for example, a desire to adhere to the "evidence" of the scriptures and the anxiety that the existence of afterlife purgation might detract from the message that all Christians must live a fully spiritual life in the present. Yet there was significant variation in the way individual authors understood the soul's progress through the otherworld and in the way such authors used language and literary genre to arrive at their understanding of postmortem purgation. The picture of purgation that emerges from this critical era in Christian thinking—from the patristic era to the eighth century—was sufficiently developed as a notion among the Christian elite that it merits consideration as a distinct era in purgatorial belief, one that crested in the work of Bede and in the cultural environment that read Bede's works and viewed their own devotional practices through the lens that Bede provided. Purgatorial thinking germinated and effloresced during the early middle ages into a critical mass of information and belief that distinguishes it from the later history of purgatory in the West. As we shall see, purgatory in late antiquity comprised a more substantial and autonomous belief system than is suggested by such a term as "proto-Purgatory" that has sometimes been applied to it.[2] Furthermore, this is an era in the history of purgatory in which visions of the afterlife begin to assume considerable theological weight alongside other forms of theological writing. Both Gregory the Great and Bede have left us accounts of visions of the otherworld to supplement their other writings on the afterlife. Both were heirs of Augustine, yet each offered different modifications of his legacy. Their efforts allowed early medieval purgatory to be attributed to scriptural and patristic doctrine. Eventually, Bede would adapt Augustine's cautious opinions on the afterlife to a new social environment.

It is important, however, that the epitome of patristic opinion that follows does not give a false impression that belief in purgatory progressed in a continuous, seamless way over the early Christian centuries. The authors whose works we will sample did not always know the works by other commentators on afterlife issues, and they did not always view their own work as continuing that of others. Rather, many of the authors we will examine addressed the topic out of dissatisfaction with different ideas, even heresies, which had gained some currency in their time.

This chapter opens with the earliest Christian sources and closes with Augustine. It was Augustine's response to early Christian traditions about postmortem purgation and the disputes among his intellectual circle concerning Origenism that set the framework of issues that were to be so important to Bede three centuries later. It is Bede who first provides purgatory with an orthodox, theological justification, an imaginative rendering of the place of purgatory in the afterlife, and a clearly articulated explanation of how purgatory operated as a place of intercession. In Bede's work we encounter the culmination of centuries of purgatorial thinking in the making. In Bede, the last patristic writer of the ancient world, we discover a true convergence of earlier thought, in an environment that looked south to the authority of Rome as representing the practices of the universal church and to the authority of the church fathers as guarantors of religious orthodoxy: Northumbria.³

Defining Purgatory

Before embarking on the earliest Christian texts, it is useful to have a working definition of purgatory in mind. For the purpose of this book, that definition is the one provided by the Bede in the 720s. It is not the definition provided by the papacy in the later middle ages. This is a purposeful choice designed to avoid, as much as possible, a teleological perspective on what was happening in late antiquity. It is Bede's definition of purgatory that marks the end point of this investigation and that sets the benchmark for later medieval definitions of purgatory. In his *Homily for Advent*, Bede penned a thoughtful description:

> But in truth there are some who were preordained to the lot of the elect on account of their good works, but on account of some evils by which they were polluted, went out from the body after death to be severely chastised, and were seized by the flames of the fire of purgatory [*flammis ignis purgatorii*]. They are either made clean from the stains of their vices in their long ordeal up until judgement day, or, on the other hand, if they are absolved from their penalties by the petitions, almsgiving, fasting, weeping, and oblation of the saving sacrificial offering by their faithful friends, they may come earlier to the rest of the blessed.⁴

In this text, Bede sketched out the essential components of purgatory in a form that would be recognizable to later medieval Catholic theology. Its main features were as follows: purgatory is a place for the purification of the elect; the fire cleanses (spiritual) pollution from the soul; additionally, the fire chastises so that purification is accomplished through the punishment of Christian bodies. This purification may last until the Last Judgement, unless the sinner is absolved from punishment through the intercession of friends and the offering of the Mass. The means of intercession are: prayers for the dead (petitions), almsgiving, fasting, weeping, and the Mass.

As we shall see, it is evident that Bede's description owed much to Augustine. But Augustine did not believe that there was a place of extended purification in the afterlife or that human intercessory activities could expunge postbaptismal sin. It is clear, then, that Bede drew not only on Augustine but on other sources also, including scripture, visions of the afterlife, and claims for the efficacy of the Mass championed by the clergy and colourfully expressed in the *Dialogues* of Gregory the Great and in other clerical writings of the period. What is clear from the passage cited above is that Bede was not tentative in his opinion; he outlined the purpose of purgatory in an authoritative way, and his strong dependence on Augustine's phrasing suggests that he believed he had the authority of Augustine to guide him.

Citing the Scriptures

Christians attributed divine authority to scripture; it was the ultimate resource for formulating and debating belief on any subject. Ideally, scripture was informative and a bulwark against heterodoxy. In practice, it was rare that the Christian scriptures fully filled these needs. Scriptural information on purgatory, or indeed on any aspect of the afterlife, was extremely sparse. Consequently, patristic commentary rapidly assumed a vital importance for Christians who sought guidance on such matters. These early Christian theologians located key passages in scripture that prompted debate on the subject, but their choices did not always coincide with later medieval theological "proofs" of purgatory.[5] The allegory of the Christian who builds on the foundation of Christ was widely, although not exclusively, used to discuss postmortem purgation. The refiner's fire and scorching oven imagery of Malachi was a frequent and uncontroversial reference point, as was a spiritualized interpretation of the three Hebrews in the fiery furnace.[6] However, the example of the Maccabees that assumed importance as a proof of purgatory in the later middle ages did not play that role in late antiquity.

That some Christians passed through some form of purifying or probative fire before entering the kingdom of heaven was expressed in the first Pauline Letter to the Corinthians (1 Cor 3.11–15):

> For no other foundation can anyone lay than that which is laid, which is Jesus Christ. Now if anyone builds on the foundation with gold, silver, precious stones, wood, hay, straw—each man's work will become manifest; for the Day will disclose it, because it will be revealed with fire, and the fire will test what sort of work each one has done. If the work which any man has built on the foundation survives, he will receive a reward. If any man's work is burned up, he will suffer loss, though he himself will be saved, but only as through fire.

This passage suggests two aspects of fire. The first is the fire that tests each man's work (often termed "probative"), and all Christians will have their work tested this way. The second is the fire through which imperfect Christians will be saved. The passage may refer to one fire that acts differently or to two fires with different functions. The action of the fire suggests differential fates for those who have built their house on the foundation of Christ. The successful Christians will be given a reward. Is this immediate? We are not told. Then there are those who have not been so successful—these latter must be saved "as through fire" (*quasi per ignem*). Although not clearly stated, the implication is that these less worthy souls will still be saved, but only after they have endured some form of penalty that is so painful that it suggests the metaphor of fire: "as through fire." But there is little precision here. The immediate, historical context of the passage was the tension between Paul and another community leader, Apollos: the building on Christ's foundation referred to the activity of leaders and teachers of the Christian community in Corinth. Later writers proposed that this passage described the fate of all Christian souls. In its transition from historical to eschatological relevance, new questions arose. Was the work burned up or was the man? Would these less successful Christians endure a fire-like experience until the Last Judgement, or would their suffering be transitory? What did the "foundation of Christ" signify? Did it refer to the church, to Christian participation in the sacraments or something else? Ultimately, the passage posed more questions than it answered. Jacques Le Goff noted that this passage was so fundamental to the development of medieval purgatory that one can simply follow the exegesis of this passage to uncover it.[7] But not all authors who wrote on purgatory used this passage as a point of reference. Bede, for example, did not.[8] Furthermore, the exegetical tradition of this passage in antiquity shows that there was no consensus on who would be subject to the fire and what the action of the fire was.[9] However, there was a certain pattern in patristic thought that underlay the variety of specific opinions on this passage. Influenced by Platonic thought, philosopher-theologians of the third century distinguished between a divine, intelligent fire that could ignite the soul with spiritual knowledge, on the one hand, from the physical, material quality of fire as it was known in earthly contexts, a base form of fire that consumes and annihilates, on the other hand. Thus it was common for patristic authors, including Jerome and Augustine, to suggest that the fire described in Corinthians referred to purification in the present life, not the afterlife. Other early patristic commentators who did consider it a postmortem fire of purification do not appear to have envisaged anything more than a fleeting transition through it. The emphasis on present-life purification was well suited to pastoral objectives, particularly because it emphasized the urgency for current penance.[10] The fire of purification was sometimes imagined physically, as inhabiting the individual like a disease or fever.[11] There was even the opinion that the probative fire was God himself or his spirit.[12] Thus in the first Christian centuries, patristic commentary generally looked to this passage in Corinthians as referring to a beneficial, saving fire, a symbol of salvation, and not a real fire. (The real fire that devours was identified as hell.) A systematic distinction between the spiritual and the physical was fundamental to Christian philosophy, as it had been to pagan thought, and this way of thinking encouraged an emphasis on the present life, the need for repentance, and the value of a life of austerity or asceticism. In the strictest sense, the passage in Corinthians offered no more than the image of fire as a metaphor for salvation. It was left to later writers to develop that fire into a system of salvation for the elect.

Intercession, more than fire exclusively, was the hallmark of early medieval purgatory. Intercession was usually effected through prayer for the dead. The medieval theology of purgatory assigned significant weight to prayers of intercession, and it is clear that Bede did too. However, it is also clear from Bede's description of purgatory that he understood prayers of intercession as something more than a simple intonation of a prayer: they required the petitioner to be in a penitential state, exhibiting contrition through fasting, tears, and almsgiving. In antiquity, too, prayers of intercession were usually accompanied by some other pious or ascetic act. Prayers intended to intercede for souls in purgatory are not necessarily the same thing as prayers for the dead, however, and it was possible for Protestant Christians of a later age to divorce one from the other just as it was for Augustine to accept some value in prayer for the dead without espousing a clear theology of purgatory.[13]

A later medieval proof text for purgatory concerned an act of intercession: 2 Maccabees 12:43–45, in which a prayer of intercession on behalf of the dead seemed to infer that the dead were in an interim state or purgatory.[14] The passage in question stated that:

> [Judas Maccabeus] also took up a collection, man by man, to the amount of two thousand drachmas of silver, and sent it to Jerusalem to provide for a sin offering. In doing this he acted very well and honourably, taking account of the resurrection. For if he were not expecting that those who had fallen would rise again, it would have been superfluous and foolish to pray for the dead. But if he was looking to the splendid reward that is laid up for those who fall asleep in godliness, it was a holy and pious thought. Therefore he made atonement for the dead, that they might be delivered from their sin.[15]

For many later readers, this passage implied an early belief in purgatory, since payment for sin was intended to alter the status of the dead. The text also affirmed that the dead would be resurrected. The value of this passage as an authority for purgatory lay in the interpretation of Judas's prayer as an intercession for the souls of the dead and in the authority of Judas as a righteous figure in Jewish history—a priestly figure (and freedom fighter) who cleansed and rededicated the temple of Jerusalem after it was polluted by the troops of the Greek Antiochus. Judas's actions in cleansing and rededicating the temple provided a powerful metaphor for the spiritual cleansing of the living from pollution and, in the sin offering, a purification of the soldiers' sin. While the analogy between what Judas did for the living and what he did for the dead is striking, there are substantial difficulties with the text and alternative interpretations of Judas's action have been suggested.

Second Maccabees is an epitome of a lost five-volume history of the Maccabees written by Jason of Cyrene in the late second or early first century B.C. The events it purports to describe took place in 164 B.C. As Jeffrey Trumbower has noted in his book, *Rescue for the Dead: The Posthumous Salvation of Non-Christians in Early Christianity*, the quoted text consists of two parts: a descriptive component (the story of Judas's offering) and an editorial comment made by Jason of Cyrene or his epitomizer, which stated that Judas acted honourably and that his actions indicated belief in the resurrection and the possibility of posthumous atonement for the sins of the dead by the living. Between the two parts of the text there was a "shift in perspective."[16] Trumbower notes that Judas's action should be seen in the context of other contemporary accounts: "The point was to protect and purify the survivors, without any concern for the postmortem fate of the sinners."[17] According to this interpretation, Judas's action was intended to protect his army and the community that had been endangered by the idolatry of some of his soldiers, and it was not until the early first century (in Jason's editing) that Judas's purificatory action was interpreted as efficacious intercession for the dead. This later interpretation, furthermore, was more in line with Hellenized Judaism of the first century B.C. than it was with mainstream Jewish practice in the second century B.C. Trumbower sees this newly expressed care for the fate of the dead as mirroring the "care and feeding of the dead in family cults from the Greek and Roman worlds, but here in 2 Maccabees an ideology of sharp differentiation of fates for the righteous and the wicked has entered into the equation.... The old criteria of national and familial solidarity are fused with the new criterion of dying in the proper religious state, and the result is an attempt by the living to rescue the dead."[18] It appears likely, then, that the portrayal of Judas's actions in 2 Maccabees was at least in part a product of a Hellenistic ideological overlay and not necessarily the practice of a second century B.C. Jewish priestly resistance fighter.[19] Thus two very different pictures emerge: one that accepts Judas' prayer and offering as intended to purify the souls of the dead soldiers, and another in which Judas' actions were intended to purify the living community through atonement to God for the idolatrous actions of the dead. The relevance of the testimony of 2 Maccabees for purgatory hangs on whether the reader accepted that intercessory prayer for the dead assumed the existence of purgatory. This is not a necessary assumption, however, and it is both striking and significant that while the book was cited as an example of intercessory prayer, it was not used as a justification for the existence of purgatory in late antiquity.[20]

There were two major contexts in which early medieval authors looked to the example of the Maccabees, and neither had to do with purification of the dead. They were: the actions of Judas Maccabaeus resulting in the rededication of the synagogue and the example of Eleazar and of the seven Maccabean "martyrs" and their mother. While both had some connection with symbols of purification (the purification and rededication of the synagogue and the refusal of Eleazar and of the seven Maccabees to eat polluted food) these avenues of thought were not taken up by early writers as a symbol of postmortem purification. The mother of the seven Maccabean "martyrs," for example, figured in some fifth-century Gallic sermons.[21] The Maccabean mother also appeared in a sixth-century poem by Venantius Fortunatus, *Ad Armentariam*, to allude extravagantly to the virtues of the mother of Bishop Gregory of Tours.[22] And there are other sporadic references and depictions in late antiquity.[23] The example of Judas Maccabaeus, while occasionally used to justify the church's prayers on behalf of all departed souls, appears to have had no significance for early preaching on purgatory and remained tied to the discourse of prayer for the dead.[24] Furthermore, Bede, who wrote on purgatory and who mentioned the Maccabean revolt and Judas's actions on a number of occasions, never alluded to the description of Judas's intercession and did not refer to 2 Maccabees when discussing the afterlife or purgatory.[25]

Another common proof text for purgatory is Matthew 12:31–32: "Therefore, I tell you, every sin and blasphemy will be forgiven men, but the blasphemy against the Spirit will not be forgiven. And whoever says a word against the Son of man will be forgiven; but whoever speaks against the Holy Spirit will not be forgiven, either in this age or in the age to come." This passage has been interpreted to mean that some sins were forgiven in the next world that had not been forgiven in this world. The passage is vague, however, and reveals nothing more than that under no circumstance will a particular sin be forgiven (speaking against the Holy Spirit). Indeed, the reference to Judgement Day six verses later underscores this view and is in line with the general expectation expressed by New Testament authors that Judgement Day was close at hand. Bede never cited this passage in connection with purgatory.

The New Testament Epistles reveal that there was a variety of beliefs about what happened to the dead in the earliest Christian communities, even to the extent of who might ultimately benefit from salvation. The Pauline tradition endorsed universal salvation in some measure, judging by Corinthians and Romans, and also accepted that baptism of living persons on behalf of the unbaptized dead had some efficacy, although elsewhere it is implied that eternal suffering awaits the wicked.[26] However, there was much in the New Testament to support Jewish converts to Christianity in the view that prayers made by the living on behalf of the dead could benefit souls in the afterlife—of Christians certainly and perhaps even of those not yet baptized.

Another example of expansive thinking about salvation that could include Gentiles and Jews is the proliferation of *descensus* narratives in the first Christian centuries, stories in which Jesus and his apostles spent time in hell preaching to the dead and offering them salvation.[27] These narratives could be interpreted as extending salvation to all Christians, but ultimately the theological use of this story for broader notions of salvation was strongly quashed by a strong historicizing impulse in antiquity: salvation for the dead had been offered only on that one historical occasion in order to permit the salvation of the patriarchs and righteous Gentiles who had not heard Christ's teachings. Since that time, sinners could not claim this ignorance, and thus they could not expect another chance at salvation after death. In the era of Augustine and Bede, it was widely believed that hell's inhabitants were confined eternally and denied any possibility of rescue.

The image of the probative fire (1 Cor. 3:11–15) that will test each man according to his work would certainly suggest purgatory to later writers, but it did not encompass all the qualities of medieval purgatory: extended purification until Judgement Day, the idea that purification involves pain and punishment, and the soul's experience altered by the intercessory actions of the living. Early exegetes, who viewed the divine fire as an image of sanctification, denied that this fire would be painful for the just.[28] They looked to the image and example of the three Hebrews in the fiery furnace who stood within flames but were not consumed because God was with them.[29] And there is no claim in the image of salvation "as through fire" that this experience could be mitigated by the prayers of the living. And we are far away from any suggestion that souls in the afterlife are affected by the offering of the Mass. Once it was posited that those with some sin could have their experience in the fire of purgation altered by intercessory acts, the nature and operation of that fire became fixed in a new way: the fire could be seen as a form of divine punishment that could be mitigated, rather than as a fire fueled only by sin and that purified by means of an automatic, cosmic cleansing of dross from the soul.

The problem with scriptural "proofs" for the theology of purgatory is that none of the passages cited encompassed all the features of medieval purgatory: rather, these passages only suggested discrete components of what would later be considered a whole. The remainder of this chapter examines what early Christian "experts" on the subject believed they knew about the fate of the soul after the body's physical death and before it joined its resurrected body on Judgement Day.

Early Christian Views

The early Christian centuries saw a steady if not prolific production of opinions on the purgation of the soul. Irenaeus, in the second century, believed that some form of education awaited the soul at death, but he did not anticipate purgation or punishment.[30] Clement of Alexandria, in the third century, argued that the soul would be purged in the afterlife by two types of fires: the educational fire that corrected the corrigible and the punitive fire that devoured the incorrigible.[31] The educational fire was a fire that did not devour but cleansed like a baptism.[32] And Lactantius, at the turn of the fourth century, wrote that the fire would not inflict pain on the just: "The power of innocence is so great that the fire retreats before it with no harm because it has received its mission, of burning the impious and respecting the just, from God."[33]

The author of book 2 of the *Christian Sibylline Oracles* imagined that all souls, both those long dead and those caught up in the apocalyptic conflagration, would pass through fire: the poet saw "all souls of men" burning in pitch and fire but then "in an instant all shall fuse together, and be separated into purity." The poet imagined the gates of hell being opened by the angel Uriel, and all its inhabitants, including the prophets and patriarchs, emerge: "And then shall all pass through the burning river, and unquenchable flame; and the righteous shall be saved, but the impious shall perish." As for the righteous, "angels shall bear them through the burning river and bring them to light and to a carefree life." Furthermore, the poet imagined that the righteous would, at that time, be able to intercede for souls—not from the pain of purgatory but from the torment of hell: "To the pious, when they ask eternal God, he will grant them to save men out of the devouring fire, and from everlasting torments."[34]

While the purificatory fire motif was developing in Christian thought, in the second century, another important idea emerged: that some souls destined for heaven would not enter heaven immediately; rather they would have to wait in some place—the grave or other subterranean location—until they were deemed ready to enter heaven. Jan N. Bremmer notes that this idea was generated in the context of anti-Gnostic sentiment, especially in the case of Irenaeus.[35] This combative stage in Christian intellectual life resulted, according to Daley, in an eschatology that "organized biblical images and popular lore into a more and more comprehensive doctrine of life after death."[36] Thus Tertullian, writing at the beginning of the third century, espoused an interim abode for the happy dead termed a *refrigerium interim*, a place under the earth where souls destined for heaven would reside restfully until the Last Judgement admitted them to eternal life. Tertullian associated this abode with the biblical Bosom of Abraham, which is "a temporary refuge (*temporale . . . receptaculum*) for the souls of the faithful." That region "though not in heaven, yet not so deep as hell (*inferis*), will in the meantime afford refreshment (*interim refrigerium*) to the souls of the righteous, until the consummation of all things makes complete the general resurrection with its fullness of reward."[37] The wicked would likewise experience a foretaste of the suffering they would experience in hell once reunited with their bodies. Both regions, the place of refreshment and the place of suffering, were located in a vast subterranean place.[38] Tertullian indicates that these regions were far distant from each other but were also within view.[39] This was not a place of punishment or a place for the education of sinful Christians but, as he explained, a sort of image of the future judgement of the soul[40]: it is a refuge, a waiting place, where souls anticipate the reward they will receive in heaven. For righteous souls that place is a *locus amoenus*, a garden with hyperfruited trees; Tertullian explicitly connected this paradise with the Elysian Fields of pagan mythology and in so doing limited the latter's role in Christian eschatology.[41] The idea that some souls waited to be admitted to heaven was enormously important for later discussions and visions of the otherworld. However, the relationship of purgatory's fire to this waiting place remained unclear even in those later works.

Some scholars have seen early intimations of purgatory in the *Passion of Perpetua and Felicity*.[42] In that text, the recently imprisoned and soon to be martyred Perpetua had two visions of her brother Dinocrates who died some years earlier when he was seven years old of a cancer of the face. In her first vision, Perpetua saw her brother "hot and thirsty, his raiment foul, his colour pale," bearing a facial scar where his cancerous ulcers had been. Dinocrates tried unsuccessfully to obtain water from a font beside him. Perpetua knew from this vision that her brother was suffering (*laborare*), and she prayed daily until she had another vision of her brother, clean and comfortable and able to drink water from a golden cup on the edge of the fountain. This cup never ran dry, and once sated, Dinocrates was able to play as children do. When Perpetua awoke she knew her brother was released from his pains (*de poena*).[43]

Scholars have long been interested in this episode. Was Perpetua's vision of Dinocrates evidence that Christians believed in purgatory at the turn of the third century? Or did the vision suggest purgatory only to later readers of her account? It is generally agreed that this is a story of an effective intercession for the suffering dead made by a woman who would later be venerated as a martyr. Early commentators focused on whether Dinocrates had died as a pagan or a Christian because salvation for non-Christians was still a hotly contested issue in the third and fourth centuries. Augustine's assertion that Dinocrates was a Christian was rooted in his need to bring the story of intercession into line with his own restricted views of salvation.

Jeffrey Trumbower has given considerable thought to the Dinocrates episode.[44] He argues, convincingly, that Dinocrates could not have been a Christian and that Perpetua's vision related the effective intercession of a Christian for a pagan—an idea that was still acceptable in her time.[45] For this reason, he argues that Perpetua's vision of Dinocrates was not a vision of purgatory as it later came to be defined:

> If Dinocrates were a baptized Christian suffering punishment to purify him of his sins, then we could say that Perpetua saw purgatory. Such an interpretation of Perpetua's visions . . . is virtually impossible for the historical Perpetua. . . . Thus, Perpetua cannot be connected with the doctrine of purgatory, except in the sense that later generations reinterpreted her vision in that direction. She did offer to posterity a notion of the efficacy of prayer for the dead, which became incorporated into the cultural construction of Purgatory, but only with limits on who could be helped that were not part of Perpetua's original conception.[46]

The idea that Perpetua interceded for a pagan also finds support in the light of Klawiter's thesis that imprisonment gave Perpetua presbyterial status and thus the power of the keys to bind and loose. At the time of the persecutions it was accepted both by the Catholic Church and by the Montanists that imprisoned confessors awaiting martyrdom could obtain Christian salvation for the lapsed and for pagans.[47] Klawiter argues that the relatively prominent position of women in the New Prophecy movement makes it likely that Perpetua would have claimed and used this power to release her brother. From this argument one would have to infer that Dinocrates was not in purgatory but in hell. Klawiter interprets the second vision as a form of baptism: "Through Perpetua's intercessory prayers and tears, her brother was pardoned and given full forgiveness of sins by the living water of baptism, the water which previously had been out of reach because he had died as a pagan."[48]

Most recently, Andreas Merkt has discussed Perpetua's vision of Dinocrates in relationship to early purgatory, and specifically its connection to the contemporaneous thought of Tertullian and Cyprian.[49] Merkt usefully catalogues the long and contentious history of the interpretation of this passage, where it can be seen that there has been a great deal of resistance to the view that this text is early evidence of belief in purgatory. Dölger, Franz, and Dronke, for example, have emphasized the pagan and psychological aspects of the visions, thereby minimizing the importance of the visions as evidence for Christian eschatology in this era.[50] Even in works in which Perpetua's actions and beliefs have received a more Christian interpretation, the case for purgatory is hardly argued. Many works now consider Perpetua's visions without reference to theological and eschatological themes.[51] One exception is Bremmer, who concludes that while the vision of Dinocrates does not prefigure purgatory, it does prefigure intercession.[52] Merkt's own conclusion is that while Perpetua's two visions of Dinocrates may not explicitly refer to purgatory, many of the key features of medieval purgatory are to be found in them.[53] How far did Perpetua's visions of Dinocrates aid in the development of later belief in purgatory? That is hard to say. We can say, however, that later sermons did not extol Perpetua for her example of intercessory prayer while alive, but rather for other qualities such as constancy in the face of death and fortitude beyond expectations of her sex and chastity.[54] As far as one can ascertain, early medieval notions of purgatory were not built on the authority of Perpetua's visions and were not influenced by their imagery.

Two great Alexandrian scholars at the turn of the third century, Clement (d. circa 215) and Origen (186–254), made influential contributions to this history of the Christian afterlife. We have already noted above that Clement of Alexandria viewed the fire of purgation as one that cleansed the sinner in the present life. But it has also been claimed that Clement intended to refer to a cleansing fire in the afterlife. Osborn put the case cautiously:

> The function of fire is to purify, to test, and to sanctify. But the notion of a cleansing fire is not carefully defined in Clement. It moves between two poles—the idea of the fiery end of the world and the idea of moral shame. It is hard to say how far the idea is spiritualised; but it is certain Clement gives us the beginning of the idea of Purgatory. However, the later development of this doctrine is completely foreign to Clement.[55]

More recently, Daley has summarized Clement thus:

In this consistent interpretation of all punishment, including punishment after death, as purification rather than retribution, Clement can be considered the first exponent of the doctrine of purgatorial eschatological suffering; he thus paves the way for centuries of speculation and controversy on the subject of "purgatory" among Christian theologians. He is also the first Christian writer to suggest, with great caution, the related prospect of universal salvation for all intelligent creatures.[56]

In view of the importance of these claims, it may be useful to clarify the limits of Clement's contribution. There are two basic areas in which Clement's ideas about a purificatory fire fall short of the medieval view of purgatory. The first is the suggestion that, in essence, Clement has eliminated hell as it was commonly understood—a place of eternal punishment without correction and without respite. As we will see in the discussion of Bede, purgatory in its eighth-century form cannot exist without an eternal hell. Insofar as Clement can be said to have accepted some notion of universal salvation, this places him in a position that is antithetical, theologically, to early medieval purgatory as defined by Bede. Furthermore, as Osborn points out, Clement's comments can often be viewed as having a spiritual meaning, so that his exact claims for the afterlife are problematic. The second deficiency, as we shall see in the discussion on Augustine, is that medieval purgatory required that "correction" of Christians could be attained through punishment in the afterlife. Clement is voluable on the good to be derived from God's correcting punishment of his chosen, but he does not envisage punishment as a method of divine purification in the afterlife.[57] The essential role of punishment in purifying the soul after death is not found in Clement's nonretributive, intelligent fire.

Clement's presumed pupil, Origen, shared Clement's preference for understanding scriptural texts, and especially eschatological issues, in a spiritualized, metaphorical way: as referring primarily to the life of the divinely inspired soul as it matures in understanding in the present life and as it continues its developmental existence in the next. Yet Origen went beyond Clement's teachings to speculate more broadly on the fate of souls after death. Furthermore, Origen was a commanding Christian intellectual who was courted as a teacher but was also liable to being misunderstood. His Christian credentials were impeccable—his father had died a martyr, and Origen himself also suffered years of persecution—and even his critics agreed that his scriptural knowledge was unsurpassed in his time, but some of his ideas invited controversy. Origen's contribution to early Christian eschatology was thus enormous and profound, while being highly controversial in his own time and beyond.[58] Indeed,

Origen's ideas and historical legacy lurk behind a great deal of early medieval speculation about the afterlife, both in terms of his positive contribution and in the strong reactions to some of his views. Jerome first embraced and then distanced himself from Origen's views, Augustine strove to answer his questions without acknowledging who had asked them, and Bede, as we shall see, had the specter of Origen very much in view when he wrote on purgatory.

It was Origen who asked the crucial question that lay at the heart of purgatory: what would be the fate of the ordinary Christian in the next life?

> What if we finish our life with sins but also with what is commendable, will we be saved through what is commendable and acquitted concerning those sins which were knowingly committed? Or will we be punished for the sins but receive no recompense for what is commendable?[59]

What, he asks, if you possess gold and silver but also wood, hay, and stubble? The answer: All souls would encounter the fire on Judgement Day after the general resurrection of the dead, and souls (possibly all souls) would continue to be purified through correction and divine instruction. First, God's fire will consume those baser elements, and then later God will compensate them (doubly) for their wrong: "For *first* that which is wrong, then that which is righteous are rendered their due."[60] Good Christians would pass through the fire of purification painlessly, and less perfect Christians would have a harder time of it, confronting the "spirit of combustion" as their sin had kindled the fire that burned them.[61] This perspective gave full scope to the idea of personal responsibility for sin and the value of penance.[62] Christians who were not perfect were distinguished in this system from those who were deeply sinful, the former being purified in the fire quickly or instantaneously, and the latter requiring more time. Thus in fundamental ways his solution for the salvation of the ordinary Christian anticipated purgatory's later theology, especially that of Bede whose account of the *Vision of Drythelm* made precisely such a distinction between those purged of *delicta* and *scelera*, but there were other aspects of Origen's eschatology that were soon deemed to be unacceptable.

Origen envisaged the divine education of Christian souls as an ongoing process, so that after death Christians would continue their schooling for some time in a *schola animarum* until they were ready to pass through a purifying, sanctifying fire that would be the final preparation needed to enable them to live with God. However, he also held to the Platonic view that the plurality of souls in the present world would eventuality reattain unity with God (*apocatastasis*). This unity would be achieved through a process of punishment and correction that would be arduous for rank sinners and would take a very long time.[63] This process was effective, however: "There is a resurrection of the dead, and there is punishment, but not everlasting, for when the body is punished the soul is gradually purified, and so is restored to its ancient rank."[64]

He also speculated on the ability of God's mercy to prevail against evil, leading to the eventual restoration of all souls to God: "For all wicked men, and for daemons, too, punishment has an end, and both wicked men and daemons shall be restored to their former rank."[65] Yet Origen's work does not show complete consistency. If the purifying fire can restore all beings to God, then hell, in a traditional sense, would not exist. Yet in some places in his work he stated that unrepentant sinners would experience hellfire, in others he implied that hellfire was reserved for devils, not for humans, and in yet others he said that hell itself must have an end and that salvation is possible even for the devil. It was this latter opinion that exposed Origen to criticism and ultimately ecclesiastical condemnation and ensured that the work that contained it, *On First Principles*, was widely condemned.[66]

Modern scholars have tended to judge Origen more sympathetically than his medieval readers, citing major problems with any analysis of his thought, namely, that his writings are not known in their entirety, that some of his writings were distorted by supporters and detractors in antiquity, and that it is important to distinguish writings that arose from speculation from those that were intended to be doctrinal.[67] It should also be expected that Origen's thought changed over time and that specific works were tailored to different audiences. For medieval writers, Origen's condemnation in 400 (Alexandria) and again in 553 (Constantinople) for his writings on universal salvation was the most salient and communicable fact about him; his condemnation removed his eschatological writings from common discourse, and, as medieval writers were wary of propagating heresy, his condemnation has obscured them also from us. It is evident that Bede knew Origen's teachings on the fire of purification primarily through Rufinus and that he chose to set up a doctrinal opposition to Origen's eschatology by characterizing purgatory's existence as antithetical to the view that the wicked would be saved.

Although varied views circulated about exactly what awaited the soul after death, writers of the third and fourth centuries do attest to the rise of certain common themes that continued to be expressed beyond their time. First, there was general consensus that when a person died, the individual soul passed on to some form of postmortem experience either before the general resurrection or (for sinners, according to Origen) after it.[68] Second, it was widely believed that the soul received some kind of judgement at death that anticipated the sentence of Christ on Judgement Day; thus no alteration of fate was possible after death.[69] Third, in this interim period the soul enjoyed an existence that could be depicted in visions (like that of Perpetua) with an incorporeal body that could be recognized by others and furnished with a similar register of sensation, whether of pleasure or pain, so that the visionary viewer could ascertain and attest that justice had seen to be done. The interim place of refreshment might be under the earth, but it was a pleasant place, a garden, a paradise.[70] Opinions varied on precisely when the soul would pass through the fire—immediately after death, before the Final Judgement, on Judgement Day, or after it. Later visionary tales depended on a narrative logic that suggested that the soul underwent judgement and purification immediately after death, and that once the right conditions were met (correct burial, punishment, or some form of intercession), the souls of the elect would rest before the Judgement Day. Those who viewed the Day of Judgement as imminent, such as Origen, tended to situate these events on the Day of Judgement itself.

In the third and fourth centuries, Christian and pagan philosophic thought about the purification and fate of the soul aligned sufficiently to suggest that a stock of common scientific knowledge existed that could be debated and refined across religious lines. Both pagans and Christians were convinced of the value of ascetic practices for reforming a fallen soul into one that reflected the divine image and that set the stage for its "return" although they disagreed fundamentally about the agency that brought it about. The pagan sage Plotinus expressed the monastic ideal of purification through detachment in terms that would have been familiar to educated Christians: "The purification of the soul is simply to allow it to be alone; it is pure when it keeps no company; when it looks to nothing without itself; when it entertains no alien thoughts . . . when it no longer sees in the world of image, much less elaborates images into veritable affections. Is it not a true purification to turn away towards the exact contrary of earthly things?"[71] Elite Christian culture absorbed much from Neoplatonic thought so that when distinctions had to be maintained it was often on purely doctrinal grounds. For example, when Augustine dismissed Platonic views of purification as represented by Porphyry it was on the grounds that Porphyry failed to attribute purification to the one "principle," Jesus Christ incarnate. There was obviously no possible compromise on this issue from the Christian perspective, but it is interesting to note that Augustine's reaction was prompted by the threat posed by Porphyry's willingness to advance what might be viewed as a trinitarian view of the "divine intellect."[72]

In the course of the fourth century, theological reflections on postmortem purgation were further refined to reflect moral, pastoral, and doctrinal concerns. The Ambrosiaster *Commentary on Corinthians* explained that the future purging fire would burn away false teaching (*mala doctrina*) and that it would be painful (*non sine poena sit*).[73] Bishop Ambrose of Milan wrote that all Christians must pass through the fire since fire in the form of a flaming sword had guarded the gates of paradise since Adam and Eve's banishment.[74] After death, souls would not lie in the grave or in the funeral pyre, but rather inhabited chambers and waited, either for punishment or for glory.[75] The souls of the just rest "in much quietness" without fear for their judgement and undisturbed by recollection of their sins.[76] The wicked would not come to judgement, however, for they were judged to eternal torment already.[77] Curiously, on the strength of his treatise *On Death as a Good*, Ambrose was held up as an icon of antipurgatorial thought in later Protestant writings.[78]

Often writers turned their attention to the afterlife as a response to heresies or views that they deemed unsustainable by reference to scripture or logic. For example, Jerome's preoccupation with hierarchies of merit resulted in a highly stratified view of the soul's reward in the afterlife. The notion that punishment should fit the crime found support in scripture, secular law, and early patristic opinion. Yet Jerome's insistence on hierarchy, even in heaven, stood in tension against the earlier dominant model of Christian Neoplatonism that emphasized final unity and "oneness" with God.[79] It was the late fourth-century struggles with Origen's legacy, however, that anticipated Bede's more limited but ultimately very significant positioning of purgatory as a response to Origen.

Augustine

It was Augustine's firm view that no alteration in the soul's fate could be accomplished after death. All Christian virtue and penance had to be accomplished in the present life in order for the soul to be eligible for God's mercy in the next. Furthermore, as Augustine developed his teaching on original sin against the background of Pelagianism, he insisted that all humans owed a debt of pain, and so all, with the possible exception of martyrs, must suffer some punishment after death. Augustine accepted that the soul might be purified in the present life through suffering; but such sufferings (*poenas purgatorias*) would be purificatory only to "those who are corrected by them (*qui eis . . . corriguntur*)."[80] Suffering experienced in the otherworld was another matter altogether; its aim was to punish, not to purify.[81] Postmortem purification was available only at the Last Judgement when a few Christians, destined for heaven, were purified by the fire of any minor impurities that remained.[82] He who passes from the devil to Christ "should not imagine that any pains are purificatory, except those that precede that ultimate and terrible judgement."[83]

Augustine's views on matters pertaining to the purgation of Christian souls are notoriously cautious. With scripture offering so little concrete guidance on such matters, Augustine was hesitant to ascribe doctrinal status to his own tentative conclusions. Because he was assailed by the views of those with whom he disagreed, he was willing to refute a flawed idea, but he often declined to propose a definitive solution to the problems that they raised.

Augustine's analysis of the fire of Corinthians illuminates his approach. The phrase "as through fire," he asserted, is a metaphor and thus may not refer to actual fire, but rather to the fire of tribulation that comes to Christians in the present life in the form of bereavement, persecutions or even death itself. It will benefit only those whose "foundation" is Christ, and those are Christians who adhere to a high standard in that they place "no earthly or temporal thing before Christ."[84] Furthermore, the image of an assaying fire was, to his mind, a way of talking about the attachment of men to worldly goods in the present life, not about the afterlife. Still, as a cautious concession to the alternative (perhaps more traditional) way of thinking about the passage as referring to the afterlife he noted in the *Enchiridion*: "That some such thing may happen even after this life is not past belief, and it may be inquired into and either ascertained or left doubtful whether some believers may be saved by a sort of purging fire, more slowly or more swiftly in proportion as they have loved with more or less devotion the goods that perish."[85] So, even as Augustine allowed himself to ponder the possibility of afterlife purgation, envisaging that souls might experience purgation differently ("slowly or more swiftly"), he held to the view that purgation was simply the soul's passage to its ultimate destination. Elsewhere he clarified that purgation would afflict the soul in a spiritual place, not the body.[86] And in the *City of God*, he expressed anew his doubts whether the fire "may be experienced perhaps only after this life, or both in this life or hereafter, or in this life only and not hereafter."[87]

Augustine lived long enough, and wrote extensively enough, that it is possible to trace an evolution in his thinking. Joseph Ntedika's study of Augustine's writings on purgatory pointed to an essential change in Augustine's attitude about the fate of the soul between 413 and 426. In those years Augustine was busy refuting what he saw as the overly lenient views of salvation tendered by "merciful" or "tender-hearted" Christians.[88] In these years of anti-Origenist debate (largely as expressed in the debate between Rufinus and Jerome, but also in the trial of Pelagius), he opposed some of the many permutations of views of salvation then circulating that suggested to him an insufficiently rigorous understanding of scripture and the power of the sacraments.[89] A digest of these unacceptable views, mentioned briefly in his *Enchiridion* 18, made its way also into the final books of his *City of God*, a work in which Augustine was finally led to address directly the subject of a purging fire after death. In the *City of God*, Augustine refuted the views of those who viewed salvation as the assured fate of those who went to church, took the sacraments, and petitioned the saints for help. He especially deplored those who believed they might avoid punishment through the merit of others. Yet even Augustine, whose views on original sin forced him to view punishment as the fate of all but a very few, was unable to consign children to the fire of purification. As long as the child is baptized he will enter Christ's kingdom, Augustine stated, and "he will not even undergo any purifying torments after death."[90] In 421 Augustine penned a work that was widely read in the middle ages, a handbook on matters of faith, the *Enchiridion*. In this work he confronted the question raised two centuries earlier by Origen: what would be the fate of those who were in some respects commendable, but who were also burdened with sin? Origen's answer to this question was clearly unacceptable to Augustine who could not subscribe to a progressive system of punishments and rewards in the afterlife. At the same time, Catholic practice (including that of his own mother) saw a value in offering prayers for the dead, suggesting that the fate of souls in the afterlife could be ameliorated by God in response to the actions of the living. Augustine's answer acknowledged the problem of the ordinary Christian in the afterlife and conceded that prayer may have some positive effect on the soul (solace) but shied away from any suggestion that amelioration of fate could be the result of such prayers:

> Now, in the time intervening between a man's death and the final resurrection, the soul is held in a hidden retreat, enjoying rest or suffering hardship in accordance with what it merited during its life in the body. There is no gainsaying that the souls of the dead find solace from the piety of their friends who are alive, when the sacrifice of the Mediator is offered for the dead or alms are given in the Church. But these means are of profit for those who, when they lived, earned merit whereby such things could be of profit to them. For theirs is a manner of living neither so good that there is no need for these helps after death, nor so bad that they would not be of profit after death. There is, however, a good manner of living which makes the use of these helps unnecessary, and a correspondingly bad manner of living which prohibits their being of any avail once a man has passed from this life. It is here, then, that is won all merit or demerit whereby a man's state after this life can either be improved

or worsened. But let no one hope to obtain, when he is dead, merit with God which he earlier neglected to acquire.[91]

In the context of a discussion of the efficacy of prayers for the dead, and in a passage reminiscent of Tertullian's views of afterlife "receptacles" in *De anima*, Augustine imagined souls anticipating the suffering or joy that would be theirs at the Final Judgement. While recognizing that sinners were of different types, Augustine did not suggest that prayers for the dead could substantially influence the experience of souls in the afterlife beyond "solace" or refreshment, which is not further defined but which may extend to nothing more than to the psychological notion that the souls know they are not forgotten by the living.[92] With tautological evasiveness, Augustine suggested that consolation is beneficial only to those who are in a position to benefit from consolation! Augustine's reticence can be best understood by reference to a treatise letter written in the same year, the *De cura pro mortuis gerenda*, in which he had argued that burial and funerals alongside other rituals for the dead, were without use except as consolation for the living and as a sign of human affection.[93] So, while Augustine, in the *Enchiridion*, appears to have conceded that some "solace" would be felt by the sinful dead when their loved ones had masses said for them and had given alms, he held fast to pastoral instruction: to emphasize that these activities could not materially benefit the deceased unless they had already, through pious living, merited such actions on their behalf.

This passage strikes one as a reluctant concession to the by now traditional idea that prayer for the dead must bring some specific benefit to them; but the "solace" that he imagines the dead may receive is so vague that it clearly arises from a desire to deflect any real value from it. The passage continues:

> When, then, sacrifices either of the altar or of alms are offered on behalf of all the baptized dead, they are thank-offerings for the very good, they are propitiatory offerings for the not very bad, and in the case of the very bad, even though they do not assist the dead, they are a species of consolation to the living. And where they are profitable, their benefit consists either in obtaining a full remission of sins, or at least in making the condemnation more tolerable.[94]

The first sentence makes it clear that prayers can benefit only one category of the dead—imperfect Christian souls destined for heaven (or as formulated earlier in the passage, those souls neither so good, nor so bad, that prayers would not be beneficial). The final sentence is difficult to interpret because it combines two different thoughts: first, that prayers for the dead may bring a full remission of sins (thus permitting the soul to attain heaven), and second, that prayers may ease the tortures of the damned. Was Augustine referring only to one category of dead here—the damned, some of whom might be released by God in an act of mercy and some who may have their suffering mitigated? In his attempt to deflect from the idea of protracted post-mortem suffering, Augustine was willing to make a fairly radical assertion: that masses and almsgiving may be effective in remitting sins altogether. Only in a sermon that was later attributed to Augustine is there the hint that prayer and its accompanying actions should be vigorously undertaken for the dead since they may stimulate God's mercy.[95]

Augustine's cautious views on the efficacy of prayer for relieving postmortem suffering, and his concession in the *Enchiridion* that there was indeed a fire of postmortem purgation, were sufficient for later writers to look to Augustine as an authority on the notion of purgatory. Ntedika noted in the conclusion to his study that Augustine addressed the two subjects of intercessory prayer and postmortem purgation separately.[96] This may have been deliberate, and therefore it is problematic to deduce a connection in Augustine's thought when Augustine clearly refrained from making it.[97] Later medieval readers of the *Enchiridion*, however, would see the two discourses as being intimately connected. It is clear from Bede's phrasing that he was reading Augustine's *Enchiridion* when he composed his own definition of purgatory in the 720s.

Conclusion

While early Christian views of postmortem purgation varied in details, such as the time, place, and action of the purging fire, and which segments of humanity would undergo it, it was increasingly the Christian view that after death, the soul would await the bodily resurrection in a state either of pain or of joy. By the late fourth century there was a tendency to emphasize the punitive nature of the purifying fire. Augustine's insistence that all humanity was sinful brought the prospect of that fire closer for Christians. Older views of progress of the soul competed with this penalty-driven theology. The distinction between notions of punishment and correction is examined in greater depth in the next chapter.

The earliest Christian writers grappled with the few scriptural passages that seemed to shed light on the afterlife. However, by Augustine's time exegetical tradition and the threat of heresy profoundly shaped discourse on postmortem purgation. Already in Augustine's time, patristic opinion as much as scripture set the framework for discussion. That tendency only deepened in later centuries. Origen, in particular, stood for all that was potentially dangerous in eschatological theology. In the East, some elements of Origen's eschatology would be refined, modified, and made acceptable in the work of later thinkers, including the writings of Gregory of Nyssa. While Origen's work continued to be plundered for its exegetical insights by western theologians, his views on the afterlife not only condemned him as a heretic in the eyes of posterity but also stimulated a reaction to any suggestion that all sins could, in time, be purged in the afterlife, or that salvation was possible for any soul that had not already been provided for by divine election.

2

Of Sons and Slaves

Violence and Correction in the Afterlife

In the early third century, Origen reflected on what the Christian's attitude to God's judgement should be: "It is my opinion, in fact, that even if someone could escape God's judgement, he ought not to desire to. For not to come to God's judgement would mean not to come to correction, and to the restoration of health and to that which heals."[1]

The role of punishment in correction, and the Christian's ideal response to human suffering, endlessly fascinated the early church fathers. Correction of the soul could be effected through punishment, but it was also possible to correct without recourse to physical violence and to punish without corrective result. Some forms of pain (penance, martyrdom) could be viewed as a good, as a purification in the present life, but how then did such a penalty (*poena*) relate to purification in the afterlife? Suffering in the present life could be viewed as purifying the soul, or it could be viewed as humanity's inevitable lot. Christians saw reflections of these distinctions all around them. They saw it in their family lives, in the empire's institutions, and even in the discipline meted out to different clerical ranks within the church. The entire world, governed by a paternal God, could be seen as a cosmic exercise in the application of such distinctions. However, it could also be an invitation to view life's trials and suffering through a valorizing lens. Choice was at the heart of the matter. The Christian should choose to come to judgement, as Origen suggested, because in submitting to God's justice, the Christian accepted suffering as a means of correction, health, and salvation. Further, because earthly trials are held to be a "copy and shadow of the heavenly," the Christian might expect to submit to correction in the afterlife. Yet there is no doubt that by the turn of the fifth century, correction in the afterlife was something that was widely feared. Choice often consisted in working to avoid it through the voluntary, preemptive embrace of pain.

In an era in which declaring oneself to be a Christian was an invitation to persecution, torture, and even death, Christians had viewed afterlife punishment primarily as a vehicle for divine retribution on their persecutors. Gehenna, an infernal place of torture, could be viewed as having been established by God for the purpose of cosmic justice—to punish individual sinners for the common good.[2] Origen expressed it thus: "God is a consuming fire and God is light, a consuming fire for sinners, a light for the just and holy ones."[3] What Christians could expect in the afterlife was the culmination of a lifetime of purification: an encounter with the purificatory fire that would "wash" the last remnants of sin from the soul. It was even possible that those who held to their baptismal vows (the baptism of the Holy Spirit) would not have to encounter a second baptism of fire. But even if the Christian would have need of a second baptism of fire, he would be saved. This view of guaranteed postmortem purification can be seen in the opinions of the church's earliest theologians. Irenaeus of Lyons, in the second century, expected that the soul would benefit from further education (*paideia*) in the world to come but did not anticipate purgation or punishment.[4] At the turn of the third century, Clement of Alexandria distinguished two kinds of fire in afterlife purgation: the educational fire that instructed the corrigible and the punitive fire that devoured the incorrigible.[5] The educational fire was a fire that did not devour, but cleansed like a baptism.[6] Origen imagined salvation effected through a long process of purifying punishments in this life and extending into the next, but culminating in a baptism of fire that would wash away sin.[7]

It might have been expected that purgatory's fires would have drawn on this tradition of an educating, correcting fire. Instead, it drew on a punitive model, one that in time would come to look very much like hell. Why was this so? Why would correction of the soul be conceived of in terms of corporeal pain? Why were the options for spiritual amendment in the afterlife so much more limited than those available to Christians in life?

The simple answer to these questions is that death changed the terms of correction. In life, Christians were encouraged to discipline themselves by whatever means best achieved the eradication of sin. In life, Christians could voluntarily seek to separate themselves from worldly things. In life, correction of the soul could become a daily exercise. In life, spiritual amendment could be tailored to the individual's sex, age, condition, and status. The impetus for such self-discipline was the uncertainty as to what kind of judgement and sentence lay ahead. The fear that divine punishment in the afterlife might exceed any known register of human pain made voluntary penitential practices in the present life a prudent calculation. Such exercises aimed at expunging the debt of pain and restoring the soul to baptismal purity.

But the western tradition was to be profoundly influenced by the perspective that even if the individual strove for purity in life, a debt of pain yet remained that could be expunged only by God's mercy. As one eighth-century penitential put it: "Christians, if they have been overtaken in sin, shall be saved after punishments,"[8] with no sense of the soul being corrected and saved *through* punishment. According to this view, death altered not only the severity with which sin would be expunged but also the means by which the debt of humanity could be paid. To some degree this was merely logical. At death the soul was no longer corrigible by voluntary efforts at purification, because it was no longer under the sinner's control. Whereas in life the sinner might feel contrition, do penance and other forms of reparation, show charity to others, and do good works to aid his soul's salvation, once the sinner had passed into the afterlife, the soul's "body" was its only vehicle for correction. Enslaved by sin in life, in death, the sinner's correction, like that of a slave, would proceed only through the most severe punishment.[9]

Salvation through Punishment and Salvation after Punishment

In life the soul was capable of amendment through education, behavioral modification, and pain. Purification through pain was the happy fate of the corrigible soul because not all souls could benefit from it. As Augustine put it, purgatorial penalties (*poenas purgatorias*) are purificatory only to "those who are corrected by them [*qui eis . . . corriguntur*]."[10] Importantly, Augustine was referring only to the purificatory punishments of the present life and to the learning capacity of the soul still in this world. Penance was punishment undertaken voluntarily. At the moment of death, however, that equation changed, and the soul's purgation was effected by punishment that was not voluntary. Augustine accepted that the living soul could respond to hardship with contrition, but it was also his belief that punishment for punishment's sake was the unavoidable misery of humanity's fallen nature, both in this life and in the next. For, by the end of his life, Augustine came to believe that pain in life and in the afterlife was unavoidable because it was the consequence of humanity's depraved condition—of original sin.[11]

Although Augustine was not the first to claim that people are born with sin because of the nature of procreation (Origen had said much the same thing),[12] it was Augustine's characterization of original sin as a debt that must be paid for through suffering that encouraged the development of an entire theology focused on pain. It was this perspective that justified the images of God's retributive justice that livened up visionary and pastoral literature. In the *Vision of Paul*, for example, the violence sustained by the bodies of the damned was explained as retribution for the physical sufferings of Christ, a debt of pain to be paid in order for cosmic balance to be restored. In its closing scenes, Christ denounced the tormented in hell: "My blood was shed for you, and you did not even repent. For you I wore a crown of thorns on my head and my hands were pierced with nails, and you did not console me. I asked for water when I hung on the cross; they gave me vinegar mixed with gall. With a spear they opened my right side . . ."[13] Christ's physical suffering demanded physical recompense. The same accusatory scene was reproduced in one of Caesarius's sermons and in the preaching of Eligius of Noyon in the seventh century. The *Vision of Paul* continues: "I was beaten with scourges, crowned with agony, in order that you might be saved from death . . . Give back to me your life, in return for which I surrendered mine."[14]

While the immensely popular *Vision of Paul* promoted a retributive eschatology based on the personal suffering of Christ, its essential message found support in Augustine's theology. Whereas some did learn from punishment in the present life, Augustine averred, "all other punishments, whether temporal or eternal, are imposed on every person in accordance with the treatment he is to receive from God's providence; they are imposed either in retribution for sins . . . or else they serve to exercise and to display the virtues of the good; and they are administered through the agency of men, or of angels, whether good or evil angels."[15] Punishment could be endured either in the present life or in the life to come in what was essentially an economy of pain. This concept was not new. It was widely believed that martyrs, who had voluntarily taken suffering upon themselves in Christ's name had repaid their corporeal debt and entered heaven without delay. In ascetic literature the lifetime hardships and deathbed suffering of patriarchs and saints were also explained in this way. Indeed, the Christian who did not suffer much in this life might want to be aware that "many sinners die quietly without having undergone sufferings in this world because of the tribulations and the punishments awaiting them."[16] As the author of one version of the *Life of Pachomius* explained, "in fact, there are also many good men who pass through these sufferings during their last illness and at the moment of breathing their last . . . and many other holy men sustained great suffering and many tribulations in the course of their lives, some on their deathbed."[17]

Such ideas were the bread and butter of holy biographies and invited rather blasé ruminations on the deaths of saints, like the comment of Pope Gregory: "What, then, does it matter to the just if they undergo harsh treatment at death, since they are on their way to eternal life?"[18] A life of affliction was to be accepted in much the same frame of mind. We are told that a sixth-century abbot named Spes (Hope) who governed a monastery close to Norica and who suffered from physical blindness nevertheless possessed interior illumination. Pope Gregory explained his condition thus: "But God sees our weakness and, in applying his sanctions, mingles severity with a father's watchful concern over our well-being; in chastising his elect he shows a merciful justice in order always to have some to whom he can be justly merciful."[19] Although God had given Spes one faculty in order to compensate him for the loss of another, Spes's affliction could not be understood as a simple exchange. His blindness was understood as a form of suffering, and God returned his physical sight to him just before he died as a sign that his suffering was coming to an end. The reader of this tale was asked to believe that the abbot's blindness was a direct result of God's paternal action: "Almighty God in his mercy saved this man from the eternal torments of hell by treating him with the utmost severity and at the same time favouring him with unusual graces."[20] God's punishment of a holy man in the present life, viewed as the act of a benevolent father, was presented as a sign of unique favour.

By the turn of the fifth century, it was widely accepted that pain was the inevitable lot of the elect and damned alike. The debt of retribution would be paid corporeally. For the damned, that debt of pain would be paid eternally and without fruit (correction). In purgatorial fires the elect would pay the debt corporeally and involuntarily, but it would be corrective and transient. Christian punishment would look like that of slaves but could be justified as a sort of paternal discipline for sons. Yet the "sons and slaves" metaphor was not that simple; it was malleable. It had shifting meaning depending on the context in which it was used. For example, when it came to life, death, and afterlife, at what point did Christians become sons and not slaves?

Sons and Slaves

The metaphorical connection of the punishment of sin with the punishment of a slave was immensely powerful to a Roman audience. In late antiquity, Christian metaphors of slavery flourished in the context of slavery's contemporary relevance as a social institution. Christians owned slaves, and some slaves were

Christian.[21] Some slaves were treated well and found security in their masters' protection.[22] Others were treated badly and tried to escape or rebel. This fact governed both the positive and negative aspects of the Christian rhetoric of slavery. The designation of the righteous Christian as son, and sinful Christian as slave, was enormously powerful to the point at which it could transcend metaphor and dictate action. Ultimately, it could dictate eschatology as depictions of the afterlife drew on images of abject servitude and the corporeal punishment of slaves.

The discourse of sons and slaves—of slavery as institution and as metaphor in ancient thought—has been the subject of significant scholarly attention.[23] The power of the slavery metaphor, as well as its limitations, for understanding slavery as a Graeco-Roman institution is generally acknowledged, as is the importance of the metaphor for understanding how Christians were encouraged to think about their relationship to God.[24] The image of slavery for depictions of corporeal punishment in the afterlife, by contrast, has received comparatively little attention.[25] A brief overview of the Christian rhetoric of slavery—what slavery signified for Roman audiences and how the rhetoric developed and changed in patristic writings—will underscore the full impact of the image of Christians as God's slaves and as bodies made for torture in the afterlife.

Patristic literature principally owed its rhetoric of slavery to the Pauline epistles in which the metaphor is used often and in a variety of ways. Most often it is used to suggest that Christians are liberated from the slavery of their illicit desires yet are bound to God as slaves. Yet, the image of the slave was also used in conjunction with, or in opposition to, the image of the son and heir. For example, in Galatians, living Christians are described as God's heirs who are "bound" to God's promise to Abraham and yet are "liberated" by the new covenant. At the same time, all Christians who were classified as God's heirs, were minors under God's law:

> I mean that the heir, as long as he is a child, is no better than a slave, though he is the owner of all the estate; but he is under guardians and trustees until the date is set by the father. So with us; when we were children, we were slaves to the elemental spirits of the universe. But when the time had fully come, God sent forth his son, born of woman, born under the law, so that we might receive adoption as sons. And because you are sons, God has sent the Spirit of his Son into our hearts, crying, "Abba! Father!" So through God you are no longer a slave but a son, and if a son then an heir.[26]

And the heir, "as long as he is a child," may be no better than a slave. Furthermore, Christians do not own their own bodies: "you are not your own;

you were bought with a price." God is the Christian's master in the way a master of slaves owns his or her slaves.[27]

Most common, however, Paul alluded to slavery as a metaphor for sin: "But now you have been *set free from sin* and have *become slaves of God*, the return you get is sanctification and its end, eternal life in Jesus Christ our Lord."[28] The Christian will be liberated from the slavery of sin through belief, but then not liberated after all, because now the Christian is (voluntarily) the slave of God. The Christian has exchanged one slave master for another. That the Christian must accept this servile condition is further emphasized in another passage: "Do you not know that if you yield yourselves to anyone as obedient slaves, you are *slaves of the one who you obey*, either of sin, which leads to death, or of obedience which leads to righteousness?"[29]

The Roman Christian is told he is a slave. Better to have God as master than the agents of sin. This is a metaphor chosen carefully for a Roman audience because Romans viewed themselves as masters, not as slaves. Indeed, slavery and Roman citizenship were antithetical conditions. Yet slavery to God made them adopted sons: heirs. Conversely, in Corinthians, Greeks are told to be "fools for God" because wisdom was what Greeks prided themselves on. There is no rhetoric of slavery in the Letter to the Hebrews: presumably Jews had regarded themselves as slaves long enough. It was to the Hebrews that Paul wrote encouragingly that "the Lord disciplines him whom he loves, and chastises every son whom he receives." And further that: "God is treating you as sons. . . . If you are left without discipline . . . then you are illegitimate children and not sons."[30] This is because legitimate sons are disciplined through punishment, and while present discipline is painful rather than pleasant, righteousness will reward those who are "trained by it."

So the Pauline letters addressed new Christians as slaves, as fools, and as sons, very aware of what those ideas meant to those respective audiences. Furthermore, slavery was a condition that immediately changed the individual's social and legal condition. As we shall see, social and legal definitions of status were important factors in the way Romans thought about religion and the afterlife.

The Pauline epistles suggest that once Christians accept God as their master, they become sons and thus heirs to God's kingdom. Yet in other places the metaphor is used quite differently to suggest that Christians will only be adopted as sons at the time of God's judgement. Commenting on the glory of the future life, Paul viewed the whole of creation as being held in bondage to decay, groaning in travail: and as for Christians, "[we] groan inwardly as we wait for adoption as sons, the redemption of our bodies."[31] The Gospel of Matthew, too, draws on the association of the slave's service to his master as a means of understanding the Christian's eschatological fate. In the parable of the talents, the good slave serves God well, while the useless slave is "thrown into outer darkness."[32] Thus metaphor of slavery readily crossed into Christian eschatology and apocalyptic literature.

It was Lactantius who fully developed the notion that God combined both master and father: "God is one: since he sustains the role of both father and master, we should love as sons and fear him as slaves."[33] It is an interesting comment in that wisdom and religion, while having the same goal in view, are viewed as distinct paths; one the path of love, the other the path of fear. In life the Christian may be a son through inheritance, but a slave in his need for religion's fear to guide him. Lactantius's comment was forceful because it drew on a clearly recognizable domestic paradigm in which sons were encouraged to be good and in which slaves were punished to amend behaviour. As Richard Saller points out, in elite Roman households slaves were punished more harshly than sons and, indeed, in lieu of sons.[34] Sons had personal and family honour to protect and were heirs to their father's inheritance. Slaves might be brought up in close proximity to sons, but they had no recognized honour to protect and were thus subject to corporeal punishment. Saller notes that to punish a son in the manner of a slave, especially whipping, would be considered so demeaning that it would bring dishonour on the family.[35] Saller's discussion focuses on the early empire, but a recent study of flogging in the patristic tradition suggests that, in rhetoric at least, such distinctions became blurred or fused by the third century. Theodore De Bruyne has charted a rhetorical change in the opinion of patristic authors from viewing flogging as a mark of servile status to viewing it as a mark of filial status.[36] He notes that Tertullian never referred to the whip as an instrument of paternal discipline but only as an indication of persecution and Christ's suffering. A generation later, however, Cyprian did: for him, lashes received in times of persecution were a punishment for Christian sin. By the end of the fourth century, Ambrose appropriated fully the idea that whipping was a "cultural sign of sonship." De Bruyne wanted to explain why it was that church authorities were willing to use the whip against their own subjects, and he asked whether the shift in rhetoric reflected a shift in brutality generally. Ultimately, De Bruyne maintained that in practice the flogging of sons would have been less harsh than the flogging of slaves and that what we see in patristic authors is a change in religious rhetoric, not in social reality. One can only hope for the sons of the empire that he is right. But we must go one step further because the idea of Christians as God's slaves and the social reality of the brutal punishment of slaves, when fused with Augustine's developed ideas about original sin, would ultimately provide justification and acceptance for visions of the afterlife in which Christians were brutalized.

Augustine also combined the images of the son and slave into a single social explanation. First, building on Paul's comments, he wrote that "it is understood, of course, that the condition of slavery is justly imposed on the sinner."[37] According to Augustine's interpretation, humankind had been created free in paradise but had lost that freedom in the fall. All humanity was thus bound in slavery to sin. Yet "slavery" to God would "save" the Christian, according to Augustine's etymological understanding.[38] This sense of "saved" slaves worked well for interpreting Christians as slaves of God because obedience to their divine master "saved" them. In his view, slavery was so fundamental to human society that it contributed to the "preservation of the order of nature," and the slave's condition would not disappear until the present world ended, "until all injustice disappears and all human lordship and power is annihilated, and God is all in all."

Until that time, according to Augustine, the good master, the *pater familias* (the image of God and the peace of human society), had the burdensome duty to maintain domestic peace.

> If anyone in the household is, through his disobedience, an enemy to the domestic peace, he is reproved by a word, or by a blow, or any other kind of punishment that is just and legitimate, to the extent allowed by human society; but this is to the benefit of the offender, intended to readjust him to the domestic peace from which he had broken away.... Hence, the duty of anyone who would be blameless includes ... [r]estraining a man from sin or punishing his sin, so that either the man who is chastised may be corrected by his experience, or others may be deterred by his example.[39]

And since orderly governance of the household ideally reflected divine orderliness, the master, like God, had the duty to punish both for correction and for example.

For Augustine, then, the institution of slavery was evidence of the present world's imperfection. For that reason the reality of slavery as an earthly institution could be viewed as a salutary sign and must simply be endured by those caught up in it. All humans were slaves to sin, and God was the Christian's master who must chastise his elect through such means as they were able to understand. In life, God, the good father, could educate through words (the scriptures) and through pain (life's vagaries) depending on the capacity of the sinner. However, as Augustine contemplated the sinfulness of human nature, he came to believe that the full measure of suffering owed could hardly be endured in this life unless one endured the trials and death of a martyr. There would always be an excess debt of pain to be paid: that pain had to be paid in the afterlife—no longer for the purpose of education but for punishment. The damned would be punished corporeally because that was how slaves were punished. For the elect, punishment would be purificatory since it would eventually expunge the debt of pain that was owed.[40] And since postmortem suffering was now considered the lot of all except a very few, most of the elect would be punished, and punished corporeally, because that is how sons were chastised.

Augustine's theology could be used to explain how the punishment of sinful Christians would be experienced corporeally like the punishment of the wicked. But Augustine himself did not dwell much on the nature of that temporary punishment. His sparse, but oft-cited comments on purgation focused on *who*, not *how*, and it is unlikely that he foresaw the variety of tortures that later Christians imagined for themselves and their sinful brethren in a purgatorial afterlife.

As we move beyond Augustine, to the fifth-century West, where barbarian kings were forming Christian kingdoms under the schooling of Christian bishops, slavery continued as an institution and as a personal fate. Church authorities sought to restrict slave access to positions of authority in the religion. In Gaul, councils stipulated that slaves could not be ordained without being first freed, a recognition perhaps of status problems as well as practical ones. However, if a slave was perchance ordained, the church had to pay double recompense to the slave's owner as penalty, a deterrent perhaps to those who might ordain an individual without the proper background check.[41] Theologically, slavery continued to be viewed as a corrupt institution since it was evidence of a corrupt world, but its existence was not often questioned by churchmen. Occasionally we hear of clerics freeing slaves or ransoming captives as charitable acts, but there is no consistent antislavery rhetoric before the tenth century.[42] It was considered a charitable act for wealthy Christians to free slaves in their wills, but this activity had a pagan past also. Christians who freed slaves in their wills probably hoped at the last to be freed by God from slave-like existence in the afterlife; their actions perhaps determined as much by the power of metaphor as by social critique or compassion.

The rhetoric of sonship continued also, of course, for those contexts in which the church leaders wanted to emphasize God's love and care for his flock. The increased emphasis on the flogging of sons in religious discourse in late antiquity was the ultimate justification for exercising and enforcing religious hierarchy and for coercing behaviour and perhaps belief. The stakes were high for real fathers who were derelict in their duty to curb their sons. The father of one five-year-old who blasphemed failed to take harsh action against him. When the boy died of plague it was clear to observers that in neglecting to discipline him, the father had made of him "a sinner worthy of the fires of hell."[43]

However, when we move to an eschatological dimension—to ideas concerning the correction and punishment of sinners in hell and purgatory—the justification for corporeal punishment by means of the rhetoric of a father's love for his son weakened. A debt of pain was yet owing, and that debt would be paid in kind. So whereas the avowed purpose behind Roman registers of punishment was to distinguish the honoured from the despised, and whereas in hell all sinners were slave bodies to be tortured, in the purgatorial afterlife, sonship (salvation) and slavery (punishment) combined.

Slaves in Hell and the Misery of Corporeality

To Greeks and Romans, slaves were bodies to be exploited, used, and ignored. Jennifer Glancy remarks, The Greek term *to sōma*, "body," functioned as a synonym for *ho doulos*, "slave."[44] Thus in Greek language and in Roman perception, slavery was most immediately recognized as a status that relegated control of the slave's body to the will and desires of another. Even though the experience of individual slaves might be varied, the slave in his "ideal" category, and thus as metaphor, was associated with corporeality. The corporeality of slave punishment is important when looking at the way punishment of sinners in the afterlife was depicted.

Visions of the afterlife tended to emphasize the corporeality of the soul because they generally focused attention on hell as a place of *bodily* suffering. This requires some explanation since visionaries believed they viewed souls at a particular moment in time. The individuals seen in visions had died; their flesh was rotting in their graves while their souls were experiencing an interim existence before the Last Judgement when they would receive their new immortal and imperishable bodies, which would complete and intensify the soul's eternal experience of bliss or pain.[45] So if it was the disembodied soul that existed in the interim otherworld, how could visionaries see *bodies* in torment? In the fifth century, at the time that the *Vision of Paul* was circulating, theologians in the West were disputing whether the soul was a material entity or an immaterial substance viewed only as a *simulacrum* of the body. Some supported the idea that the soul was a material organ but that it was (generally) invisible. Augustine's response was that souls, when seen in visions, appeared to have a corporeal likeness only so that they could be recognized by the visionary viewer.[46] In the case of a theologian such as Augustine, the "evidence" of visions and visionary literature forced a need for some kind of theological explanation. The generally anonymous authors of visionary literature, however, fretted little over such concerns. That is not to say that they were impervious to theological nuance generally. Visionary literature was just that: a literary vehicle for spiritual expression. The narrative power of these texts, their descriptive logic, their drama, and their pathos arose from a strong sense that souls in the afterlife were encased in bodies that saw, felt, heard, and reacted in the manner of earthly humans. According to the authors of these texts, it was possible to encounter such souls in travels to the otherworld, touch them, talk to them, and gain information from them.[47]

The visible, recognizable, and embodied souls who feature in visionary tales appeared to maintain personal identity and thus carried with them into the afterlife their own personal stories and sometimes their mental preoccupations.[48] Not only were the names of the righteous inscribed on golden tables, but their faces were inscribed there too.[49] But mostly they appear as bodies—as bodies that experience bliss and as bodies that experience pain. Jennifer Glancy notes that slaves often served as surrogate bodies for their owners; they acted on behalf of their owners, and they received blows intended for them.[50] There is some correspondence here with the way bodies in the afterlife received the penalty of the sinful soul. In ascetic literature and mentality, the body was viewed as the soul's doppelganger, an ally and an adversary in times of spiritual reckoning. This disassociation of the body from the soul was scriptural; the apostle Paul had stated: "Do you not know that your body is a temple of the Holy Spirit among you which you have from God? *You are not your own.*"[51] Thus the punishment of souls in the afterlife was dictated by their seeming corporeality—the bodies of the damned received the blows and pain intended for the soul. The damned, in particular, were fixed in the imagination as bodies. In this regard, it was suggested by the authors of these accounts that the torture of souls in the afterlife was akin to the punishment accorded to slaves.

I would suggest that contemporary audiences would have immediately recognized the depiction of distressed souls in the afterlife as drawn from the fate of slaves and of criminals of the lowest class. Whereas upper-class Romans could expect such penalties as exile, confiscation of property, and removal from positions of power and honour, the commodity of the lower class was the body. Lower-class criminals and slaves expected to suffer corporeally for any infractions toward the state or their owners. It was the horror of the penal system as exacted on the lowest segments of society that proved a terrifying image of punishment and a powerful deterrent. In hell, sinners were criminals, shackled and tortured, with mutilated faces and bodies. Depictions of tortured sinners in hell appear in the earliest visionary texts: in the *Apocalypse of Peter* from the second century, in the *Christian Sibylline Oracles* from the second and third centuries, and in the third-century Greek version of the *Vision of Paul*.[52] However, the variety of tortures peaks in the *Vision of Paul*, a work that claimed to be the secret revelation to the apostle Paul. The *Vision of Paul* is thought to have been composed in Greek during the reign of Theodosius I (AD 379–95) and has traditionally been dated to AD 388. The original Greek text is lost. The work was known in some form to Augustine by 416, who dismissed its claims to be a genuine work of the apostle Paul. Eventually, the work was translated into Latin, possibly as late as the end of the fifth century.[53] It seems likely that the *Vision of Paul* reflects the ecclesiastical and monastic concerns of the late fourth century, and it is against the specific background of late antique society that the long list of infernal punishments it catalogues can be seen.[54] This catalogue of violence echoes those conditions that lower-class criminals and slaves would have recognized. The underworld is described as a prison. It is held by bars of adamant[55] and contains holding cells for witnesses.[56] The deep pits are described as vast, but they are crowded and claustrophobic.[57] Individuals are strangled, mutilated with razors, blinded, tantalized by thirst and hunger, suspended from various parts of the body, impaled by three-pronged iron instruments, and torn apart by wild animals and have their hands and feet cut off.[58] Some punishments recall the execution of slaves and criminals in the amphitheatre; other descriptions recall death and suffering in pit-like prisons.[59]

In Paul's vision, much blood was spilled in activities that recalled state-exacted penalties for lower-class criminals and slaves, even if they also formed part of traditional apocalyptic imagery.[60] In the later Roman Empire, no single punishment differentiated the slave from criminals of the lowest class. Slaves and criminals alike could be sentenced to die *ad bestias* (thrown to wild animals in the amphitheater), by amputation of limbs, by crucifixion, by drowning, and by being burned alive. The only real difference was in the context of punishment—slaves could expect to be punished at the whim of their owners with no trial, no opportunity to protest, and no sense that the harshness of punishment would be appropriate to the crime. Here was an important difference that at least some visionary texts tried to claim for God's punishment of sinners in the afterlife—that it was just, that it was appropriate punishment, or even that it was lenient compared to the egregious nature of the infraction. For all such appeals to God's justice and mercy, the author of this kind of text was in fact trying to prompt a different reaction in his audience: fear—the fear that their bodies would be assaulted. These were punishments calculated to shock and deter those who had protected their persons all their lives.

It is possible to find historical examples of individual punishments meted out to slaves that also appear in depictions of torture in the afterlife. For example, it was not an uncommon penalty for theft that the offender's hands be cut off. One of Caligula's slaves had his hands cut off for stealing silver plate.[61] In the reign of Galba, fraudulent moneychangers had their hands cut off.[62] The *Vision of Paul* depicted men and women with their hands and feet cut off, naked in the snow and ice, and being consumed by worms.[63] These were individuals who had harmed orphans, widows, and the poor. In a sense, these sinners had stolen from those less fortunate, but their punishment in hell affected more than their hands.

In one important way, the tortures of hell drew from the real experience of slaves: the authors of visionary texts, like the slave owners themselves, had enormous scope for devising capricious and imaginative cruelty. As Bradley points out, "The omnipotence of the master over the slave was such that the way was open not just for the exercise of these, as it were, standard types of physical punishment and treatment, but also for the devising of exceptional acts of cruelty in which sadistic tendencies on the part of some owners stand out clearly."[64] What is interesting about this is that, judging by the popularity of visionary texts such as the *Apocalypse of Peter* and the *Vision of Paul*, there was so little recorded abhorrence for such depictions of divine punishment. Indeed, the imaginative, sadistic aspects of torture undoubtedly accounted in part for their appeal.[65] The *Vision of Paul* had its critics, like Augustine, who doubted its veracity, but the notion of hell torture was never cited as an issue of concern.

Other tortures of the damned, such as strangulation—one of the penalties of Roman law—were equally possible as penalties exacted by families as honour killings. For example, in the *Vision of Paul*, women who had abortions were strangled along with the men who consorted with them.[66] And some of the tortures are witnessed in the usual horrors of war and vengeance, such as suspending individuals by various body parts—a torture that is surprisingly common to apocalyptic and visionary literature and that was also a favoured barbarian atrocity.[67] (A later Latin redaction of the work shifts this image to reflect more Northern, ritual killings, with sinners hanging from trees.)[68]

Primarily, the torture of the underworld involves a river of fire through which sinners must pass or in which they are submerged to varying degrees.[69] Fire is particularly central to early apocalypses, and it remains a constant feature of later visions of hell even as torture methods became more elaborate. Fire was a known punishment for transgressors in the Roman world. Criminals and slaves could be burned alive as a punishment, and, under Nero, Christians accused of burning Rome were lit like human torches.

Ultimately, however, reference to rivers of fire undoubtedly owed more to Egyptian, Greek, and Jewish mythology than to any attempt to reference penalties exacted in the ancient period; after all, fire cannot normally be made to flow.[70] The fearsome sight of magma streams issuing from volcanoes undoubtedly underlay much of the river of fire imagery. In hell, the river of fire acts as an infernal parallel to the refreshing rivers of paradise, thus forming part of what was already a traditional afterlife landscape.

Chains (*catenae*) are commonly mentioned as restraints for sinners in the afterlife just as they were for slaves in life. Indeed, a common medieval image of souls being taken to hell at the Last Judgement shows the devil, or devils, leading the damned by means of neck ropes in a kind of chain gang.[71] Chains appear early in the Christian apocalypses, inherited from Jewish apocalyptic imagery. In the *Apocalypse of Peter*, those who manufactured idols "shall be in chains of fire."[72] In the *Christian Sibylline Oracle*, book 2, we learn of the sinful that "the angels of the immortal, everlasting God shall punish fearfully with flaming whips, binding them tightly about with fiery chains and unbreakable fetters."[73] In the *Vision of Paul*, girls dressed in black are approached by four angels bearing burning chains (*cathenas ignis*) that are set on their necks as they are led away into darkness.[74]

Chains and restraints of various types were a reality for slaves as they were for low-status criminals. Archaeology has uncovered many types of iron restraints used on slaves, captives, and criminals, including leg shackles, manacles, more sophisticated spring-lock handcuffs, and neck chains.[75] The exact use of any given artefact is open to interpretation; however, the vigorous trade in slaves in these centuries is not in doubt, and such trade provides a likely context for at least some of these finds. Neck chains are particularly significant because they recall the bronze collars that identified fugitive slaves and that were used throughout the Mediterranean world in late antiquity and are attested also in the early medieval West.[76] The collars served as easy and immediate identifiers of servile status. The collars were riveted and thus could not be removed by the wearer. The slave who wore such a collar could also be identified as a criminal through its use and by an inscription incised on the collar's outer surface. Finally, the collar removed from the wearer any protection against bodily assault since any freeborn person could discipline such a slave at will. In short, the neck collar was a sign of the wearer's complete corporeal vulnerability.

Another important feature of the neck chain was that it was a form of restraint that also allowed for walking and thus was used in the transportation of slaves in the slave trade. As F. Hugh Thompson notes, "neck-shackles and linking chains are clearly designed for slaves on the road to market."[77] Slaves could be transported long and short distances in this way. A line of slaves being led by their neck shackles by their slave master is depicted as part of a funerary relief on the Amphipolis stone in Greece.[78] The archaeological remains of particularly sophisticated neck shackles in Britain and Ireland show that this form of restraint was common in northern Europe too. Slaves and military prisoners could also walk while wearing manacles suspended from a chain.[79] In medieval depictions of the Last Judgement, the dead were often shown as a shackled line of sinners being led to hell by the devil or by demons. In the Last Judgment scene on the West Tympanum of Notre Dame, Paris, sinners were depicted as bound by a single massive chain.[80] The left-to-right movement of these sinners recalls the left-to-right movement of the neck-shackled slaves depicted on the Amphipolis stone. The idea of transportation is important here; slaves in transports broke all ties with their native communities and with kin. Transportation in an era of dangerous and difficult movement emphasized the captive slave's irreversible fate. Likewise in hell, damned souls were shown being led by demons from one part of hell to even darker regions of hell. They were the walking damned.

One of the most common words used for hell in Latin sources and in the liturgy is *ergastulum*, which is a prison or slave detention center. While fetters and extended prison stays were not generally the intended penalty exacted by the Roman justice system, they could become so for individuals who were retained for long periods before trial.[81] Prison conditions could be harsh, even for those with the money and connections to improve their situation, and inevitably some met their death in prison.[82] High-ranking Romans accused of minor crimes were either exempt from pretrial detention or could give surety for their presence before a magistrate.[83] Lower ranks, or those who flouted the restrictions of bail, faced a grueling pretrial detention.[84] Prisoners could be moved from one part of a prison to another, depending on the status of their case: some areas of a prison had natural light and ventilation while there was also a dark, inner part of the prison.[85] In visions of hell, visionaries reported that there was a difference between the part of hell that could be viewed by an outsider and the deeper darkness of hell that lay beyond.

Facial disfigurement was another indicator of slave status in the early empire, since slaves were sometimes tattooed on their foreheads to indicate that they had attempted to flee or resist captivity. Constantine's prohibition (AD 316) of facial disfigurement as punishment, including for slaves, may not have eliminated all memory of this. Since it is posited that the Latin *Vision of Paul* as we currently have it was based on a Greek text of the third century, it might be argued that the emphasis on this element of afterlife humiliation may date from that earlier time. However, the connection between dishonour and disfigurement, especially of the face, is as ancient as historical record, and it is especially evident among the peoples of the ancient Near East and in the Bible as a way of stigmatizing enemies. Unsought bodily mutilation and manipulation is a universal way of reconfiguring power relationships. As Tracy Lemos notes, "mutilation signaled a newly established power dynamic between the victim and the aggressor." And "by associating the victim with a lower-status group and/or by effecting an actual status change in the victim."[86] Likewise, forcible tattooing served as a marker for change in status. Tattooing had many functions in antiquity, but importantly, Greeks and Romans regarded it as a barbarian practice, so that "tattooing was always utilitarian, and usually a sign of degradation."[87] It was mostly used in a penal context. The chosen religious connotation of tattooing in some cultures was not mainstream practice in the Roman Christianity.[88]

As a metaphor in the Christian rhetoric of slavery, chains signified the enslavement of the soul to the body and to sin. Images of chains and fire were conventional in Roman mythology for depicting the divine wrath and divine power. Fire belonged to the gods. Prometheus was bound to a rock on the orders of Zeus and was tortured by a liver-eating eagle in retaliation for his gift of fire to humankind.[89] Hephaestus (Vulcan) forged chains in his workshop beneath the volcanic Mount Aetna, wielding tongs in the manner of later medieval demons. A later Irish visionary saw the island forges of hell and Judas nearby sitting on a rock.[90] In the book of Revelation and in its illustrators, Satan was depicted as being bound, for a short time at least.

Bodies in hell (and later in purgatory) were often depicted as naked. Nudity itself was not a reviled condition, although in later medieval depictions of the afterlife, souls entering heaven's gate were given clothing by attendant angels, which suggests that honour and purity were associated with clothing. In the *Vision of Paul*, some of the damned wear rags full of tar and sulphurous fire, and others wear black clothing or else bright raiment that, because they are blind, they cannot see.[91] Those who harmed widows, orphans, and the poor, however, were set in snow and ice, naked and with mutilated hands and feet.[92] In such cases, the nudity of souls in hell underscored the vulnerability of their bodies to torture and their value as spectacle. Nudity also exposed genitalia to public view. In life a man's penis (or "phallus") was a sign of his masculinity and of all the rights that pertained to manhood in the Roman world. Male slaves were sometimes castrated, despite official attempts to ban the practice, in order to delay onset of puberty and to make them more appealing as sexual objects to men.[93] Eunuchs might sometimes attain positions of great influence, but their status was still one of dishonour. Similarly, in hell, the penis was rendered useless, as all rights and honours of manhood were taken away. Thus in this way too, the man in hell was like a slave—a man with a physical penis but without its cultural power.[94]

Women were also depicted naked in the afterlife—exposure of their genitalia evoking shame, sex, and reproduction. Roman persecutors honed in on sexual shaming as a way to deter and ultimately punish female martyrs. The martyrs Blandina, Perpetua, and Felicity were displayed naked in the arena as a way to dishonour them; class and status were linked to clothing, and so female nudity suggested sexual degradation and prostitution to the onlooker.[95] Indeed, Christian women were sometimes forced into brothels during the time of persecution as a punishment specifically targeted at women.[96] The inability of a woman of any class to control exposure of her body had profound resonance as a determinant and indicator of class. It was a reality of the condition of slavery that both male and female slaves could be prostituted by their slaveholders for money, or they could be forced into prostitution as a punishment.[97] However, as far as we can tell from the visionary texts that have survived, there was no expectation of sexual activity in the afterlife. Therefore, the experience of the female soul in hell did not reflect the female slave's most constant vulnerability in life—to the sexual appetite of her owner. However, the female soul in hell is still viewed as a gendered and reproductive being, except now her relationship to her children (often depicted as aborted) is vituperative and unmotherly.

Public humiliation was another important aspect of the torture of sinners. This was not incidental to their condition. Augustine noted its importance.[98] The public nature of punishment was integral to its effectiveness, not so much to the individual undergoing it, but to the viewer. As Jill Harries has explained: "The prime motives for inflicting punishment in Late Antiquity were those inherited from the Early Empire: retribution and deterrence."[99] Public humiliation served this purpose for *honestiores*.

While the convergence of torture in hell and the punishment of the lower class in Roman law and practice is striking, I do not want to suggest that the punishment of sinners in hell exclusively mirrored the experience of slaves and criminals in life. Some of the tortures described clearly had other sources—biblical, poetic, ascetic, and imaginative. Torture was often conceived of as a collective experience. Martyrs were typically depicted as withstanding not one, but many assaults on their bodies; this was probably true in practice when they were killed as part of a public spectacle, but it was also a literary device and embellishment. Shaw cites a passage from a Greek novel in which the female heroine Leukippê goads her would-be rapist Thersandros with a catalogue of all the tortures that she claims will be ineffective to bring about her sexual submission; the wheel, whips, hot irons, fire, and axe.[100] This implies that the concept of torture required that the acts be repetitive and numerous, which was a feature of visions of hell also. What is also significant about these tortures is that they maintained a degree of realism from what could be observed in the earthly experience of criminals and slaves. In the Roman world, slave owners could avail themselves of instruments of torture from a public official who maintained them for the purpose of torturing criminals and slaves.[101] Scenes of torture were not outside the realm of normal experience, and this became increasingly commonplace as the empire wore on.

It is striking that while Roman philosophers and Christian theologians preached the unimportance of the body relative to the value of the soul, visions of afterlife punishment, with their internalized images of slavery, tended rather to emphasize and affirm the value of corporeality because the body has become the vehicle for a higher end—an expression of God's justice.

Erosion of Privilege

In the Latin version of the *Vision of Paul*, the section of the work dealing with the torments of hell (chapter 31 onward) is significantly more elaborate than the epitomized Greek text as we have it.[102] It is a pity that we cannot make a direct comparison of the full Greek version with the existing Latin texts. If one were to discover a Greek version of the *Vision of Paul* as ancient as the *Apocalypse of Peter*, reflecting a time of persecution, the Greek hell might afford some insight into the way the work would have been perceived and altered by a fourth-century, institutionalized Christian readership. A comparison of the *Apocalypse of Peter* and the *Vision of Paul*, such as that undertaken by Jan Bremmer, reveals considerable differences in preoccupation between those respective texts. We may also ask whether the tortures of the damned depicted in earlier apocalypses would have satisfied the legal and moral concerns of fourth-century Romans. Without direct evidence, however, one must be cautious about reading the fifth-century Latin text as reflecting purely late fourth-century concerns. Yet if, as Bremmer has recently argued, the Greek version was composed as late as 400, then much of this problem disappears: the *Vision of Paul* becomes a text rooted in the worldview of late antiquity.[103] Even if a full Greek were some day to come to light, it would still be useful to know how the tortures of the damned in the Latin *Vision of Paul* conformed to Roman expectations of justice and to the legal system as it operated under the later Christian emperors. This question, then, may be asked: how did ideas about slavery, corporeality, and afterlife torture intersect with late antique notions of justice and punishment as enshrined in legal opinions, imperial edicts, and other written sources?

There is a substantial body of scholarly opinion that suggests that crime was punished more severely in late antiquity than formerly, leading to a more cruel and savage era in the penal history of the West.[104] By the late fourth century, Roman law had increased the number of crimes that could be punished by death and ensured that more classes of people were subject to that penalty. It was an era that coincided with the accession of Christian emperors. This picture of a cruel and repressive legal system has been challenged and refined by Jill Harries, who suggests that much of the impression historians have about this savage era arises from a more open and vocal criticism of the legal system by intellectuals, including Christian bishops, engaged in what she terms a "culture of criticism."[105] These voices clamored for more humane treatment of criminals, or at any rate for a reduction in death penalty sentences, since death removed from the criminal the opportunity for repentance and reform.[106] The range of penalties by which the convicted could be punished diminished, and the substitution of hanging for crucifixion was certainly more humane for the victim, if less "entertaining" for the spectator. Furthermore, Christian bishops had influence in the judicial arena, which gave them opportunities to observe prison conditions and to appeal for leniency. As Harries states, "By the late fourth century, the agents of the state were themselves largely Christian, and therefore open to approaches from bishops, who backed appeals for leniency with the moral *auctoritas* inherent in their office."[107] The impact of Christian values did not always result in softer views of torture and penalties for the guilty, however. Harries notes that there was "a measure of social acceptance, at least among the elite, for what we would regard as 'cruel and unusual' punishment."[108]

The issue of personal status before the law, however, is particularly germane to a discussion of afterlife punishment and Roman law. Late antiquity saw an erosion in traditional privileges of the elite before the law, and this posed great stress for those who were accustomed to consider their bodies free and inviolable. In the time of the Republic it had been the privilege of the Roman citizen of decurion rank and above that he could not be subjected to torture or the death penalty. This exemption of decurions from corporal punishment was affirmed in late antiquity too, in the Theodosian Code.[109] Under the early emperors this privilege was disregarded in certain instances, but still the elite Roman citizen's expectation was that he should not be treated with the harshness and cruelty often accorded to the lower class, the provincial, or the slave. Thus Bradley: "The inherent bias of the Roman legal system meant . . .

that lower social categories were discriminated against as far as the application of punishment was concerned, and slaves, as the lowest category of all, suffered the most severe types of criminal penalty: 'Our ancestors have in every penalty punished slaves more severely than free men,' so a passage from the *Digest* states."[110] In the early empire the reality of Roman justice had been very harsh; and the brutalization of slaves, noncitizens, or those who had lost citizenship rights—for example, Christians—was legally endemic. By the second century, the "marginal elite" were also being threatened by loss of traditional immunities.[111]

Torture had a legitimate place in the Roman legal system. In a criminal proceeding, torture was typically used in the interrogation—the *quaestio*—and its purpose was to arrive at the truth or, at any rate, a confession of some sort. Bradley notes: "although in the imperial period the use of torture to extract evidence for criminal proceedings from free persons is documented, for slaves it was traditional."[112] The details of torture methods were often left to provincial governors or their subordinates. The torture of criminals, furthermore, was conducted in public, with execution following rapidly. In the early empire the pain and spectacle of execution might also be enhanced by the addition of theatrical elements, as when criminals were dressed up to represent figures in dramas who were killed or were made to represent religious figures to be dispatched in combat with animals and gladiators in the arena. (Such spectacles continued in the later fourth century for the execution of homosexuals.[113]) By contrast, elite Romans had often been granted some control over their punishment by having the opportunity for a private death: suicide. But Romans below the rank of decurion were liable to face public torture and death.[114]

With the arrival of the Christian emperors, certain penalties, such as branding on the face, crucifixion, and *ad bestias*, were gradually eliminated, but now the death penalty was applied more often, and this, as we have noted, eventually elicited outcries from prominent Christians. Furthermore, more people were being tortured because more crimes warranted this and because the elevated status of some perpetrators was no longer protective. Harries reminds us that immunities may have been more customary than encoded in law.[115] However, a perception of immunity and a sense of class entitlement would have been enormously important in fixing the elite's response to apparent attacks on their status. Romans citizens who believed they were to be accorded greater personal deference when they transgressed were shocked to learn that members of their own social group were treated no better than plebeians and the unfree. Once reserved for slaves and foreigners, torture and death was now a potential reality for elite Romans.

For elite Romans, this new susceptibility to torture—or at any rate, the perception that this was so—was compounded by the message it relayed: that they had lost privileges accorded to their status. In a culture in which legal notions are tied to status, an attack on one was an attack on the other. Indeed, loss of status and its legal protection—*infamia*—was a form of punishment in late antiquity. Loss of status and legal protection would have provoked alarm among the elite, and it is in elite discourse that the more vocal anxieties were expressed. As Harries and others have noted, the purpose of Roman law was retribution and deterrence, and the latter was best served by instilling fear. The elite had broadly accepted that fear was a salutary weapon when directed at the servile class and the criminal element in society (often seen as one and the same thing). However, now the well-honed machine of fear was turned on the elite, as emperors increasingly resorted to threats of torture. Such threats fed already heightened anxieties of Romans about loss of status and about slippage from the ranks of the protected to the vulnerable and from the free to the unfree.[116]

How does the perceived corporeal vulnerability of the Roman elite help us understand the impact of visions of the afterlife like the *Vision of Paul*? We might expect that the spectacle of torture would fix the gaze of its Roman readers because fear of torture was now closer to home. The *Vision of Paul*'s depiction of torture would have conveyed corporeal vulnerability, reduction of status, and loss of personal autonomy. The age-old anxiety of slipping from elite to lower status and from free to unfree was now intensified by legal vulnerability. When ascetic and theological works such as Augustine's *City of God* emphasized that Christians were slaves of a God whose justice was complete, and from whom no expectations of leniency and immunity could be assumed, they and their readers had very concrete terms of reference in mind.

By the late fourth century, then, judging by the enormous popularity of the *Vision of Paul*, Romans had come to accept that God's retribution on sinners would be corporeal and impervious to considerations of status. The Romans of the fourth century may not have invented this catalogue of fear, but they readily internalized it. The rhetoric of fear that had been viewed as a salutary strategy for keeping the lower classes in line had come back to haunt the elite. God's retribution would be violent. Religious texts emphasized that while sin was a condition of the soul, in the afterlife, its punishment would be inscribed on the body. Death had become indeed a great leveler—for all the damned, irrespective of what their earthly status had been, were now slaves of God.

Conclusion

When Pope Vitalian wanted to encourage the Anglo-Saxon king Oswy and his queen in their devotion to Rome, he sent a cross as a gift to Oswy's wife. The cross was fashioned out of fetters and was accompanied by a gold key.[117] Vitalian expected the queen to understand the message. Peter's fetters, a symbol of slavery, were welded to form the cross of salvation. The pope offered the key to heaven.

The rhetoric and reality of slavery flourished into the early middle ages, providing an ongoing source of reference for motifs of afterlife punishment and salvation. In the West, the barbarian invasions of the fifth century brought anxiety and social disruption. Hagiographic and ecclesiastical sources indicate that captivity was a constant danger, so that the resources of the church, and sometimes the intercession of saints and holy people, were put to the service of ransoming captives. The slave trade continued and expanded, with a constant flow of people around the former empire and its periphery.[118] The rhetoric of slavery continued to be popular and topical with Christian writers. Reflecting on a future life in heaven, Julianus Pomerius considered it a place where the soul would experience a "blissful freedom of movement," contrasted with his view of hell as a place where souls were "fettered to eternal bodies."[119] Caesarius of Arles, writing in the first third of the sixth century, preached that "out of a slave you were made a friend, so reject what you have been born, and pay attention to what you have been reborn."[120] Gregory of Tours could talk of Mitrias of Aix as a slave in rank but a freeman through righteousness.[121] Thus, visionaries, authors of visionary texts, and missionaries were intimately involved in slave-owning concerns. We know that the missionary Lull and his father freed two slaves when they departed for Rome; Pope Gregory III wrote to Boniface decrying the practice of selling slaves to pagans for sacrifice; and Boniface described a man's desperate condition in the afterlife when his brother did not honour a manumission requested in his will.[122]

Although purgatory did not emerge as a place of individual judicial-style torture until the turn of the ninth century, the roots of those images of violence were to be found in antiquity, in its visions of hell, and in anxieties of the Roman elite as they faced and feared the erosion of traditional protections. Romans citizens were increasingly told that they were now to regard themselves as citizens of heaven[123]—but this new regime held out no guaranteed protections from the violence of its penal system.

Before the ninth century, the central image of purgatory was fire: a fiery furnace, a wall of fire, a river of fire, or a valley of fire and ice. Invited to gaze on the spectacle of Christian sinners in hell, Christians had come to accept that torture was the fate of the transgressor who was unrepentant or who had delayed reincorporation through the sacraments. They were also told that other avenues for spiritual amendment were closed off at death. As purgatory slowly became more defined in subsequent centuries, the path of postmortem recompense through pain was in place. In purgatory, as in hell, sinners would receive no privileges based on earthly rank. Indeed, the higher one's rank, the more impartial God's justice must have appeared. The powerful were not entitled to any legal immunities in the afterlife. But it was not just the rich who were humbled: in crossing from life to death, all Christians risked taking on the misery of corporeality and changing their status from sons to slaves.

3

O *Purgatorium Caeleste!*

Purging Body and Soul at St. Martin's Shrine

We have seen that the violence meted out to the Roman slave provided a potent template for God's punishment of the damned. Slaves and the damned were outcasts alike, their fate to endure the misery of corporeality. Christians, by contrast, were insiders, the perfectible, the elect. But they, no less than the outsiders, were victims of suffering and corporeal affliction. It was clear that Christian pain would require a different interpretation from that of the damned. That difference could be found in its soteriological purpose and in the individual's Christ-like acceptance of suffering. Christian pain would be transitory and purificatory, it was argued. Pain could be a means for the Christian to achieve spiritual perfection. Eventually, pain would be alien to the perfected, incorruptible resurrected body.

What constituted Christian purity and perfection? That was not an easy question to answer in late antiquity, and, indeed, it was much debated. The pursuit of spiritual perfection and the possibility of attaining it in the present life were certainly viewed very differently by the various Christian groups, largely based on different interpretations of Christ's life, New Testament teachings, and by the church's early history. The story of humankind's fall from perfection and exile from paradise and the human desire for reformation and return to the divinity suggested the path that must be taken: detachment, as far as it was possible, from distractions and distortions of the soul created by human needs and desires.[1]

Identifying the ideal path to Christian perfection was complicated in late antiquity by the church's history of martyrdom that advanced the idea that torture and death were the ultimate symbols of self-sacrifice. Yet from the fourth century onward the church had become a privileged institution, one that increasingly governed important areas of public and private life. As the church evolved as an institution, many of its symbols of integration and resistance were to change, yet at its core the church strove to maintain its hold on the moral superiority of its members associated historically with the time of the martyrs. The efflorescence of the cult of the martyrs from the fourth century was in part an expression of the church's desire to promote, in an era of greater security, the salutary benefits of personal sacrifice and pain. This was not to say that pain was considered a desirable goal.[2] Yet, as redemptive, Christ-like figures, martyrs were thought to have taken upon themselves the pain of others. Thus they were also figures of intercession capable of alleviating pain. This power was most visibly demonstrated in the cures at their shrines. If it was a sign of faith to endure bodily suffering as the martyrs had done, it was also a sign of faith to seek out a cure from suffering at the shrine of a saint. An end to suffering, a cure from pain, testified to God's power in a different but complementary way to that of the martyrs and was furthermore a proof and acknowledgment of the martyr's presence in heaven. Thus it was that the alleviation of pain through the intercession of the martyrs and the violence of purgation became connected polarities in the Christian's quest for purification.

The appeal of the martyrs and their cults was that they represented an ideal relationship to their body and to pain. Their voluntary suffering had perfected them, cleansed them of sin, and earned them immediate access to heaven. This was the reward for their "correct" attitude toward the body: purification through suffering. Yet access to heaven was every Christian's highest hope. Christians wanting to emulate the martyrs could turn to the "white" martyrdom of the ascetic life as their passport to heaven. Ascetic literature embraced the image of violence against the body and internalized it. Christian perfectionists, fascinated with the possibility of achieving spiritual and bodily purity in their earthly existence, voluntarily took on a regimen of deprivation that might achieve it. It was commonly thought that the angelic life could be prepared for and to some extent anticipated in the present life through fasting, and chastity.[3] Those who achieved spiritual purity were judged to be holy, and immediate access to heaven was their reward. Together with the martyrs, holy ascetics became part of the community of saints in heaven.

Ordinary Christians were encouraged to take their own tentative steps in the direction of perfection: fasting in observance of feast days, eschewing marriage and property, avoiding the obvious pitfalls of poor behaviour (like working on Sundays or washing one's face on Good Friday), trusting that the teachings and sacraments offered by the Church would cleanse them, and hoping that the intercession of the saints would make up for any deficit. As one might expect, we encounter those who worried that the number of the elect were few and that they would be found fatally wanting when they came to Judgement Day. Others appear to have held a more optimistic assessment of Christian instruction as a successful path to present perfection, believing that the pursuit of the contemplative life on earth was within the reach of any Christian who desired it.[4] But whatever the milieu, the advice given to all who sought spiritual perfection was that the key to salvation lay in the present. Absolute purity could be achieved only by a process of purification, which was held to be lengthy, and that was achieved through spiritual living and bodily "death" or "mortification." Those who aspired to join the ranks of the saved were advised that it was surely better to purify the body on earth within a known register of pain than to be subjected to unimaginable and unquantifiable pain in the hereafter. Those who sought healing at holy sanctuaries learned in a very concrete way that purification of the body in the present life could be a violent and messy enterprise.

While Christian writers had only limited ability to describe the pain of purification in the next life, they were well placed to observe the pain of purification in the here and now. If they wanted to know what purification of the body would look like, they had only to look around them. And that is precisely what they did. Christian writers were keen observers of suffering, including sometimes their own maladies, and they drew ready eschatological analogies from what they saw. Dramas of purification were easily viewed in public and private fora for those inclined to look. Christian public life appears to have offered ample opportunities for such display. The transportation of relics, the processions of clergy, or the sudden appearance of a holy recluse in the streets of the city could stimulate a flurry of cathartic activity among the inhabitants: demoniacs confessed their crimes and were exorcized, captives were miraculously released from their chains, the mute could suddenly shout out, and the lame could walk. Within sacred enclosures—at church altars and at holy shrines—the sick were healed under the clergy's scrutiny. Those responsible for shrine documentation pondered the meaning of such displays and sought to craft moral lessons from them. Their efforts are preserved in miracle lists and saints' lives. But no corpus of miracle literature appears to have been so clearly shaped by personal eschatology as the miracle stories penned by Gregory, the sixth-century bishop of Tours. Under Gregory's pen, the healing miracles at saints' shrines, particularly that of St. Martin of Tours, was evidence of nothing less than God's purification of his people. In Gregory's writings we find a loose but fairly consistent theology of bodily purgation tied in very explicit terms to the soul's fate in the afterlife.

Healthy Body, Healthy Soul

Christ is the physician who heals the soul. This image, so familiar to ascetic works and the penitentials, drew heavily on traditional Graeco-Roman medical ideas that connected mental health with bodily health, and moral and philosophical literature that linked bodily health with the "health" of the soul, a condition that would allow it ultimately to be "saved."[5] Medical and philosophic ideas were often intertwined as complementary disciplines and discourses.[6] Indeed, physicians and ascetics were often part of the same intellectual Christian communities as once physicians had been part of philosophic circles in antiquity.[7] A soul that was healthy (*salus*) was also one that was preserved (*salvus*).[8] This traditional body-soul connection was underscored in the Christian theology of corporeal resurrection. The resurrected body would be a perfected version of the earthly body and a suitable vessel for the soul in the afterlife.[9] Thus the healthy body was a body clean from the "stain" of the sin that caused disease. The body that was tormented by disease or by mental illness was patent evidence of, at best, the frailty of present existence and, at worst, its sin and damnation. Medical views of disease routinely attributed its presence to external causes, both demonic and divine. Both demonic and divine afflictions caused the body to contort and become repulsive to normal society. The demoniac was *par excellence* the symbol of the consequence of being "open" to evil: his limbs flailed out of control, his teeth gnashed and bit, and he caused self-harm and harm to others.[10] The demoniac's cure was signaled when his body was "cleansed" of the demonic intruder through the matching divinely ordered contortion of purgation, often resulting in liquid evacuations. But the divinity could also afflict the body, punishing it for sacrilegious behaviour. The apparently reversible punishment of the sacrilegious person was often the twisted, contracted hand or other limb viewed as the immediate vehicle for offense. The divinity might also use bodily suffering to purify the soul. Even the saint might have to undergo the purification of disease or fever in order to gain immediate entrance into heaven. For example, Bede commented of St. Cuthbert that at the end of his life "he was suddenly felled by disease, to be prepared by the fires of internal pain for the joys of everlasting bliss."[11] The ordinary afflicted person was driven to seek out the divinity and his saints at the shrines in hopes of a cure. This "blame the victim" mentality of Christian medicine was displaced only in the case of congenital deficits, which were viewed as the inherited sin of the parents. Whatever the perceived causes of affliction, the divine remedy was to purify the body and soul of sin. The body's return to health, like that of the soul, restored the individual to God and made it fit for heaven. Gregory of Tours liked to say of some of the sick that when they were healed it was as if they had been "born again," by which he meant that is was as if the clock had been set back and creation had been set aright.

Cure of the body, like cure of the soul, was thus God's work. This work was often performed through the saints at their shrines. Not only did cures at the shrines of the saints provide the material for churchmen to craft dramatic narratives of purification, transformation, and restoration, but also their observation of these activities provided them a crude empirical method: just as miracles in which dead people were brought back to life suggested the truth of Christ's resurrection, so did miracles of healing and their often violent course suggest the painful means by which sinners could be restored to the promise of heaven. In short, the divine method of purification, evidenced in the miracles at holy shrines, foreshadowed the soul's purification in the other world.

Purging at St. Martin's Shrines

The philosophical teachings of the ascetic elite may have provided a theological explanation for the divine conjunction of body and soul, but there is no place where those ideas found more concrete expression than in the healing miracles attributed to the saints at their shrines. It is at the shrines that we see how deeply ideas about the connection of body and soul were rooted in late antique culture, how far the fate of the soul could be viewed as being etched on the living body.

Substantial shrine documentation survives from Gaul. Early Gallic saints and their relics appear to have been popular resources for the sick, and their hagiographers and relic guardians took account of healing miracles when crafting their cults. The cult of St. Martin of Tours was the most spectacular healing cult in Gaul. This posthumous reputation may have had some basis in Martin's personal history and methods. Noting his use of herbs, Aline Rouselle has suggested that Martin's early military training may have equipped him with rudimentary medical skills that could have been put to use in his community.[12] He was also familiar with natural purgatives, as Martin's nearly fatal self-medication with hellebore shows.[13] Medical opinion at the time viewed purgatives as essential means of treating gastrointestinal disorders as well as an array of other ailments including madness, and Martin may have known of this remedy from his time in military service. Thus it is possible that this medical remedy lay behind some of the healing miracles attributed to Martin and other saints.[14]

Saint Martin's reputation as a healer was such that after his death, his body and other relics were thought to be infused with his healing power.[15] His tomb became a cult site from at least the fifth century on as Martin's episcopal successors, starting with Bishop Perpetuus, set to the task of recording miracles associated with the saint's relics.[16] Of these, Gregory of Tours's collection of miracles is by far the richest, since the miracles are numerous and sometimes documented in great detail.[17] Although Gregory pressed his theological interpretation of the cures intermittently, the work as a whole is entirely informed by his view of Martin as a healer and as a Christ figure. Furthermore, Gregory not only documented healing miracles but also was a petitioner for cures at St. Martin's shrine.[18] Afflicted by headaches and stomachaches, he regularly sought and received healing from the shrine he supervised. These cures were often explicitly connected to purges. The medical culture in which he lived promoted cupping, among other forms of purgation, but he resisted blood purges when he was able, viewing it as a demonic temptation.[19] Gregory's hopes for healing rested on the efficacy of purges supplied in the form of a mixture of water and the dust that settled on Martin's tomb. This purging concoction was practiced at a number of shrines in Gaul, activating healing that was considered both physical and spiritual.[20] As we shall see, Gregory's personal medical concerns dovetailed with his writing on miraculous cures, and this make his works particularly illuminating on the perceived connection of bodily and heaven-sent purgation.[21]

Another dimension played an important role for Gregory in his compilation of miracle stories: pastoral teaching. No sermons by Gregory have survived, although his hagiographic vignettes may have provided the substance of some of his preaching. It seems likely that Gregory viewed miracle accounts as seeds for pastoral instruction. It is certainly the case that Gregory viewed his authorship of the miracle books as a holy and public act, an activity he did for St. Martin's honor. He hoped his reward for undertaking this task would be forgiveness of his sins.[22] But he also viewed Martin's healing miracles as a continuation of Martin's preaching in which Gregory himself could partake by recording them. Read collectively, the miracles could be understood as a kind of extended sermon for those who would read and understand them. Gregory's miracle "sermons" drew on an intimate and circular connection: the bodies of the sick were the raw material upon which Martin displayed his saving power and from which Gregory created his theology. At the same time those same bodies and individuals were the audience for Martin's and Gregory's message. Once written down, the miracle became a sacred text, an *exemplum*, fit for religious contemplation and instruction. We should not be surprised, then, to discover that in Gregory's hands, Martin's miracles provoked theological and eschatological reflection.

We have already seen that purgatives were a common medical remedy for a wide variety of conditions in antiquity.[23] In Gregory's work, the holy dust purge cleansed the body of impurities caused by disease and demonic infiltration. Indeed, Gregory used the terms *purgatus est* and *mundatus est* frequently and interchangeably when describing the outcome of both medical problems and exorcisms. Thus, when the priest Nannius approached the church of St. Ferreolus, singing psalms and bearing with him newly acquired relics of St. Julian of Brioude, Gregory informed his readers that a possessed man nearby was cleansed of a demon (*mundatus est*), and that at the church a girl was *purgata* of the same affliction.[24] Likewise, whether the miracle recipient was healed of an identifiable physical ailment or was afflicted with a demon resulting in exorcism, Gregory used purgation terminology for both. A girl whose eyes had become inflamed with crying was brought to St. Julian's shrine for healing and rose from the ground *purgatis lippitudine oculis*.[25] The medical terminology of purging was thus applied equally to a cure aided by the intervention of a physician or the intervention of a saint. How unique was this terminology to Gregory? A quick glance at other contemporary miracle lists shows that it was common to associate healing with purging. But it is also clear that the healing purge was far more common in Gregory's work than in other texts of the same kind. Whereas other authors used the terminology of purging when referring to effluence, Gregory used purging terminology not only to describe the manner in which a person was cure but also as a synonym for the act of healing itself. This suggests that Gregory saw the purged body as a powerful metaphor for health.[26] Sulpicius's Martin who had induced the dead and mute to vomit was now, in Gregory's works, the saint who purged the sick with heaven-sent purgatives.

In describing the purgative cures, Gregory's desire for personal and community purity was closely knit with a fascination for all that is conventionally repellent. If we are to believe that these stories of spectacular spewings, bloody vomit, putrefactions, and so on reflected practice at the shrine, we must accept that effluence of every kind was deposited within the holy precincts and even in front of the altar.[27] Obviously there were housekeeping issues involved, but the altar railings that are commonly mentioned in the sources must have provided the altar and relics some protection.[28] The odor of vomit and excrement is sufficiently abhorrent in its own right, without recourse to its symbolic interpretation as evidence of mortality and as a sign for sin; but fascination with the saint's cure supercedes any expression of disgust in Gregory's accounts, and there is no desire to gloss over even the most minute details of bodily eruptions. In the quest for purity, the consequences of impurity were apparently tolerated. Thus we must accept that in the view of one prominent bishop of the time, displays of bodily infirmity and liquid explosions were appropriately found on holy ground and provision was made for the sick to stay at the very core of the various shrines dedicated to St. Martin. Gregory informs us that those suffering from chills and fevers customarily lay the whole day between the altar and the holy tomb, at the very epicentre of holy power.[29] There is a very pragmatic, utilitarian aspect to this cultural acceptance of effluence: St. Martin's tomb was the right place for the vomiting sick. It was the requisite, necessary place (*loca necessaria*) for a woman who suffered from dysentery for five months.[30] It was the appropriate place for farting as a demon was expelled; it was the place where Gregory could record unabashed fascination with strings of bloody goo hanging from the mouth. Saint Martin's cell at Candes, a shrine that contained the bed upon which the saint had died, was where a possessed man could stay overnight and be cured after much shouting and coughing and vomiting of bloody pus.[31] Saint Martin's basilica was where a possessed man spewed up fetid blood from his mouth and was thereby purged of a demon. The shrine was a place of holy work, and the resident saint's purging remedy was as powerful and explosive as the sickness that had afflicted his petitioners to begin with.

When confronted with the graphic nature of these details we may get a sense that we are witnessing the genuine experience of shrine-goers, yet this can only be partly true. For all the verisimilitude of the healing miracles, the reader of the miracle accounts is distanced from the reality of shrine cures by the author's overarching narrative perspective and by what is left unsaid. Any shame felt by the individual suppliant goes entirely unexpressed in Gregory's narrative because his perspective is entirely focused on the positive message of the miracle. Further, we are not informed about any medical treatment that might have been offered in conjunction with St. Martin's dust and alongside prayers. The intimate connection of sacred spaces with bodily effluence, which is distasteful to modern sensibilities, may even have been felt by those involved, but it was not viewed that way by the shrine's greatest guardian and promoter, nor was it expressed, in Gregory's account, by the many sick people who flocked there or were carried there by their parents, spouses, and employers.

Medical purges purified the body with violence.[32] Purges that arose from the body's natural response to toxicity were also violent: the purge prompted an involuntary reflex that could be spectacular and ugly. When demons were purged from the body, the consequences were particularly violent.[33] Dust from St. Martin's tomb consumed on site was so immediately effective that one boy needed help getting to a privy quickly to relieve his bowels of air and two worms.[34] Purgation cured both the willing and the unwilling.

Purgation also rendered the individual fit and healthy for the proper work of the church: prayer, psalm singing, and sacramental life. The unfortunate Theodomund, whose ears and throat were obstructed by illness, had those orifices spectacularly unobstructed when he approached the altar. With his mouth still bloody from vomit, he praised St. Martin's name aloud much to the astonishment of bystanders. Gregory tells us that this man was subsequently helped by Queen Clothilde so that he went to school, learned the psalms, and eventually became a cleric.[35] Gregory often observed that those healed at the shrine dedicated their lives to St. Martin and to the church in some way after their cure. It was doctrinal obstruction that held some others back: Arianism was the leprosy from which the entire Suevic nation was cured at the elevation of St. Martin of Braga to episcopal office.[36] For one man, theft of property belonging to St. Martin's church was a "leprosy," as was Gregory's own self-confessed extravagance.[37]

Thus purgation from sickness and other impurities suggested a path to salvation. Gregory bluntly states that the blind man Ursulf's sight was restored in two ways; in his physical eyes and also in the eye of his heart.[38] A paralyzed woman who was healed by the sign of the cross and the stroking of her limbs was healed by the "touch of salvation."[39] These cures relied on private accounts. By contrast, purgation of the sick body propelled interior sickness to public view. The violence done to the body was visible to all. From the perspective of public instruction there was good reason not to want to hide such drama from view. A violent process, one that contorted the face and limbs, drew the observer's gaze to the spectacle of purgation and the lesson that linked bodily health with salvation.

Yet such stories were not the only evidence that divine power might work on Christian bodies in a powerful and coercive way. Gregory related two stories that viewed the violence of purgation from a different angle: the demoniac's subjection to a purging plunge.[40] At their core, the two stories were not Gregory's stories. Gregory opened his collection of Martin's miracles with a prose rendition of some miracle accounts recorded by Paulinus of Périgueux in verse in the 470s.[41] Two of these involved men being flung into water by demons before being rescued by bystanders and restored to health by their experience. The first account related a phenomenon that was observed many times at St. Martin's church.[42] Gregory tells us that Paulinus had written that "when possessed men were being driven to leap in the air over the railings in the church, often they were hurled into a cistern (*in puteum*) because of the compulsion of a demon. Then they were pulled up unharmed and, while the people watched, were restored [to health]." Gregory adds the comment, "I have seen this happen in my times too."[43] Gregory's prose rendition of Paulinus's verse makes a few minor alterations, but in both versions the water in which the demoniacs are propelled is a *puteus*. In his translation of Gregory's miracle accounts, Raymond Van Dam renders this as a "cistern." The word was most commonly used for a well, although it also had the sense of a deep pit or even a dungeon or a deep, confined space that could become stinky if polluted.[44] Thus it was also a word commonly used for the "pits" of hell.[45] This is significant, as we shall see. It is unclear where either the cistern/well-pit was located in relation to the church and its precincts. It was not the baptismal font although it seems to have supplied the church with water. In a related aquatic story, Gregory explained how a possessed man was lead to a river (the Loire) by a demon who intended to submerge his prize. The man struck out for the other bank and emerged in dry clothes. Once he came to Martin's cell at Marmoutier, he appeared cleansed (of the demon).[46]

Both stories are manifestly about unfortunate people supposedly possessed by a demon and then impelled to self-harm.[47] In both cases significant risks were drowning or death from the fall. Furthermore, in the case of falling down a well or cistern, there were added obstacles to recovery. The shock of the water "cleansed" the men of their demons. Therein lay the miracle. Therein may also have laid the cure. Immersion in water is recorded as a therapy for the insane in ancient as well as in modern times.[48]

At first look we can imagine that these two stories appealed to Paulinus and Gregory as a kind of baptismal story. However, the violence of the actions suggests that we should look further. I would suggest that these are eschatological stories—stories of death, renewal, salvation, and restoration.[49] The men are said to be possessed by demons, so their plunge is involuntary and alarming. Their stories are reminiscent of stories of postmortem purgation that came to characterize later medieval visions of the afterlife. The vision of the monk of Wenlock, in particular, springs to mind because after plunging into stinking water, men were seen emerging on the other bank, cleaner than when they went in. The dry clothes of the demoniac as he emerged from the Loire, like the cleanliness to be obtained from the stinking river of the otherworld, suggested the violence of divine action. Exorcism by means of violent plunges, in contrast to the voluntary immersion of baptism, displayed the needful purification of those who were not in concert with divine desire. As we have noted in the previous chapter, sinful souls were thought to have no personal volition in the afterlife. The sick and possessed were clearly victims of violence, yet that violence would ultimately heal them. It was violence that could bring the sick to health. Eventually, long after Gregory's time, the violence of corporeal purgation would provide a useful reference point for the means and purpose of purgation in the afterlife.

Will It Suffice?

As grave sickness approached, Gregory became panicked by the thought of his sins. What fate awaited him at the Last Judgement? Early in his clerical career, before he became bishop of Tours, he had had a close call.[50] He had fallen sick with sores and fever and believed he was going to die. He set out to make a pilgrimage to St. Martin's tomb, determining that if he did not recover, that would be the place of his own burial. One senses true panic as he ploughed through forests with his traveling companions, determined to complete the journey once begun. He arrived safely and was cured. But at the worst of his sickness he had feared he would die and face the Final Judgement—the judgement, he said, that all the guilty must fear.[51] Yet Gregory appears to have feared it more than most. Gregory certainly believed that he was a sinful man—fearful yet hopeful that his patron saint would protect him. He may have been sensitive to an explicit failing beyond the general sinfulness of mankind. In one text he admitted to the "lurid leprosy of luxury"—a phrase with deep scriptural resonance and also a realistic temptation to a man of his status.[52] In his eyes, his frequent illnesses erupted from personal failings, and he thanked God for having given him a doctor, Martin, "who cleanses our infirmities, washes away our wounds, and bestows effective remedies."[53]

Dust from St. Martin's tomb was Gregory's medicinal weapon. This dust (*pulvis*) collected from the top of Martin's tomb was mixed with water to create a potion.[54] On some occasions it appears to have been mixed with medicine. Sometimes the potion had an opposite effect, binding up the intestines to save the person afflicted with dysentery.[55] But it was the dust's purging properties that Gregory most admired. In life Martin was said to have cured the sick with his own hands, but now, almost two centuries after his death, Martin offered purgative power from beyond the grave. After coming to Martin's shrine to counteract a pounding, headache-inducing toothache, Gregory was cured and, in effusive gratitude, praised the holy remedy: this dust, he claimed, "overwhelms the subtleties of doctors, surpasses sweet scents and is more powerful than strong ointments."[56] This dust acted as a physical purge, cleansing the stomach and the head: "Like scammony it purges the stomach, and like hyssop, the lungs; and like pyrethrum it cleanses even the head."[57] But the purgative dust was much more: the miraculous dust was, in truth, the heaven's purgative: *O purgatorium, ut ita dicam, caeleste!* It was a purgative that not only strengthened limbs but also cleansed the stains of conscience (*conscientiarum maculas*).[58] Gregory's claim makes one wonder precisely how he thought the conscience worked. He speaks of it here as if it were a bodily organ. Yet, the purging dust, in cleansing the "conscience," did something more than cleanse physical and spiritual ailments; its active power cleansed the mind of that very pollution of sin that ascetic literature proclaimed would stand in the way of salvation.[59] It was truly heaven's purge.

Gregory prayed for the connection that he hoped would be true: that bodily cures in the present life and their power for spiritual cleansing would be a sign that he would be saved in the next. In a moment of reflection at the end of book two of the miracles, Gregory addressed his celestial patron:

> I pray that the confessor generously grant to me, a sinner, what he has often bestowed upon the people, and that he cleanse me from the illnesses that he often notes and contemplates, that he restore to me the light of truth, that he snatch me from mistaken unbelief, that he purify my heart and my mind from the ghastly leprosy of extravagance, that he cleanse my thoughts from wicked desires, and that he dissolve and overturn my entire mass of misdeeds.[60]

Gregory's deepest desire for salvation was expressed in his healing from sickness, but a related image of salvation also occupied his mind: freedom from bondage. Accounts in which prisoners and slaves were freed from their chains and their confinement were important miracles in the dossier of any Merovingian saint, but they found a prominent place among Martin's posthumous miracles. In these miracles, the promise of healing, spiritual rebirth, salvation, and resurrection were interwoven. When the paralytic Foedamia was visited by the apparition of St. Julian of Brioude at his shrine, "it seemed to her as if a load of chains fell from her limbs to the ground."[61] Van Dam comments on the connection between bondage and sickness in Gregory's thought: "Illnesses led to constriction, bondage and darkness, much like being confined in a prison . . . and [Martin's] healings resembled the liberation and redemption that the Lord had offered through his own death and resurrection. Each ritual of healing was a re-enactment of the original Easter, and the Easter festivals that Gregory and his congregation celebrate often included both healings and releases from captivity."[62] The most common story told of slaves was that they were healed of physical affliction by St. Martin, and that in gratitude or awe their owner or another patron freed them from their bondage. Prisoners (imprisoned for whatever reason) tended to be freed miraculously as they called out for help when Martin's relics were close by: they then took asylum in a church that protected them before a judge or other civil authority.[63] Failure by the authorities to provide mercy on such occasions was viewed as lack of respect for Martin's power. In a few cases slaves were not freed by their masters and were returned to their former duties, or they were freed but their manumission was not respected by the heirs of the estate. The sickness from which the slave had been cured then reasserted itself, not as a punishment of the slave, but as punishment for the master's lack of respect or faith.[64] The slave whose paralysis returned was a slave who could not work. Yet a slave who had been crippled from birth and was cured by St. Martin's power and freed from slavery was saved: "you might think that he had been born again."[65] The release of the political prisoner Wiliachar from the iron chains clapped on him by King Clothar prompted Gregory to consider his own vulnerability: "If only the blessed confessor should deign to show such power to me, so that he might release the bonds of my sins just as he crumbled those massive heavy chains on top of Wiliachar!"[66] Gregory felt that his sins bound him. Every story of release from bondage represented the promise of freedom, renewal, and rebirth. As we shall see in the next section, such promises of renewal and rebirth were closely interlocked with eschatological images and expectations generally, and specifically with the eschatological figure of Martin as exemplar of Christ.

Judgement Day

If purification occurred in the present life through the kindly (yet violent) action of the saints, postmortem purgation appears not to have figured in Gregory's afterlife. Gregory hoped that Martin would intercede for him on Judgement Day. Martin's intercession would be a shield from torment. Indeed, Gregory envisioned God's judgement as swift and harsh, and he believed he saw evidence of that finality when he observed the death of the patently sinful. Gregory tells a story about a church custodian who received the alms designated for the care of those registered on the church's poor list. The custodian pocketed a gold coin, lied about having taken it, returned it, and then died.[67] Gregory's comment was that he lost the reward of life because of his greed; he imagined the man thrown into Tartarus (eternal torment). The story's purpose was to highlight the sin of greed (a man submerged in hell because of a single *nomisma*); consequently Gregory took no account of the man's returning the coin. One might argue that the custodian must have repented of his deed because he returned the coin but that there was no time for him to make full penitential satisfaction. Penance was a privilege tied to longevity—a sudden death was a judgement of God in that it nullified that hope. It was precisely the ruthless nature of future judgement that appears to have panicked Gregory when he considered his own likely fate. Gregory's fear reveals a lot about Gregory's eschatological views and in particular the role of St. Martin in the events of the last day.

It is difficult for the modern reader to determine precisely what Gregory's thinking was when he imagined his own damnation. Was he genuinely fearful that a bishop who had been so carefully educated in his religion, whose family included so many saints as models, and who had lived a life in the service of his patron saint, would be damned for eternity? If that were so, what hope could there be for the great mass of people Gregory encountered in his pastoral work? Conventional wisdom linked the salvation of the bishop to how well he guided his flock. The good bishop, like Aaron, prayed for the salvation of his charges and in the process assured his own.[68] No one could accuse Gregory of ignoring the spiritual health of his flock—his observation of their behaviour at the shrines and his protection of them in the political arena absolves him of that charge. Yet in Gregory's writings there is an absence of self-identification with his flock, a quality that was thought to characterize the ideal bishop. When Gregory turned his mind to the day of judgement, his thoughts were only for himself. Did Gregory inflate his fears out of personal humility or to add urgency to the spiritual improvement of his flock? Was Gregory's intrusion into his own work, as a petitioner expressing dire fear, a conscious attempt to provide a template for his flock so that they could adopt an appropriate religious attitude?[69] Did his awe of the martyrs and the saints lead him to diminish the moral probity of those who achieved only ordinary piety? Was salvation, in short, only to be obtained through the protection of the saints? Certainly, we know that the relative spiritual merits of various lifestyles were debated in the fifth and sixth centuries. Was the ascetic recluse who lived a life of contemplation a holier person than a bishop charged with the care of his flock? In answer to precisely that query, Julianus Pomerius strove to reassure an anxious bishop: he pointed to the different, but equally meritorious, path taken by those who assumed religious office to guide their congregations. Yet contemplation was still the key. Julianus Pomerius's insistence on it may have served more to emphasize the gulf between the paths of the ascetic and cleric than to see a bridge between them.[70] It is possible, however, that Gregory's abject reliance on saintly intercession arose from a "compassionate" mode of thinking influenced by the *Apocalypse of Peter* in which, at the Last Judgement, the saints would intercede successfully for the damned.[71] Richard Bauckham sums up this position: "According to this group the wicked are rescued from hell by the prayers of the saints immediately on being consigned to hell at the Day of Judgement. Their punishment is revoked, not implemented at all . . ." While the *Apocalypse of Peter* is not generally supposed to have great influence on theological thought in the West, it is not inconceivable that the work, or its mild universalism, was known to Gregory and others who were deeply committed to the cults of the saints.

Reflecting on his cure from a pulsating headache, effected through pressing his head against the shrine curtains, yet contemplating the advisability of having his blood let, Gregory prayed to St. Martin for health and purity. As he prayed, he imagined that he had been called to the Final Judgement. Huddled among the herd of the damned (a goat, not a sheep) he hears the sentence that confirms his worst fears: he is to be condemned to the eternal flames. But then he imagines that Martin will shield him with his cloak and do for him what Martin had once done for a dead "monk": obtain a reprieve from punishment (*excuset a poena*).[72] The reference was to Martin's first miracle, told by Sulpicus Severus, in which he had resurrected a dead catechumen.[73] This miracle suggested Martin's chthonic powers. Like Paulinus before him, Gregory viewed Martin's resurrection of the dead man as reason to petition for his own salvation. In Sulpicius's account, the resurrected catechumen had already received his sentence at the heavenly tribunal, and Martin's intercession had saved him even from Christ's judgement. Likewise, Gregory believed that Martin (and other saints, too) could intercede to save the sinner even after he was "buried" in hell. Martin's saving power was thus equal to Christ's. Martin, like Christ, could reach into hell to save his own:[74]

> We do not doubt not only that we are worthy to acquire this remission for our sins through their prayers, but also that we are saved from the infernal torments through their intervention. For we believe that just as they restrain [all] kinds of illnesses here, so they deflect the ruthless penalties of torments there; that just as they alleviate bodily fevers here, so they quench the eternal flames there; that just as they cleanse the horrible ulcers of ghastly leprosy here, so through their intervention they obtain relief for the blemishes of sins there; and that just as they restore to life the bodies of the dead here, so there they extend their hand, dig up from the waters of Acheron those buried in sin, and restore them to eternal life.[75]

It would be hard to find a clearer statement on the power of the saint. The saint straddled two worlds: the human and the divine, the sick and the healthy. Martin is believed present at his shrines, in his relics, and in the dreams of his devotees, yet he is also in heaven, and the healings he performs in association with his relics are miracles that stretch his hand to the living from beyond the grave. The tomb is the source of eternal life.[76] Gregory's utter confidence in the intercessory capacity of the saints is revealed in how he believed it was done: "just as they restrain [all] kinds of illnesses here, so they deflect the ruthless penalties of torments there." That is to say, that what is brought about by a process in this life (cleansing, alleviating, restraining) results in a completed remedy (remedy, quenching, deflecting) in the afterlife. The saint's rescue of the sinful appears to be complete, although it depends on cleansing here on earth: the cleansing of blemishes in the present life corresponds to a remedy for the blemishes of sin in afterlife. This does not mean that a bodily cure here corresponds automatically to salvation there; rather, Gregory describes degrees of human failing and degrees of supernatural aid in the present life. It is that cure of the body prefigures the potential health of the soul. The clue to the saint's activity for humanity in the afterlife was to be found in the saint's miracles in the present life; put another way, miracles in this life lit the path that led to salvation in the next.

Yet, Gregory did not imagine that having been saved by St. Martin he would join the company of the saints. He imagined a lesser place for himself: "Because I am not worthy to be clothed with this splendour, let it rather be the case that I am worthy to be freed from the threatening agents of the underworld. And may I not suffer from such a punishment that I am separated from the kingdom of God whom I have piously relied upon in this world."[77] What kind of place will give refuge to the less exalted? Gregory imagines it as a place where he will be safe from demons, but it may yet be a place of punishment—only not to such a degree that he is separated from God's kingdom. It is a curious conception because Gregory's hope for his imagined future home is a place in heaven, not simply a lesser existence in heaven (as might be denoted figuratively as a smaller mansion, for example) but a place in which punishment may yet occur—a continued punishment meted out in heaven's domain but not by demons. This description might have some claim to represent a middling existence for the less than perfect soul if Gregory had imagined it as the place his soul went straight after death, but this was clearly not the case: the setting is not an interim judgement but the Last Judgement at which all humans will be divided between the saved and the damned. Was Gregory's modesty a stumbling block to eschatological consistency?

We may imagine why it was that Gregory may have drawn some personal consolation from the thought that he would be protected by St. Martin in the event of the worst possible outcome. If we look at Gregory's approach when addressing an audience, when Gregory came closest to articulating an abstract idea or theology, we find much the same advice being invoked. He urges his reader to seek the patronage and thus the intercessions (*suffragiis*) of the martyrs. He anticipates that their assistance will bolster (or perhaps substitute for) a deficiency in merits: "What we are not worthy to obtain by our own merits, we can receive through their intercessions."[78] The full meaning of this comment is unclear. Did Gregory hope that the martyrs could top off an evident shortfall of merit, so to speak? Or is this a garbled reference to the Augustinian notion that salvation is not obtained by personal merits alone and that in taking on the sign of the cross, the martyrs have become the vessels for God to impart divine grace to his people? The precise identity of the martyrs becomes somewhat confused when in this passage Gregory imagined that all his listeners could become martyrs if they took on the sign of the cross and resisted vice (a somewhat modest criterion).[79] At the Final Judgement, however, God would listen to the martyrs who had spilled their blood and who petitioned for their devoted followers that they would not be damned in perpetuity (*nec damnet in perpetuo*): "At the moment of judgement *(in illo examinationis tempore)* when eternal glory surrounds the martyrs, either the mercy of their mediation will excuse us or a lenient penalty will pass over us."[80] Here Gregory anticipated either a complete dismissal of the sinner's crimes or a light sentence (*levis poena*). It is the light sentence that is suggestive here and that may echo Gregory's personal hopes for a place in heaven with only minor punishment. Was this purgatory? Logically, this would seem not to be the case—the imagined scene is at the Last Judgement.[81] Nor can Gregory be thinking of the fire of purification through which all the souls of the saved must pass because, again, it is clear that the punishment forms part of the judge's sentence. Gregory seems to imagine that at the Last Judgement, God can still sentence Christians who are deemed saved to experience light punishment—whether temporarily or eternally is not made clear.

Conclusion

Gregory of Tours's world of purgative-driven salvation is never considered in studies of purgatory. Yet his perspective on health and salvation is an important dimension in our understanding of what purgatory was to become: a place in which bodies were made healthy through the application of the medicine of purgation. Gregory's thinking on health and miracles was entirely theological and even eschatological.[82] Gregory saw God's power, and that of his saints, in every facet of his environment; and that environment was replete with evidence that God purged the faithful of bodily infirmities and spiritual sickness in preparation for salvation. Purgation was a means to "restore" bodies in preparation for their future life. Can we say that Gregory's works, widely read as they were, formally contributed to the intellectual development of purgatory? That would be hard to prove. Rather, Gregory illuminates social perceptions of purgation as a means of restoring the body and soul to health. How far were Gregory's views representative of his time? The question is often asked but cannot be fully answered. I would suggest that at one level Gregory represents a particular way of thinking about the world that had ancient roots and was deeply ingrained in Mediterranean culture: a world that saw a connection between one's bowels and one's salvation. His ideas about bodily purgation had roots in pagan philosophy and even distant parentage in the thought of Origen who was also drawn to metaphors of bodily purgation. On another level, the fullest flight of his eschatological reading of Martin's miracles appears to have been peculiar to him. Furthermore, Gregory's view of his own activities at the saint's shrines avoids expected models of behaviour. Prior to a purge, Gregory's sickness would not allow him to eat. Perhaps as a sign of honesty, he does not link these episodes to fasts. But he also does not take away a message from these episodes that fasting or other ascetic acts should result from the crisis. Crisis induced devotion to the saint. The cure is all.

In a prosaic fashion, Gregory's focus on Martin's miracles suggested that God's plan was to be read in nature and in humanity's experience of the natural world. Gregory, like other shrine scribes, depicted the writhing bodies as they were purged of demons, of foul odours and liquids, as they vomited out blood and pus, and as they were wracked by coughs, fevers, and chills, and in so doing recognized that what he was seeing was the hand of God forcing the bodies of the spiritually sick to become healthy and whole in preparation for the resurrection. Heaven's purgative was not a pretty sight, but it was a holy thing, a healthful agent, a violent stimulus to health. Poised between sickness and health, the petitioners at St. Martin's shrines were struggling to be restored. Gregory's miracle stories stand at a midpoint between those who imagined afterlife purification as some kind of neutral refining agent and those who viewed it as a place or state of torment. They point to a cultural attitude that expected God to act violently to save the bodies and souls of the elect. Gregory expected purification to occur in this life, and he documented its violent swath through the sick. It was left to others to explicitly extend the idea of the healing torments to an afterlife venue, but in Gregory's account of Martin's healing miracles we view an anticipation of the images of the purging torment that was to characterize visions of the afterlife in centuries to come.

4

Purgation in the Sixth and Seventh Centuries

Although purgatorial theology continued to develop along its own lines in the East—a tradition that retained sympathy for Hellenistic ideas, including Origenism—and although eastern ideas and texts continued to make their way West, Christian culture in the medieval West was distinctly heir to Augustine's eschatological thinking.[1] Augustine's legacy is evident in the earliest Gallic sources to discuss purgatory and was transmitted through the centuries through the work of, among others, Gregory the Great, Isidore of Seville, and Bede. These works testify to a common corpus of concerns that persisted over time. Furthermore, visionary accounts of the afterlife began to make their impact in these centuries as the *Vision of Paul* found imitators. Finally, the sacramental life of the church, especially baptism and penance, which offered purification but also required it from its members, kept images of spiritual cleansing firmly in view of the faithful.

Julianus Pomerius and Caesarius of Arles

Augustine's theology of sin and grace grew in uneven influence over the course of the fifth century, but by the early sixth century his views were receiving official recognition. At the Council of Orange in 529, largely due to the efforts of Bishop Caesarius of Arles, the Gallic bishops rejected "semi-Pelagianism." Caesarius was a vocal promoter of Augustine's theology and, in his own sermons, a promoter of his scriptural interpretation. Behind his dedication to Augustine's legacy stood the shadowy figure of his tutor, the African émigré rhetor, Julianus Pomerius.

Julianus Pomerius is an interesting figure because he wrote a treatise on the soul that discussed postmortem purgation (*De anima et qualitate eius*.) Unfortunately, the work and three other treatises by him have not survived. He is primarily known for his surviving book, *On the Contemplative Life*, which was admired and widely copied, although mistakenly attributed to Prosper of Aquitaine in the Middle Ages. Yet Julian of Toledo quoted from Pomerius's lost treatise on the soul in his *Prognosticon*. There, Julian attributed to Pomerius the view that the church's prayers can effectively intercede for those who are not so perfect that they can go directly to paradise, nor so criminal that they deserve to be damned. The prayers of the church, and the imposition of penance, will allow them to participate in God's kingdom.[2] Julian reiterated Augustine's formula that masses said for the very good are thank offerings, when said for the not very bad, masses are propitiatory, and when said for the very bad, they are consolation only for the living.[3] It appears, then, that Julianus Pomerius was as Augustinian in eschatological matters, as he was in other, better-known facets of his teaching.

We know Caesarius to have been Pomerius's pupil around 497.[4] In 499 Caesarius was made abbot of a monastery in Arles; three years later he was made Bishop of Arles, in which capacity he served for forty years. The sermon collection of this early sixth-century bishop is a treasure trove of exegetical thinking put to the service of moral education.[5] The sermons were addressed to the entire Christian community, lay and clerical, and held up the ideals of Christian living to both. His sermons emphasized that sins could be purged in the present life through continuous penance and good works, especially almsgiving: repentance in this life could even restore the lost grace of baptism.[6] For those who failed to atone adequately through penance, there was the possibility of purgation through pain after death.

Caesarius's fidelity to scripture yielded a fire-centered eschatology. "Depart from me, accursed ones, into the everlasting fire" is a favourite phrase from Matthew's Gospel. Yet this threat of hellfire is never evoked without very concrete advice on how to avoid it and a highly developed sense of what divided heavy sins from lighter ones. Heavy sins included sacrilege, murder, adultery, perjury, theft, robbery, pride, envy, and avarice. Habitual sins such as drunkenness and slander were also included in this list. Light sins included gluttony, garrulousness, carnal relations with a spouse without desire for children, irritable behaviour, and gossip.[7] Both categories of sin could be atoned by penance performed in the right frame of mind and especially if accompanied by almsgiving.[8] However, Caesarius insisted that Christians could only be purged of light sins after death.[9]

This purging fire presented a pastoral problem, however. Caesarius was evidently concerned that this latter option of a purging fire might be viewed by his audience as a reason to defer penance in the present life since it might appear (erroneously) that salvation could be achieved after death. Consequently, he explains the characteristics of this purging experience. This fire is extremely painful, he warns: "that fire of purgatory will be more difficult than any punishment in this world can be seen or imagined or felt." Furthermore, it may last a very long time indeed. From Peter he quotes, "One day will be as a thousand years, and a thousand days as one year," and asks, "how does anyone know whether he is going to pass through that fire days or months or even years?"[10] Caesarius appears to have viewed this fire of painful purgation as the fire of Judgement Day the "rational" fire that will merely "lick" the chaste bodies of the just.[11] In suggesting that the fire of purgation might potentially afflict the sinner for months or even years, Caesarius was giving to the fire of purgation a duration, a "thickness," that was to become a central feature of medieval depictions of purgatory. In this, Caesarius lent authority to Augustine's suggestion that purgation was a feature of the afterlife that for some would be more than transitory: "we will have to stay in that purging fire as long as the abovementioned slight sins are consumed like wood and hay and straw."[12] If the purging fire was the fire of Judgement Day, what happened to the souls of the dead as they awaited resurrection? Caesarius is not aways crystal clear on the matter. In some places, Caesarius made reference to the Bosom of Abraham as the resting and waiting place of the elect. Yet in other places Caesarius appears to suggest that there is an immediate judgement.[13] The split between just and damned may suggest the fates of those who would not undergo purgation: the just (Caesarius identifies as martyrs, virgins[14]) would pass through the fire directly to heaven while the damned would go directly to hell. Those who must be purged are not included in this depiction. Elsewhere, the crowning of the just occurs on Judgement Day: "when the Day of Judgement comes, a good life will be able to crown the Just."[15] The compacting of postmortem events (from worms to judgement) may also simply have served to enhance dramatic effect. In the many sermons in which Caesarius addressed the fire of purgation, it was always in the context of Judgement Day.[16]

In a sermon on 1 Corinthians 3:12–15, Caesarius carefully considered who would be able to go through this purging fire and how painful it would be. The saints will pass through that fire "without any violence" and "as though through pleasant pools, untouched by the burning flames which do not even observe their true nature."[17] Only those encumbered by slight sins will be able to be purged of them after death. These are sins of which even saints cannot always be free. They are represented in the parable by those who build on Christ's foundation with gold. Good Christians who are careless in present penance are those who build with wood, hay, and straw; it is they who can expect a delay of months or years in the fire of purgation. Caesarius offered these potential sufferers the remedy of present penance.

In his adherence to Augustinian theology and the concept of original sin, Caesarius adopted Augustine's emphasis on afterlife pain as punishment for sin. He viewed as correction only those tribulations that lead to spiritual reform in the present life: "men will not be able to escape intolerable punishments and eternal flames unless they have first extinguished in themselves the fire of various carnal passions."[18] The slightly sinful Christian who is not so "purified" by bitter tribulation in this life must expect to be tortured by purging fire in the next. The damned will go directly to hell. Based on Matthew 25:41, Caesarius (like Origen) emphasized that hell was not prepared for mankind, but for the devil and his angels. Yet sinners, if they do not reject the devil's "rags" by taking up the "stole of good works," will forfeit God's grace and be condemned to hell together with the pagans, heretics, and Jews.[19]

It would not have served Caesarius's pastoral purpose to couple his depictions of afterlife events with explicit statements about the mitigation of postmortem pain through prayers of the living. There is a hint of the idea in an interpolated sermon: "'If you pass through fire,' I am with you 'and the flames shall not consume you.' If you ask through prayer, you will find, and if you knock through giving to the poor, Christ opens the doors to you in order that you may enter and possess paradise." It is possible that the later interpolator sought to remedy the deficit. More characteristically, we find in Caesarius's prayers for his sister's nunnery the view that in the commemoration of those departed who had lived a holy life under the guidance of the church, suppliants could bring to mind God's "indulgence" in bringing the soul the reward she deserved.[20]

In Caesarius the sermon-writer we are presented with the measured tones of episcopal authority, exhorting his flock to be mindful of Judgement Day. We glimpse another Caesarius in his biography, written within a few years of Caesarius's death by five members of his clerical staff.[21] His deacon Stephanus recalled how one night, on his way to check the time for the night office, he heard Caesarius whispering in his sleep: "There are two places, there is no middle place, only two: either one ascends into heaven or descends into hell." Upon waking, Caesarius was aware that he had been shouting out to someone in his dream. Stephanus thought Caesarius was always addressing God. But one wonders whether the stressful moment was perhaps connected with his old tutor Pomerius. Was he dreaming his disagreement with him on this issue, as he had once, in the schoolroom, dreaming himself out of having to confront the "dragon" of the classics? It is a rare and tantalizing glimpse of an author of purgatory grappling with its theology.

Gregory the Great and the "Dialogues"

Whereas Augustine was tentative about the soul's destination before the Last Judgement, Pope Gregory offered new certainties about the afterlife arising, broadly speaking, from a combination of two sources of influence: a strong but sometimes modified Augustinian theology and supernatural narratives—essentially, ghost stories.[22] Although Gregory discussed the postmortem fate of souls in other works, including the *Moralia in Job* and the *Homilies*, it was his representation of the afterlife through visionary tales in the *Dialogues* that caught the imagination of his medieval readers.[23] Its style and approach is so different from Gregory's other works that it has prompted generations of scholars to find ways to explain it.[24]

Gregory devoted the final book of his *Dialogues*, to discussing the fate of the soul after death. This last book, probably written in the mid-590s, is undeniably choppy in style; the questions and answers of the "dialogue" do not always fit smoothly.[25] This may be due, at least in part, to the inherent difficulty of grafting anecdotal narratives onto a framework of Augustinian theology that has been adjusted to suit the dialogue form. It was an experiment that was not always successful and that may have been misleading in some instances. Some of the stories arose from Gregory's personal experience, and others were sent to Gregory by friends and religious acquaintances; at times they preserve their narrative coherence at the expense of the theological framing. However, Gregory clearly states his aim for this final book: to demonstrate that the soul lives on after the death of the body. The theological portions of the book and the three colourful stories examined below fulfilled that aim for Gregory's readers.[26]

Gregory wanted his stories to support and illustrate an eschatological scheme in which the individual's death was followed by immediate, personal judgement. The souls of the just would go directly (or with slight delay) to heaven, while the souls of the wicked would also be punished immediately. Gregory conceded that some of the elect might be temporarily delayed in attaining heaven because they lacked perfect justice.[27] However, on Judgement Day, the souls of the just would receive their bodies, which would double their bliss. This was illustrated by the clothing they would wear: after death the elect would wear a single white robe and be allowed to rest; a double white robe representing body and soul together would be theirs on Judgement Day.[28] This white-robed, restful fate for the just immediately after death would be mirrored infernally in the immediate torture of the damned.

On hearing of this immediate, postmortem judgement, Gregory's interlocutor, Peter, was prompted to comment: "I do not know what Christ has taught us in this regard, but from human reason we should conclude that the souls of sinners could not be punished until the Day of Judgement."[29] Rather than address the apparent inconsistency between his own view and that found in scripture, Gregory merely affirmed that if the souls of the saints are already in heaven it follows that "from the day of their death the reprobate burn in fire."[30] Yet Peter's question was a good one: scriptural references to the afterlife generally assumed that the second coming was imminent and that Christians waited in their graves for the resurrection and judgement of all souls. Gregory's response (drawing on Augustine) supposes that there is an immediate, individual judgement at death and that the Last Judgement merely confirms and augments the experience of the soul by adding to it the sensation of the body. In the narrative context of the book, Peter appears satisfied with Gregory's response, yet between Peter's assumption and Gregory's reply yawned the gap between scripture and early medieval thinking about what happens to the soul after death. Tertullian had already expressed the notion that the dead had a foretaste of their future judgement. Gregory, like later medieval thinkers, believed that an immediate, individual judgement at death anticipated the outcome of the soul's judgement at the Last Judgement. In fact, the entire corpus of western visionary literature in which individuals traveled to the otherworld presumed this to be the case, often including elaborate judgment scenes of individuals, which clearly preceded the universal judgement of Judgement Day.[31] Rather than debate Peter on scriptural grounds, Gregory's anecdotes sought merely to affirm his belief in immediate judgement. It becomes clear that immediate, individual judgement was a necessary component in Gregory's stories and was necessary for developing ideas of purgatory, since it gave an opportunity for intercessory prayers to aid the souls of the dead before the Last Judgement.

Having established that souls were judged immediately, Gregory proceeded to discuss afterlife purgation. Peter asks whether "we are to believe in a purging fire after death."[32] Peter's question whether such a thing is to be believed (*credendus est*) indicates that what follows will concern doctrine rather than opinion. Again, Gregory's answer was evasive, consisting of a string of quotations from the Old Testament (Isaiah, Ecclesiastes, the Psalms) that did not broach afterlife purgation but rather the need for repentance. Only one quotation from the psalms ("For his mercy endures for ever") could even remotely refer to recourse beyond the grave.[33]

Each individual will be presented to the Judge as he was when he left this life, writes Gregory, "yet," he continues, "there must be a cleansing fire before judgement, because of some minor faults that may remain to be purged away."[34] These minor faults include idle chatter, immoderate laughter, and minor errors of ignorance.[35] Gregory turned to the image of fire given in 1 Corinthians 3: 11–15 as scriptural evidence for a future purging fire. Gregory struck an Augustinian chord with the comment that this fire may indeed refer to tribulation in this life, but he then proceeds to his true interest, the future purgatorial fire. Echoing Augustine and Caesarius, Gregory explained that the sins that may be purged in it are minor. Paul did not intend major sins (*peccata maiora*) to be understood since such sins are indestructible by fire, and minor or very light sins (*peccata minima atque levissima*) are consumed by fire easily.[36] However, even such minor sins are purged only if the individual has merited such a cleansing through good works, he states.

Gregory chose to illustrate his points about postmortem purgation with stories. The stories he chose, however, fall short of this intention on a number of counts. Only one of them refers unambiguously to a fire, and the others are not easy to reconcile with Gregory's stated theology of purgatory.

The first of three stories to be examined here concerns the unfortunate fate of a pious man, the deacon Paschasius, who had sinned out of ignorance, not malice. Gregory's purpose in telling the tale was to provide an illustration of the principle that intent was an important qualifier of sin. Paschasius had been extremely generous in almsgiving, but he had a single fault: he had chosen to support the wrong candidate in a papal election and had continued in his loyalty to his candidate (and his objection to the duly-installed pope) until his death. When Paschasius died his soul did not find peace. Bishop Germanus of Capua (died c. 541) visited the baths of Angulus a long time later, *post multum vero temporis*, and saw Paschasius there working as an attendant. Paschasius explained that his one fault had been his support for Laurentius over Symmachus, and he begged Germanus to pray for him: "when you come back and no longer find me here, you will know that your prayers have been heard." Germanus did as he was asked, and when he returned to the baths a few days later, Paschasius did not reappear. Gregory commented that "[Paschasius] could be purged of this sin after death because he had sinned not through malice but through ignorance,"[37] and he added that Paschasius's previous record of almsgiving allowed him to be forgiven a light sin when he was no longer in a position to work to this end himself.[38] Thus Gregory added a second, very Augustinian lesson to the story: posthumous purgation was available to Paschasius only because he had merited such consideration through his pious activities in life.

There is nothing in Gregory's account to suggest that he believed Paschasius was purged through fire. Paschasius stood in the heat of the baths, but this heat was not apparently painful either to Germanus or to Paschasius.[39] The use of the baths as a symbol for purification might seem appropriate for a purification that is akin to a baptism than to a purging fire. Yet Paschasius explained that he was in a place of punishment (*in hoc poenali loco deputatus sum*). It is not clear whether this is a place of physical torture, psychological penalty, or simply confinement.[40] The true nature of Paschasius's affliction was presented primarily as demoted status. The audience's reaction was primed by Germanus's reaction to the scene: he was shocked (*vehementer extimuit*), to discover that such a man (*tantus vir*), was performing such a task. Bath attendant was a job that in the ancient world was conventionally relegated to slaves.[41]

Paschasius's purgation was evidently protracted. Gregory tells us that Germanus saw Paschasius a long time after the deacon's death (*post multum vero temporis*). The schism over the competing claims of Symmachus and Laurentius started in 498 and became particularly violent in 502; Paschasius is believed to have died in 511.[42] Germanus of Capua evidently knew Paschasius well enough to immediately recognize him in his vision and must have been a younger contemporary. In 519 Germanus was already a bishop and one of a group of papal legates sent by the new pope, Hormisdas, to Constantinople at the conclusion of the Acacian schism.[43] We are not told when in Germanus's long career he saw his vision of Paschasius, but Pope Hormisdas reconciled many of those disaffected by the Laurentian schism, and it would be plausible that Germanus's vision took place at a time when reconciliation both at home and abroad was on everyone's mind. Germanus died c. 541.[44] Paschasius's job as an "attendant" (*stantem et obsequentem*) certainly underscores the impression that a long time passed, for his job is to wait and serve. By contrast, the bishop's prayers of intercession on his behalf act quickly. Paschasius no longer appears at the baths after only a few days. The protracted time element in this story anticipates later visions of extended postmortem purgation coupled with swift release after an act of intercession. The clearly articulated connection of prayers (and elsewhere, masses) of intercession and the release of a soul from punishment is an important development.[45]

Later in the *Dialogues*, Gregory and Peter resumed their discussion of Paschasius's case. Peter wanted to know how a miracle could have occurred publicly at Paschasius's tomb when Paschasius himself was undergoing punishment privately. Gregory reminded Peter that Paschasius was indeed punished "for some time," which, although vague, is not the same as his previous statement that Paschasius suffered a long time.⁴⁶ It appears that Gregory was trying to reassert the notion of brief purgation at this point in the story. Furthermore, it was at this point that Peter introduced another question prompted by Paschasius's punishment in the baths, namely, the location of the place of postmortem punishment. After brief hesitation, Gregory offered the solution: there are two places of punishment. One is an upper place of punishment on earth (thus explaining Paschasius's situation), while a lower place of punishment exists *sub terra*.⁴⁷ The upper place of punishment was clearly temporary, and by being situated on earth, on the same plane as living humans, it neatly accounted for traditional ghost stories in which souls were hindered from passing to their ultimate destination.

Paschasius's story has a double in another story in the *Dialogues*. This time the story was told to Gregory's friend Bishop Felix by an unnamed priest about an unnamed sinner, the former proprietor of the baths at Tauriana. The priest entered the hot springs and saw a stranger there who tended to his needs. Wanting to thank the attendant on his next visit to the hot springs, the priest took two (consecrated) loaves of bread with him, one of which he offered to the man. The stranger declined it because he could not take holy bread. He explained that he had been sent back (from the dead) to the springs because of his sins, and he asked the priest to "offer that bread to God on my behalf, so that you may intercede for my sins."⁴⁸ Echoing Paschasius, the sinner affirmed that "when you come back and do not find me here, you will know that your prayers have been heard." The priest spent the week in prayer and offered Mass for him every day. When he returned to the springs, the man was no longer there.

The similarity between this story and that of Paschasius is so striking that it can hardly be coincidental. It is a variant on the earlier story, possibly a traditional story, recycled and given new authority. In the earlier story of Germanus of Capua's encounter with the deceased Paschasius, the sinner asked for the bishop's prayers, which he received. In the story of the anonymous sinner, the priest was asked to make an intercession that, we learn, included the saying of daily Mass for one week. The first story relates the personal intercession by one member of the elite for another, of one holy person for another. The second story, by contrast, generalized the remedy of masses for the ordinary sinner said on his behalf by a priest. It is a plebeian version of the earlier story and thus more interesting in its implications for the avenues of recourse offered to ordinary Christians. Like the earlier story it likened purgatorial suffering to a job at the baths-evidently just about the worst job you could have in sixth-century Italy. Furthermore, while this second version of the story lacks precision about the nature of the sin being punished, Gregory does emphasize its quality: it belongs to an alarming, double-negative category of faults, namely, those "not incapable of being unbound."[49]

In later centuries, the story that most closely linked Gregory with the theology of purgatory was an account of his pastoral dealings with a monk at his monastery named Justus. This was another tale in which a dead man returned to the living in a vision, but this time it was Gregory himself who consigned the man to his punishment.

The story, in brief, is as follows. A monk in Gregory's monastery, Justus, who served as his personal physician, confessed on his deathbed to having kept three gold coins hidden away, contrary to the rule of the community. The money was later discovered in his medicine supply. Gregory was greatly distressed at this and began to wonder what he could do to purge the dying man of his sin.[50] He decided to resort to a harsh treatment in order to save him. It was Gregory's belief that the fear of death was "sufficient to purify [the soul] of its minor faults."[51] Thus, in this case, Gregory ordered the monks not to talk to him, thus depriving him of one of the most valued aspects of monastic life, the consolation and support of the community at the moment of death. "The bitterness of this experience at the moment of death may serve as a penitential scourge to cleanse him from the sin he has committed," commented Gregory.[52] He ordered that once Justus died, his body be cast on the dung heap with the gold coins thrown after him and the monks say, "take your money with you to perdition."[53] The first order, Gregory explained, was for the sake of the sinner: "The bitterness at the hour of death was to bring about the forgiveness of his sin."[54] The abuse of the dead body was intended as a lesson to the living. Gregory noted the good effect of his harsh sentence: When told of it, Justus wept bitterly and "passed out of his body in his sorrow."[55]

Justus's fate returned to Gregory's mind thirty days later, and he ordered masses to be said for the monk for thirty days consecutively. Gregory explained to his community that "Justus has now been suffering the torments of fire for a long time and we must show him our charity by helping as much as we can to gain his release."[56] After thirty days of consecutive masses Justus appeared to his brother Copiosus in a vision and stated, "Up to this moment I was in misery, but now I am well because this morning I was admitted to communion."[57] Copiosus reported his vision to Gregory who remarked with satisfaction that the monks knew that "the brother who had died was freed from punishment through the sacrifice of the Mass."[58]

Justus's release from the fire's torture after thirty days of masses led, in later medieval England, to the popular belief that thirty masses, termed trentals, would release a soul from purgatory and that this had been the custom since Gregory's time. In fact, there is no evidence that there developed a systematic belief in the efficacy of thirty masses in the early middle ages. The story was powerful, however, and alongside similar stories of the saving and miraculous quality of the Mass, this story underscored the view, endorsed later by Bede, that the office of the Mass was a vital feature in gaining a soul's release from purgatory.

Was Justus in purgatory or in hell? Gregory is not clear on the matter, and scholars have made the case each way. In favour of the "hell" interpretation, the point can be made that Gregory damned Justus and his money to perdition—that is, to those "lost" to salvation in hell. He also removed the man from the protection of the community—a monastic excommunication. Gregory tells us his severe actions were aimed at purging the man through sorrow before death and, at the moment of death, through fear, thus releasing him from his sin. Gregory does not specifically indicate that he was purged after death. This fit the conventional, penitential view that purgation must be accomplished before death. There is no indication that Justus would be released in time anyway through the cleansing power of purgatorial flames. Thus it is not clear that Justus was being purified in the fire; but he was certainly being tortured in it. Was it precisely the tragic fate of damnation that preyed on Gregory's mind? He had personally ordered the masses (he was not abbot of the community) as a means of reversing his own previous sentence of damnation: "take your money to perdition." The "hell" interpretation had support in the seventh-century anonymous *Whitby Life of Gregory*, whose author gives a slightly different account of the dying physician and his three coins. In that work it was clear that the unfortunate physician was in hell although, dramatically, "still living"![59]

In favour of Justus being in purgatory, we have Gregory's comment that Justus had now suffered enough. Gregory was able to engineer Justus's release by offering masses. When Justus appeared to Copiosus he stated that he had just received Communion, which must be understood as a reversal of his earlier excommunication by Gregory. It is possible that Gregory had rescued Justus from purgatory. That was certainly the view that held sway through the middle ages.

Gregory's most significant contribution to the development of early medieval purgatory arose from stories that suggested that Christians could still be helped by the living once they had passed from the world of the living to the world of the dead. In Gregory's stories the dead are still visible to the living and can be recalled to mind; the living are still a recourse for them and can improve their fate. When Pope Gregory condemned and then released from suffering his intimate Justus, his story took on the overtones of institutional authority; and later readers pointed to the story as a critical illustration of the pope's power to bind and loose. When a similar story was told about a former owner of the local hot springs establishment, it was the supernatural efficacy of the Mass that came to the fore. In that respect, the minor tales told by Gregory of how a drowning man was sustained by the host and survived, and how a captive was loosened from his chains every time his wife ordered that a mass be said for him, played just as important a role in broadening the common perception of the efficacy of the Mass as did the more famous stories of Justus and Paschasius.[60] If the Mass could save the living from peril, it could do the same for the dead: "deceased persons, too, can be absolved from sins through the Mass, provided their sins are pardonable."[61]

Gregory's stories of posthumous aid are solidly viewed from the perspective of the living. The two bathhouse stories do not suggest that the interim time between death and Last Judgement is tortuous in anything more than a social sense, and thus they do not do the work of illustration that Gregory intended them to. Only in Justus's story does the reference to the monk's torment in fire appear in what might be viewed as a more traditional example of postmortem purgation through fire, except that the story was more effective in illustrating the pope's power of the keys than the routine operation of purgatory. In many ways the three stories we have examined here illustrate a transition from one level of intercession story to another, in which simple prayers of intercession (Paschasius) are displaced by prayers strengthened by the sacrifice of the Mass (the hot springs owner) and finally multiple masses (Justus).

The *Dialogues* is an interesting work because it preserves, like archaeological strata, fragments of debates and ideas about hell and purgation that harken back to Augustine's time and even earlier. For example, Augustine's influence is readily seen in passages in which a discussion of the eternal nature of hell intersects with ideas about correction and purgation. The early Christian view that punishment must be linked to correction is revived in Peter's question to Gregory about the purpose for God's punishment of sinners and whether it is just to punish someone eternally for a sin that took place in a finite period of time on earth.[62] One might wonder how far these concerns about alternative views were still "live" at the end of the sixth century, rather than a sort of antiquarian theological exercise. Gregory did not mention Origen by name in the *Dialogues*, yet concerns about Origenist views lay behind some of Peter's queries, for, as de Vogüé noted in his edition of the *Dialogues*, the same questions are voiced by "Origenists" in a comparable passage in his *Moralia*.[63] Origen's second condemnation at Constantinople in 553 was a relatively recent event, yet debates on ideas that might be termed "Origenist" had been aired closer to Gregory's time. For example, when insisting on the corporeality of the resurrected body, Gregory undoubtedly had in view the Eutychian dispute that he had been personally involved in refuting.[64] There are times when it seems that the final book of the *Dialogues* is little more than a collation of fragmentary notes taken from reading Augustine's works. Gregory's answers to Peter are hardly satisfactory summaries of Augustine's views, and there is a habitual slide away from real explanation to raw assertion. When Peter points out that the just man punishes his servants for the purpose of correction, not cruelty, Gregory defensively asserts that God is not cruel—"Almighty God, being a God of love, does not gratify his anger by torturing wretched sinners"[65]—and attributes this torture, as did Augustine also, to a comprehension of justice only attainable to Christians once they have become absorbed into the Godhead, for then "his severity will penetrate their minds."[66]

Looking backward and forward, we find in Gregory's *Dialogues* features both consistent with, and at variance with, previous traditions and the fullest expression of purgatorial workings in Bede. On the one hand, Gregory's stories give copious voice to the desire of the dead to return to the living in search of help, whether it be to request simple prayers of intercession or the sacrifice of the Mass. Gregory was much more interested in giving evidence for the efficacy of intercession than Augustine and Caesarius, although he drew directly from them in his insistence on the importance of good works and on the lightness of the sins that could be purged. In particular, Gregory laid great emphasis on the Mass as a time when Christians renewed their personal connection to God. Robert Atwell made an important distinction when he commented that "Gregory can consider the eucharistic sacrifice divorced from the liturgical commemoration of the departed, and as a specific offering with a specific intention" and in seeing this as a shift toward "the notion of a priest being specifically requested (eventually paid) to make propitiatory offering on behalf of an individual or a group, especially after death."[67] The importance of the Mass as a means of intercession is important to Bede. On the other hand, there are ways in which Gregory's discussion of purgation did not fully anticipate notions of the purgatorial fire that were to be familiar to Fursey and Bede. The fire of purgation that was kindled by the excrescences of human sin, which was to be so important to Fursey's vision, is viewed by Gregory as God's creation.[68] Gregory's stories were about removing impediments to safe passage to the otherworld. Paschasius was stuck waiting on earth, whereas he should have been waiting in heaven. Indeed, if Gregory had not introduced the story of Paschasius as an illustration of purgation, the reader would not have made such a connection. The torment of the monk

Justus comes closest to the idea of a hellish torment that is temporary and accessible to intercession, yet there is no sense in this story that Justus's fate represents the generic fate of Christians. Rather, the account suggests a different kind of story in which a community's ritual curse on a wrongdoer consigns a soul to hell and that is ultimately redeemed by the efforts of the entire community to bring the soul back. Justus's return to the state of the "just" presumably earned him a more honourable burial than his first resting place. Gregory's confidence in the value of burial in church was a clear departure from Augustine's views, and it explicitly expressed the value of practices that were, by Gregory's time, widespread.[69]

Gregory offered the explanation that abuse of the sinner on his deathbed was intended as a penance. Without penance before death, the soul was damned. Yet, the salutary, purging benefit of deathbed suffering was a favourite theme in the *Dialogues*: "the very dread that grips a departing soul is sufficient to purify it of its minor faults."[70] God's hand was at work in this. Gregory told this most compellingly in a little story about a man of God who disobeyed God's word and was killed by a lion. When his body was discovered, the lion was standing next to it, but it had eaten neither the man nor his donkey. Gregory's comment was that the man was "sanctified in the death he suffered as a punishment for his disobedience" but that the lion stood guard over the body of the just man since no further punishment of him after death was permitted.[71]

While Gregory's writings never achieved Bede's precision about the function and operation of purgatory, his tales in which the dead returned to the living begging for sacramental intercession, and his emphasis on the efficacy of the Mass to save souls after death, were enormously influential for future writers on the afterlife. We know that Bede was deeply immersed in Gregory's writings, as he was in Augustine's writings. For Bede, as for Gregory, visions of the afterlife and theology intersected, but along very different lines. Gregory's theology as presented in the popular *Dialogues* is a truncated version of Augustine's theology, and his stories are still in transition from traditional ghost stories to ecclesiastical ghost stories. By contrast, Bede's theology of purgatory is rooted in antiheretical argumentation, and when he provides an account of a layman's vision of purgatory it clearly illustrates and supports the view of purgatory that he presents.

Purgation in the Seventh Century

Outside of the visions of the afterlife that were quite informative on purgatory, formal works of theology in the seventh century offer only fragments of information on what people were thinking about afterlife purgation, and yet this must have been a crucial century in the development of ideas of afterlife purgation, standing between the work of Gregory the Great and that of Bede. The few works that have come down to us suggest that Augustine, Caesarius of Arles, and Gregory the Great were considered the essential authorities on postmortem purgation, and their ideas and phraseology infuse the works produced in this era.

The seventh century saw the first documented generation of Irish monks and scholars settling in Gaul, establishing and reforming monasteries. They were *peregrini*, wanderers from their homeland for God's love. Of them, Columbanus's life, works, and writings had considerable influence on the ascetics and politics of continental monasticism. Personally afflicted by forced wanderings, when Columbanus came to describe the soul's itinerary after death, he adopted a somewhat rambling style, layering and repeating ideas and phrases, as if continually uprooted and moved on. Human life is a tiring journey with identical miseries, he maintained, but at the end of that journey, a trial will divide fellow travelers into different orders: "You see the scheme of the misery of human life, from earth, on earth, to earth, from earth to fire, from fire to judgement, from judgement to hell or else to life," repeating it a few lines later, "from earth you shall arise, in fire you shall be tried, you shall await judgement, and thereafter you shall attain either an eternal punishment or an eternal reign; for there it behoves us, as the Apostle says, to appear before the judgement seat of Christ, that each may receive his body's due reward."[72] Whereas previous writers had looked at the soul's fate in the afterlife from the moment of death, Columbanus framed it within Creation entire. His vision of the soul's fate is set on a cosmic canvas, even an elemental one, in a way that recalls the framing of the *Vision of Paul* and, later, the *Vision of Fursey*. Earth, fire, judgement, life or torment. At the time of the resurrection, man "shall at the last be tried by fire, so that the fire should be some art dissolve both earth and clay, and should show by melting the counterfeit whether it has any gold or silver or other of earth's precious things." The fire of 1 Corinthians 3:11–15 is fused with the smelting, furnace imagery of Malachi: "the day of the Lord comes scorching like an oven . . . He draws nigh as the fire of a furnace."[73] Meditating on such a sight is terrible, but not to fear these things "is the part of dead and hopeless minds." His imagined path for the soul is apocalyptic, without the staging points imagined by Caesarius and Gregory.

The seventh century was an age of *epitomies, florilegia,* false attributions of authorship, and downright plagiarism. Taio of Saragossa, for example, appears to have appropriated the work of Peter the deacon quite openly for his *Sententiae* and consequently offered nothing new.[74] Bishop Isidore of Seville (bishop 600–636) wrote little specific on the subject and was in any case deeply indebted to Augustine; in Hillgarth's words, "Isidore was not greatly exercised by eschatological problems."[75] Nevertheless Joseph Ntedika recognized in Isidore a new willingness to believe that the fire of purgation could cleanse more serious sins that had not been fully expiated through penance.[76] Julian of Toledo wrote more extensively on purgation in his *Prognosticum* (AD 688–89), a work that addressed issues relating to life after death and that pieced together quotations from the church fathers, particularly Augustine and Gregory the Great, including Gregory's *Dialogues*. There was artistry to his compilation, elevating it above the ranks of many early medieval *florilegia*, and judging by the number and geographical range of extant manuscripts it appears to have enjoyed significant success, however, it did not aim to diverge in opinion or theology from its sources.[77] Julian's excerpt from Pomerius's work has been mentioned above.

The fact that purgation continued to be discussed in these seventh-century works, and that these works were themselves copied, disseminated, epitomized, and falsely attributed to others, must have done much to consolidate the view that purgation was an essential element in discussions of the fate of the soul and that prayers for the dead alongside masses were anchored in concrete ways to the alleviation of afterlife suffering. However, the direct connection of prayers and masses as efficacious aids to the living, and the discussion of the purging fire, is not yet made explicit. This is to a great degree a reflection of how seventh-century authors used earlier texts. When Julian of Toledo discussed prayers for the dead (*Prognosticum*, 2. 10), he drew on his source Julianus Pomerius, in which the efficacy of such prayers was discussed.[78] When he wrote about the purging fire, he embarked on a different set of ideas drawn from his sources—Augustine and Gregory the Great—and situated them, furthermore, in a different part of his book (2. 19). He did not make any crossover comments or connections between the two discourses, because he assembled his information in separate conceptual blocks. Thus in Julian's work, as in Augustine's before him, we cannot prove conclusively that such a connection was made.[79] Now, it might be argued that such a connection was inevitable, that prayers for the dead have no meaning unless set alongside a belief in purgatory, but there are many arguments to be made to the contrary. Prayers for the dead were a cross-cultural, cross-religion phenomenon that did not depend on a clearly articulated doctrine of purgatory. Indeed, since the papacy did not accept purgatory as doctrine until the later middle ages, at the institutional, dogmatic level, medieval prayers for the dead long existed in a cautious relationship to the notion of purgatory. The connection of prayers for the dead with a fully developed view of purgatory was first accomplished by Bede who finally brought together the parallel discourses of prayers for the dead and the fires of purgatory.[80]

A Carolingian sermon attributed to the learned bishop of Noyon, Eligius, shows that afterlife purgation continued after Caesarius's time to provide a fruitful topic of moral teaching in Gaul.[81] As with Augustine and Gregory, seventh-century writers generally tracked their way through this topic by fixing on categories of sin and sinners and by raising that old chestnut of how souls could be bodily tortured by a real fire in the afterlife when they had no physical bodies. It is something of a relief, therefore, to come across a seventh-century writer who framed his information on purgatory in a somewhat different way.

The Liber de Ordine Creaturarum

Sometime in the last two decades of the seventh century, an anonymous Irishman wrote a treatise outlining the order of the cosmos and the ranking of the creatures that inhabit it.[82] Each creature occupied its own particular habitat—the place where it had been assigned by God and that reflected the nature of its inhabitants. Incorporeal creatures, including the righteous dead awaiting resurrection, occupied the tranquil upper air (where jet-propelled aeroplanes cruise today), while demons occupied the lower air where the atmosphere is roiled by storms and turbulence.[83] From their lower vantage point, demons could trouble the dreams and composure of humans on earth.

The author of this unusual work included an account of sinners and their punishment in the cosmic overview, including hell and purgatory. But whereas the first part of his treatise located angels and demons in specific zones in the sky, he did not offer a precise geography of hell or purgatory.[84] In particular, we learn nothing of purgatory's location or its relationship to heaven and hell. Rather, when he reached his discussion of hell and purgatory, he turned his thoughts in a different direction: to categorization of sin (closely mirroring contemporary ascetic literature), to crowd control and transportation issues (who goes where, when, and how), and to divine judgement. Even if the author did not specify a location for purgatory, however, the fact that he included heaven, hell, and purgatory in a work broadly conceived as cosmologic suggests that he was thinking in spatial terms and regarded these places as part of the natural world, in the same way that he imagined the physical location of the garden of Eden on earth.

Three major routes led to hell, only one of which required examination by the divine judge.[85] Those who did not receive baptism were fast-tracked to hell, without need for examination. Likewise, those who had lost the cleansing of baptism through committing capital crimes and who had not availed themselves of penance went directly to hell, passing from the present life directly to torment. The author considered these two groups to have already been judged—to have judged themselves, in effect—by failing to abide by scripture. The impious were already judged by unbelief. Those who committed capital crimes were judged by scripture. The third group—those who were baptized but had lost the grace of baptism through other grave sins—were liable to examination by the divine judge, and it was from God's court, as it were, that they were condemned and taken away to hell.

The anonymous author further identified three major routes to heaven for the baptized: immediate entry to heaven, without judgement, was available to the first group, to those who had suffered "tribulation." Interestingly, saints and martyrs are not specified here; perhaps the author was thinking of monks. The second group are the baptized who fulfilled the scriptural command to feed the poor and perform other positive acts of mercy. They will be called to judgement but only after they have passed through the fire of purification. The third group are those whose souls are marred by having attained a lesser degree of the full spiritual life. They will undergo purification in purgatory. The author portrayed this third group vividly: they married, were not perfectly abstemious, laughed too much, slept too much, and sometimes held opinions that were not quite right. It is tempting to identify in this description of forgetful, disorganized Christians, a portrait of the pious laity.[86] These latter will be purified, as by fire, and, echoing Augustine and Caesarius of Arles, we are informed that the fire of purgation will be longer and harsher than we can imagine in the present life. No mention is made of judgement here; presumably, this third group, like the second, would be called to judgement after purification.

The significance of this work for a study of purgatory is not glaringly obvious. The work's author was obviously very concerned with clarifying who would go to judgement and who would immediately go to heaven or hell and relied heavily on Gregory the Great's *Moralia* to do so. A secondary purpose was achieved in reconciling scriptural passages that might otherwise appear inconsistent. At first glance it may appear that little new was added to purgatorial lore by this work. It does not appear to have spawned a new literary framework for discussions of purgatory in the immediate future, for example. Nevertheless, the work was copied and found its way into numerous monastic libraries in England and on the continent. Was it viewed as a curiosity? Was it read with admiration? We cannot know. For the writer seeking information on afterlife purgation, Augustine's *Enchiridion* would always be a handier guide, and Gregory's *Dialogues* a more gripping read. This treatise did not connect the fate of souls undergoing purification with prayer for the dead, and thus it did not provide the important connection of purgatory with liturgical intercession. However, this little text did do one thing that was unique and significant for purgatory: it specifically connected one group of souls from Gregory's fourfold schema of souls with purgatory, which Gregory had not done. Thus it stands at a midpoint between Gregory the Great and Bede.[87] The treatise has one other important claim on our attention, however, and that is the possible light it sheds on Bede. The earliest copy of the *Liber de ordine creaturarum* was written in Northumbria around 700, and that means that Bede may have known this Irish work. In view of Bede's subsequent pronouncements on purgatory he would certainly have found it lacking. However, he may also have found its connection of the Gregorian schema of the fate of souls with purgatory useful. The Northumbrian connection for this Irish work is a reminder that Irish scholars continued to maintain connections with centres of learning in Northern England. But with respect to discussions of purgatory, the influence of Bede and other proponents of continental, patristic scholarship ultimately took the framing discussion of purgatory in a different direction.[88]

Visions of the Afterlife

The seventh and eighth centuries were an era of intense interest in visions and in visionary literature. It is no coincidence that purgatory began to emerge as a more fixed feature of the afterlife at a time when visionary literature found a ready audience among monks, clerics, and the laity. In the early middle ages visionary literature was a popular, powerful, and reputable source for information on the afterlife.[89] With roots in Jewish and Christian apocalyptic literature, the visions of saints and sinners came to occupy an important place alongside patristic writings, sermons, and treatises as a literature of spiritual edification and clarification for the fate of the individual.[90] The authority of these accounts was sometimes questioned. Pope Gregory, among others, warned that somatic causes could underlie visions, especially if they came in the form of dreams.[91] However, early Christian visionary literature was known, admired, and appropriated in the seventh and eighth centuries. The second-century *Shepherd of Hermas*, for example, was known in the early medieval West and was used by Bede.[92] The enormous popularity and appeal of the Latin *Vision of Paul* is evident from its many manuscript copies, the many variant works it spawned, and the inspiration it gave to authors of other vision texts. It was possibly known in Ireland as early as the first half of the seventh century.[93] Medieval writers believed the work had the authority of the apostle, and they set it alongside the visions of the martyrs as an authoritative source of information on the afterlife. Its influence can be seen in the seventh-century visions of Fursey and Barontus and in the eighth-century vision of a monk at Much Wenlock.[94] Furthermore, the *Vision of Paul* was almost endlessly reconfigured to reflect the interests of later eras.[95] Pope Gregory's *Dialogues* enjoyed a similar popularity although its text was generally handled with greater fidelity than the *Vision of Paul*. The many accounts of supernatural events in the *Dialogues* furnished stories of effective intercessions that were addictive reading for monks and nuns. The *Lives of the Fathers of Merida* explicitly acknowledged its inspiration, as did the *Vision of Barontus* (678 or 679) and the *Vision of Wetti* (before 824). From ancient times, visions had been integrated into the fabric of history, and there was the recent example of Gregory of Tours's *History of the Franks*. Bede included a number of visions in his *Ecclesiastical History*, including the *Vision of Drythelm*, intending them to reach wider audiences than the monastic circles in which they were produced. And finally, hagiographies, which had always included visions of death and personal transformation, began to show great interest in accounts of sinners being released from torment by means of prayers of intercession and masses.

Visions were central to the Christian culture in that they arose from ascetic and penitential practices that monks and clerics preached.[96] Their recent proliferation was explained by Pope Gregory as a sign that the end of the world was drawing close.[97] The literature that recorded them served useful purposes, for example, as reification of obscure scriptural promises making them comprehensible to regular folk.[98] As a recorder of visions, Pope Gregory's comment that "we aim at a true understanding through images" is particularly apt. Gregory was clearly willing to view visionary images as having elements that were literal, metaphorical, spiritual, and scriptural all at the same time.[99]

Visions of the afterlife also supplied solutions to eschatological problems. In the patristic survey we have noted that patristic authors were not always clear how the immediate judgement of souls at death related to the purgatorial fire and the day of judgement. Visions provided one kind of answer. Immediately upon death, the soul was claimed by holy figures (usually saints or angels) or by demons and was taken to its interim destination. Much drama was extracted from tales in which angels and demons fought over the less-than-perfect soul.[100] The disputed soul was then taken to trial. This trial was not a trial of fire: it was modeled on the judicial trial system in which accusers and defenders and witnesses all played their part. An element of uncertainty still entered the picture once the soul had made its case (or had it made on his behalf). Often the vision ended before the conclusion of the trial was known.[101] Alternatively, a penitential remedy was prescribed. At first, the visionary Fursey appeared to pass muster, passing beyond the accusing demons so that he could converse with two clerics on pastoral matters. But on his return he was burned by a man being tortured in the fire. With the notable exception of Fursey, visions in which the fate of the visionary's soul was being actively decided did not depict purgation by fire as the trial through which they must immediately go.[102] The *Vision of Paul* with its extended trial scene was an influential model for all these visions, yet the authors of these visions of the afterlife were also making imaginative choices; and by omitting the fire's depiction at the immediate judgement of the soul, they chose to reserve the fire of 1 Corinthians 3:11–15 to Judgement Day.

This literature may have been produced almost exclusively in monastic contexts, but they reached further afield. In Anglo-Saxon England in particular, where monasteries were deeply engaged in pastoral and missionary work, and where monks often remained very much integrated into family and social networks, the opportunities for vision accounts to reach broader audiences were many and varied.

Sacramental Purification

Baptism and Penance

The sacramental life of the Church aimed to identify and purify its members to prepare them for eternity. The promise offered by baptism was nothing less than eternal life. Yet Christians who availed themselves of this promise were required to be pure. To that end they were asked to renounce the devil and his works, to repent their former ways, and to offer themselves as pure sacrifices at God's altar. Since baptism could be undertaken only once, penance was the way most sinners experienced their quest for purity.

The two sacraments—baptism and penance—were viewed as having parity with regard to the remission of sins for "in each the mystery is one."[103] Yet baptism had a special status as a cleansing ritual. Prudentius waxed lyrical on the subject: "From this washing, which removed all stain of sin, men became renewed and resplendent like raw gold when it has been refined in a furnace, and bright as the brilliance of silver when it is purified of dross and polished with soft cloths."[104] The image of refined gold linked baptism with postmortem purgation as the path to eternal life. Even before Augustine gave his authority to such ideas, it was widely believed that all Christians needed the purification of baptism—even infants, since children of pure parents are not born pure.[105] Those who died immediately after baptism, *in albis*, could be viewed as particularly blessed. One West Saxon king abdicated after reigning only two years and at about the age of thirty traveled to Rome to be baptized, "for having learned that the road to heaven lies open to mankind only through baptism, he wished to obtain the particular privilege of receiving the cleansing of baptism at the shrine of the blessed apostles. At the same time he hoped to die shortly after his baptism, and pass from this world to everlasting happiness." Bede quotes his epitaph: "Now, robed in white, he moves among Christ's sheep."[106]

For Christians who long survived baptism, penance was a needful purification. The path from sin to purity was not the same for all, but there was a general order of events. First, the sinner would become aware of his sins and feel remorse. This would raise doubt in his mind and perhaps in the minds of others, concerning his ability to partake of the eucharistic sacrifice.[107] The repentant Christian then prayed for divine guidance or sought out and confessed to a spiritual guide who would determine his penitential path. Penitential exercises might follow if the gravity of the sin required it, culminating in absolution that "washed away" the postbaptismal stain. This allowed the Christian to return to the status of the "just" and to enjoy the full benefit of the purifying sacraments offered by the Church. Indeed, in Caesarius's opinion, penance had advantages over baptism since survival beyond baptism gave Christians the ability to augment their dossier of good works.

The question of how and when penance was to be undertaken was the subject of much debate. In the case of canonical, public penance, the earliest and most persistent difficulty arose from the Church's desire to create a system that was rigorous as a means of discipline and yet merciful in making it an attainable goal for even the most compromised sinners. In the era of persecutions, many Christians had abandoned their way of life, and as bishops sought to reintegrate these "sinners" into the fold, they strove to recognize distinctions of merit among the lapsed. For example, those who resisted their persecutors but were ultimately compelled to sacrifice to idols were to be treated differently from those who had not resisted. Penitential activities were to be tailored to the context, circumstances, and motive that had lead to the offense. Even the gravest of sins could be washed clean through penance, for "greater sins are washed away by greater weeping."[108] Early councils such as the Council of Ancyra (AD 314) sought to provide guidance on these matters and, together with the rules and ascetic writings of the early church fathers, were the progenitors of the sin-classification literature and the penitential manuals of a later age.

Bishops were advised to use discretion when applying sanctions and to use their judgement when reconciling the penitent. Bishops "purged" the community of grave sinners through excommunication and reconciled them through the imposition of hands, a baptismal gesture.[109] While bishops were responsible for setting normative standards and rituals of reintegration, it is likely that in the case of ordinary Christians the work of penitential satisfaction was carried out in less public ways.[110]

Even when the crisis of postpersecution society was a distant memory, ecclesiastical authorities struggled to maintain a balance between standards that were so strict that they discouraged integration of the sinner and those that were so lax that the sinner was given insufficient cause to fear. As Ambrose argued when dealing with one rigorist group, "no one can repent to good purpose unless he hopes for mercy."[111] This compassionate approach favoured metaphors that saw penance as the medicine for sick souls. The physician does not despair of his patient, and with proper care the patient may recover. A harsher conventional metaphor compared the sinner to a debtor. Matthew 5:25–26 was often cited: "and you will be put in prison; truly, I say to you, you will never get out till you have paid the last penny." Yet, as Ambrose was quick to point out, it was better to be in debt to God than to man because God could be repaid in intangibles such as the "affection of the heart" and by a penitential attitude. What was important was that the sinner was inclined toward God by first making confession of his sins. Confession started the sinner on his path out of debtor's prison: "If you have confessed at the call of Christ the bars will be broken, and every chain loosed, even [though] the stench of the bodily corruption be grievous." If the penitent stayed the course, God's forgiveness was assured.[112]

"Doing" penance (*paenitentia agere*) required the sinner to purify himself through various acts, external and internal. These included external activities such as good works, especially almsgiving and self-mortification, and internal ones such as prayer, recollection of vices, weeping, and groaning. "Prayer, fasting, and tears are the resources of an honest debtor," wrote Ambrose.[113] Fasts were required of all Christians at various times in the Church's calendar, but penitential fasts were supposed to be supererogatory and sufficiently severe to mortify the flesh. There were probably few who could contemplate it with Prudentius's relish: "Surely there is nothing purer than this rite by which the heart's tissues are cleansed and revived and the undisciplined body is compelled to sweat so that fat will not constrict our minds and choke our souls with the foulness of its stench."[114]

Prayer was at the heart of the Christian's connection to God. From the careful structure of the Lord's Prayer to the interior "wordless" prayer of ecstatic contemplation, prayer was supposed to be constant and unending. Drawing on 1 Timothy 2:1, ascetic literature recognized and ranked four types of prayer: supplications, prayers (sometimes interpreted as a "vows" or "pledges"), intercessions, and thanksgivings.[115] Constant prayer was the ideal held out to monks who might engage in these different kinds of prayer at different stages in their spiritual careers and according to specific circumstances. Supplications and prayers were related to the monk's own spiritual needs, especially sorrow for past vices and fear of future judgement. Prayers of intercession and thanksgiving moved the monk to identify with the broader needs of the Christian community, and finally to achieve pure, fiery, wordless prayer that sparked interior illumination.

Tears and groans were expected to adorn prayers of every sort, although they should not be so loud that they disrupt the prayers of others. Tears evoked baptismal cleansing. Quoting one of the penitential psalms, Cassian stated that "forgiveness of sins is obtained by the shedding of tears, for 'every night I will wash my bed; I will sprinkle my resting place with tears.'"[116] And Ambrose had written that "he shall be saved in the future who has wept most in this age."[117] While providing an obvious image of purification by analogy with baptism, tears were also an outward sign of compunction, a spiritual state produced when "the thorn of sinfulness pricks our hearts."[118]

When the bishop was satisfied that the penitential remedy was complete, the sinner was absolved of his sin and could once again approach the altar. In the fourth century, when penitents stayed for years in penitential grades, inching their way closer and closer to the altar, the ritual of reconciliation and the bishop's blessing must have provided a moment of high drama. In later centuries such dramatic moments continued, especially in the arena of high politics. For the ordinary penitent, however, who was assured of absolution and who could now take his place beside his fellow Christians, his readmission to Communion must have been intensely felt. Such were the outward symbols. But for Cassian, true confidence in absolution came from interior knowledge. "Here is the full and perfect definition of repentance: that we should never again commit the sins for which we do penance," and when the Christian knows that his disposition toward that sin has been eradicated. "Therefore" he continues, "the truest judge of repentance and the mark of forgiveness resides in our conscience, which reveals to us who are still living in the flesh the absolution of our sinfulness before the day of recognition and judgement and discloses the end of reparation and the grace of pardon."[119] No official rite of absolution is required, since true penance is negotiated between the sinner and God, and because human penitential efforts must always fade in comparison to God's gifts: "Sins are purged away by mercy and faith."[120] Above all, Cassian was concerned that a sense of guilt must not keep Christians away from Communion. Harkening back to the motif of penance as medicine for the wounds of the soul, Cassian cautioned that if the penitent is too fearful to come to Communion it constitutes a kind of arrogance in that he relies too heavily on his sense of his own efforts, whereas it is in fact the sacrament that makes him pure. The penitent who does not avail himself of the sacred mysteries as a "remedy for sickness" does not heal his soul.[121] So, while Communion should not be sought by those who are "polluted with impurity," bishops were counseled that "we are bidden by the teaching of the Lord to confer again the grace of the heavenly sacrament on those guilty even of the greatest sins, if they with open confession bear the penance due to their sin."[122]

In Ambrose's day, one-time canonical penance was the norm, although it is clear from his treatise *On Repentance* that there were already those in his time who sought to "abuse" the sacrament by repetition. In fact, as Richard Price has pointed out, private, informal penance was a more common recourse for most Christians even in the early Christian centuries. Increasingly, monastic cultural norms permeated Christian culture, and the pious were encouraged to live lives conditioned by a recognition of their own sinfulness. " 'There will be no end of penance for those little offenses by which the righteous person falls seven times' as it is written, 'and gets up again,'" wrote Cassian.[123] Repeatable penance becomes more commonly attested in later centuries, especially in the penitential handbooks popularized by Irish monks, but the foundations of tariffed penance are rightly to be sought in the practices of the early church.[124]

While significant variations in penitential advice and method coexisted throughout these early centuries, penitential literature had one firm rule: penance was an option available only to the living. From the second-century Shepherd of Hermas ("the repentance of the just has an end") to the sixth-century poet Venantius Fortunatus (there is no penance "*in futuro*") the rule was known.[125] Indeed, Cassian went so far as to suggest that the one hundred-fold reward for perfect renunciation was to be found only in this life, not "in the millenium."[126] Death changed the terms by which reparation for sin could be made. In life, penance and the sacraments purified; in death, purification came only by fire. In life, the discipline of penance might be harsh, but this could not compare to the torture suffered by the sinner who must be purged in the fire to come. In fact, penance was very much viewed in terms of alleviating afterlife suffering. The register of that compensation was completely different, however. Whereas penance could expiate even the gravest of sins, in the early centuries purgation in the afterlife was restricted to cleansing only minor ones.[127] Reflecting on the value sinners derived from penance, Julianus Pomerius commented that by such means "they will exchange eternal torments for temporal."[128] Cyprian had maintained that in the afterlife, "there is no longer any place for repentance, and no possibility of making satisfaction."[129] This was to become the Church's official position in the West, a position that only intensified in the anti-Origenist climate after Jerome and Augustine. It is true that some visionary tales suggested that some of the damned might indeed feel belated remorse, but the emphasis remains clear: remorse in hell bears no fruit. Their cries will not be heard.[130]

Intercession

Of the four types of prayer, prayers of intercession were the type that linked the individual to the broader Christian community. The traditional interpretation identified prayer of intercession as the one the individual made for others "when our spirits are fervent, beseeching on behalf of our dear ones and for the peace of the whole word."[131] Yet the individual also sought the intercessory prayer of others. For slight sins, a living person could intercede for himself through prayer, through the prayers of the church and the prayers of ordinary Christians known to them. Intercession for grave sin required the intervention of a holier person, someone for whom Moses or Jeremiah would be the model.[132] We have already noted that Gregory of Tours placed enormous reliance on the intercession of his patron saint St. Martin.[133] For the genuinely repentant, the entire church could bring together the combined efforts of its priest, the congregation, and the saints in heaven—what would be termed the Communion of the Saints. As Ambrose termed it, "If the punishment that is inflicted by the many is sufficient for condemnation, the intercession which is made by many is also sufficient for the remission of sins."[134]

As we shall see in the next two chapters, prayers of intercession involved those who asked and those who helped, in relationships that were variously dangerous or supportive. Fursey's relationship with a penitent would place him in grave moral peril, and Bede's circle was heavily involved in ties of mutual intercessory obligation.

It is clear that some Christians invested great hope in the intercession of saints, the church, and even their family and friends. At the nunnery of Faremoutiers, a daughter prayed her mother out of torment.[135] Readers of Wetti's vision were warned: "Do not be confident when your life is over, the fires which you build by your own evil deeds will be dispersed by the pleas of another. Though there are many whose sins may be purged by intercession, no-one can confidently rely on this, since no-one knows how heavily his sins will weigh."[136] Furthermore, Wetti was instructed that intercessory prayers must be free. This did not deter him from asking his friends for 100 masses and 100 psalms, which was a considerable inflation of intercession judged by petitions made a century earlier.

To be effective, intercession for oneself or for others was to be approached in a penitential frame of mind. "Pay first that which you owe, that you may be in a position to ask for what you have hoped," advised Ambrose.[137] Bede would specify that those who wanted to intercede on behalf of their loved ones do so with alms, fasting, weeping, and the celebration of the Mass.[138] A rather more long-term rescue plan was anticipated by one man in torment: he smiled in the knowledge that three thousand years hence one of his male descendants would become a priest, and on his saying of his first Mass he would be released from torment to eternal life.[139]

Burial and Funerary Liturgy

Prayers and psalms brought images of purification to the deathbed and the grave site. They did so in the earliest liturgies and continued to do so in later centuries through the traditional prayers of the community. Having said that, it is extremely difficult to identify changes in eschatological ideas by reference to burial practices and the funerary liturgy.[140] We must acknowledge that our picture will always be incomplete. In the case of burial practices, geographic diversity in burial forms, social and gender distinctions in commemorative methods, and problems with artefact survival from these early centuries have left archaeological evidence that is often more suggestive than truly evidentiary. In the case of the liturgy, and thus for its funerary aspect, texts and practices were diverse. Gaul, Spain, and Italy[141] provide a greater abundance of liturgical texts than, for example, Ireland or Anglo-Saxon England, leading to geographic *lacunae* in our knowledge of this most important aspect of Christian practice.[142] Even when liturgical texts are available, significant problems of interpretation remain associated with their use and their representative nature. Yet in some respects Merovingian liturgical productions are more amenable than others to discussions of variety and change since prayer content and options were fluid before the unifying trend of early Carolingian productions.[143] Nevertheless, accepting these limitations it is still possible to investigate purgatorial ideas, purgatorial images, and fear for the soul's fate in the funerary documentation that has survived.

Burial Practices

The desire for burial *ad sanctos* accompanied the belief that the saints could offer the dead special protection at the resurrection and the Last Judgement. The saints were believed to inhabit heaven immediately after death. Consequently, they were well poised to intercede for their devotees. We have seen examples of such intercessory hope in the previous section. Burial *ad sanctos* increased as relic veneration increased and as it became a legal requirement and a religious expectation that churches be endowed with relics.[144] Monasteries and nunneries were serious importers of relics both locally and from abroad, and they also benefited from a degree of self-generating relic activity as the bones and contact relics of holy founders and holy patrons were added to their collections. Dust, cloths, shoes, and even beds provided the focus for holy veneration. By the seventh century, monks and nuns who stayed the course could expect burial within the monastery's protective *vallum*.[145] Burials within churches and close to shrines are also recorded, and requests for special places of burial are recorded in visionary literature at this time. Such privileged burial was not available to all, and there is some evidence that requests for special burial by secular elites in the seventh century put pressure on monasteries and churches, which in turn sought to preserve their sacred space.[146] While the desire for burial *ad sanctos* was clearly linked with the hope of saintly protection, it may also have been linked to other religious, social, and even emotional needs, such as identification with a particular community, the security of protected sacred space, and ongoing liturgical "participation" after death. It would be hoped that proximity to the bones of the saints might excite the compassion and protection of the saints at the resurrection. Such burial may also have been linked with the idea that the saints would protect the soul's passage to the afterlife. Barontus, for example, had benefited greatly from the protection of his own monastery's patron, St. Peter.

Funerary epitaphs and grave markers affirm family and community desires that the deceased will evade hell and await the resurrection in peace.[147] The hopeful phrasing of these monuments was clearly intended to evoke liturgical prayers.[148] Burial with holy objects has a similar range of possible explanations. Crosses are often found in association with burials, whether as grave markers or as gold foil crosses sewn onto shrouds, embroidered onto clothing, or worn around the neck.[149] They identified the body as part of the Christian community, as blessed, and they undoubtedly also functioned as a protection against evil. Such practices aligned with concerns to protect the individual within the community, perhaps suggesting anxiety about individual judgement. Desire for the body's protection was certainly congruent with belief in a final, physical resurrection. Desire to protect the body may also have been related to fears for the journey to the afterlife—the presence of demons at the deathbed or in the air. It is unlikely that protection of the body was linked specifically with purgation since while Christians may have feared purgatory's fire, they were also taught to accept it as a necessary prelude to life in heaven. Funerary prayers requested God to cleanse the soul of any stain clinging to it; they did not ask that the soul be spared that cleansing. To suggest connections of burial practice with specific ideas about purgatorial belief runs the danger of going beyond the evidence. Mourners prayed for, and corpses dressed for, success. Their best hope was a quick transition to paradise.

Prayers for the Dead

For most ordinary Christians the liturgy, and the prayers contained therein, was the most important way they learned the spiritual language and doctrinal elements of their faith. "Let my hymns link the days," wrote Prudentius.[150] In church, communal prayers for the dead revived the memory of loved ones and consoled them with the expectation that the soul had found peace. Foremost, the prayers affirmed that the dead who died within the discipline of the church were an integral part of the Christian community—the living connected to the dead. As Augustine expressed it: "souls of the pious dead are not separated from the Church which is even now the kingdom of Christ"; death posed no boundary.[151] From the church's perspective, an individual who participated in the sacraments was assured liturgical assistance and commemoration after death. Indeed, in these centuries, funerary services were reserved for communicants and were refused to penitents and catechumens.[152] The names of those who could be legitimately prayed for were inscribed on church diptychs alongside the living and later on parchment in the "books of life."

Liturgical sources also preserve prayers and psalms that were said over individual Christians from sickbed to grave. The audience for these prayers was probably largely confined to monastics and clerics in the sixth and seventh centuries as the church's role in burial of the ordinary dead was slow to take hold. Yet despite their restricted audience, the abundance of prayers and masses from which the celebrant could choose offers insight into attitudes toward the soul's final journey. The choice of psalms and prayers in use for the end of life —sickness, the agony, at death, as the corpse was taken from the dwelling to the church, and as it was deposited in the ground—has provided scholars with a rich area of study both for an understanding of the connections between liturgical texts and ancient traditions, for changing interpretations of ancient rites, and for understanding changing attitudes toward death and the fate of the soul after death.[153]

Psalm choice for funerals was extremely varied, but they usually comprised a balance of hopeful and penitential psalms. Important for the Roman tradition were Psalm 113 [114] (*In exitu Israhel de Aegypto*) and the joyful and triumphant, psalms 114–19, which appealed to God's promise of help and salvation. Psalm

64 [65] (the *Te Decet*), confidently reads: "Praise is due to thee, O God, in Zion. To thee shall all flesh come on account of sins. When our transgressions prevail over us, thou dost forgive them." And Psalm 4 (*Cum invocarem*) says, "In peace I will both lie down and sleep; for thou alone, O Lord, makest me dwell in safety." In these psalms, God's majesty is evident: he is King, he is Lord, he is safety. These psalm choices continued to be made in later funeral *ordines*. Penitential psalms were also regularly used in funeral services. The use of Psalm 50 [51] (*Misere mei, Domine*) is particularly interesting, however, in that it implores God for purification: "Wash me thoroughly from my iniquity, and cleanse me from my sin! For I know my transgressions, and my sin is ever before me . . . purge me with hyssop and I shall be clean; wash me and I shall be whiter than snow . . . Create in me a clean heart, O God, and put a new and right spirit within me. Cast me not away from thy presence, and take not thy holy spirit from me." The psalm was used for various elements in the mortuary ritual including the agony, in the church service, and over the grave site. Perhaps most telling was its use for the funeral procession from the dwelling to the church, or from the church to the burial site.[154] Its processional use was particularly apt for the soul's purificatory passage from the cares and sin of the world to the peace of the heavenly Jerusalem. Its use is widely attested in the Latin liturgies of Spain, Italy, and Francia.[155]

The purificatory theme is continued in prayers that asked that the soul be cleansed to prepare it for its heavenly home. While the exact form of the prayers varied in length and detail, their general outline is seen in the form found in the appendix to Caesarius's *Rule for Nuns*. The *Pio recordationis effectu*, which was said over the dead body, asks that God may remit all her offenses and remove any worldly error.[156] In the *Old Gelasian* the request is that sins be "washed away."[157] Similarly, the prayers of the *Sacramentary of Gellone* and the *Gelasian Sacramentary* (both from the eighth century) asked God to wash away the minor sins of the soul: "and if this soul has contracted any thing from the mortal region, which is contrary to you, . . . may you wash it away through the indulgence of your piety . . . that through your piety you will hand over [the blemishes] to perpetual oblivion."[158] That this cleansing might be effected through fire is not mentioned.

Prayers and psalms in funerary contexts evoked images of spiritual purification that were transitory and painless. They focused on the slight sins that any soul must contract by living in the world. They do not delve into the problem of serious sins or purgatorial punishment.[159] This may have begun to change by the eighth century. Damien Sicard notes that the *Berlin Sacramentary* contains a reference to an interim period of rest: "ut usque ad resurrectionis diem, in lucis amoenitate requiescat." He comments that this passage and a similar passage in the contemporary *Book of Cerne* "oriente vers la croyance en un lieu intermédiaire de repos, en un paradis suave, où dans la douceur de la lumière, l'âme rachetée de tous ses péchés attend le jour de la résurrection." Yet, he sees a critical distinction between this idea of the soul in a pleasant place of light, and the pains of purgatory traditionally associated with "l'idée actuelle de purgatoire."[160] The hope expressed in both the *Berlin Sacramentary* and the *Book of Cerne* is so close to the depiction of pious souls in the *Vision of Drythelm*, that it is hard not to attribute this new expression of hope to developing images of the afterlife in which the soul, purged of its sins, would find rest in celestial meadows. For most Christians, the liturgical prayers with which they were familiar did not have to change to accommodate the idea of purgatory as a place of protracted and possibly painful cleansing. The formulation of traditional prayers was not inconsistent with a developing notion of extended purgation or purgatory as a place. Prayers that the soul safely pass the portals of hell, or that asked that sins be removed, did not preclude the later idea of protracted purgation. The sixth-century Caesarian *Te Domine sancte* prayer asks God to allow the soul to pass by the portals of hell, and the eighth-century *Tu nobis Domine* from the *Bobbio Missal* asked that God's servant might "evade the fire of hell." The Verona version of the latter prayer asks that the soul evade the place of punishment (*locum paenalem*), but this is hell (*flammamquae tartari*) not purgatory, although it may eventually have been understood that way.[161] Later Christians hearing these prayers would find nothing in them to contradict the developing idea of extended purgation. Purgatory could slip into Christian devotional life, threading its way into the Christian's understanding of the liturgy. The prayers would stay the same: imagination supplied the context of purgatory that was missing.

Conclusion

In the sixth and seventh centuries, incremental steps were taken that bound the idea of postmortem purgation with the efficacy of prayers for the dead and masses for the dead to intercede for somewhat less than exemplary Christians. There was also an increasing concern to situate the penitent's place in the commemoration offered by the Church and by private prayer. At the beginning of the period, the unreconciled penitent (even the catechumen) was excluded from the comfort of the Church's efforts on his or her behalf. The *Vision of Fursey* would witness the tension this caused, as we shall see in the next chapter. By Isidore's time, however, the penitent could hope to make good on penitential debt owed by being purged after death. This trend would come to full fruition in Bede, whose *Vision of Drythelm* assured salvation to the penitent (even the deathbed penitent) through a long process of tortuous purgation.[162] The fire of purification, which cleansed the light sins of the elect, would eventually be supplemented by the tortuous purgation of grave sinners in Bede.

Importantly, all these incremental steps were made by authors who believed they were transmitting the authentic teaching of Augustine, particularly as it was expressed in the *Enchiridion*. Indeed, they believed they had Augustine's authority behind them as they made the very connections that Augustine had eschewed. Visions of the afterlife began to reflect the concerns and conceptions of afterlife purgation in imaged form, and the eschatological authority they were accorded helped fix common perceptions about what happened to Christians in the afterlife.

5

Purgatory, Penitentials, and the Irish Question

There is a school of thought that views the emergence of purgatory as a seventh-century Irish phenomenon. This view relies heavily on the evidence of visions of otherworldly travel that were recorded in the seventh century—visions that began to include a purgatorial fire as part of the imagined landscape of the afterlife.

Not all major visions of the seventh century included a depiction of purgatory—the *Vision of Barontus*, for example, did not. But in the seventh century detailed accounts of visionary travel began to circulate widely, and they were accorded authority on eschatological matters. That meant that visions that included descriptions of purgatory were instrumental in "fixing" purgatory as a focus of interest in the afterlife. Scholars now widely value visionary literature for understanding seventh-century religious culture. The seventh-century visions of Fursey and Barontus, in particular, have been invoked as evidence for the rise of the individual, of purgatory, and the "end of the ancient other world."[1] This new focus on the seventh century has given rise to a number of important publications about the afterlife that are simultaneously stimulating and problematic. In particular, the notion that purgatorial descriptions arose cap in hand with Irish (or as it is sometimes expressed more generally, "northern") institutions and modes of thought, in an oppositional and even antithetical relationship to continental "Roman" trends, warrants scrutiny. This chapter, then, seeks to question the weight that is sometimes given to what may be termed the "clash of cultures" model for purgatory's formation.

Scholarly Watersheds

In his *Le voyage de l'âme dans l'au-delà d'après la littérature latine (ve-xiiie siècle)* published in 1994, Claude Carozzi saw the seventh century as a crucial moment in the development of views about purgation. Indebted to Le Goff's discussion of the "infernalization" of purgatory, although differing from it, Carozzi characterized a changing perception of purgatory in these centuries as a move "from purgatorial fire to a purgatorial hell."[2] Early ideas about purgatorial fire differentiated the punishment of sinners based on duration in the fire, but Carozzi argued that the rise of a "purgatorial hell" was inevitable once differentiated tortures were introduced into it.[3] This stage in purgatorial teaching was framed by the *Vision of Fursey* written in 656 or 657, and the *Fragmentary Vision of 757* (Letter 115) written a century later. His analysis of the *Vision of Fursey* revealed a hybrid text dependent in part on the *Vision of Paul* but also informed by the classifications of sin promoted in Irish penitentials. Furthermore, in its more imaginative elements, Carozzi saw resonances of northern pagan culture and Germanic mythology. His views on the northern, and Irish character of the *Vision of Fursey* underlie much of the newer thinking on the Irish contribution to purgatory.

In 1999 and 2000 Peter Brown published two papers in which he outlined an original theory about purgatory's origins.[4] His argument hinged on a massive idea: that about 700 the clash and intersection of two very different cultural attitudes, that of the Mediterranean and the Irish, resulted in a shift in afterlife thinking. In these papers he argued that Christian expectations of the afterlife were rooted in two concepts: "amnesty" and "purgation." For Brown, the seventh century marked the period when the weight between these two concepts changed, that is, when Irish ideas of individual recompense jarred against an older world of community-wide hopes for divine amnesty. This clash of imaginative structures, according to Brown, signaled the true end of the ancient otherworld and the beginning of the more "familiar" medieval representation of the afterlife in which purgation of sins dominates. In his words: "Our own notions of the other world go back, effectively, to the seventh century and no further."[5]

Marilyn Dunn has also focused on the *Vision of Fursey* as an important text in purgatory's development. She sees the work reflecting Irish ideas concerning the afterlife in that "it depends on the evolution of systems of tariffed penance promoted on the Continent by British and Irish monks and clerics."[6] Thus for Dunn, a key argument for the rise of purgatory is to be found in the connection of purgatory with the tariffed penances. Indeed, Dunn presses the penitential evidence even further than Carozzi and Brown by claiming that Irish penitential tariffing and "quantifiable intercession" help explain not only Fursey's milieu but also that of the Gregorian *Dialogues*. My analysis of the *Vision of Fursey* presents a challenge to these views of purgatory in the seventh century.

The "Vision of Fursey": Evidence for Postmortem Penitence?

The *Vision of Fursey* is a crucial visionary text for discussing the early medieval afterlife and for developing ideas of purgation in particular. It is widely accepted as being the first surviving 'independent' visionary text of the middle ages to describe the individual soul's travel into the otherworld and indeed the first to describe such a journey in cosmic terms since the *Vision of Paul* and that work's widely circulating variants.[7] Written about 657 at the monastery of Péronne, the *Vision of Fursey* is a long and substantial narrative incorporated within the hagiographic *Life of Fursey*. It predates the next visionary epic, the *Vision of Barontus*, by about twenty years, and it was widely known and copied.[8] Bede reproduced Fursey's vision in an abridged version in his *Ecclesiastical History*, thus testifying to the work's presence in Northumbria by the early eighth century.[9] Through Bede's synopsis at least, the vision would have been familiar to the Anglo-Saxon missionaries in the early eighth century. The *Vision of Fursey* is thus a document of great interest and importance to our understanding of the seventh-century afterlife and a vital document for the representation of purgatorial ideas in the mid-seventh century.

A few words should be said about Fursey, his career, his sphere of influence, and the environment in which his vision was recorded. Obviously, the primary source for Fursey's life might be said to be the work he purportedly dictated himself: his vision. The visionary event upon which the later written account was based took place in the early 630s, possibly in East Anglia. The vision narrative as we have it, however, gives few clues to Fursey's natal environment or to the external circumstances of Fursey's career. Most of what we know of Fursey comes from the continental *Life of Fursey*, in which a full account of Fursey's visionary journey was presented, and from Bede's brief comments in his *Ecclesiastical History*.

Fursey (Fursa) was an Irish monk who had lived in his native land many years before his move to East Anglia, possibly in the Irish tradition of becoming an "exile for God."[10] His choice of East Anglia, a territory within the orbit of Frankish politics and Merovingian-style religious culture, suggests that he and his companions were already ideologically in tune with continental religious culture and not somehow outlandish foreigners. After some political upheavals, he moved to northern France where he founded the monastery of Lagny-sur-Marne in Neustria. Fursey's patron in this foundation was the Neustrian mayor Erchinoald, an advocate of reformed monasticism, a man with Irish sympathies and extensive Anglo-Saxon connections.[11] Perhaps Erchinoald sought Fursey out: headhunting a charismatic holy man—a man who could be reliably feted as a saint after his death. Fursey may have been a rare coup for the mayor who seeking to extend his influence through the patronage of monasteries and their relics. Four years after Fursey's death in Neustria in 649/50, his body was exhumed and found to be incorrupt. It was deposited in the basilica of the monastery of Péronne, and it was at Péronne that the account of his life and visions was composed in 656 or 657 and where his cult was fostered in the early middle ages.[12] Fursey's career was thus a long one—much of it spent in Ireland and East Anglia. Some version of his vision was likely told to audiences in England and may be responsible for alternative versions of his vision that are later cited in Britain. However, the extant version is best described as a continental work.[13]

As Merovingian texts go, the *Life of Fursey* was a remarkably contemporary composition having been written only a few years after Fursey's death at an institution in which he was well known and at a time when the saint's life would have been a living memory for its author and his informants. Fursey's brothers continued to be associated with Péronne, providing vital access to information. Nevertheless, the information supplied by the *vita* is sparing on details about England and Ireland and relatively speaking much richer on details relating to the monastic experience in Gaul. It may be presumed that other versions of the vision circulated during Fursey's lifetime, but it is important to keep in mind that the full written version of Fursey's vision that will be examined here was written more than a quarter of a century after the visionary event that inspired the account.

This background is important for a number of reasons: first, because it makes the text's most immediate context the monastic concerns of a continental Irish monastery in the 650s, and second, because it shows that using the work as evidence for a distinctly "Irish" way of thinking is, at the very least, problematic.[14]

At first sight, the early history of the monastic community at Péronne favours the likelihood that it would have preserved a distinctively Irish text. Péronne was founded by Fursey's brother, Foillan, and eventually another brother, Ultan, was its abbot. It was one of a small number of monasteries that retained a reputation as a centre for Irish monasticism for some generations.[15] We may assume that the *Rule of Columbanus* was used in it, alongside others, and that the *Benedictine Rule* may also have been introduced early on.[16] There were undoubtedly also a significant number of Anglo-Saxon monks there, since Erchinoald's primary foreign contacts were among the Anglo-Saxon elite and since Fursey and his brothers had come to Neustria via East Anglia.[17] The political disturbances that compelled Fursey to leave East Anglia anticipated those that brought the Anglo-Saxon Balthild to new prominence in the Neustrian kingdom as Clovis II's queen.[18] Still, Péronne was about as "Irish" a monastery as one could find in northern Gaul.[19] But what would this mean, precisely, for the character of a work written there? The work was written in Latin. Was its author Irish? Possibly, but what would such an identity signify? Was there such a monolithic thing as an "Irish" character either at home or abroad?[20] Would an intense dedication to penitential practices among its monks, and a love of scriptural learning, distinguish it from other monasteries in Gaul influenced by Columbanus's reforms? In short, was there anything in Irish culture that would be considered sufficiently alien that it would account for distinctive features in Fursey's vision? As we shall see, such questions are not readily answered.

It is important to bear in mind that the *Vision of Fursey* as related in the *Life of Fursey* is a carefully crafted text. Whatever core of "genuine" experience might be argued to be preserved in Fursey's narrative, the written account we have must have undergone later editing and embellishment. Furthermore, the text is not a document of vague recollection but a carefully argued treatise on eschatological and pastoral issues. This is seen not least in the complex structure of the work. The visionary narrative opens with a short description of a vision that Fursey experienced when he first fell sick. That vision is vague in detail, although it included angels and celestial singing. But three nights later darkness once again enclosed him, and he experienced the very elaborate vision that is described here. This second vision has a fairly complex sixfold structure. (i) Fursey saw a valley of four fires, (ii) angels and demons debated God's mercy and penance, (iii) Fursey asked about the end of times, (iv) he heard a mini-treatise on the pastoral responsibilities of teachers and rulers concluding with an itemization of the failings of the lax teacher, which continued (v) when Fursey met two clerics whom he recognized, Beoanus and Meldanus, who conversed with him at length and gave him spiritual and pastoral advice, and (vi) before his soul could return to his body, a demon hurled a burning man at him—a man from whom he had once accepted a gift—and Fursey was burned by contact with him. This visionary narrative does not appear to be the product of a single event, nor is it probable that it was a fully contemporaneous account. While the first vision is vague and retains a dream-like impressionistic quality, the second is laborious and overly scripted. Fursey's cosmic vision of the valley owes much to classical models, and the mini-treatises reflect long-standing pastoral and ascetic debates. The responsibilities of those who teach are outlined both in ascetic and earlier visionary texts. The danger of accepting gifts from sinners was likewise a perennially relevant issue for both seventh-century Ireland and seventh-century Francia. The involvement of Beoanus and Meldanus in the vision makes sense in the context of Péronne, where relics of those saints were interred alongside those of Fursey and were the objects of cult reverence there. But was there any reason to think they would have been named by Fursey in an account of a vision twenty years before?[21] In short, the long visionary text preserved in the *Life of Fursey* is a highly constructed, literary piece, which undoubtedly had some genuine experiences underlying it, but which was nevertheless a text for which many opportunities had been presented for theological reflection and cultural framing.

A Tricky Debate

The element in the *Vision* that has attracted more attention than any other is its debate scene. The scene is framed in a dramatic fashion, with a full-scale battle between angels and demons taking place as the conversation progressed. While angelic troops deflected the fire-tipped arrows of the demonic army, the demons and angels immediately surrounding Fursey were engaged in a war of words as they stood protected within the fire that "tried each according to his works." The immediate accusation was a serious one: Fursey had accepted gifts from individuals who were unrighteous because they had not completed their penance. Fursey's angel advocate countered with the claim that Fursey had believed that each one had done his penance. The purpose in this defense was to make a moral distinction between an intentional act on Fursey's part and an innocent, false assumption. Such an assumption would also mean that the gifts, while tainted, were innocently accepted by Fursey on behalf of the church. The devil's retort was to push the blame back onto Fursey as a failure to do due diligence. The conversation continued:

> The holy angel replied, "We are judged before the lord." The deceitful demon falling into blasphemies against the creator, burst forth saying: "Up until now we thought God was truth." The holy angel responded: "What else is he? The demon said very impudently: "Because it is promised that every fault (*delictum*) that has not been

purged on earth will be avenged in heaven. The prophet Isaiah proclaims: *If you are willing and listen to me, you shall eat the good of the land; But if you refuse and provoke me to wrath, you shall be devoured by the sword.* (Is. 1, 19–20) This man has not purged his faults on earth, nor has he received vengeance (*vindictam*) here. Where, then, is God's justice?" The holy angel rebuking them said: "Do not blaspheme, for you do not know God's hidden judgements." A devil responded "What kind of hidden judgement?" The holy angel said: "As long as penitence (*penitentia*) is hoped for, divine mercy accompanies mankind." Satan responded: "But there is no penitence[22] in this place." The angel replied: You do not know the depth of the mysteries of God: perhaps, even indeed, there will be." The devil replied: "Let's go then, for there is no rationale for judging."[23]

Later, the demon modified his case, accusing Fursey of not loving his neighbour as himself. The vision's author makes it clear that this was a "perverse" accusation, but in fact it was connected with the appropriate reconciliation of a sinner, as we shall see.

This crucial passage in the *Vision of Fursey* has prompted considerable discussion, in particular, the angel's comment that appears to affirm that there might indeed be penitence (*paenitentia*) in the afterlife. What could this mean? Brown saw the debate between the angels and demons in terms of traditional antagonisms in ascetic culture, proposing that the angel's comment was possibly "a corrective to the penitential rigorism introduced into Gaul, a generation earlier, by his compatriot, Columbanus."[24] Dunn goes further, stating, "The point has now been made clear: those who have completed penance in this life may continue to do so in the next. On to the ideas of post-mortem purgation or purification and intercession which had been developing for centuries has now been grafted the new concept of post-mortem penance, instantaneous upon death and limited in its duration."[25] Although the term *paenitentia* means "penance," it is clear that Dunn's argument relates to penitential-style satisfaction ("tariffed and quantified penance") rather than the broader meaning of penance as a sacrament.[26] There is no problem viewing this exchange between demons and the angel as a reflection of contemporary debate, but it is harder to claim that this view was promoted by the author of Fursey's vision, as we shall see below. It certainly becomes more problematic when this hint of an idea is viewed as an "extension of the concept of tariffed and quantified penance into the afterlife."[27] For a work that was evidently crafted with care, the ambiguities of the passage in the *Vision*, both in terms of its wording and its framing within the larger narrative, are striking and, one suspects, deliberate.

Before we can assess the claim that this text testifies to a change in beliefs about the afterlife, it is important to consider the form and nature of the debate. The dialogue was a favorite monastic tool to present an authoritative discourse between two unequal participants, in which opposing views could be presented rationally and elegantly, but in which a particular theological view invariably trumps the "misguided" view. In hagiographic narratives, debates between saints and demons presented antagonistic views, with the saint generally speaking for the desired view, and the devil's advocates taking the contrary view. A familiar example would have been Sulpicius Severus's *Life of Martin of Tours*, in which a similar debate about penance took place between the saint and some demons; the demons argued the rigorist position, and the saint argued a more relaxed, compassionate position.[28] In hagiography, then, such a debate was an effective way to flag the rights and wrongs of a theological disagreement.

In the case of visionary narratives, the debate was taken to a different level of urgency and intensity. Fursey's was a soul in danger. In his unfamiliar environment he did not have the knowledge or authority to engage in the debate himself: the angels spoke for him. This dislocation of the conventional model of debate allowed for some liberty with the convention. Most notably, it allowed the angels to argue a position that might trick a demon while not being strictly truthful. Demons were notoriously tricky and used truth and scripture to deceive. Consequently, angels needed to be wily, even to the extent of sidestepping the truth in order to save a soul. As a dramatic tool, trickery enlivened a narrative. The audience could relish an angel's trick over a demon. The desert fathers were often said to have issued saucy retorts to challenging demons, and somehow this tactic had confounded them. We see something of the same humour in another visionary narrative, the *Vision of Barontus*.[29] Barontus was a Merovingian nobleman who had entered the monastery of Lonrey late in life with a long slate of dubious activities to account for, including having had three wives. When demons attempted to drag his soul to hell, Barontus was saved by St. Raphael, who summoned St. Peter to join the defense. Saint Peter dismissed the demons' claims because, he noted, Barontus had confessed his sins to a priest, done penance, and entered the monastery. When the demons refused to give up, calling on God's justice, St. Peter concluded his defense of the woefully compromised Barontus by hitting the demon on the head with his keys. The demons retreated, as they had in the *Vision of Fursey*, similarly disgusted with the tack being taken in the proceedings. What transpired immediately afterward was that St. Peter knew all along that Barontus was in flagrant violation of monastic regulations, having evidently lied about having held back a small fortune of twelve gold solidi, presumably for his own use. Yet, here is the point. Saint Peter had told the demons that Barontus had given away all his money in alms. Saint Peter lied. The lie tricked the demons so that Barontus could be given time to make amends and, in so doing, redeem St. Peter's lie.

The point of these comparisons is to indicate that dialogues between angels and demons in visionary tales are not as easily interpreted as dialogues in other forms of monastic literature. In placing the discussion of afterlife penitence in this format, the vision's author was setting the conversation within a context that appears deliberately ambivalent: a context in which the rights and wrongs of the case were not immediately evident, and a context that did not have a more authoritative placement, such as the section of the work in which Fursey was given instruction on penitential issues by Beoanus and Meldanus.

Next, we should look at the principal accusation brought against Fursey by the demons: that Fursey had accepted gifts from sinners. The demon twice quoted scripture in order to accuse him, first, quoting Ecclesiasticus 34:19, stating: "The Most High is not pleased with the gifts of the unrighteous," and second, quoting Deuteronomy 16:19, "a gift blinds the eyes of the wise and subverts the cause of righteousness."[30] The angel cut off the accusation with the comment, "We are judged before the Lord." Despite the angel's bravura, the accusation that Fursey had accepted gifts from a penitent stuck. Toward the end of the vision, Fursey was punished for this infraction. As Fursey was passing back through the unitary, probative fire, his angelic guides held back the walls of fire to the left and right so that Fursey could pass through unharmed.[31] But suddenly, a burning man hurled by a demon broke through the fiery wall. Fursey was burned by the contact. According to Bede, this encounter left Fursey with a scar that he bore for the remainder of his life.[32] Fursey's encounter is a very telling episode because it concludes, through action, the verbal debate initiated earlier. The demons had accused Fursey of accepting gifts from sinners, and here now was one such sinner. Fursey was thus presented with the truth that his angel-advocate had tried hard to evade. The demons immediately seized the moment to gloat that this man was Fursey's known associate: "It is unlawful to reject him who you earlier accepted, and just as you accepted his goods, so you must share in his punishment." But the angel protested the action: "Not because of greed did he accept it, but for liberating this man's soul." And at this declaration, the fire ceased.

Here, then, is the conclusion of the debate on penance. Fursey had evidently accepted gifts from those who were deemed unrighteous because they had not completed their penance, but Fursey had used the donation in the will for the release of the man's soul. One of the angels pointedly remarked to Fursey that latecomers to penance must keep to their penitence right to the moment of death and that they must not be allowed burial in a holy place.[33] Was this a prohibition against Christian burial for penitents? The regulations governing funeral services for penitents were traditionally strict.[34] However, it is also possible that the allusion was to burial *ad sanctos* and to the church's intercession for the souls of the dead—both ways in which the worldly and rich might attempt to improve their chances at the Final Judgement.[35] Had Fursey accepted the gift in return for giving the man privileged burial and access to intercession? Two parts of the work addressed the problem of gifts to the church and their appropriate use. The first part involved the priest, Beoanus, advising Fursey that alms given by the unjust (sinners) for the sake of their souls should be distributed to the poor.[36] The implication is that the goods of the unreconciled should not be accepted for church use or for liturgical purposes.[37] The second part is at the conclusion of the discussion about holy burial. An unreconciled sinner will give alms to the poor as part of his penance, "however, nothing shall be accepted by the priest preaching for him, but his goods shall be divided among the poor next to his tomb, lest others partake in his iniquities."[38] In short, the alms of sinners, even those donated in a will, must be segregated from monies available for other "purer" uses in the community. We have already seen that the distribution of alms and other church revenues was a long-standing concern.[39] Indeed, there is a quality to this discussion that suggests that the customary rules for such finances were becoming increasingly rigorous and complex in cases in which sin was attached to the donor. The scriptural basis for this concern was quoted by the demon in accusation.[40] Fursey's fault lay not so much in accepting the sinner's gift, but in dispersing it in an inappropriate way. Recall that the damned man was thrust against him jawbone to jawbone, a graphic way of explaining that an intimate bond existed between the fate of the intercessor and that of the one for whom he made intercession. If so, it was a warning for all priests who entered into mutual bonds of obligation with sinners.

The *Vision of Fursey* is a very interesting work. It comprises many elements that made it notable and much copied in the early middle ages: battles between angels and demons, the horror of contact with fire, and the pastoral advice drawn from contemporary ascetic debates that gave pause for thought to both priests and sinners. It is also the first visionary text to incorporate a visual rendering of the fire of purgation through which souls pass and that tried each Christian according to his works. But does the work testify to an emerging theology of postmortem purgation that involved a notion of penitential practice in the afterlife?

When the angel retorted to the devil that there may yet be penitence after death, the angel's meaning was unclear. If the angel meant that a soul in the afterlife could become a penitent in the afterlife, that is to say, initiate a state of repentance that had not begun on earth, then the angel was expressing a view that was distinctly at odds with prevailing theological opinion. The entire thrust of ascetic proscriptive literature, the penitentials, and visions of the afterlife was to urge the need for present penance precisely because it was impossible to repent and make satisfaction after death. One of the prayers in the *Bobbio Missal* expressed this quite explicitly referring to the departed soul being in a hidden receptacle, "which is not a place of penance."[41] Nor did this message change in any formal pastoral literature throughout the seventh century. When Paul encountered the weeping souls in hell who had been too involved in the world to do penance but now belatedly acknowledged Christ, he had pity on them, but the Archangel Michael challenged them: "Where are your prayers, where are your penances?"[42] In hell, souls might regret past actions, but they could not initiate true remorse. Consequently the tormented souls stimulated Michael's pity and even some alleviation of suffering, but no alteration in their fate. The inclination toward God and the long process of penance had to be started before death. Interestingly, even Fursey in his function as visionary is not depicted as confessing to the sin of which he is accused, nor does he express remorse. Like a modern defendant, Fursey is silent while the angels and demons debate his case. Fursey's life as a monk made him a perpetual penitent, and his worthiness may be inferred from the fact that he can be purged by the fire. But this penitential state was begun before his "death." Fursey's purgation was pain that bore fruit. But this was not to be expected for those who failed to do penance in life. Indeed, there may be some inkling of a formal rebuttal to the idea of afterlife penitence in a sermon attributed to Eligius of Noyon, which states: "There may be some penitence in hell, but completely without any fruit, and there may be those who suffer the pain of penitence, but without having medicinal value from it."[43] Set within the context of Neustrian *kirchenpolitik*, Eligius's comment is possibly even more interesting. Eligius was part of a faction opposed to Fursey's patron Erchinoald and to Erchinoald's landgrab around Péronne.[44] Eligius's refutation of the value of penitence in the afterlife might then be seen in the context of a rebuttal of views being expressed in a major work composed at Péronne. How better to oppose Erchinoald and his new foundation than to suggest that Fursey, the saint whose relics were the primary cultic focus of the institution, was in some measure tainted by unorthodoxy? Any idea that the soul could count on spiritual progress in the afterlife smacked of Origenism. Even the monks, who in Francia and England had retained moderate elements of Pelagian thinking, had never suggested (as indeed, Pelagius also emphatically did not) that the business of earning merit extended beyond the grave.

Did the angel's comment refer to penitential satisfaction being conducted after death? The idea that there might be penitential-style penance in the afterlife is actually quite extraordinary. Of what would it consist? If it involved remorse, then that would be nothing very new—the damned in ancient visions were often depicted lamenting their lost chances. If it involved punishment, such as Fursey received, how would that be different from Augustinian-style postmortem purgation as it was already imagined? If we look at the Irish penitentials such as the *Penitential of Finnian* and the *Penitential of Cummean*, both texts that Carozzi believed were known to the *Vision*'s author, we find no evidence for this extraordinary claim. Indeed, Irish penitentials were strikingly Augustinian in their theology and, like the *Bigotian Penitential*, were quite clear on the notion that after death souls could only be saved after punishment, not through it.

How seriously, then, should we take the angel's comment that "perhaps, even indeed, there will be (penitence)" as a new theological direction in postmortem restitution? And why did the author tuck it within an appeal to "God's hidden mysteries" where it could not be examined? Perhaps strangely, but not uniquely to this type of text, the devils were proved right in the end. Just as the monk Barontus was indeed guilty of a hidden sin for which he had to make restitution, so Fursey too had something to hide. The angel's arguments may have aimed to confound the "demons" who would legalistically diminish God's jurisdictional autonomy, but this did not alter Fursey's fate one wit. Fursey was punished for his fault—that is to say, he was purged. His purging punishment was to be burned by the fire.[45] He was not given penance to do on earth (as Barontus was made to do), but rather he received advice from the two clerics Meldanus and Beoanus. Fursey was punished for his transgression, but he was also purged of it having preemptively sustained the penalty he would have been due in the afterlife, and indeed the work does not end with the notion that further penance or postmortem purgation will be needed. Like Salvius in the previous century, Fursey was stricken with fear about regaining his earthly body. But the angel soothed him with the promise that he would return to heaven with joy: "Fear not to take up this body, which, though infirm, you may assume without any revulsion of sickness nor of repugnant sins. In this tribulation you have overcome unlawful lusts, so that old sins will not prevail against you." Fursey's sin had been purged permanently in that great fire. He had been at fault in a matter that mattered not only morally but also to the norms of his religious culture. He had returned to earth and to his community a whole person, pure once more, able to preach from a position of authority and impervious to possible criticism. His vision had purified him of error. He could now become a saint. The story ends on an orthodox note after all.

Irish Influence?

How far, then, can we take the *Vision of Fursey* as evidence for those claims that have been made for it? Is the vision evidence that a new, and lasting, direction in afterlife thinking had emerged that conceived of purgatory as a form of penance after death? Is it evidence that the values of tariffed penance had seeped into a purgatorial afterlife? Is the *Vision of Fursey* evidence that such views might be due to a distinctively Irish spirituality? Unfortunately, as we have seen, the text resists easy characterization. Written in northern Gaul at a monastery that, while inspired by Irish ideals, was probably by no means a reservoir of untainted "Irish" ideas, the work shows its deep debt to traditional continental sources, as is also common in Irish hagiography written in that century.[46] Brown terms this kind of literature a "newly perfected hybrid plant" with roots in the Christian Mediterranean.[47] This includes the struggle between angels and demons and the debate itself, which was a strong feature of Egyptian and Merovingian hagiography.[48] Clare Stancliffe comments that "there is nothing from seventh-century Ireland (including Iona) comparable to the developed treatment of the soul's out-of-the-body experiences such as we find in the *Life of Fursey*, a continental product."[49] Indeed, it is extremely problematic to identify some kind of unique Irish spirituality either in Ireland or on the Continent, since there must have been regional and generational differences. Individual ecclesiastical careers in this period often show mobility across Ireland, England, Gaul, Italy, and even the East.[50] Continental sources had noted peculiarities in the Irish ecclesiastical hierarchy and in ascetic practices, but it does not follow that Irish Christianity was fundamentally different in its teaching.[51] By the mid-seventh century most Christian communities were in line with the main festivals in Rome or at any rate conformed or did not conform at about the same rate as any other region outside Rome itself. It is now generally accepted that the "Celtic Church" of England and Ireland had largely accepted Roman practices well ahead of the Synod of Whitby, making Iona and Lindisfarne somewhat anomalous by 664.

The *Vision of Fursey* is embedded in ascetic and pastoral concerns that were traditional and long-standing within late antique Christian culture. Concern for the proper treatment of penitents was always topical. It was certainly true that penances that required three or five or more years to complete ran the risk that the penitent would die before the penance was complete. It had always been so, even when penances were played out on the steps of ancient churches. But when it seemed likely that a sinner would die before penitential satisfaction was complete, the church had been committed historically to reconciling the penitent preemptively and dispensing the host to aid the soul's journey to the afterlife.[52] That extended penance caused anxiety is seen in the stories of Gregory the Great and in many seventh-century visions including the visions of the nuns of Faremoutiers and the *Vision of Fursey*. Many seventh-century stories played with this notion of time. Could penance be hastened, or commuted? In some cases it appears that it could. This must have been the laudable aim behind the commutation literature that envisaged payments in lieu of penance in just the way that Roman citizens once were able to give produce in lieu of military service! Yet ultimately, reconciliation with the church was available to the penitent as long as he lived, even on the deathbed, and even if the host had to be manually laid on the dying person's tongue. Had Fursey really done wrong in reconciling a penitent, or were there other issues at stake?

What is perhaps most remarkable about the advice given in this text is its ambivalence about priestly intercession, and this may have become a more timely issue as lay access to priestly intercession increased. Penitents could expect reconciliation on their deathbed, but a lapsed penitent was in a much more hazardous situation. In the early church, penance, like baptism, could be performed only once. The idea of the need for continuous penance slowly took hold from about the 430s onward.[53] Repeatable penance must have blurred the edges of what constituted full reconciliation. The devil accused Fursey of accepting gifts from sinners whose penance was not complete and who had perhaps returned to ordinary life. Relatedly, we have noted above that the text reveals concern about how the goods of sinners were used when given to the church for their souls. If we look at the *Penitential of Finnian*, we find advice about reconciling the laity: a layperson who had committed every kind of foul deed and who was "converted from evil-doing" must do three years of penance, after which he must give money for the redemption of his soul, and that money will be given to the priest.[54] The penitential did not go on to say how the money should or should not be used, although elsewhere the money is said to have been used for alms. There is no mention of priestly intercession or burial *ad sanctos* in the penitential. Perhaps these were issues of more pressing urgency in seventh-century Gaul than in seventh-century Ireland.

Had Fursey's actions aided the man he sought to reconcile? The man whose soul Fursey had attempted to rescue by accepting gifts had not been liberated from punishment. Perhaps his presence in the fire was evidence that he had been liberated from hell to purgation. Was the message to be careful what you wished for? If Fursey saved a soul so that it could be purged rather than condemned to hell, the intercession was effective, but Fursey must pay a personal price for that deed since the man's penance was not complete. If the man's soul burned in hell, then Fursey's fault was even more grave. The teacher's responsibility for his flock's actions was a fixed idea in the monastic life. The secular world was less easy to control. But what then was the message, since for whom were the clergy to intercede if not for the sinful?[55]

To support an argument that a penitential-style penance in the afterlife signaled a new and lasting direction in afterlife thinking, we would want to find evidence that later texts incorporated this new idea. There is none. Any mention of postmortem penance through penitential practices, such as we find in Eligius's sermon, is made in order to deny it. So while a debate may indeed have occurred, and while the debate in the *Vision of Fursey* recorded it, the outcome of the debate appears to have been determined by the vision's continental redactor. Perhaps the debate scene was too well known to be left out, but the proof of the purging was in the fire, as Fursey soon discovered. It is surely significant that when Bede summarized Fursey's vision he did not include the debate scene, or even its essential points. We do not know precisely which version of the vision Bede had access to, but it was evidently some form of the long version produced at Péronne. The author of Drythelm's vision well knew how to frame a visionary narrative along orthodox lines. Further, if the debate was in fact a reflection of the tension between Eligius's and Erchinoald's faction, then the continental context for the debate, and perhaps for the work more generally, seems assured.

The influence of the penitentials on the rise of purgatory must now be addressed. Carozzi's comments on the influence of the penitentials arose from his examination of the various ways that sins were classified in ascetic and penitential literature. There is no question that penitential literature relied heavily on models of ascetic instruction, since it is acknowledged and evident in most of those works. Cassian's eightfold classification of capital vices, in particular, offered a familiar structure for penitential discussions, although other models were also used. Rather than looking as far back as Cassian for the *Vision of Fursey*'s enumeration of sins, Carozzi pointed to the more immediate influence of the penitentials of Finnian and Cummean. He noted that healing vices with contrary virtues was a common trait of the Irish penitentials, that the *Vision of Fursey* did not use Cassian's eightfold classification system, and that the *Vision* focused rather on distinguishing capital sins from lighter ones. Indeed, Carozzi's preference is always to look to more contemporary sources for the *Vision*'s inspiration, which can hardly be argued with except to note that it has a particular effect: it ensures a distinctly northern and Irish view of the work. A fuller acknowledgment of the direct influence of the works of Cassian and of other continental ascetic texts tips the balance a different way. For example, Cassian, too, was greatly concerned to distinguish grave sins from lighter ones, as indeed were Augustine and Caesarius. The *Vision*'s instruction that minor sins were being treated severely when more serious sins often went unpunished was a critique of the way penances were assessed and applied, rather than a problem of classification. Indeed, the solution suggested by the *Vision* offered precisely the kind of humanity and gentleness that lay at the core of the teaching of the great monastic abbots such as Martin of Tours, Romanus of Condat, and Benedict, whose rule, we might speculate, may have been contending for position at Péronne in the 650s. Likewise, the notion that sins feed on one another, augmenting one another, an image that Carozzi saw reflected in the augmentation of the fires in the *Vision*, harkens back quite clearly to Cassian's work, among others.[56] The point is, of course, that choosing a shorter versus a longer perspective can greatly influence the context in which a text such as the *Vision of Fursey* is viewed.

That the author of Fursey's vision was influenced to some degree by the *Vision of Paul* is in little doubt, and the areas of coincidence are carefully established in Carozzi's work.[57] The *Vision of Paul* was a widely copied text in the early Middle Ages. Its contents were endlessly epitomized, embellished, transformed, and made relevant to the prevailing religious culture. Carozzi noted that the long version of the *Vision of Paul* was known to Aldhelm of Malmesbury and his correspondent, Cellanus, who was abbot of Péronne after Fursey's brother, Ultan. Thus there is evidence that the long version was known in both England and at Péronne at the turn of the seventh century. Carozzi saw evidence for knowledge of the *Vision of Paul* in the basic structure of Fursey's vision, as well as in its details. He saw a strong influence of baptismal themes in the *Vision of Fursey*: the four fires at the beginning of the vision were stoked by faults committed since baptism; Fursey's questioning by the demons was comparable to the baptismal examination, and Fursey's ordeal in the fire was a kind of baptism by fire (as, indeed, purgation had been called by Origen and others). Furthermore, Carozzi identified in Fursey's vision a fire that "condensed" multiple elements that had been discrete in the *Vision of Paul*: a combination of punishment, purification, trial, and judgement. For Carozzi, this fire was regenerative, a quality that Carozzi attributed to very ancient ways of thinking, both pagan and Christian, even Indo-European. Turning to prohibitions against pagan practices in the Germanic Council of 742 amongst others, Carozzi proposed that the pagan "Niedfyr" was a purificatory fire, allowing for a transposition of images (the purging fire of purgatory) that would ultimately facilitate the process of converting pagans. Any discussion of the meaning of the Niedfyr in the early to mid-seventh century is necessarily speculative, however, since we have no contemporary sources to indicate what this fire symbolized to the inhabitants of Germany, Scandinavia, and Ireland, let alone if it held the same meaning in each of those places.[58] Carozzi notes that in medieval times the church accepted the tradition of lighting fires at Eastertide, a concession that he linked to the church's accommodation of certain pagan practices in the hope of converting pagans. Conversely, one might argue that at Easter the church imposed on such fires a meaning that they in turn found acceptable. Fires were lit at other times, such as the summer solstice bonfire that came to be associated with the festival of St. John in north Atlantic countries, an ancient bonfire tradition that has lasted into the present century.

Carozzi's interpretation of Fursey's vision sought to accentuate its non-Roman context: penitentials, Germanic law, and church councils.[59] While I am not convinced that he was able to show the direct or exclusive influence of any single penitential, he certainly demonstrated that the discussion of sins in the *Vision of Fursey* was not out of place with that in other contemporary works, such as in certain penitentials that were undoubtedly known to the author and the *De duodecim abusivis saeculi,* which was probably not.[60] Carozzi was cautious in interpreting the debate between the angel and the demon concerning afterlife penitence and saw the angel's comment (that there may indeed be penitence in the afterlife) as a reference to the fire that Fursey encountered later in the vision. But ultimately, Carozzi did not shy away from attributing to the *Vision of Fursey* an "Irish" character. He concluded his discussion of Fursey with the comment that Fursey and his companions were part of a non-Romanized people, only recently converted, and that this work was part of creating a new language—an acculturation of the sort recommended to Augustine of Canterbury by Gregory the Great. As we shall see later in the chapter, this cautious Irish characterization was substantially augmented in the contributions of Brown and Dunn.

Bede's Epitomized "Vision of Fursey" (AD 731)

Bede summarized Fursey's vision in his *Ecclesiastical History* among events of the 630s.[61] Thus Bede's work was published a century after the date of the events described and three generations after the Péronne account was penned. It is evident that Bede was using some form of the Péronne account written around 656/57 since he included the detail that Fursey's body was found to be uncorrupted when it was moved, and this fact had been observed when Fursey's remains were moved to Péronne.[62]

By including Fursey's vision in his *Ecclesiastical History*, Bede brought Fursey's vision to new audiences, thereby enhancing the saint's reputation and his vision. However, in abridging the text, Bede excised significant portions of the vision, including the debate between the angel and the demon about afterlife penitence, and reduced the instruction narrative involving Meldanus and Beoanus to the simple comment that "from them he learned many things valuable to both to himself and to those who might be willing to listen."[63] In view of Bede's known views on purgatory, and especially his sensitivity to error in eschatological thinking, his excision of the debate of the angel and the demon appears deliberate and not an attribute of brevity.

Bede's own interest in the account is revealed in his focus on the cosmological aspects of Fursey's ascent and on Fursey's encounter with the man from whom he had accepted a gift. He was also very interested in the four fires of falsehood, covetousness, discord, and injustice, which merged as one in the vision.[64] He repeated the angel's explanation of the fire: "That which you did not kindle will not burn you; for although the conflagration seems great and terrible, it tests each man according to its deserts, and the evil desires of everyone will be burned away in this fire."[65] Bede's account supplied additional information not known from the Péronne account of the vision: that the name of Fursey's monastery in Anglia was Cnobheresburg, that one of the monks in Bede's monastery claimed to have spoken to someone who had met Fursey, and that Fursey would sweat while telling his tale. Bede also contextualized his account in a characteristic way: He introduced Fursey with a synopsis of his preaching mission. Writing in a missionary age at the beginning of the eighth century, Bede readily understood the vision's injunctions about preaching in the context of foreign missions. In fact, Fursey's career did not really bear out his characterization as a missionary.[66] As far as we can tell, Fursey's preaching career centred largely on repeating his vision to penitents.

The "Fragmentary Vision of 757"

In view of the claims for long-term shifts in views of afterlife penitence, it is instructive to examine a later visionary text that described purgatorial punishment. Such a text is found in the *Fragmentary Vision of 757*, a work whose author is unknown to us.[67] The work was collected among the letters of Boniface and Lull. The text's author was not the visionary, but rather someone who had heard the vision and who wrote down what he remembered of it. The author conceded that his memory was shaky about details and that he could make no claim to understand the vision's full meaning. Undoubtedly, he was addressing an audience that knew something about the Anglo-Saxon queens and bishop mentioned in the work. It seems likely that his informant was an Anglo-Saxon monk.

The visionary tale is well underway at the point the reader joins it. The text opens with a description of tormented souls: "some souls up to the armpits or to the neck; and over the heads of others rose a seething whirlpool of fire and blackness." The souls of many prominent men and women were seen in those pits including abbots and abbesses and counts. They were being tortured there. However, this place had one clear distinction: "All the souls in the pits were to be set free at some time, either on the Day of Judgement or before." One woman was released from the pit when Mass was celebrated for her, "and this, he [the visionary] said, was the highest good for souls who had left the body."[68] The obvious comparison for this text has been the *Vision of the Monk of Wenlock*, preserved in the same collection; however, the comment that the souls would be set free at or before judgement is strikingly reminiscent of the *Vision of Drythelm*, a text that we can be sure was known in these circles.[69] Indeed the *Fragmentary Vision of 757* seems to combine elements from the *Vision of Paul*, the *Vision of the Monk of Wenlock*, and the *Vision of Drythelm*.[70] Its attention to the Mass as a particularly effective mode of intercession is also a feature of Gregory's *Dialogues*. In short, this fragmentary work is a mishmash of earlier visionary texts whose composition appears to have been strongly motivated by a political agendum, the contours of which are evident in the naming of individuals but whose full political substance eludes us. After viewing these temporary pits, the anonymous visionary was taken to the first, second, and third heaven by means of a rainbow.[71] The text becomes very strange at this point because the visionary arrived before a judge at the monastery of Ingedraga where he had to confess all his omissions and sins. Then he saw three troops of demons preparing torments for the places of punishment.[72] In these pits of punishment (*poenalibus puteis*) he saw former queens Cuthburga and Wiala: Cuthberga was stained up to her armpits, and Wiala was seen with a flame above her head burning her entire soul at once. They were being punished for sins of the flesh. There, too, was Count Ceolla Snoding bent back, his head and feet bound by hooks.[73] None of these individuals has been identified, although some plausible suggestions have been made.[74] However, also in these pits was found the royal tyrant "Ethilbeald," presumably King Aethelbald of Mercia, murdered in 757, and it has been proposed that the Bishop Daniel mentioned in the vision, who had failed in his duty to baptize children, was Bishop Daniel of Winchester (705–45).[75]

The torturous punishment of Aethelbald and the two queens and especially the contortion of Count Snoding, are reminiscent of earlier depictions of hell, and indeed, I would argue that the punishments at this point in the text are indeed intended to be understood as a depiction of hell. Thus I disagree with Carozzi, who interpreted the account of these pits as a continuation of the description of purgatory at the beginning of the text.[76] While the fragmentary nature of the text makes definitive identification impossible, Carozzi's interpretation of these pits as purgatorial seems highly unlikely. There is a significant change of gaze between the beginning and end of the vision as we have it. After viewing the temporary pits at the beginning of the text as we have it, the visionary saw a place of the living, of happiness, and of fragrant flowers. Then the visionary moved on to another place having been led through the three heavens by means of a rainbow. He is then told that he will have to confess his sins. Only then is he shown this last place that, being presented as pits of punishment with torments prepared by demons, fits the conventional visionary view of hell, and is a suitable warning to the visionary monk. The identity of the queens and of the count have eluded the historical record, but we know very well what Boniface and his circle thought about King Aethelbald, and hell would not have been considered too severe a place for him. It is important to make a distinction between a place of purgatorial torment at the beginning of the fragment and the graphic depictions of torture of individuals in hell at the end of it because it means that the work cannot be used as evidence for the intrusion of individual, penal-style tortures into purgatory by the mid-eighth century. The tortures of the souls of purgatory in this text, as far as a fragmentary description can allow, are cosmic in nature: whirlwinds of fire. This is very different from Count Snoding's torture. Differentiated, penal-style torture was a feature, it seems to me, that was characteristic of purgatory only from the early ninth century in visions such as the *Vision of Wetti*.

The *Fragmentary Vision of 757* supports the view that purgatory as envisaged by Bede in his *Vision of Drythelm* had become incorporated into Anglo-Saxon visions of the otherworld by the middle of the eighth century. The text's emphasis on the Mass as a means of releasing a soul from purgatory shows its indebtedness to the Gregorian-Bedan intellectual tradition. Finally, it is quite clear that the text does not support the notion that postmortem "penance" was ever considered an option for sinful souls in the seventh and eighth centuries.

Vision of Paul, Redaction 6

Redaction 6 of the *Vision of Paul* is a somewhat later work, probably late eighth century in inception, but it is an important text for some of the issues discussed here.⁷⁷ It is also a work that some scholars claim to include a depiction of purgatory. That identification, as we shall see, is highly debatable.

The only complete manuscript of the work dates to the ninth century, but, as Theodore Silverstein noted, it was made by a blundering copyist "who apparently had before him a Merovingian original which he did not fully understand."⁷⁸ This was then corrected "with a hand hardly distinguishable from the original."⁷⁹ Carozzi has offered convincing arguments that the text may have been composed originally in the second half of the eighth century.⁸⁰ Both Silverstein and Carozzi have argued that the nine torments described in the text related to a purgatorial place rather than hell (although retaining Paul's intercession for his Jewish parents as a release from hell.)⁸¹ I disagree. The interpretation of the nine places of torment as purgatory while plausible is not proven, and it is important to keep in mind that their interpretation hangs by a slender thread. My examination of that thread, which follows, leads me to a different conclusion.

The title of the work, probably added to the work in the ninth century, suggests that Paul's vision was indeed of a place where sinners were capable of amendment: "The chastisement of sinful men (as shown to) Saint Paul. Those who sin and amend."⁸² This is the basis for the attribution of the text's torments to purgatory by Silverstein and Carozzi. However, unlike the title, the body of the text does not make it clear that a purgatorial place was being described. The work opens with the sentence: "Saint Paul is taken to the Kingdom of God that he might see the works of the just and the penalties of sinners."⁸³ Immediately following a brief description of the first heaven filled with fruit-bearing trees, Paul was shown the realm of punishment introduced with the phrase: "and he came to another place." Each new category of sinner and punishment is introduced with this phrase. At the end of the work, Paul asks where his parents are and on being informed that they are burning in hell, he cries and begs to enter hell to see them.⁸⁴ Instead, he is granted their release. The suggestion in this final passage that Paul's parents may be in an infernal place other than the one he was shown may indicate a distinction between the earlier place of torments he was shown and the hell where Paul's parents burn. It is not clear. Much hangs on section 7 of the work, a passage that discusses penance:

> And Paul asked: "These are those who sinned against chastity; how indeed do they pay?" The angel answered him: "If they do penance while they live, the Lord will forgive their sin." And Paul asked "If you are a presbyter, or deacon, subdeacon or virgin, or bride of Christ who sin, how indeed do they pay?" The angel responded: "You should

lie four years on pure (sacred?) ground, two of them on stone and during those very years the unjust should reconcile, fasting on bread, salt and water, and the lord will forgive their sins."[85]

Silverstein suggested that *enim dare* ("how should they pay?") should be changed to *emendare* ("how can they make amends") in section 7. This introduced a correction that is not necessary for the meaning of the text and profoundly altered it. Rather, when confronted by clerics who have sinned against chastity and did not simply fail to do penance, but despised it, Paul asked the question, "how indeed do they pay for this?" The angel responded that if they do penance while they are living (*dum advixerit*) God will forgive them. Likewise the angel's advice for presbyters, deacons, subdeacons, virgins, or brides of Christ who sin is that they lie four years on the ground, two of them on stone, and fast on bread and water, and God will forgive them. This advice for the living, a break from the vision's focus on the dead, certainly intrudes into the rhythm of the journey, but it may also have been a purposeful address to his audience who, with him, would be shocked at seeing churchmen in hell. Furthermore, on the issue of penance, the angel's message is clear: penance must be done by the living, and punishment awaits the impenitent dead.

It may fairly be argued that the scribe who added the title in the ninth century understood the vision through the lens of purgatory. *Redaction 6* was copied into a codex that included texts with a penitential focus. However, the original text of *Redaction 6* most likely referred to hell. In the end, *Redaction 6* is a unique if obscure snapshot of changing belief in the afterlife at the turn of the ninth century. Textually, the work was a dead end. Silverstein established that *Redaction 6* of the *Vision of Paul* arose independently from other works in the *Vision of Paul* tradition and had no textual descendants.[86]

Was "Tariffed" Penance Connected to the Rise of Purgatory?

As we have seen, purgatory's rise in the seventh century has sometimes been explained by reference to the proliferation of penitential literature in that century. For example, Dunn argues that

> The ecclesiastical view of post-mortem purgation began to change in the seventh century as the use of the system of tariffed penance pioneered in Britain and Ireland began to spread. Once the idea of repeatable and quantified penance began to gain currency, the vista of the afterlife began slowly to change as the idea spread that

penance—as opposed to simple purgation—could be continued in
the afterlife. This perception only evolved slowly . . .[87]

Significantly, Dunn assumes but does not prove a direct connection between purgatory and the penitentials. This version of the Irish origin theory is highly problematic. It rests largely on the view that the penitential culture of the seventh century was dominated by Irish ways of thinking that were distinguishable from the traditional practices on the Continent. This is by no means an established fact, and indeed, there are good reasons to view much of Irish penitential culture as developing similarly to the way it developed on the Continent.[88] Furthermore, tariffed penance was not new. Richard Price sums up this view succinctly:

> The tariffed penance which is conventionally attributed to the originality of Celtic monks derived in fact from eastern practice developed in the fourth century, notably in the penitential epistles of Basil of Caesarea, which lists specific offenses with a set period of penance for each, and make no reference to any need for formal reconciliation at the end of the process.[89]

The problem is that once the Irish origin theory is assumed, it is a short step to attempt to link purgatory to other Irish institutions such as Irish law with its 'long lists of compensations.' Here, Dunn strives to include the Gregorian *Dialogues* into the worldview occupied by Fursey:

> Tariffed penance possessed similar characteristics to Irish law, sharing its private rather than public nature and its automatic penalties for specified offences.[90] Such concepts would lead to the development of the concept of quantified periods of intercession which would automatically obtain the release of the soul from its purgatorial state-the basis of the three stories relating to post-mortem purgation in the *Dialogues*. The radical elements in the *Dialogues*' view of the afterlife are conditioned by a belief in the continuance of penance post-mortem which in turn had its basis in the system of tariffed penance which originated in northern Europe.[91]

As we have seen, there is no reason to suppose that a model of postmortem penitential practice was widely accepted in the seventh century, nor that penitential practices influenced the way afterlife purgation was viewed in subsequent texts. Further, as we have seen, the "Irishness" of the *Vision of Fursey* is questionable. The assumption here is a common one: that there is a connection between the tariffed penitential system and a radically new way of conceiving postmortem purgation. This notion must be reevaluated, and so, in the remainder of this section, I shall address a few of these interrelated lynchpins of what may be called the "penitential/Irish" origin theory.

We have seen that there is no evidence that postmortem penitential practice was an idea of authority and influence. To a great extent this is because religious leaders were so emphatic that the time for repentance was in the present and that penitential satisfaction could not be made after death. After death, the lot of souls was improved only by undergoing the "correction" of punishment. Indeed, this view is extremely strong in the very documents that Brown and Dunn view as having influenced seventh-century ideas about the afterlife.[92]

Penance had a very real connection to the postmortem fate of the soul, but it was a traditional, ascetic one requiring the soul to be purified in the present life to prepare it to encounter whatever fate it met after death. Penance, after all, was the means by which the living soul was purged of postbaptismal sin. However, the advice and prescriptions set down in the penitentials drew inspiration from a combination of ascetic literature, monastic ethos, and ancient penitential practice as legislated by church councils. Penitentials were guides to present life amendment, not a template for the future satisfaction of sins. In visions of the afterlife, sinners were always warned to undertake penance before time ran out, and in those visions in which the visionary was in personal danger of damnation, they were sent back to earth to confess and make penitential satisfaction there. The exception to this rule was the *Vision of Fursey,* since Fursey's future punishment was anticipated and carried out in his purging in the fire, allowing him to return to earth with no penitential debt owing. Penitentials emphasized that all sins could, with time and effort, be forgiven. Even the most heinous crimes imagined by the penitentials, such as the loss of a child's soul because it was not baptized before death, could be atoned for: "its expiation through penance is possible, since there is no crime which cannot be expiated through penance so long as we are in this body." And "if a cleric is wrathful or envious or backbiting or gloomy or greedy, great and capital sins are these, and they slay the soul and cast it down to the depth of hell. But there is this penance for them."[93] Indeed, penance did more than bring the penitent back to a neutral status: the successful penitent was restored to the status of being "Just."[94] By contrast, it was widely held that only minor sins could be purged in the afterlife and that capital sins that were not expiated before death damned the soul.[95] The salvific scope of the penitentials and of purgatory was therefore conceived to be altogether different.

The problem lies with the argument that suggests that tariffed penance (and relatedly, tariffed Irish law), with its lists of infractions and their corresponding compensations, helps us understand the way sinners made satisfaction for their sins in purgatory. For the proposition to be true we would want to find some evidence that the infractions and compensations listed in penitentials were replicated in visions of purgatory or that making punishment commensurable to the crime was novel. Neither is the case.[96]

Penitential tariffing offered a way to differentiate degrees of infraction, often by distinguishing the level of intent or the social consequences of the transgression. They offered a practical refinement of the larger organizing principles upon which they were founded. The discriminating issue of intent had informed Roman law and was consistently applied to issues of religious justice by bishops in council and by patristic authors. The idea that sins could be individually weighed and satisfaction made in the form of penance or its equivalent in coin was not new. Commenting on the injunction, "redeem your sins in alms," Salvian, writing in the early fifth century, advised his listeners thus:

> Think most diligently of all the faults you have committed. Think of the different kinds of sins. See what you owe for lies; what for cursing; what for perjury; what for carelessness in thoughts; what for foulness of speech; finally, what for every desire and evil wish. Take into account also ... adultery, fornication, impurities, drunkenness, uncleanliness, hateful to God, avarice, the servant of idolatry, and after these sins perhaps others contracted by the shedding of human blood.[97]

Salvian then addressed satisfaction: "When you shall have computed the number of all, weigh the price of each one. After this I do not ask that you give all you have to God for your sins. Give only what you owe." In light of the long history of penances and the rise of penitentials, it is interesting to reflect that Salvian was probably a monk at Lérins at the same time that St. Patrick was there.[98]

The penitentials, like the ascetic literature upon which they were based, determined intent and imagined exceptions and mitigating circumstances within the broader work of classifying sin. The principle of exception and merciful modification of penance had been traditionally enshrined in the personal discretion accorded to bishops in such matters by church councils. A bishop might be guided by precedent but was not bound to it. In light of the extraordinary diversity of penitential satisfactions contained in penitentials, and the evidence of monastic libraries that copied and preserved many different penitentials, it is hard to imagine that penitentials were intended to be applied "automatically." The early visions that incorporate purgatorial depictions invoke God's discretionary power.

Perhaps the most striking difference between the penitentials and purgatory is the method of purgation. In penitentials vice was cured by its contrary virtue, or, as the *Penitential of Cummean* termed it: "Contraries are cured by contraries."⁹⁹ Sinners were encouraged to achieve a spiritual life through behavioral reeducation. This approach arose directly from ascetic literature, ascetic models, and ideally, at least, from ascetic practice. Penances were tailored to fit the strengths and weaknesses of the individual: abstinence for the lustful, fasting for the gluttonous, almsgiving for the avaricious. However, in visions of purgatory, sin was not counterbalanced by an instructive penalty but simply was punished. In hell, in fact, the vice of the sinner was sometimes punished by a corresponding vice or by being immersed in pitch or the river of fire up to the level of the offending member, but we have to wait until the turn of the early eighth century (*Vision of the Monk of Wenlock*) for purgatorial punishments to achieve a similar correlation.

There is correspondence between penitential practices and the confession of sins in visions of the afterlife. Visionary travelers to the otherworld were often informed that their sins were many and of a varied sort.¹⁰⁰ The monk of Wenlock heard his many sins cry out with individual voices: greed, vainglory, falsehood, idleness, sight, stubborness and disobedience, sluggishness and neglect in sacred studies, drowsiness, negligence, carelessness. The monk would need to be purified of all these. Yet when sins were punished in visions, for rather obvious logistical reasons, suffering souls were represented only by a single sin: list, greed, anger, and so on. There is no indication in the visions that sinners would suffer punishments serially for their different crimes. However, establishing categories of sin was important to the authors of both kinds of text. In the *Vision of Barontus*, for example, the damned were assembled (classified) in bundles for the fire, echoing the scriptural image of the tares.¹⁰¹

The sufferings of souls in hell and in purgatory shared a common trait: their mode of punishment was imagined to be outside human control. Yet the emphasis on voluntary self-discipline and voluntary penance is strong in the penitentials and in the long history of Christian penance. Julianus Pomerius instructed priests as follows:

> If, however, they become their own judges and, as though avengers of their own iniquity, here exercise the voluntary penalty of a most severe punishment against themselves, they will exchange eternal torments for temporal; and with their tears flowing from true contrition of heart they will extinguish the flames of the everlasting fire. . . . Therefore, those will more easily reconcile God who . . . bring sentence of voluntary excommunication against themselves; and separating themselves not in heart but in duties from the altar they ministered, mourn for their life as though it were dead. . . .¹⁰²

It was this voluntary aspect of penance that souls in purgatory precisely lacked.

The So-Called Bigotian Penitential

Up to this point I have argued that connections between the penitentials and developing notions of postmortem purgation are either weak or nonexistent. However, there is, in fact, one text that combines a list of penances with a description of postmortem purgation and advice on intercession: the *Bigotian Penitential*. This penitential has not received attention in scholarly discussions about purgatory, yet this is the only penitential that actually presents a textual connection of present penance, postmortem purification, and priestly intercession for penitent souls.

The penitential is not easily dated, although it is generally ascribed to the late eighth or ninth century.[103] The work is profoundly shaped by issues arising from Leviticus. The prologue of the work contains the usual appeal to the authority of the church fathers (especially Jerome) on vices and remedies.[104] There are two elements to the prologue that are specific to this text, however. The first is a rumination on purifying images that were conventionally used to refer to purgatory: 1 Corinthians 3:15 ("though he himself will be saved, but only as through fire.") and Malachi 3:2–4 (the refiner's fire). The second is an unusual digression on the seventh remission of sins (from Cassian, see above) concerning the priest's relationship to the one for whom he seeks to make satisfaction. The prologue is disjointed, but its meaning can be discerned.

The first rumination is intended to support the prologue's earlier point that the wounds of sin can be remedied by means of penance. It continues:

> Hence it is written: *Many are the scourges of sinners*, and not everlasting destruction, according to this (word) of the Lord: *For what does it profit a man if he gain the whole world and lose or cast away his own soul?* Whence it seems to be indicated that some sins involve loss, but not destruction; for he who has suffered loss yet is said *to be saved* though (only) *by fire*.[105]

Having established that some sins do not lead to destruction but are open to penitential satisfaction, the author moves on to the second image, that of gold refined through fire (Mal. 3:2–4). Here it is unclear whether the author intends present purification or afterlife purification; at one point the furnace represents temptation. However, the text then turns to what appears to be a discussion of afterlife purgation

Therefore all must come to the fire—must come to the proving; but truly: It both melts and cleanses the sons of Juda. But if one comes thither many good works will follow. And if he brings but little unrighteousness, that little is dissolved and is cleansed as is lead by fire, and what remains is all gold; and if anyone bears more of lead thither, he is burned more, so that he may be melted down more and yet that some little purified gold may remain. But if anyone comes thither who is all lead, it happens to him as is written: *He is plunged into the deep as lead in a mighty sea.*[106]

There are some obvious parallels with Fursey's vision here: the more he is sinful the more he is burned. The confinement of the damned in the sea (an image from Exodus 15:10 relating to Pharoah's host) is reminiscent of the *Fragmentary Vision of 757* in which troops of demons were seen preparing torments in the sea. In juxtaposing a list of penances with scriptural images of the purging, probative fire, this penitential makes a connection between penances and the soul's experience in the afterlife that is not articulated elsewhere. There is not, however, any suggestion that the purification is like penance, only that penance in this life will cleanse sin that otherwise must be cleansed after death through fire.

The need to be cleansed from the fate of being birthed (original sin) is then addressed:

While we are placed there in the flesh we cannot be to perfection, unless the eighth day come, that is, unless the time of the pure future arrive; on which day, however, he who is a male and acts as a man is cleansed immediately on the coming of that future word. And immediately the mother who bore him is made clean; for he shall receive in the Resurrection his flesh purified from its vices.[107]

This section of the penitential is a direct (and unacknowledged) appropriation of Origen's eighth homily on Leviticus in which Origen had interpreted the levitical teaching on a woman's impurity after childbirth (Lev. 12:1-5) from an eschatological perspective.[108] Coming as it does, directly after the discussion of the saving fire of Corinthians, the addition of this sermon fragment further develops the theme of postmortem purification. Yet the author of the penitential appears aware of the dangers of using Origen, for the comment soon follows that "Therefore also the Lord saith that both the devil and his satellites and all wicked men and transgressors shall perish for ever."[109] And at this point the penitential's author turns to the subject of punishment.

And the Christians, if they have been overtaken in sin, shall be saved after punishments. The nature and extent of these punishments shall, we doubt not, be weighed, as I have said, not only according to the diversity of the faults but also according to the difference in strength of each of the sinners, or of training, or of age.[110]

In weighing the punishments according to the capacity of the sinner, we find penitential philosophy being applied to the saving punishments of the afterlife. Yet, as this passage makes clear, Christians are saved *after* punishments and not *through* them, maintaining Augustine's emphasis that in the afterlife the soul's punishment is distinct from its purification. In this one penitential, then, we encounter a discourse on post-mortem purification that though clumsy is not unthinking. The long list of penances that follow, however, are no different from those in other penitentials in that they advise only on the means of atonement in the present life.

The second digression concerns priests and intercession. Cassian had enumerated twelve remissions of sin, but in the Bigotian prologue, after reaching the seventh remission on the list, there is a long digression, and there is no return to consider remissions eight through twelve. The seventh remission is: "when anyone converts a sinner from the error of his way":

> For thus saith the divine Scripture: He that converteth a sinner from the error of his way shall save his soul from death and has covered a multitude of his sins. This also is written in Leviticus: The priest who offers this and brings about reconciliation, it shall be for his own sin. The priests of the Lord, who preside over the churches, should learn that their share has been given to them together with those whose misdeeds they have caused to be forgiven. But what is it to cause a misdeed to be forgiven? If thou take the sinner, and by warning, exhortation, teaching, instruction, lead him to penance, restrain him from his error, amend him of his vices, and render him such that God may be rendered favourable to him after his conversion, thou shalt be said to cause forgiveness for a misdeed. When, therefore, thou art such a priest and such is thy teaching and thy word, there is given to thee a share of those whom thou has corrected, that their merit may be thy reward and their salvation thy glory.[111]

The fate of the priest and the sinner were bound together in a relationship of mutual dependence. In undertaking to instruct and convert the sinner, the priest might augment his heavenly reward, yet the converse was equally true. The priest risked loss when he worked for a penitent who was not found satisfactory before God. The priest's responsibility for the penitent spoke directly to Fursey's case, and the fate of the sinner he had schooled. Like the sons of Levi who must be refined in the refiner's fire (Malachi is about purification of priests), the intercessor must be purified so that he will present suitable offerings to God.

Finally, in seeking God's intercession for the sinner the priest also entered a penitential state. Later penitentials would spell this out: "As often as we assign fasts to Christians who come to penance, we ourselves ought also to unite with them in fasting for one or two weeks, or as long as we are able."[112] As Bede's formula for appropriate intercessory activities (prayer, almsgiving, tears) indicates, intercession was effective because the intercessor approached the altar also as a penitent. However, as the *Vision of Fursey* so vividly illustrated, the priest who granted absolution too easily might share in the sinner's debt.

A Seventh-Century Watershed?

As the idea of extended postmortem purgation solidified in the imagination of seventh- and eighth-century Christians, we may suppose that Christian attitudes toward death, and in particular the preparations they made for the afterlife, may have shifted. In these centuries, as we have seen, postmortem purgation was still envisaged in terms of time spent in purifying fire, but now, through the imagination of visions, this purgatorial fire began to acquire greater detail as a place where the Christian soul might be detained before achieving perfection. How are we to understand the receptiveness of our seventh- and eighth-century sources to such an idea?

Peter Brown's articles have done more than any other work to suggest an explanation for this phenomenon from a broad historical and cultural perspective.[113] He saw new preoccupations with "merit, sin and identity" in the seventh century, requiring a "different imaginative world," a world in which purgatory emerged out of the contact, overlap, and friction between two basic cultural models' ways of thinking: the Mediterranean "empire of God," with its hopes of radical acts of amnesty, and its contrast with the northern (Irish) focus on individual sins and hope for postmortem purgation.

Prior to the seventh century, Brown has argued, Christians believed or hoped that God occasionally granted "amnesty" for sinners in the afterlife. Brown proposed that this was characteristic of late Roman mentality—the suppliant's hope for, and reliance on, imperial or patron-delivered "amnesty," which would relieve him of distress. This relationship of dependence took on a deeper dimension in the Christian mind when applied to hopes for the mercy of God and the intercession of his saints. Brown proposed that just as imperial amnesty could release the individual from arrest, from poverty, and from other obligations, so divine amnesty could release the individual's soul from the consequences of sin through a single act of mercy. The relationship of patron to client was one of exercised power. Amnesty offered by the ruler was a dispensation for the client from the full force of that power—which, paradoxically, underscored how truly absolute the ruler's power was. Brown argued that imperial power and occasional amnesty was the model for human expectations of the divine in late antiquity before the seventh century and that just as the emperor could cancel taxes, so God could nullify sins.

Brown saw purgatory standing within the "inconclusive juxtaposition" of two imaginative structures: the idea of postmortem purgation and "God's exercise of his sovereign prerogative of mercy."[114] Further, postmortem purgation could only arise, in Brown's view, as the "imperial" model of the amnesty-granting God had weakened, and as "appeals to God's power of *indulgentia* no longer provided a solution for the problem of the un-atoned sins of the faithful."[115]

In the seventh century, Brown argued, visions of the afterlife testified to a shift away from these individual hopes for amnesty toward a model of individual purgation. This shift, he remarked, marked the end of the late antique otherworld and the beginning of what to "us" is a more "familiar" system of otherworld purgation. The impetus for this shift, he argued, came from Ireland, a "land without amnesty," a society whose "own self-image precluded mercy."[116] In Brown's interpretation, Fursey's understanding of the afterlife was of a system of justice in which "every debt must be paid and every wrong atoned."[117] As a result of this Irish thinking, Brown claimed that amnesty was no longer central to views about the afterlife, only a last resort: it was the penitential system that had come to centre stage. As hopes for divine amnesty faded, Brown discovered a "peccatized" world "with the definitive reduction of all experience, history, politics, and the social order quite as much as the destiny of human souls, to two universal explanatory principles, sin and repentance."[118]

Some cautions are in order. First, it should be noted that the waning of older hopes for "divine amnesty" did not converge as neatly with the rise of a northern "peccatized" culture as Brown's model suggests. The possibility of "amnestic" gestures was both argued and put to bed rather earlier than the seventh century. The idea that God could cancel sins (and thus their consequences in the afterlife) was complex in ancient sources and quite variable. Augustine's discussion in book 21 of the *City of God* suggested seven variant Christian opinions about God's "merciful" powers in late antiquity.[119] For example, some Christians believed that all humans would be saved from hell by God's mercy. Other Christians believed that all who participated in the Christian sacraments would ultimately be saved—or at least those who took the Eucharist, or at least those who performed good works. Most radical was the belief of some Christians that God would forgive not only Christian sinners but also the devil and his angels in a final amnesty, leading to the dissolution of hell altogether. All of these views were condemned by Augustine as Origenist, or as tending logically to Origenism. As a result of Augustine's condemnation, and the pastoral concerns that might arise as a result of the publication of such ideas, radical amnestic views of this sort did not disappear entirely but were very much weakened after 400.[120] We find, then, that the idea of God's amnesty as a final release of all Christians from punishment fell out of favour much earlier than the seventh century. As Augustine rather succinctly expressed it, "the more merciful the theory is, the more it contradicts God, and therefore, the farther it is from the truth."[121] God's mercy was not limitless, and it was not for everyone. In the western provinces hope for divine amnesty tended to be displaced to the power of the saints who, like Martin, might be thought to plead, or even act, on behalf of their clients before God at the Final Judgement. The sacrament of baptism remained the one truly amnestic ritual for Christians in the early middle ages. All sins were purged at baptism. Even deathbed rites could not promise this boon. The increasing normalization of infant baptism left most Christians in need of postbaptismal purgation through penance.[122] Thus the "peccatization" of the afterlife that is so evident in the visions of the seventh and eighth centuries had long roots that ultimately extended back to Augustine and to the reception of the Augustinian teaching on original sin.[123]

Conclusion

The reason why purgatorial images began to find their place in visions of the afterlife in the seventh century eludes easy explanation, yet many of the explanations that have been offered in recent scholarship are deeply problematic. The arguments made for a clash of Irish (or northern) culture with that of "Roman" regions does not acknowledge the considerable unifying effect of cultures deeply dependent on monastic, biblical, and patristic literature. At the same time the considerable diversity of practices and rituals that characterized the whole of western Christianity at this time makes for a certain unity in divergence. Furthermore, geographic distance did not imply doctrinal marginality by the seventh century, any more than proximity to Rome guaranteed orthodoxy.

The Augustinian pessimism that is often thought responsible for the expanding rigors of purgation is offset by the optimism of Bede's theology of purgation (in the next chapter). The intense narratives of personal sinfulness portrayed in visions of the afterlife are found already in the fifth and sixth centuries. Gregory of Tours's self-excoriation, examined in chapter 3, must give us pause when considering such attitudes as a peculiarly seventh-century phenomenon.

One might argue that the popularity of Irish penitentials had a profound influence on the way penance was viewed and that they encouraged a greater awareness of the role of the clergy in assessing and administering penitential activity. However, no good case has been made to support the claim that the penitentials were crucial in the development of purgatory. Furthermore, "tariffing" of individualized penalties did not have an analog in visions of purgatory until the ninth century. Indeed, it was not until the *Vision of Wetti* in the early ninth century that a clearly described differentiation of torments finds a place in a depiction of purgatory.

Fursey's vision does indeed appear to have floated the idea of "penitence" in the afterlife, but it is not clear from the text what this comment meant precisely, whether it was conceived as an element in purgation or an alternative to purgation by fire. It was certainly not a notion that held sway in immediately subsequent visions of the afterlife or in the doctrinal foundation that would be developed by Bede. Thus, the claim that the *Vision of Fursey* exemplified a new, penitential direction in afterlife purgation, and that the underlying mechanism of purgatory was directly related to tariffed penance, cannot be shown. That there were debates we can be reasonably sure of, but in the end, the earliest visionary depiction of purgation by fire was closely tied to ascetic and patristic tradition.

6

Purgatory in Bede and Boniface

In the early years of the eighth century, two English monks made important contributions to the development and widespread acceptance of a purgatorial afterlife. Bede was a historian who included visions in his work, including the vision of a layman named Drythelm, but he was also a theologian, a biblical commentator, and a writer of sermons. Boniface's contribution was of a different sort. He recorded an account of a monk's vision that became widely known, and his long career as bishop and missionary did much to disseminate Anglo-Saxon intellectual culture abroad.

Bede and Boniface were more or less contemporaries, having been born in the decade after the Synod of Whitby (664).[1] Both were monks in an age when monks were sometimes extensively employed outside their monasteries, as pastors and missionaries at home and abroad. Bede was a monk who was also an ordained priest, and Boniface was a missionary monk who eventually became a bishop. Their descriptions of purgatory, together with Bede's theological justification for purgatory, helped solidify its place in the Christian afterlife for future generations.

Bede (c. 673–735) was born in Northumbria. He joined the monastery of St. Paul at Wearmouth at the age of seven, later transferring to the joint monastery of Wearmouth-Jarrow as a young man. His physical, spiritual, and intellectual life was lived under the guidance of the Benedictine Rule.[2] His intellectual and historical sensibilities were forged by a post-Whitby, pro-Roman

Northumbria. Bede only rarely left his monastery, but he had access to books, and he wrote copiously[3]: sermons, commentaries, hagiographies, and his most famous work, *Ecclesiastical History of the English People*, completed in 731. In his *History* Bede told the story of Britain's conversion to Christianity from early contacts with Roman Christianity to the seemingly miraculous success of the Roman mission sent by Pope Gregory the Great in 596 to convert the pagan Anglo-Saxons to Christianity and bring the rest of Britain's inhabitants to the joys of Roman order. We now know that much of Bede's story of the conversion was distorted by his intense desire to elevate the importance of the Roman mission in England, but his political vision of a unified Christian nation living happily under Roman order had enormous appeal and political longevity.[4]

At the time Bede was writing, missionary zeal was high. In the closing years of the seventh century, Anglo-Saxons had begun to look to the continent for new converts. On the eastern front of Merovingian Francia they found wavering Christians, and beyond that, especially Frisia, they found pagans. With papal and Pippinid help, missionaries such as Boniface and his predecessor Willibrord would establish new churches in German territories.

Wynfrid, who took the name Boniface, left the supportive company of Anglo-Saxon nuns to take up missionary work on the Continent in 716. After 718 Boniface never returned to England, preferring to live the ascetic ideal of an exile for God. Like Bede, Boniface had become a Benedictine monk at an early age, first at a monastery in Exeter and then at Nursling, and he only left that environment in his forties when he joined the efforts of other Anglo-Saxons, such as his distant relative Willibrord, in the ongoing attempt to convert the Frisians to Christianity. Thereafter his life was that of missionary, church reformer, and church organizer in those German territories that the Franks claimed as a sphere of political influence. He was martyred in 754 at the age of eighty when, after decades of administration and church politics, he returned to the ideals of mission cultivated in the prime of his life. Much of his correspondence with a succession of popes, kings, nuns, and friends has survived, and they give us a uniquely personal view into the ideals and mechanisms of missionary work.[5]

There is no evidence that Bede and Boniface ever met, but they had many friends in common. It is interesting that both writers penned descriptions of purgatory at about the same time. While their accounts differ in some important details, they both appear to have accepted purgatory's place in the Christian afterlife. Neither writer commented that he was introducing something new or speculative, and it is unlikely that either thought he was breaking new ground, so to speak. Indeed, in view of Anglo-Saxon historical loyalty to Rome and St. Peter as representing the authority of the universal church, and their well-honed resistance to any theological deviation deriving from their contact with Christianity in Celtic areas or from pagan beliefs, it is likely that in their view, at least, their descriptions of purgatory were fully orthodox.[6] Both Boniface and Bede introduce new elements and bring new complexity to the topography of the afterlife. Both authors show knowledge of the *Vision of Paul* and Gregory the Great's *Dialogues*, and Bede knew the *Vision of Fursey*. However, it was Bede's positioning of the concept of purgatory in terms of anti-Origenist debate that was to be the most critical contribution of all.

Boniface: The "Vision of the Monk of Wenlock"

Boniface recorded the vision of a monk from the monastery of Much Wenlock in a letter to the abbess Eadburga in 716.[7] It was a tale he had first heard in England from abbess Hildelida and that he had been able to verify personally by talking to the visionary shortly before the man's death.

The monk related that during a violent sickness he had felt his soul leave his body and was carried up by angels until he could see the entire earth surrounded by fire.[8] He observed demons fighting angels over departing souls. He then found himself before a kind of tribunal in which his accusers were personifications of his major vices, and his defenders his paltry virtues. Without any resolution to his fate, his journey continued. He was shown four destinations: upper hell, lower hell, then lower heaven, and upper heaven.[9] The description of the two hells and their relationship to each other is an interesting feature of this vision. In upper hell, souls that looked like black birds were tormented in pits of fire, clinging to the rim of the pits for relief from the heat, weeping and wailing before falling back down into the fire. Their brief respite at the edge of the pit anticipated the refreshment they would receive at the Last Judgementwhen they would be guaranteed "eternal rest."[10] Much is left unsaid about their fate. The *requiem perpetuam*, which they obtain at the Last Judgement, consists of relief from torture. This is not the same as saying that these souls will be saved. If they are to be saved, how have they achieved this boon? It is possible that the author, in envisaging rest from torture, imagined that these souls would simply not exist after Judgement Day—that they would succumb to a second death and be forgotten. This annihilation is a fate that those who will suffer eternally will envy. That is the fate of those in lower hell (*inferno inferior*), a place of eternal torment without respite, where the release of death never comes because the mercy of God does not reach them. It is likely that there is no hope of eternal life in this description of the two hells. The souls there are truly in hell, and the respite enjoyed by those in upper hell is only fleeting.

Leaving the infernal regions behind, the monk journeyed to a fragrant meadow where handsome men enjoy extraordinary happiness. The angels confirmed that this was paradise.[11] Close to this place the monk was shown a scene in which souls were being purified of their minor sins. These souls crossed a river of boiling pitch by means of a log-bridge[12] in order to reach the city of Jerusalem on the other side.[13] Some fell into the pitch but emerged from it "far more brilliant and beautiful" than when they fell in. This progression from filth to purity was accompanied by the angels' explanation that "light sins" were being removed by the "kindly chastisement of a merciful God." Once purified, the souls evidently joined the angels in their work of protecting beautiful souls from demonic assaults.[14]

It is quite clear from this description that the work of purification was accomplished within the confines of heaven, not hell. The fragrant paradise nearby with its handsome men seems to indicate that it is a destination. Yet, at the same time, a great assembly of souls sought to cross the bridge in order to reach the heavenly Jerusalem. As Claude Carozzi has pointed out, positioning purification between paradise and the celestial city makes no logical sense, because it suggests that some souls can stay in paradise while others undergo purification and reach the city.[15] One solution to the unusual topography and itinerary is that the vision was not intended to be understood in a fully linear manner.[16] For example, although the purification takes place in heaven, the river of pitch in which souls are purified is described as the *Tartareum flumen*, which seems to bring the viewer back to hell. The text states that the monk "also saw" the place of purification and the souls crossing the river, just as he "also saw" the fragrant paradise after having seen souls groaning in the pits of lowest hell. Another possibility is that at this point in the text the itinerary owes a debt to the *Vision of Paul* which also situated a place of purification between its description of paradise and the celestial city. The author of the *Vision of Paul* relates that after Paul visited paradise, he was taken down to the second heaven, to the land of promise where the souls of the just, on leaving their bodies, were allowed to rest temporarily. Closer to the City of Christ was the Acherusian Lake, with its whiter-than-milk water, in which the repentant were baptized by the angel Michael who then lead them to the celestial city "alongside those who have never sinned."[17] The precise identity of the men in white who inhabited the fragrant paradise in the monk of Wenlock's vision is still unclear, however. Were these the white-robed righteous who awaited the Day of Judgement when they would receive a second robe, as Pope Gregory had described in the *Dialogues*? Had they already undergone purification or did they not need it? These details were not fully worked out.

One of the more important innovations of the vision is its appropriation of the ancient bridge imagery for the new purpose of representing purgatory. The immediate model for the monk's vision was Pope Gregory's description of the soldier's vision in the *Dialogues*. Gregory had described a bridge crossing a stinking river over which the souls of both sinners and the just attempted to pass. The just souls crossed over the other side, to a heavenly city with dirty suburbs, and the wicked fell into the pitch and remained immersed there. In Boniface's account of the monk's vision, by contrast, all the souls that crossed the bridge were destined for heaven: the souls that are holy cross over with ease, and those who have light vices not yet expunged plunge into the infernal river from which they emerge cleansed. The bridge has retained its probative function but now the division is not between those who are saved and those who are damned, but between those who require purification before they enter God's city and those who can journey there without it. Both the bridge and the river contribute to the sense of motion in this part of the vision. Those who cross the bridge continue their progress toward the city, while those who must be purged are plunged into a flowing river of pitch which temporarily impedes their movement but from which they ultimately emerge. All the souls in this part of the afterlife are moving, whether quickly or slowly, in the direction of their heavenly destination.

Another interesting feature of the purification of souls in this vision is the lack of emotion that attends it. This is evident in the absence of sound. Purification requires a plunge into fiery river, but, as the souls fall off the bridge into the pitch, there are no screams of pain, even though the river is described as "boiling" and the plunge is described as a "chastisement." The souls' progression appears curiously mechanical. No emotion except happiness attends their purification, and thus it is unclear whether they experience pain. The river plunge is represented as only a fleeting obstruction to the joy to be experienced on the other side. By contrast, the vision's emotional register is entirely in the screaming souls in the two hells and in the happiness of the men in white.

The absence of pain would be significant, of course, because it harkens back to a much older conception of purification as painless for the elect.[18] By contrast, in late antiquity most Christian writers were stressing purification's painful attributes. After Augustine there is a chorus of agreement that souls must suffer pain and punishment in order to atone for (original) sin.[19] Caesarius of Arles warned his listeners not to believe reports that the fires of purification would be painless. On the contrary, he argued, pain experienced in the afterlife would be felt many times more intensely than in the present life.[20] Thus, the silence of purification in the monk of Wenlock's vision places it strangely in relation to other vision texts of that era. For example, in the *Vision of Fursey*, Fursey was burned by the touch of a wicked man from whom he had accepted the gift of clothing. He carried the scar of that encounter when he returned to earth and would show it to visitors who wanted to hear his tale. In the *Vision of Drythelm* also, the souls destined to be saved spring back and forth between two extremes of pain. The silence in Boniface's account shares with its model, the soldier's vision in Gregory's *Dialogues*, the silent ordeal by which souls that were saved would reach their heavenly destination.

Purgation appears to occupy time in this vision. Did souls in this place benefit from the intercession of the living? That is unclear. Intercession is not addressed in the purification scene, but it does arise as an important element later in the vision. After the monk had seen the various places of the afterlife, an anecdotal section follows in which the monk identified some of the inhabitants of that place. One of the people he saw was a certain monk who had recently died. The monk of Wenlock had performed funeral rites for this monk and had given a message to the man's brother with whom he shared a bondswoman in common, that the woman should be freed for the repose of his soul. The woman had not been released, and now the monk cried out in deep distress. We are not told where this monk resided in the otherworld. Having lived a life of penitence as a monk, and having received funeral rites on his deathbed, the monk would have been saved from hell, according to the expectations of the day. However, he was in present distress, and the sense of the passage is that if his brother were to release the bondswoman as the monk had desired, then the dead monk would be able to pass into a state of repose. This vignette suggests that there is a place of interim salvation where suffering could be relieved by a significant act of charity performed by someone living. In that respect it is very like the stories of intercession told by Gregory in the *Dialogues*. As for the monk-narrator in Boniface's account, he was instructed to relate his experience to the priest Begga and to confess and expiate his sins under that priest's guidance.

Bede: The "Vision of Drythelm"

Bede recorded Drythelm's vision as an event that had occurred in the 690s.[21] As in the case of the monk of Wenlock's vision, Drythelm's story had been circulating for some time before it achieved written form. According to Bede, the pious layman died one night and returned to life in the early morning hours. He reported having seen a vision that so affected him that he decided to dispose of his property and his wife and enter the monastery of Melrose. Like the monk of Wenlock, Drythelm toured four regions in the otherworld, but unlike the monk of Wenlock's vision in which purification took place within heaven, Drythelm's purgatory was situated in hell.

Purgatory was, in fact, the first destination Drythelm was taken to. There he saw a valley of fire and ice. Bede narrates:

> Both sides were full of souls of men, which were apparently tossed from one side to the other in turn, as if by the fury of the tempest. When the wretched souls could no longer endure the fierceness of the terrific heat, they leapt into the midst of the deadly cold.

Drythelm thought at first that this must be hell, because the souls were in such misery and had no respite from their pain. But his guide later informed him that:

> The valley that you saw, with its awful flaming fire and freezing cold, is the place in which these souls have to be tried and chastened who delayed to confess and make restitution for the sins they had committed until they were at the point of death; and so they died. But because they did repent and confessed, even though on their deathbed, they will all come to the kingdom of heaven on Judgement Day; and the prayers of those who are still alive, their alms and fasting and especially the celebration of masses, help many of them to get free even before the Day of Judgement.

Drythelm was then taken some distance to a place of great darkness where he saw roaring flames "full of human souls which, like the sparks flying upward with the smoke, were now tossed on high and now, as the vaporous flames fell back, were sucked down into the depths." At this point, Dythelm's guide disappeared without explanation, leaving a terrified Drythelm to watch condemned souls being taken down to the pit, and he was threatened by spirits brandishing tongs. Then he saw what appeared to be a bright star approaching; it was his guide who continued with him on their journey until they came to a great wall "endlessly long and endlessly high everywhere." There were no openings in it—no windows or doors. But suddenly Drythelm and his guide were on top of the wall looking down onto "a broad and pleasant meadow." Drythelm reported that "in this meadow there were innumerable bands of men in white robes, and many companies of happy people sat around." Drythelm's first thought was that this was heaven, but his guide, divining his mistake, stated, "No, this is not the kingdom of heaven as you imagine." It was later explained to him that this is the place where "the souls are received of those who depart from the body practicing good works; but they are not in such a state of perfection that they deserve to be received immediately into the kingdom of heaven; nevertheless all of them at the Day of Judgement will enter into the presence of Christ and the joys of the heavenly kingdom." Drythelm was promised that if he lived rightly and simply, he would return to this place after his death. By reference to Bede's writings elsewhere, we can identify this place as paradise.[22] Drythelm's glimpse of heaven, occupied by the perfect, was sensual and elusive: light, soft singing voices and a wonderful fragrance.

The fundamental elements of medieval purgatory are found in the valley of fire and ice. The polarity of torment seems to suggest a middle place—alternatively hot and cold, but neither fully one or the other. Fire and hail and blood feature in apocalyptic passages and may underlie this imagery, although it is possible it was drawn more directly from Jerome.[23] However, the medical condition of fever and chills was also used as an eschatological motif representing divine punishment or hell itself.[24] Oscillating between one moment of pain, intermission, and then pain again is reminiscent of the comment Bede made about the punishment of the whip that strikes the back but then is removed while the next blow is prepared. This intermittent pain he distinguished from the constant torture of the damned.[25]

The intermittent torment suffered by these souls is exacted for inadequate and delayed penance, but, Bede makes clear, the postmortem suffering of these souls can be remedied by the actions of the living. All these souls will attain heaven on Judgement Day: their fate is assured. Their hellish habitation is reminiscent of the souls in the monk of Wenlock's vision of upper hell, except that in Drythelm's vision their future as saved souls is clearly expressed and intercession will aid them. Their condition is further reminiscent of Augustine's comment in his *Enchiridion* that there is a manner of life "neither so good as not to need such helps after death, nor so bad that [prayers] cannot be of benefit."[26] Yet Bede's group of those "not so bad" as to deserve damnation are clearly worse sinners than Augustine's group. They have committed crimes (*scelera*) that they have failed to confess and emend except on their deathbed. For this they must be tried and punished, but they will still be saved. In offering heaven to grave sinners through extended purgation, Bede widened the net of salvation. Was Bede influenced in this by Isidore?[27] Was he influenced by prayers that increasingly universalized prayers for the dead?[28] Or was he perhaps, responding to the appeal of a broader net of salvation, a moderate form of Origenism? This last possibility is discussed further later in the chapter. It is sufficient to note here that Bede's vision of the purgation of sinners is very different from both that in the *Vision of the Monk of Wenlock* and that in the *Vision of Fursey*. Unlike the *Vision of Wenlock*'s upper hell in which souls will only receive future reprieve from eternal torment, Bede's upper hell contains souls whose suffering will be mitigated by intercession and who will be saved at the Last Judgement. While Fursey (in the continental *Vision of Fursey*) was purged painfully for an omission (*delictum*), the souls in Bede's upper hell are being purged for serious crimes (*scelera*) in a distinction that recalls Origen's between those who are instantaneously purified and those who must endure longer purification. Fursey's vision may reflect the view that the fire of purification that immediately precedes the Final Judgement is the fire that is reserved for cleansing the just, fleeting but painful. The fire experienced by Fursey is a fire that feeds on sin, like fuel; its activity on the soul will end when the sin is incinerated off. In Bede, however, the purgation by torture of those with grave faults takes place in a geographical landscape—a deep valley of great length—they are being punished, and their stay will be a long one. These souls have been there since their death, and they will remain there until Judgement Day or until they are aided out of it. Their place of punishment is not the purificatory fire that cleanses the just. When Judgement Day arrives, the fire of purification may still await these scelerous penitents, so that for them also, those minor faults not yet purged will be cleansed.

The happy men in the flowery plain enjoying their mansions in sunlight are those who have done good works but who have not attained perfection. Are they awaiting the fire through which they will pass for purification on Judgement Day? Seemingly not. Elsewhere, Bede indicates that such souls will be purified first and then await Judgement Day.[29] Thus, for Bede, judgement and purgation immediately follow death.[30] This happy group has no need to fear Judgement Day. They are not yet perfect enough to enter heaven, but they are conversing. Is this, as suggested elsewhere in Bede's works, a version of the *schola animarum*, a place where souls will learn the true mysteries of the Trinity?[31] These happy Christians enjoying lectures on the lawn seem to include all pious Christians, including Drythelm, even though he has been married and will live a life of monastic penance to deserve it.

Although the images and even the categories of sinners are different in the accounts of Boniface and Bede, both are representations in which the soul's purification includes chastisement. The punitive purpose of purification, temporary but possibly lengthy, and its accessibility to the actions of the living make these two accounts quite striking testimony to a general acceptance among the clerical elite at least of the idea of protracted purgation in the afterlife. If we accept that Bede's account preserves elements of Drythelm's personal experience, we may suppose that such ideas may have taken longer to come to the attention of laymen. That we are witnessing the cusp of lay awareness is suggested by Drythelm's comment that "I began to think that perhaps this was hell, of whose intolerable torments I had often heard tell," but he is informed by his guide that "this is not hell as you imagine." For Drythelm visits the otherworld expecting to see heaven and hell but is introduced instead to four regions that include purgatory and a pleasant meadow outside the city of God. Drythelm's comment suggests that his vision was grappling with an idea that was new—to Drythelm at least—and that the otherworld was not quite as he had expected to find it, that it represented a challenge to what a layman, the recipient of clerical instruction, "had often heard tell." Still, it is to Bede that we must attribute the vision's theological consistency and fully articulated system of intercession.[32]

What Kind of Purgatory?

Bede's account has attracted attention for its four-part structure and the absence of a conventionally purificatory image in the account.[33] There are no rivers of fire. Referring to the description of upper hell, Le Goff insisted that "this place is one of examination and punishment, not of purification in the proper sense of the word."[34] This is a true characterization of the description, but not a true distinction. We have seen that writers after Augustine accepted his view that purification and correction in the afterlife was achieved through, and possibly in addition to, punishment. Bede's fire and ice purgatory is certainly distinct from the scriptural fire that proves and purifies those who have done good works. The monk of Wenlock's vision, with its description of a purgatorial plunge into the infernal river, offered an image more suggestive of purification, but its narrator also insisted on interpreting it as chastisement.[35] Claude Carozzi, too, balked at labelling Drythelm's upper hell as a place of purification. He noted, as had Jacques Le Goff, that the term "purgatory" or "to purge" is not used in this text.[36] But assuredly the strongest argument for identifying upper hell as purgatory in Drythelm's vision is the fact that by reference to other works, Bede himself clearly did so, and he associated purification with punishment. When he described the forms of intercession that would relieve the fate of those souls, he paraphrased the words he used in his *Homily* and in his *Commentary on Proverbs* in which he discussed purgatory.[37]

In Bede's *Vision of Drythelm*, we are presented with a fully developed depiction of purgatory as a location in the otherworld that is temporary, punitive, but available to the intercession of the church and the intervention of the living. This was not protopurgatory; it was a fully operative system of intercession. In Bede's time, the notion of purgatory as a destination in the afterlife before the Last Judgment had gained currency in some circles, but it may have not been an essential element in what laypeople such as Drythelm would be routinely exposed to in church.[38] One might speculate that Drythelm's vision was precisely the result of a pious layman's first imaginative encounter with what appeared to him to be a relatively new idea.

Readership

Boniface and Bede wrote for monks and nuns, but they also wrote for knowledgable lay audiences. Bede's *Ecclesiastical History* had a fairly immediate audience. The *History* was dedicated to the Northumbrian King Ceowulf (who later resigned his throne and became a monk at Lindisfarne) and, with its account of good kings and bad, was intended to be read with profit by a secular audience. Drythelm's vision had come to Bede circuitously, from a monk-priest named Haemgils who had questioned Drythelm, and whose oral or written account Bede had used.[39] The vision had been told earlier to King Aldfrid who had arranged for Drythelm's entry into the Melrose community, and we are informed by Bede that Drythelm told his story many times to those who visited him and listened with a spiritual attitude. The other works in which Bede discussed purgatory were also known beyond his immediate circle. Bede's *Homily for Advent* (see below), if it was delivered orally at all, may have had a monastic audience to begin with.[40] However, as a written work, Bede's homilies circulated widely in the years after their composition. Boniface requested a copy of Bede's homilies, and they were quickly incorporated into other homily collections in England and on the Continent. Likewise, a copy of Bede's *Commentary on Proverbs,* which may at first appear purely to the tastes of monks and accessible only to the educated elite, was requested, by Boniface no less, as an aid to preaching.

Similarly, Boniface's letter describing the monk of Wenlock's vision, written to the Abbess Eadburga in 716, probably had a fairly broad audience. Letters that have survived from the early middle ages were rarely private documents, and it is clear from the persons writing and receiving this letter, and from the enormous length and detail of Boniface's description, that the letter conveyed information to a larger audience than just Eadburga herself. We learn from the opening lines that Eadburga had requested the account from Boniface and thus that she already knew about the monk's vision. She knew also that Boniface could provide more details. Boniface explains that he had recently spoken to the monk and that the monk had told him of a number of visions, many of which he could no longer recall. Boniface had heard the man's account in the company of "three pious and venerable brethren." It would appear, then, that the account had been rehearsed many times before Boniface heard it and that at least on one occasion the vision was repeated before a small audience of monastic notables. It is likely that the account was a well-integrated version of a number of the man's visionary experiences and thus represents a viewpoint that was considered notable, privileged, and orthodox. Boniface's purpose in writing the account, and Eadburga's purpose in requesting it, must have been the edification of the community she ran and as an instruction for them in otherworldly matters. Boniface's relationship with Eadburga and her community was one of enormous trust. Boniface relied on this impressive cadre of holy women to provide materials and prayers for his mission. To them he stood in the relationship of friend, mentor, and spiritual advisor. These were people he cared about and would not mislead. It is significant, then, that no caveats about this vision are expressed, no suggestion along the lines of "take this for what it is." Rather, the vision is related in an authoritative manner to a religious person whom he esteemed.

The media in which these visions of the afterlife were disseminated, then, presumed a larger audience than the monastic and may represent a shift or period of transition in which purgatory—an idea that had a significant monastic tone—found a broader audience. There is no indication in either case that the narrative was supposed to be restricted in audience or to be read with caution. As we move to Bede's theological perspective on purgatory in the next section it is particularly important to bear this in mind. When Bede set down Drythelm's vision in writing, he authorized it, literally, with his theological credentials. Bede was quite willing to edit the vision narratives he incorporated into his work, like the *Vision of Fursey*, as we saw in the previous chapter. Thus Bede's narrative should not be viewed as distinct in authority from his sermons or his biblical commentaries even if, being a more literary medium, the visions may have had a different audience in mind. Bede did not dismiss the authority of visions or their importance for religious instruction; properly edited, he embraced them. In a figure so widely respected for his historical craft, it is sometimes difficult to reconcile Bede's "medieval" attention to the instructive value of the supernatural in visions. We must not cleave Bede the theologian from Bede the recorder of visions.[41] Bede included Drythelm's vision within his own work without apology. Evidently he viewed it as instructive, and in recording it, he guaranteed its theology also.

Bede's Theology of Purgatory

In previous chapters we have sketched a variety of Christian opinions, views, and interpretations on the subject of purgatory-what it was and what passage through it entailed. Undoubtedly, some held their views on purgatory as a matter of personal belief, others were merely summarizing the views of others, and yet others were speculating. But before the Gregorian *Dialogues* indicated a particular view of postmortem purgation *credendus est*, no earlier author expounded a particular interpretation of purgatory as a matter of doctrine—a belief required of all Christians.[42] Many earlier writers did, in fact, write on purgatory as a way of refuting alternative ideas about salvation. But it is not until Bede that we encounter a view of purgatory that positions it theologically as an explicit expression of orthodox belief. This was Bede's contribution: to frame purgatory as an orthodox response to heresy.

Homily for Advent

Bede wrote his collection of *Homilies* in the 720s or early 730s. In the *Homily for Advent*, purgatory is presented quite simply as fact:

> But in truth there are some who were preordained to the lot of the elect on account of their good works, but on account of some evils by which they were polluted, went out from the body after death to be severely chastised, and were seized by the flames of the fire of purgatory [*flammis ignis purgatorii*]. They are either made clean from the stains of their vices in their long ordeal (*examinatione*) up until Judgement Day, or, on the other hand, if they are absolved from their penalties by the petitions, almsgiving, fasting, weeping, and oblation of the saving sacrificial offering by their faithful friends, they may come earlier to the rest of the blessed.[43]

Bede sketched here the essential components of purgatory in a form that would certainly be recognizable to later medieval theology, possibly even to the extent of using purgatory as a noun.[44] The fire seizes on the soul's sin to purge it; the examination or ordeal it endures is long and will last until the Final Judgement unless the intercession of friends succeeds in bringing it an earlier rest. The list of pious activities performed by the living recalls the explanation given by the angelic guide in Drythelm's vision: alms, fasting, and the celebration of the Mass can aid in the release of the soul. Added to this list is weeping—a sign of repentance and thus the sincerity of the petition or prayer.[45] It is clear from this account that purification of souls was obtained either by a long process of painful purification (that is, it was not instantaneous) or by the petitions of their friends. This either/or formulation had the potential to mislead since it suggested that some souls might evade punishment in the afterlife if their friends petitioned for it. Carroll suggested that Bede rectified this mistake in his *Commentary on Proverbs*, presumably a later work.[46] In the *Commentary*, Bede confirms that punishment awaits less-than-perfect souls, even those helped by their friends' petitions. This places Bede's writings in line with Augustine's view that souls are sinful and must be punished, even if only briefly.

Bede wrote his *Homiliary* in his later years, at a time when he was working on his *Ecclesiastical History*, with its account of Drythelm's vision in the final book.[47] The sermon's theme was God's grace, commenting on John 1:15–18: "This was he of whom I said to you, 'He who is to come after me ranks ahead of me because he was before me. And from his fullness we have all received grace for grace.'"[48] Bede noted the particular importance of the phrase "grace for grace," *gratiam pro gratia*. He writes that John "is testifying that we have received a two-fold grace, namely one grace in the present and another for the future." The present grace, he explains, is faith, love, and good works, all of which are accomplished only with God's help. The future grace is eternal life that will be the reward of receiving the first grace (of faith, love, and good works.)

In its scriptural context, the meaning of the enigmatic phrase "grace for grace" was that the first grace was the law of Moses, the second was Christ, but the phrase was subsequently reinterpreted. Augustine, who was Bede's source here, took this phrase to refer to faith as the first grace and "grace for grace" to be eternal life.[49] This interpretation recast the scriptural phrase into a context that was eschatological. The result was to emphasize that even the means (faith, love, and good works) by which the Christian may seem to "merit" eternal life are supplied by God's grace, and therefore eternal life, being a reward for these qualities, is also a grace—a grace built on another grace, as it were. The discussion of merit and grace signals that access to heaven is to be found through the sacraments and through predestination as one of God's elect. For Bede, as for Augustine, the issue of grace, and the grace needed even for good works, distinguished orthodox thinking from the views of Pelagius and, more importantly, those of Origen.[50] They are not named, but their presence is felt by reference to the terms of the debate. At this point in the sermon, however, Bede takes a slightly different trajectory. Bede explains that Christ will introduce the elect to the vision of God, not just at the Last Judgement, but indeed as soon as they have left their bodies. It seems that Christ will then come to them and instruct them in the afterlife, "after they have been released from the corruption of the flesh," because Bede states that Christ will reveal to the elect an understanding of the Trinity in which the mortal Jesus will be acknowledged as part of the Trinity.[51]

Bede ends the homily with a passage that is not found in Augustine. He states that there are many just people in the church who "immediately gain the blessed rest of paradise" but that there are a few who were "preordained to the lot of the elect on account of their good works," but who became polluted on account of some evil and must be purged by fire. It is interesting to note Bede's optimism—many will enter heaven immediately, but only a few will need to undergo purgatorial suffering.[52] Once these souls have passed into the next life, they must rely on the faith, love, and good works of the living who, in making up any previous deficiency, earn the release of these souls from purgatory. Presumably, the "faithful friends" who undertake such good works on behalf of the dead also receive grace by doing this good work.

Thus Bede explained that it was the lot of some souls to suffer a long period of chastisement until the Last Judgment. That trial would ultimately cleanse them, and it might be shortened by the charitable intervention of their friends. These souls have a longer or shorter stay in this place, but they will eventually join the blessed. Thus Bede described here a system that is fully recognizable as purgatory, not just because he delineated an interim time for souls, but because he described the mechanisms by which that stay could be shortened and affirmed that the final destination of these souls was heaven. Bede's description is important because it clearly articulated the function of this place, the reasons why a soul might end up there, and the means by which it might be released. In so doing Bede formulated a very different idea from the idea of hell in which souls in torment may receive temporary refreshment.[53]

Commentary on Isaiah and the Proverbs of Solomon

Bede's eschatology, and his mental framing of purgatory in particular, was intimately connected with his determination to refute Origen. He did this by emphasizing the eternity of hell.[54] His approach can be appreciated in two works: a letter containing a mini-treatise on Isaiah addressed to Bishop Acca of Hexham and his *Commentary on Proverbs*. The letter to Acca was a response to a particular difficulty. The *Commentary on Proverbs*, by contrast, was a densely argued work. It was probably intended for a more restricted audience than the homilies and letter, although we know that it was subsequently viewed as an aid to preaching.[55] In the *Commentary on Proverbs*,

Bede presented purgatory as the antithesis of Origen's teaching on universal salvation.

Bede's engagement with Origen's eschatology can be seen, obliquely, in his letter *On Isaiah*.[56] In about 716, Bede had found himself having to correct his bishop for having misunderstood comments he had made on hell in another work, his *Commentary on Samuel*. Bishop Acca of Hexham queried Bede, and Bede clarified his position based on his reading of Isaiah 24:21–23. In so doing, Bede added a footnote to a long, august, and sometimes contentious patristic tradition of commentaries on the book of Isaiah. The passage debated was a key text for those who refuted the eternity of hell. Isaiah 24:21–23 states:

> And on that day it shall come to pass that the Lord will visit upon the host of heaven on high, and upon the kings of the earth who are upon the earth, and they shall be gathered together into a gathering of one bundle into the pit, and they will be shut up there in prison, and after many days they will be visited, and the moon will blush, and the sun will be confounded, when the Lord of hosts will reign on Mount Zion, and in Jerusalem, and will be glorified in the sight of his elders.[57]

Earlier works had debated the meaning of the visitation of the sinners in the pit or prison. When had this visit occurred? To what purpose? Could this passage imply that souls in hell would be released at some future time? Jerome, Augustine, and Bede would all agree that the answer to this last proposition is no. Bede looked to Jerome's *Commentary on Isaiah* to aid him in interpreting this passage, accepting Jerome's suggestion that "they will be visited" meant that these souls would not receive relief or rescue, but rather would be "visited" with eternal punishment.[58] In his quotation from the work, Bede included Jerome's comment that the passage may appear to support the view of his "friends" (enemies) "who grant penance to the devil and to demons, because after some time they are visited by the Lord." The "friends" Jerome refutes are followers of Origen, but in this case quite pointedly Rufinus.[59] By including this passage from Jerome, Bede showed not only his knowledge of the Origenist context but also his interest in preserving it.

Bede's letter offered a division of scriptural statements concerning God's wrath and mercy according to how they related to the final days. In particular, statements that suggested that God would be merciful were to be understood as relating to present times "in which the saints sing to the lord of mercy and judgement," and did not refer to the future life.[60] When scripture stated, "In wrath you will receive mercy," Bede wanted his reader to understand that this referred to the present age in which God might punish but would also be merciful to the penitent. This was a neat way to dispose of scriptural statements that might otherwise be interpreted as a reprieve for sinners from eternal punishment in hell. The only hiatus in torture experienced by the damned would be when they were removed temporarily from hell to join the general resurrection when their souls would be joined with bodies so that they could be consigned again, and for all eternity, to the pit. Yet this dire prediction is softened for those who repent before death. Turning his concern once again to his reader, he urges penance because those who do not bear the "adversities of penalties" of penance essentially deny eternal life. "But let him rather be diligent," Bede cautions, "and take care for himself and for his own, so that, once they have been purified from faults and adorned with good works, they may await the last day."[61] Thus Bede closes his letter expecting that the repentant sinner will take care of both himself and his own *(suimet suorumque)*, a community-driven sentiment that, as we shall see, was important to the way he viewed the path to purification, both before and after death. Once cleansed, those souls will await the last day. Echoing Gregory's *Dialogues*, Bede envisaged that purified souls would indeed rest before the momentous events of the general resurrection.

Bede's eschatology never lost sight of Origen whose teaching appeared vivid to him. Nor did he ever seem to relax his determination to protect fellow Christians from the "plough of heretical deception." In his *Commentary on Proverbs*, Bede returned to his task of asserting the eternal nature of hell. Except in this single work he made a conceptual leap that was new: he linked the eternity of hell with the existence of purgatory.

"When the wicked man dies, his hope perishes" (Prov. 11:7) provided Bede a proof text allowing him to assert, in the strongest terms, that Origen had been wrong in his view that the wicked would be saved.[62] The wicked (the "homo impius"), in Bede's view, would certainly not be saved.[63] He went on to describe a situation in which he makes clear that in alluding to purgatory, he is proposing a view that is antithetical to Origen's view: "Nevertheless, it should be noted," he writes *(notandum autem)*, that if the wicked will not be saved, "still there are those" *(sunt tamen qui)* who die with slight sins attached who can be absolved after death.[64] It is interesting to ponder the choice of conjunctions by which Bede cements a refutation of Origen to a consideration of purgatory because it suggests that Bede viewed purgatory's existence as a response and as a correction to the theological proposition of universal salvation. Purgatory is set up in this passage as antithetical to the idea of universal salvation—and posited as an alternative to it. Bede evidently did not acknowledge, or know, Origen's complete views of purgation and purification; these would at least have complicated the matter. For Bede, the opposition of an orthodox view of hell as eternal and a heterodox view of it as possibly being redemptive is fully exploited in order to make his case for purgatory. Thus these short conjunctive phrases are enormously telling because they reflect on Bede's frame of reference; they signal how purgatory's existence was viewed, at least in Bede's mind, as a response and correction to a particular theological proposition that was associated in the West with Origen—that of a noneternal hell that was linked to the idea of universal salvation.[65] It is not at all certain that Bede had any source of knowledge about Origen beyond what he could have gleaned secondhand from Jerome, Augustine, Rufinus, or Gregory the Great.[66] It is unlikely he knew Origen's works in their Greek form.[67] Yet he was aware of a distinctive but perhaps not obvious feature of Origen's view of purgation—that the wicked would be released long after Judgement Day—and he refuted it.[68]

Bede's emphasis on the power of intercession in these descriptions may also be related to his anxiety about alternative, cosmic notions of salvation. We have seen that an important image for both theological and visionary texts was the fire that is fuelled by sin. The idea behind this image is that sin attaches to the soul like a stain but is burned off when the soul comes into contact with the fire of purgation. This image suggests that cleansing the soul is an automatic function of a cosmic process. Logically, the fire will burn out once the fuel of sin is exhausted. This image, with its philosophic and theological heritage, had the potential to be viewed as an expression of universal salvation, since the fire tests each soul and removes that which hinders it from unity with the divinity. Conversely, the idea that the job of the fire of purgation can be adjusted by human and sacramental activity—by intercession—produces a fire that is different in its function and operation. Bede linked intercession with the fire of purgation and thus removed from it the capacity to burn sin automatically as a kind of universal barrier through which all souls pass. In its place he emphasized that the fire of purgation was a tool for spiritual cleansing that was operated by divine agency—a punitive fire that can be mitigated by human activity under the direction of the Church. This very fundamental change in the way the fire is viewed once intercession is so clearly linked to it aided Bede in building his anti-Origenist perspective on purgation.[69]

The thread of ideas that connected the rejection of universal salvation and a noneternal hell to the rise of a more fully developed notion of purgatory is probably lost in the paucity of document survival in the early middle ages. But Bede made the connection very clear in his *Commentary*. In Bede we have the evidence that the rise of purgatory in the West could be viewed as a direct response to, and repudiation of, universal salvation and the Origenist views of purgation that had supported it. Repudiation of universal salvation provided purgatory with a theological justification. Bede, and perhaps others, saw purgatory as a positive response to, and clarification of, Origen's unacceptable but possibly appealing theological idea. In so doing, Bede moved beyond Augustine's disapproval of the lax views of salvation circulating in his time to point the finger directly, and only, at Origen. Indeed, as if to underscore the importance of this connection, Bede named Origen in his text, breaking ranks with some medieval authors who avoided even mentioning the heretic's name.[70] Origen had opened the door to the ultimate salvation of all souls. Bede's purgatory, with its ability to purge even serious crimes, by contrast (as described in Drythelm's vision above), offered salvation to many souls: an assurance to Christians that they would be admitted to heaven if in life they partook in the sacraments, confessed their sins, and expressed willingness to do penance. After death they could continue their path to salvation through pain in purgatory and through the charitable offices of living friends who could offer prayers, tears, alms, fasting, and masses. Purgatory was, in essence, a highly limited and circumscribed response to the appeal of universal salvation: it was an orthodox variation on universalism. None of the postmortem remedies mentioned by Bede for imperfect souls were new; each had found a place in earlier literature.[71] (Bede's reliance on the charitable offices of friends that he saw as so intrinsic to purgatory, for example, is examined further below). However, Bede combined the Gregorian fourfold distinction of souls with purgatory, and purgatory with the postmortem efficacy of the prayers and the Mass.[72] In so doing, Bede made the connection between prayers for the dead and the fire of purgatory in a way that Augustine had failed to do, but which Isidore of Seville and Julian of Toledo had seen.[73] Furthermore, Bede's account of effective intercession elevated the contribution of the individual intercessor—thus distinguishing that activity from the general prayers for the dead intoned by the priest in church. Not only was the existence of purgatory now made very clear, but also the means of escaping it, or at any rate escaping from its full intensity and duration.

Set alongside the *Vision of Drythelm*, in which even the most serious sinners could be saved providing they repented before death, Bede's theology of purgatory cast a wider net of salvation than many of his sources had envisaged. Perhaps Bede was confronting not just Origen, but his own universalizing desires; opening salvation to most Christians, while expressing the most orthodox, anti-Origenist sentiments. In such a context, Bede's emphatic repudiation of Origen may have been something more than a simple statement of orthodox belief: it raised the specter of Bede's own personal optimism and longing. Bede's modified universalism proved popular and flexible to diverse audiences.

The new "universalism" would prove useful in the missionary activities that both Bede and Boniface identified with.

Bede's contribution to early medieval purgatory was vital to the way it would be understood by subsequent generations.[74] In Bede, two discourses that only seemingly belonged together—prayers for the dead and relief from purgatory—were fully expressed. Bede's work provided not just a theological justification, but a justification rooted in antiheretical orthodoxy.[75] While varied opinions and interpretations of eschatology may have circulated (both Acca of Hexham and Drythelm were represented as confused), still Bede could insist that the wicked would suffer eternally and that hell was closed off from any remittance. The "impious" would go to hell, but the "scelerous" could still be saved. Bede's authority as a scholar and holy man, the dissemination of his works (particularly those in which purgatory was discussed), his attachment to the missionary objectives of prominent Anglo-Saxons abroad, as we shall see in the next chapter, and the importance of a rhetoric of certainty places his views of purgatory at a crucial moment in the history of Anglo-Saxon and Continental Christian belief and practice.

Friendship, Gift-Giving, and Intercession in Bede

We have seen that Bede firmly believed that intercessory prayers could benefit the soul in purgatory. This belief had practical consequences. Bede envisaged that the fasts, alms, prayers with weeping, and masses would be undertaken by a Christian's "faithful friends."[76] Who were these *amici fideles*? What was expected of them? And what was the relationship between the request for the prayers of "friends" and gift-giving practices in a religious culture?

Classical antiquity offered fine models for understanding the ideals of friendship and gift-giving.[77] Cicero and Seneca in particular wrote works on these subjects that were much admired in antiquity and that set the stage for the later development of a Christian ethos.[78] Cicero, for example, had much to offer the medieval reader in understanding the codes and expectations of friendship and patronage. As he tells us in his book *On Friendship*, "the Latin word for friendship—*amicitia*—is derived from that for love—*amor*."[79] Friendship arises from mutual affection and a recognition of mutual virtue and "from a natural impulse rather than a wish for help." It was a sentiment repeated in monastic literature: "the grace of friendship in its fullness and perfection can only survive among perfect men of like virtue," wrote Cassian.[80] But in Bede's time, as in Cicero's time, friendship had many facets and advantages, including the desire for help and for benefits.[81] Early medieval sources record a wide array of relationships that were described as exhibiting bonds of *amicitia* and for which love was not the foremost impulse. There were the formal friendships, called "friendship alliances" by scholars, that were concluded between peoples or parties who had not displayed notably friendly activities prior to the agreement.[82] The strategic use of gifts to consolidate such friendships points to the pragmatic nature of these bonds.[83] Such political friendships lay at one extreme of friendship. At the other extreme were those friends who clearly knew one another well, or were kin, who expressed their friendship in the language of longing, desire, and love and whose effusiveness exceeds most modern expectations of friendship.[84] Cicero had insisted that virtue was the bond of true friendship and that its sign was loyalty. In the Christian world that virtue was faith, and loyalty accompanied it: *amici fideles* were friends who were both loyal and of the faith. For such friendships, personal acquaintance was not necessary: a man's status, or virtue, as a Christian could be sufficient to nurture a feeling of friendship from strangers. In that sense, Christian sentiments about virtue and fame were very much like those expressed by Cicero. Telling different forms of friendship apart is not often easy. Many types of friendship were accompanied by the giving and receiving of gifts whose material value might be great or small, but whose value as a token of friendship was often made explicit, and whose value derived in great measure from the status of the person who gave it.[85] Friendship and gifts went together. And we may also now add, so did friendship, gifts, and preparations for the afterlife. But who were these *amici fideles* who would supply the tears, the fasts, and the masses, and what lies behind Bede's specification that friends must do this duty?[86]

In order to answer these questions we must consider Bede's social environment. Bede lived almost his entire life in a monastery, and it would be natural to seek his closest acquaintances among the monks, priests, and even bishops who lived in such communities. If by "friends" Bede intended to refer to those he knew most intimately, that is to say, fellow monks and priests, he could have made that clear by using the usual term for a fellow monk, *frater*, or he could have cited the monastic *familia*. But he did not. As Brian Patrick McGuire pointed out in his study, *Friendship and Community*, the Benedictine Rule emphasized relationships of hierarchy rather than of peers.[87] In this, it may be further said, the rule did not differ significantly from norms outside the cloister.[88] So Bede does not appear to have been restricted to fellow monks when he wrote of "friends."

Bede's social network was not particularly confined by his monastic profession. Wearmouth and Jarrow were centres of learning, culture, and possibly trade. They were probably already centres of hospitality—for pilgrims and for travelers—and may have provided accommodation for lay as well as clerical visitors. The monks and priests there served the local community in a pastoral capacity. Bede also traveled in a limited way; he had spent some time at the episcopal monastery of Egbert, Bishop of York, and he was on friendly terms with the monks at the island monastery of Lindisfarne, forty miles to the north.[89] It seems likely that he personally knew King Ceolwulf of Northumbria to whom he dedicated his *Ecclesiastical History*, and his long list of correspondents is well known. So it is possible to imagine that Bede's landscape of friendship might be broad indeed and that he would have expected to find friends among secular and religious leaders outside his community. Indeed, it has been shown that some Christian authors reserved the term *amici* to designate classical, secular connotations of friendship.[90]

Another factor to consider is Bede's indebtedness to Augustine's *Enchiridion*, which states that "Nor is it to be denied that the souls of the dead find solace from the piety of their living (*suorum viventium*), when the sacrifice of the mediator is offered for the dead or alms are given in church." In fact, Augustine referred to the piety *suorum* (which meant "of their own people," but which is often translated as "of their friends").[91] Indeed in his *Commentary on Proverbs*, in the passage that paralleled that in the *Homilies*, and in his letter to Acca concerning Isaiah, both cases in which he may have had Augustine's text before him, Bede used *suorum* just as Augustine had. But in his *Homily for Advent*, Bede substituted the prayer *amicorum fidelium* for *suorum viventium*. What is the significance of this change in the *Homilies*? Was his use of the prayers of "faithful friends" in his *Homilies* intentional? Was it a revealing slip? Or did he simply view the terms as synonymous? In any event, in changing Augustine's "own people" to "faithful friends" in the *Homily for Advent*, Bede fixed the meaning of Augustine's term as "friends."

Bede did not live in the same social environment as Augustine. In understanding a man's "own people" as referring to "friends," he would have understood the social context of that friendship very differently. Presumably this new language did not rule out actions performed by those bound to the dead person by different ties of affiliation like slaves, followers, or family since the broader meaning of *amicitia* and the Old English *freond* also had the meaning of kin.[92] Yet, when referring to kin, Bede most often used the term *familiaritas* (thus, McGuire). So in appealing to friends rather than one's kin, Bede seems to challenge the trend in the early middle ages of having kin and subordinates fulfill these duties.[93] That is to say that in referencing friendship, Bede appears to shift the burden of that duty from the place where it generally resided. Most often, according to McGuire, Bede used the term *amicitia* to refer to political associations in which "friendships give benefits, rewards, gifts and concrete material help," using it "almost as a synonym for *beneficia*."[94] Terminologically, then, it is political friendship that most closely explains Bede's assertion that friends can bestow benefits and help, and this is important as we consider friends' duties with regard to the afterlife: friends are those who will act for you because they are impelled by social bonds and hierarchical obligations to do so and who are friends because they can be relied upon to act.

Finally, the request that one made of these faithful friends was that they petition God for mercy. These friends must be worthy to approach the altar. The gift that they bring is themselves, their prayer, and the sacrifice of the Mass. On a personal level they must feel a genuine penitential stirring in the soul. Bede would certainly have kept the liturgical aspect of these acts of friendship in view. A gift must be acceptable to the recipient. For example, in his chapter on friendship, Cassian three times brought his reader's attention to the passage in Matthew about bringing gifts to the altar: "So greatly, then, does our Lord wish us not to treat someone else's annoyance as if it were nothing that, if our brother has anything against us, he will not accept our gifts—that is, he will not permit us to offer him our prayers—until by a speedy act of reparation we remove the annoyance from his mind, whether it has been conceived justly or unjustly."[95] God accepted gifts (i.e., prayers) only if the person offering them was in personal harmony with those around him: that is, by definition, acceptable prayers were those of friends.

Another way to approach Bede's meaning is to look at his own preparations for death. To whom did he entrust the masses and almsgiving that would aid his soul's progress?

We have an account of Bede's last hours in a letter penned by a later abbot of Wearmouth-Jarrow named Cuthbert. Cuthbert had been one of Bede's pupils and by his own account was present at Bede's death.[96] His letter, written about 760 in response to Cuthwine's request, is simple, moving, but also intensely literary. There are many quotations from scripture and from the psalms. But Cuthbert includes enough details to suggest that he based his information on good recollection or records of some sort.

Cuthbert tells us that as death approached, Bede asked him to fetch "the priests of our monastery." When they arrived he distributed to them some personal items and asked that each of them say masses and prayers for him after his death. These priests are not named in the letter, nor were they such intimates that they naturally formed part of the huddle of people attending Bede in his last hours. Bede had called for priests, and according to Cuthbert, Bede made arrangements for the postmortem ceremonies himself.[97]

Bede's requests were accompanied by gifts to the priests who would say masses for his soul. Bede owned certain treasures that he kept in a little box: pepper, napkins, and incense (*piperum, oraria et incensa*). These he described as "little presents which God has given me": *munuscula, qualia mihi Deus donavit*. The priests promised to say the masses, and they all wept. This distribution of items to the priests and the request for prayers and masses prompt comparison with the later medieval practice of paying for masses, an economic system that allowed laypeople also to participate in rescuing loved ones from purgatorial pains. We may ask whether Bede distributed these items (which he had received as gifts) for the personal use for the priests, for their professional use, or for further distribution as alms? It seems to me that at least the pepper was most likely intended for the priests' own treasure boxes—that they were gift-payments to the priests for the services they were about to undertake. Pepper was a luxury commodity in the early middle ages, although as a recent article has pointed out, it was not the most rare of spices.[98] The pepper may have been for his personal use to flavour food or as a commodity that could be regifted. Pepper is often mentioned as a gift-item in Anglo-Saxon letters. For example, the missionary Lull sent frankincense, pepper, and cinnamon as "little gifts" to Abbess Cuniberga around 740.[99] The gifts accompanied a request Lull made of her regarding two freedmen who had once belonged to his father. Napkins could have liturgical uses, but the context suggests that these were a personal accessory (why else were they in his personal box?). Bede was a priest and thus may have had use for liturgical accessories, but we have no evidence that Bede performed services outside the monastery, so why have them among his personal possessions? Incense was used to accompany prayer in church,[100] but this could have been stored in the church or vestry. It is more likely that the incense was used for his own cell as an aid to meditation, since we know that Bede had allotted a particular place in his cell for prayer, and indeed it was not uncommon at this time for monk-priests to have a small altar in their cell.

Strictly speaking, monks were not permitted to own personal items under the Benedictine Rule, not even books and pens. This may not be quite as damning an infringement of the monastery's rules as may at first appear, if we take to heart the cautions of Patrick Wormald and other scholars about considering any English monasteries to be exclusively Benedictine at this date.[101] However Cuthbert relates that Bede identified them as gifts that God had given him: *qualia mihi Deus donavit*. They may have been given to him in the context of pious gift-giving or as a gift for prayers he had said for someone else: a kind of pepper-for-prayer exchange. It would appear that some small gifts constituted a special category, exempt from regulations about private property.

In the past decade, religious gifting has received some belated attention from early medievalists: Bernhard Jussen and Florin Curta in particular have recently addressed the vocabulary of the gift in the early medieval West.[102] According to Jussen, the term *munus* (for which our source has a diminutive) expressed an unequal power relationship—a gift relating to human existence as God's creation, a gift that was not intended to be reciprocated, and in Jussen's words, a word used to denote "a wholly free, unmerited transaction."[103] This meaning does not translate well to this particular description since the passage relates to specific objects that must have been given to Bede by a human hand. God's gifting, in this context, must be understood as being at some remove—perhaps in the sense of their being items connected with church matters. When Cuthbert noted that Bede "distributed" them to the priests, he used a term that was common to legal wills.[104] And Anglo-Saxon bequests almost always expected a service in return from beneficiaries; here the form of service is clearly expressed as prayers and masses.[105]

It is also clear from other sources that masses were said on behalf of the living as well as the dead and that gifts routinely accompanied such requests. Bishop Torthelm of Leicester wrote to Boniface in 737, stating that he was sending him a small gift as a pledge that his community would remember Boniface in the celebration of Mass and in their daily prayers.[106] Thus relationships between religious people were consolidated in life through exchange of gifts and masses, in the hope that when death intervened, there was no suspension of activity.

It would be naive not to view Bede's distribution of gifts for what it was: a compensation for the masses and prayers that the priests would undertake and an exchange of gifts for masses that friends already engaged in during their lifetimes. And Bede's gifting *does* have to do with reciprocity since Bede prepaid a debt that he hoped to incur. Giving items that had real value—rather than token value suggests that in an exchange that crossed the boundary of death, a service of real burden was being imposed on the priests. That this was a burden and not an act confined to some romantic, altruistic[107] sense of friendship further illuminates Bede's statement that friends would work for a soul's release from purgatory.

Furthermore, I do not think that the fact that Bede gave gifts rather than coin to pay for masses is a relevant distinction here. In the early eighth century coinage was not as plentiful as it was by the end of the century, so gifts were often payment in this period. Nor did coinage always appear to have negative connotations. Bede tells a tale of the noble nun Earcongota, daughter of King Eadbald of Kent, who was evidently quite "the gold coin"!

Earcongota had a vision of her imminent demise: men in white robes entered the monastery of Brie and, when questioned, replied (referring to Earcongota), "We have been sent to bring away with us the gold coin (*aureum... nomisma*) that was brought here from Kent."[108] And when Bugga wrote to Boniface in 720 she asked him to offer masses for the soul of a dead relative, sending along fifty *solidi* and an altar cloth.[109] The fifty *solidi* were undoubtedly a pious offering akin to almsgiving, not a personal gift to Boniface, but the gift was still being made. Statements of friendship and gift-giving removed any suspicion of simony from these requests. But in any case, a theology of sacred commerce gave a framework for pious Christians to understand their own giving and getting.[110]

Gifts clearly imposed a heavy obligation on the recipient. Herefrith's account of St. Cuthbert's last hours revealed that Cuthbert was very concerned that he might have accepted gifts for which he had made no return and that he relied on a priest named Beda to keep a mental tally of them all.[111] The status of gift exchange weighed heavily on a person who was about to die.

I do not want to obscure entirely the element of personal, sentimental friendship in such matters,[112] but time and again it is the usefulness of friends that is praised in sources. At the death of Wilfrid of Ripon in 709, an intimate, Abbot Acca of Hexham, "celebrated a private Mass daily for the repose of [Wilfrid's] soul and had every Thursday, the day of his death, kept as a feast just like Sunday." Such testimony suggests that a friend of Acca's station (and Acca was also the direct recipient of Wilfrid's patronage) performed masses for him both as head of the monastery and as a private person. We are not informed how long daily masses were said for Wilfrid, but this enormous investment by Acca was seen by Wilfrid's hagiographer Stephanus as actions that reflected "the depth of the love he bore" Wilfrid, his "father in God."[113] Wilfrid in particular was a bishop who valued hierarchy, and his hagiographer tells us in one episode that Wilfrid's "faithful friends" were two abbots, some monks, priests, and kin.[114] These were people of "lower" status who had benefited from Wilfrid's patronage; they are a reminder that Anglo-Saxon bishops were usually accompanied by a retinue, just as were secular notables and that their faithful companions were there to receive largesse and to perform duties. For a powerful cleric such as Wilfrid, this retinue was the most obvious gathering of his "faithful friends."

In conclusion, Bede's writings may prompt a number of questions about friendship, gifts, and the afterlife that cannot be fully answered. But we can say this: Bede's idea of friends were those who could be relied upon to help you after you were dead. And they operated in an orbit of obligation and reciprocation that may or may not have been entirely mutual. Early on, it seems, petitions for intercession by friends took on an institutional character. When Bede was commissioned by the bishops and monks of Lindisfarne to write the *Life of St. Cuthbert*, he sent it to them with a prefatory letter that stated, "Moreover, when I am dead, deign to pray for the redemption of my soul, and to celebrate masses as though I belonged to your family and household, and to inscribe my name among your own."[115] The *libri memoriales* that are so well attested in monastic communities on the Continent from the ninth century on were clearly being kept already in Northumbria at the beginning of the eighth century and were integral to Anglo-Saxon commemoration of the dead. In important respects, these *libri memoriales* were a continuation of the ancient and ongoing principle that the living Christian community pray for the Christian dead—community prayers, commemoration, and expectations of continued community in heaven. Church liturgies contained general prayers for all the faithful departed, but by means of these books the living hoped to be remembered by name long after they were gone.[116] Bede would expect to be remembered in the prayers of his brethren after death, but his contract with the priests for prayers and masses suggests that he sought a more personal, individual intercession than would otherwise have been available.[117]

It could be argued that in moving from the language of kin and dependents to the language of friendship, Bede effectively broadened the landscape of postmortem help, creating a theology of purgatory well positioned for the future involvement of the laity. For example, friendship could also include women. But it may also be true that the language of friendship served to purify (or obscure) the contractual dependencies that continued to bind people and made petitions for prayers and masses appear less commercial than they really were. Still, Bede's contribution to ideas of friendship and the afterlife is important because his writings coincide with the emergence of purgatory as a more clearly imagined place in the Christian afterlife. There is no call in Bede that prayers be intoned in perpetuity, although Anglo-Saxon charters were beginning to take this long with respect to property donation. The request for the prayers of individual friends imposed human life-span limits on the length of the intercession being requested; requests from friends who headed monastic foundations could promise something more. But whether one relied on kin, fellow monks, distant monks, or friends (however defined) for intercession, the provident Christian ensured that for the near future, at least, his corpse's surroundings would be filled with the sound and intent of prayer.

Wider Connections

One of the challenges of studying Bede is the enormous gap in our knowledge of the intellectual culture of Anglo-Saxon England in the seventh century. It was a century in which many influences, both domestic and foreign, may have brought firmer outlines to the notion of purgatory than we can now recover. Was Bede the first to juxtapose purgatory's orthodoxy with Origen's heterodoxy? Is it possible that such thoughts circulated in the aftermath of the anathemas against Origen at the Second Ecumenical Council of Constantinople in 553? Is it also possible that a modified form of universalism, such as was made popular in the East through the "orthodox" Origenism of Gregory of Nyssa,[118] circulated among those who would eventually have a profound influence on the ecclesiastical culture of Britain?

One can only imagine the ideas that might have come to Bede by way of the book collections and tradition of personal teachings of early seventh-century figures such as the Greek monk Theodore of Tarsus (602–90), who became Archbishop of Canterbury in 668, and Greek-speaking Abbot Hadrian (c. 637–709), who became abbot of the monastery of SS Peter and Paul in Canterbury. During his early years, before he sought refuge in Italy, Theodore may have trained in the schools of Antioch, Edessa, and Constantinople, where he would have had access to the enormous corpus of exegetical work associated with some of the great eastern theologians.[119] His own theological knowledge was widely respected; it appears likely that he was engaged in antimonothelete research and that he took part in the Lateran Council of 649.[120] His presence in Canterbury brought to Anglo-Saxon England firsthand knowledge of the major figures and controversies of the seventh century. Like Theodore, the North African Hadrian had probably fled to southern Italy ahead of Arab invasions. He was probably from Libya, and it is likely that Greek was his natal tongue.[121] Taking up residence in Naples, Hadrian lived at the heart of the cultural cross-currents of Mediterranean trade and scholarship, especially from the Greek- and Syriac-speaking worlds. By the time he left Naples for England in 670, Hadrian was "the intimate and trusted confidant" of the pope and of Emperor Constans II. Bernhard Bischoff and Michael Lapidge's study of the *Canterbury Biblical Commentaries*, with its predominance of Greek patristic sources, has illuminated the intellectual environment that Hadrian and Theodore fostered in England in the late seventh century. Unfortunately, key figures for eschatological learning such as Origen and Gregory of Nyssa left only little trace. The Canterbury school did not retain its Greek foundations after the deaths of Theodore and Hadrian. Some memory of their teachings survived to Bede's time to be attributed to them, and their influence may have been greater than can be ascertained by the survival of the sources. Once Greek language was forgotten (there were just a few who could read it in Bede's time); the Greek language library they brought with them would have been neglected and no longer copied. Yet, while the manuscript sources do not exist to affirm any specific intellectual connection between Bede's Northumbria and Greek eschatology, they certainly existed for a time, and any insights Bede or others might have derived from them would have carried with them an authority that texts from other sources might not have had. Theodore and Hadrian had included Lindisfarne in their tour of England, perhaps supplying books to that monastery, whose library Bede used.[122] Furthermore, Theodore and Hadrian may have brought something less tangible, but equally important to the formation of purgatorial thinking: a tendency in seventh-century Greek religious culture for clarifying doctrinal issues, a process that was ongoing in the time of Theodore and Hadrian.[123] Theodore and Hadrian used their considerable administrative experience in the task of organizing the church in England, bringing their knowledge of church councils to England, and using the model of Roman councils in their new environment.[124] Conciliar pronouncements were an important source of authority on doctrinal issues for Bede, as they had been for Augustine in his later years.[125] The condemnation of Origen at Constantinople in 533 had the effect of distilling fears of heterodox eschatology onto a single individual.

Closer to home, Bede's monastery's library was enriched by Latin works brought to the monastery of Wearmouth and Jarrow toward the century's end by Wearmouth's founder, the avid book collector Benedict Biscop, among others.[126] Benedict had also spent time at Lérins, a monastery that attracted an international body of monks. Finally, there was the rich and continuing connections of Wearmouth-Jarrow with Irish scholars and texts.

I hope to have shown that it was the patristic habit of interpretation of scripture, perhaps more than scripture itself, that fed the idea of purgatory in late antiquity and the very early middle ages; that stories about the dead returning to the living, and visions of the afterlife, illustrated a developing sense of an afterlife in the early middle ages and of purgatory's place in it; and that Bede was an important figure in giving purgatory a theological purpose as well as meaning. Bede recorded a view of purgatory that, by his time, fit the passion of monks and nuns for petitioning friends for prayers, creating a spiritual commerce of major and minor liturgical offerings, and emphasizing the importance of monastic interdependency, both at the level of individual monks and nuns and at the institutional level as monasteries recorded and prayed for the inhabitants of fellow institutions. By the time Bede and Boniface described visions of purgatory, the idea had become sufficiently familiar, at least to Anglo-Saxon monks, that not only was the orthodoxy of this view not questioned, but also the idea of purgatory had become a rigorous statement of orthodoxy.

Whether we see Bede as a theological innovator or as a learned editor of accepted opinion, his influence on the future acceptance of early medieval purgatory was profound and lasting. His works found their way into missionary libraries by the second half of the eighth century; a fellow Northumbrian, Alcuin, disseminated Bede's work to the Carolingian world; and when Hincmar of Rheims wrote on purgatory, he had Bede's work before him and quoted it verbatim.[127] In the Carolingian age there would be a cluster of politically inspired visions of suffering souls in purgatory that could rely on the existence of antecedents brought to the Continent by Anglo-Saxon missionaries.[128]

Finally, it is important to recognize that Bede's and Boniface's accounts of purgatory were written down and distributed in the context of Anglo-Saxon missionary work. Bede's narration of Drythelm's vision is found in the last book of his *Ecclesiastical History of the English People*, directly following a sequence of chapters in which he described the mixed success of early Anglo-Saxon missions to the Frisians in the 690s: of Egbert, who was warned through the dreams of one of his monks not to undertake the mission at all, and he didn't; of Wictbert, who went to the Frisians but, having no success with them, returned to voluntary exile in Ireland; and of Willibrord, who had major successes among them, having wisely visited the court of Pippin II (d. 714) first and gained that mayor's protection and aid. This latter was also the mission that Boniface may have joined briefly in 716 before his career took him to Rome and on a different missionary path. Is it coincidence that our two earliest accounts of purgatory are to be found in the context of Anglo-Saxon missionary efforts abroad? In the next chapter I address the missionary context for these English authors of purgatory.

7

Missionary Eschatology and the Politics of Certainty

In the last chapter we saw that purgatory as an imagined place and as a theological concept acquired sharper definition in the work of two English monks who, in different ways, were deeply committed to furthering the success of missionary activities to the continental Germans. Indeed, the waning years of the seventh century and the early eighth century was a time when missionary fervor was high among educated churchmen. Spurred on by successes at home, missionaries turned their gaze to their continental pagan "kin" who, in their eyes, had not yet received the blessing of conversion from Rome. The anonymous author of the Whitby *Life of St. Gregory* believed that the apostle who converted a people to Christianity presented that entire nation to the God on Judgement Day.[1] According to this kind of reasoning, and their own conversion mythology, Anglo-Saxons would be presented to God by their own teacher, Pope Gregory the Great. They must have hoped their continental brethren would stand beside them on that day.[2] As these Anglo-Saxon missionaries crossed into German and Frisian territory, they took with them a devotion to Rome and a commitment to strictest orthodoxy.[3] Alongside the necessary accouterments of sacramental life (missals, vessels, altar cloths, portable altars, and so on), they also took their learning and their religious culture with its books, penitentials, calendars, and the strong connections of spiritual friendship that would support their activities abroad. As they founded monasteries they set up schools, staked out cemeteries, and recorded names of the faithful in their Books of Life. The missionaries were mindful of their own salvation, too. They were trained in scripture and theological issues, and as the correspondence of Boniface's circle shows, they continued to look for books and advice on spiritual and practical matters.[4] Eschatological issues must have loomed large in their world: it would be a poor missionary who was ignorant or in doubt about what happened to the soul after death or who failed to know the signs of the "end times." Yet, it is the great frustration of any investigation into missionary eschatology that the rich sources for this era do not often address eschatological issues in great detail, and in particular they do not often discuss belief in purgatory. Boniface's account of the *Vision of the Monk of Wenlock* is evidence that there were those in the missionary field who believed in postmortem purgation as represented in that work, and it contained views that Boniface himself undoubtedly assented to.[5] Yet, being guided by different concerns, the sermons and letters that survive are poor records of postmortem purgatorial belief. Still, even if our eighth-century missionary sources are not voluable on the subject, we must at least attempt to account for the ready assimilation of this belief by missionaries and attempt likewise to account for the religious culture that supported it.

Boniface and his companions crossed to an established missionary front.[6] The territories east of the Rhine were already dotted with monasteries founded by earlier Merovingian and Anglo-Saxon missionary initiatives, largely sponsored by the political piety of the Austrasian mayors. Depending on where they went, they encountered Christians and pagans of various sorts, although it is not always an easy matter to determine the precise religious affiliation of the communities they encountered; the very terms "pagan" and "Christian" pose problems for interpretation and for providing an exact vocabulary for the historian.[7] "Paganism" was in the eye of the beholder. As Ian Wood warns, "allegations of paganism are at times no more than identifications of alternative Christianities."[8] Furthermore, in written sermons Christian missionaries routinely recycled the language and concerns of earlier "authorities" on paganism, such as Caesarius of Arles and Gregory the Great, with little attempt to refresh their rhetoric in new circumstances.[9] Archaeology is an imperfect tool for identifying Germanic communities since Germanic peoples (possibly with the exception of the Anglo-Saxons) did not invest in durable religious buildings of the sort that archaeology can now uncover. Even when structures of some sort have survived, it is usually open to debate whether the site should be interpreted in religious terms. Thus, in trying to understand the religion of the Germans, we are inevitably left to make sense of Christian written sources that arise from distinct, and often hidden, ideological perspectives. Sometimes those perspectives can be partially uncovered through literary studies.[10] In other cases we are almost totally in the dark. We are also at the mercy of our sources for the vocabulary and identifications that we must work with. It is as though we are hearing only one side of a conversation—a conversation that may not have been going anywhere. Yet in questioning the purpose of what we hear, it may be possible to learn something of what the afterlife meant to Christian missionary preachers and how they might view it as part of their task of educating both Christians and pagans. As we shall see, Christian missionaries undoubtedly preached on the afterlife, and, as they confronted Germans of various religious complexions who presumably held their own distinct views on the subject, they sought to sharpen their own understanding of the fate of the soul after death.

This chapter examines the environment in which the Christian theology of the afterlife was given the task, the challenge, and the stress of persuading others to accept a view that may have appeared alien to anyone not immersed in a long tradition of biblical exegesis and patristic thought. Yet we must also ask whether the religious desires and human impulses were so very different among the groups in this "conversation" and whether the desire for an afterlife in which family and friends would be met again was not at the very heart of any religious and cultural contact. Because of the nature of the sources, this chapter is largely about the Christian missionaries themselves—their needs and their desires—but they did not fret in a vacuum. Thus the story of the missionary contact with the Frisians is a starting point for this chapter, but a telling one, because in the semimythologised figure of the Frisian king Radbod, Anglo-Saxons encountered, or perhaps created, a conversion subject that they both desired and feared: a pagan with the desire for an afterlife of his own.

The Frisian Mission

Our sources attest that the life of the early medieval missionary was often a hard one.[11] For every story told of grateful pagan communities sinking to their knees in praise of a newfound God, there was another in which the missionary encountered incomprehension, resistance, and even death. Early medieval missionary accounts of the seventh and eighth centuries are remarkably candid about the failures, as well as the successes, of the missionary movement east of the Rhine. Indeed, many missions failed at first encounter or a short time after. A mission's success depended greatly on the toleration of the local ruler and his leading men to missionary presence in their territories and, in time, on their acceptance of its aims and message. There are many accounts of missionary encounters with kings, neatly dialogued. But perhaps the most famously recalcitrant subject of a missionary offensive was Radbod, a pagan Frisian king or duke who stepped away from the baptismal font at the last minute when informed that his unbaptized ancestors were consigned to hell.[12]

Radbod's removal of his toe from the baptismal water became an iconic moment in the later history of the German missions—more important perhaps for imagination of posterity than for the outcome of any Christian surge of the time.[13] Indeed, the account is to be treated with great caution. It has been long known that the dates of the missionary Wulframn's life and those of the Frisian king do not correspond.[14] Radbod's story is viewed by some as being largely fictional. Yet, as Stéphane Lebecq points out, the *Life of Wulframn of Sens*, in which Radbod's baptism is described, may reflect authentic tradition concerning the king because it had been related to the author of the *Life*, Jonas, by an eyewitness—a Frisian priest, Ovo, who claimed to have been saved from human sacrifice by Wulframn many years before, and who had come to live at the monastery of Saint-Wandrille where the work was eventually produced.[15] It is possible, then, that there may be a germ of truth to the story: it is equally possible that it is purely an imagined event. But this is a secondary concern. The power of the story lies in concerns that were not confined to a single event: family, ancestors, and the afterlife.

Radbod's supposed encounters with the missionaries took place in the years before his death in 719, at a time when Christian missionaries east of the Rhine operated under the protection of the Mayors of the Franks, Pippin II and Charles Martel, and when missionary work in the area was intimately linked with Frankish and papal politics. If the *Vita Wulframni* is to believed, missionaries were beginning to have success with many Frisians accepting baptism, including Radbod's own son. Radbod was about to join the list of new converts when the afterlife issue suddenly arose. Radbod asked Wulframn a simple question: where were most of the Frisian kings, princes, and other nobles to be found? In the heavenly kingdom? Or in that other place of damnation, Tartarus? Wulframn answered: "Only the exact number of his elect are with God. Your predecessors, the Frisian kings, who died without having received baptism have certainly received the sentence of damnation. But he who would believe and accept baptism, certainly he would know eternal happiness with Christ." Hearing this, we are told, Radbod was *incredulus*! Radbod declared that he could not deprive himself of the company of his predecessors, the Frisian princes, and that he could not give his adherence to these new words, and that he would rather stay with those whom he had known for so long and with the rest of his people. Our source for this fine speech is a Christian text, but its substance is plausible.

The tale of Radbod's refusal takes on further complications when one remembers the political background to Radbod's position as *dux* or *princeps* at the edges of the Frankish Empire and the danger to his royal status that might result from abandoning his ancestors and royal (possibly divine) geneaology. Germanic leaders rested their claims to rule on royal bloodlines and on the often highly constructed sacral claims of their kingship. But we should not overlook the obvious here. Radbod's avowed reason for rejecting Christianity was clearly stated: the Christian afterlife did not appeal to him. Radbod may have had political reasons to hold the Frankish missionary at bay, but the excuse he offered was a good one—an unarguable objection to the Christian offer. It pointed to a weak spot in eighth-century Christian afterlife belief: that the past was not recoverable and that family forebears would not join new converts in salvation. This was a concern that would have been as relevant to the era of Frisian missions as it was to be at the time of the Saxon initiative almost a century later when the work that has preserved the story was penned.

While the hagiographies were written to extol the virtues of the two missionaries, it is Radbod, the antihero of these accounts, who catches our attention. His withdrawal from the new religion at the moment of baptism confronts us with an iconic story of royal hesitation, of the intersection of religious identification, social accountability, and political calculation. But it is also a story about conflicting views of the afterlife: of differing expectations of the nature of that experience, of what the kingdom of heaven will be like, of who will inhabit it, and of how allegiance to a particular vision of that future existence may influence the status and identity of the living.[16] The afterlife mattered for pagans. Yet that fact is not always fully appreciated in studies of pagan belief.

Representations of Pagan Belief in an Afterlife

This is not the place to discuss at any length what pagan afterlife belief may specifically have entailed: the problems of sources and geographical variation are too large to be given space here. It is sufficient to say that our knowledge of Germanic religion is woefully lacking, and what we do know is compromised by the nature of our sources. In the absence of written records, eighth-century paganism is particularly obscure. We know (or think we know) more about Germanic gods, cults, and rituals from the time of Tacitus in the first century than we do about the eighth century—and that earlier information is unreliable for the eighth century because of its distance in time and because of Tacitus's political and ethnographic agendum. Conversely, we have a good sense of what thirteenth-century monks thought Scandinavian-Germanic religion was about, but their information is certainly unreliable for an earlier age. This source gap has opened the field for historians to supply their own interpretation of what Germanic religion would have been like and how it meshed with Christian teachings at that time. The variety of scholarly opinion on this matter is overwhelming, ranging from those who see an accommodation between Christianity and Germanic culture occurring in the early middle ages, to those who see the benchmarks of transformation occurring only in the twelfth and thirteenth centuries. Much depends on the literature and locality being studied and what criteria for "accommodation" are set.

Even if such an investigation is ill served by its sources, it is useful to consider the way in which Christian sources responded to paganism in Christian literature and how it has served to obscure pagan afterlife beliefs from view.

There is a strong trend in scholarship to hone in on the ways in which Germanic religion was different from the Christian religion—in its values and its mythology. Germanic mythic personages and images could, in time, transfer or be accommodated to the new religion, and examples can be found in the material artefacts of communities in transition. That process of transformation is almost always attributed to the imagination of medieval monks who sought to preserve or neutralize (according to one's perspective) the power of ancient ideas in newly assumed contexts. The work of accommodation, then, is viewed as a one-sided effort to build a bridge between two distant poles—a binary opposition that must inevitably result in a clash when the two are brought into contact.

A particularly strong and uncompromising statement on the antithetical nature of the Germanic and Christian religion has been advanced by James Russell.[17] Russell characterized the Germanic religion as having a "world-accepting, folk-centred, magicoreligious orientation," whereas the Christian orientation was "world-rejecting, individual-centred, soteriological." With Christianity explicitly advanced as a counterpoint to the Germanic religion, Russell's vision of the German religion was that it was somehow deficient in transcendent opportunities and in the way its afterlife views meshed with other aspects of the religion. Indeed, such a perspective implies that the pagan and Christian religions were so incompatible that mutual incomprehension and deception were inevitable.[18] Furthermore, Russell claims that Christian missionaries knowingly misinformed prospective converts about the full implications of the new religion (no evidence is adduced for this) and that a policy of mass baptisms went hand in hand with a decline in the catechumenate—the instruction that converts received prior to baptism—leading to further ignorance of Christian tenets among the converted. These are strong claims, and there may have been some individual cases that would bear this out. Some qualification is in order, however.

First, in the absence of informative sources, it is important that we do not underestimate or discount the importance that afterlife beliefs must have had for pagans. As portrayed in the *Life of St. Wulframn of Sens*, Radbod's unwillingness to forgo the company of his ancestors in the afterlife surely suggests that Christians understood that there was a powerful imaginative component to the pagan conception of what lay beyond death. The Christian kingdom that Wulframn presented to him, a kingdom whose inhabitants were limited in number (to the elect) and that included paupers as well as kings, did not compare with the place that otherwise awaited him. Radbod's identity as king appears to have been rooted in his people's history, and it was his desire that in death he would keep company with the great kings and heroes of the past. We have no way of knowing whether Radbod's beliefs and perspective were typical of all Frisians or of any other Germanic group.

Archaeological evidence poses its own problems for understanding Germanic conceptions of the afterlife. Burial practices and their relationship to settlement patterns can suggest changing attitudes toward the dead—fear of the dead, neutralization of chthonic powers, solicitation of the dead for protection, and so on—but they can tell us little more when unaided by written sources. Likewise, grave deposits are open to multiple interpretations. Not every good-looking bead is an amulet. Archaeological studies that offer a long chronological overview can reveal subtle but clear differences in burial and votive practices over time, among different status groups and with substantial local variation.[19] When pressed to interpret afterlife beliefs from burial evidence, archaeological studies often resort to anthropological insights, sometimes those deriving from very different eras and cultures.[20] This strategy is an admission of the difficulties of interpretation. The varied beliefs of the Germanic peoples about the afterlife (there is no reason to suppose them unchanging) elude us, and they can become confused with other aspects of Germanic culture such as the desire to represent status, gender, economic competition, and ethnicity in a mortuary context.

Preparations for death in the pagan world, especially for elite burial, could be time-consuming and costly. Some graves and corpses were lavishly appointed. There are many ways to interpret this: a desire to display real or aspired-to status, individual and community concerns, desire to appropriate the power of real or imagined ancestors, or to comply with accepted norms. Yet lavish graves sometimes incorporated vehicles for transportation, which suggests that a future journey was envisaged. Thus it is hard to account for the richly adorned graves of Germanic princes who took their weapons, their personal finery, and their horses, ships, and wagons with them into the grave if they had no evolved concept of an afterlife, and if that future existence did not seem fully real to them and fully worth sacrificing for.[21] The desire to display individual and community status may have played a role in lavish burials, but it is unlikely to have been the only motive.

There were important ways in which Christian and pagan practices were aligned. In the seventh century many Anglo-Saxon Christians were buried with weapons and other objects, and churchmen appear to have permitted it—these Christians do not look very different to pagans in a mortuary context.[22] Indeed, their social practices, and their reliance on kinship and honour evidenced in Anglo-Saxon law, makes it clear that Anglo-Saxon Christianity was very "Germanic," so that acculturation preceded the export of Anglo-Saxon Christianity to the Continent. Boniface's letter to the English, written in 738, requesting help for the mission makes the point that these Saxons are kinsmen—"of one bone and one blood" with the Anglo-Saxons.[23] Commercial contacts had a longer history than religious differences; the Frisians were renowned traders in slaves, furs, Frankish swords, and Frankish wine and grain, lending opportunities for pagans and Christians to mix and for the pagan religion to assimilate some Christian features, too.[24] So, although our sources on the Germanic afterlife are scarce, it would be shortsighted to discount its importance or its power to rationalize other aspects of Germanic culture and religious practice. Recent studies of the Anglo-Saxon burial at Sutton Hoo give greater weight than previously to the importance of the burial as a "voyage to the other world."[25] Was it a Christian voyage or a pagan one? Or something in between? When we cannot answer such questions confidently for a site as rich and as well-studied as that at Sutton Hoo, it must clearly be wrong to make too sharp a distinction between the culture and religious modes of expression of the missionaries and that of their missionary audience.

What was Christianity's appeal for prospective pagan converts? Historians have long noted the short-term or long-term political advantages of conversion for the elite and of the technological culture of stone building, glass, and writing that must have impressed them. Yet when we look at what missionaries themselves believed they promised potential converts, it was not political and technological advantage or even the persuasiveness of a new religious myth, but rather the claim that they had more certain information about what happened in the afterlife than did their pagan competitors. When presenting conversion stories to Christian audiences they invested heavily in a powerful rhetorical program: one that pitted Christian "certainty" against pagan "doubt." For example, Bede tells the story of King Edwin's long road to conversion.[26]

The Northumbrian king was hesitant to accept the new religion, even though he had a Christian wife and was subjected to the constant arguments of the missionary Paulinus who had accompanied her. Finally, Edwin would not make a move until he had consulted with his council of chiefs. He was helped in this by the defection of the pagan high priest Coifi who argued that the pagan religion was "valueless and powerless." Then, one of the chiefs famously compared the present life to a sparrow flying through a banqueting hall: "While he is inside, he is safe from the winter storms; but after a few moments of comfort, he vanishes from sight into the wintry world from which he came. Even so, man appears on earth for a little while; but of what went before this life or of what follows, we know nothing. Therefore if this new teaching has brought any more certain knowledge, it seems only right that we should follow it." Coifi added: "this teaching clearly reveals truths that will afford us the blessings of life, salvation, and eternal happiness." This was the conversion issue that Bede wanted to promote. Bede would have us believe that both the anonymous nobleman and the pagan high priest were impressed by Christian certainty about the afterlife just as they doubted the teachings of their natal religion. In discussing what happened to souls after death, Christian certitude was being forged quite deliberately as a response to pagan "doubt."

Bede's insistence on public Christian "certainty" and on pagan "doubt" may still have the power to mislead.[27] In burial practices as revealed in archaeology, we are routinely confronted with a picture of a noble, materialistic, consumer pagan culture. This is contrasted with Christian texts that present saints and ascetics. Yet the archaeology of Christian burial does not reveal a picture very different from that of pagans. The emphasis on ascetic dress in Christian texts does not correspond well with the actual furnishings of Christian graves. Cuthbert's burial with its luxurious textiles, jewels, carved coffin, and protective outer coffins is a good example of the way archaeology and text do not coincide and has to be explained by reference to community considerations. It is widely recognized that burial customs have more to do with the community that buries than they do with the afterlife belief system of the individual person buried.[28] Indeed, the connection between burial rites and afterlife belief is extremely difficult to argue convincingly, and, as noted above, historians of archaeology most often have recourse to anthropological insights or later cultural models to make sense of enigmatic finds.

Of course, it is not possible to detect belief in spiritual purgation in burial sites, pagan or Christian. Yet were such ideas necessarily lacking? What did it mean when Tacitus stated that Isis was worshiped by some of the Suebes in his time, except that some Germans adhered to a chthonic cult that had purification and resurrection as significant features?[29] It is reasonable to ask whether pagans were as doubtful and vacillating about what awaited them at death as some of our Christian sources would have us believe. Were they lacking in afterlife imagination? Is it not possible that it was, in fact, Christian missionaries who were forced into clarity about the afterlife precisely because the pagan view of it was particularly accessible? What our sources are clear on is that Christian missionaries and writers wanted to promote Christianity as a purveyor of certain knowledge about the afterlife. It suggests that *certainty* was a greatly valued *Christian* cultural commodity and that certainty about the afterlife in particular was a component of that belief that was expected to carry much weight.

Christian Preaching and the Bedan Connection

While Christian missionaries were firming up their own views of the afterlife, they were also striving to become effective teachers. This meant requesting and receiving advice from those who claimed some knowledge of the undertaking, requesting books and prayers and the practical accouterments of the job. The survival of the letters of Boniface, Lull, and their correspondents allows unique insight into the importance of social networks and spiritual friendship for the success of keeping missionaries connected abroad. Yet, while we can trace exchange of certain goods, such as manuscripts, linens, and spices, we are woefully ill-informed about what missionaries actually preached. Those few Christian sermons that appear to address pagans (or, what is more likely, "pagan" practices) are highly literary and derivative pieces: the sermons of Augustine, Caesarius of Arles, and Gregory the Great were plundered for material by eighth-century homiletic writers as written sermons essentially became *florilegia*.

Still, there is ample evidence that sermons to Christian communities readily addressed the fate of the soul after death and that such thoughts occupied the minds of those who preached. For example, a sermon penned by the missionary Pirmin of Reichenau addressed recent converts and threatened its audience with the torments of hell.[30] In the mid-eighth century, Alchfrid the anchorite wrote a letter-sermon and sent it to the priest Hyglac and his fellow monks, asking them to consider the course of human misery "on earth, from earth into fire, from fire to judgement, from judgement either to gehenna or to glory." Appearing right at the beginning of the letter, this attention-grabbing description was in reality a direct quotation from a sermon by Columbanus, but it shows how thoughts of postmortem purgation could enter sermon literature.[31] In a series of mid-seventh-century sermons by Bishop Eligius of

Noyon, the Final Judgement is kept in close view. Almsgiving is the consistent theme: Christians are to feed the poor because in that way they feed Christ. They will be secure on Judgement Day because they will be able to say: "Give, Lord, because we gave; have mercy because we were merciful; we fulfilled your commands, you (*tu*) give back to us what you have promised."[32] The urgency of this exchange in the present life—food sent to heaven rather than to the stomach—derives from the fact that "no one can redeem you after death."[33] Thus, when the author quotes Ecclesiasticus (Sirach) 3:30, stating that "just as water extinguishes fire, so almsgiving extinguishes sin," it is the fire of hell that he has in mind. Another sermon by Eligius, which is included in a second *vita*, lists the by-now traditional Caesarian list of "pagan" practices that Christians must avoid, but there is no discussion there of the afterlife.[34]

Boniface was the recipient of two significant pieces of advice about preaching, both in letters. The first letter written by Pope Gregory II on May 15, 719, charged him with his mission to the pagans (unspecified but probably in Germany) and openly declared what his preaching should entail: "you will pour into their untaught minds the preaching of both the Old and the New Testament ... with reasoning suited to their understanding." In another letter, Boniface was advised by Daniel, bishop of Winchester, how to handle pagans as prospective converts. Daniel had been Boniface's bishop when he lived at Nursling, and the letter advises on preaching content and forms of argumentation specifically targeted to pagans. Its recipient was to avoid discussion of genealogies of ancestral gods.[35] Whether this was knowledgeable and practical advice is debated, but written almost a decade after Radbod's refusal, the letter seems to confirm that the issue of ancestors was held by at least one church authority to be a tricky one.

Boniface's own writings are our best evidence of the link between postmortem purgation theology and missionary work. His transmission of the *Vision of the Monk of Wenlock* is the most obvious testimony to the connection. But we also know that in the last decade of his life, Boniface became aware of Bede's work. Three letters have survived in which Boniface wrote to contacts in northern England asking that copies of Bede's work be sent to him. One request was to the abbot of Wearmouth-Jarrow asking for some of Bede's treatises (unspecified). Two were to the archbishop of York requesting Bede's works, one of them specifying Bede's *Homilies* (*lectionarium anniversarium*) and *Commentary on Proverbs* (*proverbia Salomonis*).[36] As we saw in the previous chapter, these two works are significant because Bede had discussed purgatory in them, and in the *Commentary* in particular, as we have seen in the previous chapter, Bede linked the theology of purgatory with the condemnation of the theology of universal salvation. Boniface may have known the general content of the works, for he stated confidently in his letter that they would be useful to him in his preaching.

The context of preaching, of course, is significant. If Boniface and his circle used Bede's works in their preaching, then we have a point at which we can be assured that some of Bede's ideas crossed from monastic culture to a wider audience. The fact that Boniface authored a text that included purgatory, that he requested further works that discussed purgatory, and that he was a powerful preacher and renowned ecclesiastical authority, all place Boniface alongside Bede as a key figure in the early dissemination of postmortem purgatorial belief. We do not know if Boniface ever referred to purgatory or to the monk of Wenlock's vision in a sermon. We might not expect to find such content in exhortatory sermons.[37] However, it is very likely that visionary accounts served a purpose in early medieval preaching. Eligius of Noyon's *De supremo iudicio* featured a long speech in which Christ accused sinners of their crimes on Judgement Day. The speech is so reminiscent of Christ's speech in the *Visio Pauli* that it seems likely that the pastoral value of sermons and visions found a natural link there. Claude Carozzi has proposed that Redaction 6 of the *Visio Pauli* may have been penned in the Anglo-Saxon missionary environment of Boniface and Lull.[38] And it was someone in that same circle who, sometime after 757, recorded a vision that described torment-filled purgation.[39]

What are we to make of this connection between missionary work and the sharpening of ideas about purgatory? How might Bede's discussion of purgatory have been viewed by those dedicated to missionary outreach? Both Bede and Boniface operated in intellectual communities that accepted that some kind of postmortem purgation awaited the Christian soul and that they consequently accepted and supported the religious and social ramifications of such a belief. Was there a closer connection?

Purgatory, Universal Salvation, and Posthumous Salvation

For all the Christian emphasis on pagan doubt about the afterlife, it was in fact the Christian theology that traditionally admitted of some uncertainty. Heaven and hell were clearly established in the Christian scriptures, but the precise nature and function of postmortem purgation still needed resolution in late antiquity. No Christian thinkers doubted that some form of purification awaited the soul and that there were some who would be saved *per ignem*, but what exactly was its scope? We have seen that many views were expressed about when and how the fire would operate, but the most contentious question was who was eligible for this posthumous purification. The offer of universal salvation was one end of the spectrum, with Origen standing for the most radical position that even the devil could be saved. At the other end of the spectrum were those who believed only a few would be saved. In the middle were the so-called merciful Christians who believed that participation in the Church's sacramental life was close to a guarantee of eventual salvation. There is evidence that some of these ideas did not go away. Origen was first condemned by an Alexandrian council in 400.[40] Yet, it was thought necessary to anathematize Origen's teachings again in 533. And Boniface wrote to the Roman synod held in 745 about an Irishman named Clemens who "contends that Christ, descending to the lower hell set free all who were imprisoned there, believers and unbelievers, those who praised God and the worshipers of Idols."[41] Evidently there were still some who taught that heaven's gates were open even to those who had not been baptized. It is easy to see how appealing such a message would be in a missionary environment: even Radbod's ancestors might be saved by such theology. Yet by Boniface's time that view was clearly unacceptable.

By contrast, Bede's formulation of purgatory offered assurance to Christians that they would be admitted to heaven if in life they partook in the sacraments, confessed their sins, and expressed willingness to do penance, even if only on their deathbed. After death they could continue their path to salvation through pain in purgatory and through the charitable offices of living friends who could offer prayers, tears, alms, fasting, and masses. Ironically, then, the tools of purgatory were prefigured in the arguments of some of the earlier "compassionate Christians" who had held that partaking in the sacraments would ensure eternal life, even if taken only on the deathbed. We have many stories in the early middle ages that would support that view. In the formation of purgatory, one might argue, the "compassionate Christians," much ridiculed by Augustine, had ultimately won. Bede offered a "compassionate" purgatory that cast its net wide. It offered hope of salvation to categories of sinners who were hitherto believed to be ineligible, unless God in his mercy chose to intervene. Adult converts to Christianity were required to do penance for their former sins both before and after baptism. Bede's purgatory offered assurance that they would, after all, be saved.

The importance of cultivating "softer" views of salvation in conjunction with missionary work is underscored by reference to the past. Trumbower rightly sees the arguments of the so-called merciful Christians in Augustine's time as a response to the transition from pagan to Christian culture at the end of the fourth century. Missionaries needed inclusive ideas of salvation. It is surely significant that one of the last western individuals to openly embrace the Origenist view of the salvation that included salvation of the devil was Martin of Tours, Gaul's most successful missionary.[42] Martin was not knowingly heretical; his views on this matter were formed before Augustine's condemnation of them and before the official condemnation of Origen at the Council of Alexandria in 400. For a missionary like Martin, seeking to convert the Romano-Gallic population of the fourth century, the prospect of universal salvation may have alleviated concerns about the salvation of family members that were later to surface in the refusal of Radbod in the eighth century. We may surmise that like the idea of universal salvation, a "compasisonate" theology of purgatory had some use for missionaries. A fully developed idea of purgatory, bolstered by the authority of visions, offered a certain and positive answer to the questions, "Who will go to heaven and how?" It was not as easy an answer to the problem of deceased ancestors as was the offer of universal salvation, but it was an answer. At a time when pagans were depicted as suffering from religious doubt, Christian missionaries needed a certain message to impart. The notion that postmortem purification could eradicate even severe sins allowed adult converts with a bad history behind them to be integrated into the Christian fold. Good Christians would still be purified gently upon death and await heaven in a flowery paradise. Through the Augustinian emphasis on punishment for sinners, essential distinctions of merit among the sinful were thus maintained.

Conclusion

Early literary depictions of purgatory emerged at an interesting historical juncture. The idea of purgatory as a place to which Christians went to suffer, perhaps for a very long time, had begun to firm in the course of the seventh century. These ideas began to move beyond the realm of monastic theology in the eighth century. Purgatory's role in the afterlife of the soul became more widely known at a time when missionaries were preaching on the Continent—and at a time when the rhetoric of certainty about the afterlife was being strongly promoted in Christian sources. It was also an era during which ideas about universal salvation were still sufficiently dangerous to need official disavowal.

In the western context, conversion of Germanic peoples has generally been seen as a two-step phase. In the first step, the missionary convinced pagans to accept baptism (often mass baptisms), with the intention that further education would follow. The second step of conversion had to do with teaching converts a Christian way of life and Christian behaviour and ethics.

Purgatory was particularly important to this second step of missionary work. A two-tiered purgatory worked as well for poorly acculturated converts and for well-assimilated penitentially minded monks. It also provided missionaries with a means of backing up their promise that their converts would indeed gain the kingdom of heaven.

Belief in a purgatory that could be mitigated also involved the newly converted population in a set of postmortem rituals (of masses, prayers, and alms) that further served to foster cultural assimilation. Since the theology of purgatory was linked with ideas of original sin, and it was increasingly common to baptize children, purgatory was also a way of explaining why new converts must allow their children to be baptized also, thus speeding up the process of assimilation.

Radbod, with whom we started this chapter, ultimately emerges as a curious figure. At a time when many of his family, his nobles, and his ordinary subjects were accepting Christianity, he resisted. His earthly kingdom was being baptized away from him—alienated from his kingship to that of a new immaterial king. He could have accepted baptism and identified with the future of the Frisian nation (as a Frankish satellite), possibly maintaining some modicum of independence by removing the easiest excuse the Franks had to get rid of him. But he did not. He looked to his nation's past and abdicated from its future. Always on the brink of cooperation and armed resistance, Radbod was finally defeated in battle by Charles Martel and his territories annexed to the Frankish kingdom.

Ultimately, Christians would handle the problem of pagan ancestors in a number of ways. Historical revisionism in the form of reburial of pagans in Christian cemeteries was one.[43] Since early Christian cult sites were often built over pagan ones, Christian burials often shared space with those of pagans. Pagan burials surreptitiously entered the Christian sacred fold.[44] At the end of the sixth century, Pope Gregory the Great had advised Augustine of Canterbury to engage in religious and cultural syncretism when confronted by pagan Anglo-Saxons. One can imagine that ordinary people and the priests who served them could be equally resourceful. In the fourth century, Ambrose of Milan had touted the idea of the "baptism of desire" for a "Christian" emperor who died without baptism.[45] Early medieval accounts of the miraculous resurrection of dead children so that they could receive baptism, and legislative prohibitions against giving the host to the dead, speak to the desire of ordinary Christians to bend the rules to allow their deceased love ones to join them in heaven. And the famous story of Gregory the Great's prayer for the emperor Trajan, which saved the pagan emperor from everlasting torment, was found in the biography of that pope written by an anonymous monk of Whitby: a late seventh-century Anglo-Saxon work. In a later age, Charlemagne forced the conquered Saxons to inter their dead in Christian cemeteries.[46] Pagans were getting into the Christian fold one way or another! In the eighth century we see a peculiar nexus of developing ideas in Christian circles: the ideological investment by Anglo-Saxons in the conversion of the Germanic peoples, the need for an ongoing logic of salvation for those entering the fold through baptism, the stress of bringing monastic theology into the public sphere, and a need to be certain of what awaited the soul after death. Anglo-Saxon missionaries held a highly developed, if still evolving, idea of purgatory, as is clear in our sources. That they included such information in preaching is likely. What it entailed in practice for those with whom missionaries came into contact is unclear. But the significance of the missionary phase for disseminating Anglo-Saxon religious culture abroad, with its strong emphasis on prayer networks, gift and exchange, Books of Life, and possibly purgatory itself, must not be underestimated.

8

Barbarians, Law Codes, and Purgatory

"We are judged by God with immediate judgement and therefore a most craven race has been raised up for our destruction and shame," wrote the presbyter Salvian, in fifth-century Marseilles.[1] The barbarian penetration of the western provinces of the Roman Empire in the early fifth century was viewed almost immediately as a sign of the impending *eschaton*. Aided by ever-adjusting mathematical calculation regarding the Second Coming, the destructions and disruption wreaked by the Vandals, the Goths, and other threatening tribes were viewed as framing events—the sign that the end of times was near.[2] Whether the barbarians were viewed as pagan or, worse, heretics, the anxiety that their military successes caused church apologists was acute. Many Christians believed that their communities had suffered because it was God's judgement on their sins. Perhaps influenced by this sort of reasoning, Paulinus of Pella tried to be thankful for all the deprivations he suffered in the wake of the invasions.[3] The pious scolding of fifth-century Christian commentators such as Quodvultdeus and Salvian was repeated by successive church leaders who found themselves trying to explain the success of subsequent barbarian attacks on Christian kingdoms. The connection of barbarians with the end of times as described in John's Apocalypse was thus very clear for contemporaries. But were the barbarians also responsible for changing views of the afterlife; more pointedly, were barbarians responsible for the rise of purgatory?

As far as we know, no early medieval author connected purgatory with the barbarians: the earliest barbarians they encountered were either Arian Christians or held to beliefs and practices that could not be accounted for in Christianity. Indeed, while a priest such as Salvian could use a barbarian "virtue" such as chastity as a stick to beat his wayward community, no quarter was ever given on matters of faith, Christology, or eschatology. Among historians, however, the connection between barbarians and the rise of purgatory does find occasional, if sometimes oblique, support. The first historians to make this connection were sixteenth-century reformers seeking to justify their rejection of the Catholic doctrine of purgatory. They focused on the "barbarism" of the barbarians. In more recent times, the barbarian explanation for purgatory has been taken up in a rather different guise: that barbarian culture and institutions, especially the law codes, undergird the "infernalization" of purgatory. Sometimes it is the structure and organizing principles of barbarian codes that are identified as providing a model for purgatorial tortures; more often it is simply the tariffing of the law, which, alongside the penitential tariffing, is accorded a kind of typological connection to purgatory. While the reasoning for this view is rarely articulated in print, the possibility that barbarian law codes may help us understand purgatory is worth evaluating.

The roots of the theory that the barbarian invasions were responsible for the early medieval view of purgatory are found in the Reformation. At that time, a "barbarian invasions theory" took its place alongside the many other "causes" of purgatory. What makes the "barbarian" theory of purgatory's rise so interesting is that it signals the first attempt at what might be called a "historical" interpretation of purgatory's rise, even while being very much informed by confessional interests. The basic outline of this theory was that the barbarian invasions triggered a decline in intellectual life and that this in turn led to a decline in theological sophistication. A theology of the afterlife that included purgatory was thus seen as a symptom of this decline and "barbarism." However, modern scholarship has not always viewed the collapse of the Roman Empire and the barbarian kingdoms in such calamitous terms. It is supposed that the non-Roman world was also spiritual and that its institutions and society had positive values to contribute to the medieval afterlife. The sudden appearance of purgatorial descriptions in seventh-century visions has suggested to some that purgatory's rise arose from non-Roman values penetrating the afterlife. Hence we have in the modern view of the barbarian thesis, the antithesis of the Reformation disparagement of "barbarians": barbarian values and institutions, such as they are represented in law codes, are now viewed as positive influences on the formation of purgatory.

Barbarian Invasions and Theological "Barbarism"

When seeking to explain purgatory's rise in the early middle ages, some Reformation Protestants subscribed to a form of catastrophe theory: in the wake of the barbarian invasions, higher learning had collapsed and was replaced with simplistic (or devilish) solutions. The contours of the barbarian thesis can be seen in a remarkable treatise with a very long title that I will simply refer to as *The Waters of Siloe*.[4] This was an English translation of a French work by the Huguenot Pierre du Moulin (1568–1658), and it sought to refute three Catholic treatises, one by a Portuguese friar, and two others by doctors of the "Sorbon." After establishing the absence of discussions of purgatory in the writings of the church fathers, and seeking to account for the practices of oblations, sacrifices, and almsgiving that became attached to prayers for the dead, Du Moulin explained:

> And thus errour begat abuse which sprang from the love of friends yet without any conceit of Purgatory; and without any foresight of such abuses as might ensue, and did befall in the daies of Gregory Bishop of Rome, who lived in the yeare of Iesus Christ six hundred. For then learning being smothered by the inundation of the barbarous nations, the Gothes, the Hunnes, the French, the Vandales, etc. And these light of the primitive Church extinct, whiles there were no more Basils, Cyprians, or Augustins, etc. The divell taking his time, and making use of the covetise of the Clergie, cosened the world with visions and aparitions of soules returning from Purgatory, as we see in Gregories dialogues, and Beda his workes; who made report of a soul that apeared mufled in a cloke of fire; of another that had beene a master of the bathes and being there in Purgatory, offered to pull of a mans hose.[5]

Here, then, we have the crux of purgatory's beginnings viewed from a Protestant perspective: Gregory the Great's *Dialogues* were a by-product of the demise of learning that accompanied the barbarian invasions. When there were no more Basils, Cyprians, or Augustines to guard against the barbarization of Christianity, the devil deceived the world, making use of Gregory and Bede and their accounts of apparitions and visions to introduce the "error" of purgatory. Thus the devil, it would appear, caused or made use of the barbarian invasions to wrest the Catholic Church from its earliest roots. Such apocalyptic imaginings aligned well with early seventeenth-century religious combativeness, and the work's English translator may have taken comfort in the use of "etc." that concealed the

Anglo-Saxon barbarians from mention.[6] Permutations on the decline motif are still found into the nineteenth century, although now the "heathenism" decried was that of the ancient Greek and Roman philosophers.[7]

The barbarian explanation still has legs in the scholarly world. Commenting on Caesarius of Arles's sermons, Le Goff proposed that the bishop's emphasis on the eternity of hell and the pain of purgatorial fires could be explained by a "barbarization of society and religion."[8] The barbarian foreigners who invaded Roman territories were not entirely to blame for this "barbarization"; the "barbarians within," the democratizing influence of peasant thought, was also a factor. In this context, sermons such as those by Caesarius, preaching hellfire, were a symptom of the contemptuous reaction of the clerical elite:

> Hell was better suited to this climate than was a process intended to bring about a reduction of punishment. For a long time the purgatorial fire discreetly lighted by the Church Fathers, particularly Augustine, smoldered in secret without finding the fuel that it needed to take hold of a world beset with insecurity and divided by fundamental conflict, a world illuminated by the brighter blaze of judgment, which was in part confounded by the sinister light of the flames of hell.

Le Goff also considered the later "barbarian" elements of the Germanic and Celtic world.[9] His cautions about the difficulty of using the later Latin accounts of Celtic, Germanic, and Scandinavian myth to illuminate early medieval visions are well to heed, and he made no concerted attempt to invite a detailed comparison of Latin works of the seventh century with those of non-Latin cultures.[10]

Carozzi also sought to situate the new texts describing purgatory in the context of the barbarian invasions that placed the West "in a new situation of acculturation."[11] We have noted in a previous chapter that he proposed that the contact of Gallo-Roman Christian culture with that of Germanic pagan culture produced a fusion of images such as the Irish Beltain fires and Germanic Notfyr with a Christian belief in a purificatory fire, and that in a missionary context this fusion was part of a purposeful acculturation to pagan practices on the part of Christians. We have noted that Peter Brown has been a prominent exponent of the seventh-century "clash of cultures" view; he also addressed the earlier decline motif with the important comment on Gregory the Great, that: "Gregory's decisive "tilt" toward the other world, as it was taken up in the seventh century, does not necessarily reflect the anxiety of Christians reeling under the blows of a declining world, as the lamentable state of late sixth-century Italy, seen through the lens of Gregory's own poignant rhetoric of the end of time, might lead us to suppose and as many outline histories of the Dark Ages seem to imply."[12]

Influence of Barbarian Institutions and Law

In chapter 2, we saw how Roman social issues and late Roman concerns about legal status had informed popular images of the fate of sinners in hell. As depicted in the *Vision of Paul*, the infernal regions operated in a way analogous to Roman criminal law and late Roman legal practice: torture, punishment, and deprivation of status. By contrast, the earliest visions of purgatory in the seventh century did not draw inspiration for its images from the damned in hell. Drawn from a scriptural and patristic palate, the earliest images of purgatory focused on fire and, in some case, ice.[13] This changed in the late eighth century, however, when specific faults began to be punished by specific, and often poetically appropriate, penalties. This development allowed social and legal concerns to penetrate the theological understanding of purgatory.

To date, there is no study that examines the connection of barbarian law codes to afterlife belief in late antiquity in any depth.[14] Nor is this such a study. However, the influence of barbarian legal institutions and ideas, and of the codes themselves, alongside penitentials, is often evoked by scholars as having a formative influence on purgatorial notions, and so we will consider the question briefly here. But first, it is important to be clear on the kind of documentation we are dealing with when using the "barbarian law codes" as evidence. To what extent were these documents transmitters of barbarian culture and law?

Our knowledge of the legal systems of the sub-Roman, Germanic kingdoms before 800 is hampered by a number of factors: the meagre survival of written laws; the impossibility of establishing what was oral law or customary usage; the paucity of recorded legal cases and settlements; the localized elements in the laws; and the general problem of manuscript survival and transmission. However, in broad terms modern scholars of the law have tended to downplay the survival of archaic Germanic elements in the "Germanic" law codes. As Patrick Wormald's excellent historical introduction to Anglo-Saxon law in the early middle ages indicates, "what was once identified as Germanic legal life-forms tend to be reclassified as species of Roman provincial custom stripped of classical plumage."[15] Even the dispute resolution of Merovingian *placita*, once viewed as Frankish, is now thought to have deeper roots in Roman practice than previously thought.[16] The aspect of Germanic law that is most clearly a departure from its Roman roots is the centrality of the feud to conflict resolution.[17] But compurgation through oath-giving and the ordeal, both means by which such disputes could be resolved, is also likely to reflect the influence of the Church and Roman vulgar law.[18] Furthermore, even though they were written in the vernacular and appear local in inspiration, even the earliest Anglo-Saxon laws were not immune to continental influences, as Patrick Wormald has shown. Bede claimed that Aethelberht's law was written after the example of the "Romani," that is to say, the Merovingians whose elite dominated southern English and, in particular, Kentish politics.[19] While geographic distance from the Mediterranean was an important factor in determining the degree of influence exerted by Roman law (as Wormald pointed out), even northern "barbarian" law is likely to have had its roots in the unrecoverable legal customs of Roman provincial courts.

It is far harder to find any element of Roman legal thinking in Irish law, such as it can be reconstructed for this early period.[20] Oath-taking, compensation, and the legal priority of high status were elements that Irish law shared in common with sub-Roman law and other barbarian laws. However, except as it is sometimes intellectually bundled with penitential tariffs, there has been no attempt to my knowledge to make a direct comparison of Irish law codes and seventh-century developments in purgatorial depiction. The political and institutional connections that have been attempted—the "peccatization" of the afterlife and Ireland as a "stateless" society and a "land without amnesty"—have been discussed already in chapter 5.

Legal Tariffs

While the principle of tariffing infractions can be found to some degree in earlier legislative documents, it is certainly characteristic from the seventh century on to see a keen dedication to tariffing in all sorts of documentation. List mania possessed the Irish, the Merovingians, and their western contemporaries. Long lists of infractions are common to barbarian law codes, penitentials, church councils, monastic rules, tables of consanguinity, and so on. The deliberative parsing of legal principles into precise contingencies sets this kind of documentation apart from the imperial rescripts of an earlier age. There was a reinforcing quality to this. As Kate Dooley notes, "The idea of tariffs was intelligible to the people because of the civil laws of fixed retribution for particular transgressions. The church took up the format of civil law, but substituted a specifically religious kind of penance."[21]

Thus the similarities between law codes and penitentials make their connections apparent at some level. Indeed, their links go beyond the simple fact of tariffing. Both were forms of legislation seeking to secure compensation for crimes: the law seeking compensation for the victim and his kin, from the perpetrator and his kin, and the penitentials seeking to impose on individuals a compensation for personal deficiencies that were tantamount to crimes against God's rule. In both penitentials and law codes even violent crimes could be compensated for (as had been the case in Roman civil law), in each case as a means of averting the threat of vengeance. The penitentials threatened excommunication of the sacrilegious from the community of the faithful, while secular law outlawed the offender, ejecting him from the protections of the law and the community. A desire to codify infractions was common to both, although the penitentials sought more comprehensive statements of morality alongside penalties, whereas the law codes were more perfunctory responses to circumstance.

Outwardly, the connections between ecclesiastical and secular legislation are strong. Both were written down by churchmen who had an important role in the administration of both secular and church law. Both documentation types had deep precedents in Roman law and in church councils respectively. The two forms of legislation often aligned on issues in which secular and ecclesiastical interests intersected, which was most cases. However, while the case is sometimes made, it is unclear how far one form of legislation actually influenced the other.[22]

Most scholars who have commented on penitentials and the laws appear to have in mind not so much direct connections of content, but rather a diffuse sense that this type of documentation reflects the "character" of the society in view. For example, "Germanic" law codes with their lists of compensation are "Germanic" in character, and Irish law codes and penitentials are somehow indicative of "Irish" values, whereas they are probably all simply indicative of shared early medieval values. In the case of Germanic law codes embodying some pristine sense of archaic Germanic law, those ideas have been quite soundly put to rest. The Anglo-Saxon laws, once seen as being distinctive and progenitors of revered English legal institutions of a later age, are now shown to have had far greater connections with continental "Germanic" law codes than once believed. The Irish case is different—not because it was written in the vernacular (see Anglo-Saxon law) or because it was tariffed, since that is common to all these early medieval laws, but because its provisions often pertain to very different kinds of issues. Even so, Irish law, as it has survived from the seventh and eighth centuries, was largely a product of a Christianized society, written in a monastic environment, appealing to God's justice through the administration of oaths and ordeals just as the other barbarian laws did. Dunn's comment that "tariffed penance possessed similar characteristics to

Irish law, sharing its private rather than public nature and its automatic penalties for specified offences," to the extent that it is accurate, can be equally applied to the tariffed clauses of barbarian law generally.

Finally, one might point to the very obvious connections that this documentation has with its precedents: the earliest forms of Roman law, pre-Imperial law, were tariffed law; levitical prohibitions, church councils, and monastic rules could also be viewed as being tariffed. When barbarian laws and penitentials are described as being "tariffed" then, it is largely a designation of degree. Germanic law was written down by Romans who, in most cases, had identifiable Roman legislation to work on. It is possible that in the case of barbarian groups who had lived on the Roman frontiers for any length of time, that some form of frontier-style or marcher legal custom had developed and was available to them. Indeed, such a hybrid form of legal custom may account for the elements in the law that have appeared most "Germanic."

The Purgative of Justice

Just as the rhetoric of penance suggested that it was a spiritual purgative, so also the law had the capacity to "purge." In Roman law punishment could be viewed as purgative: "customarily, punishment purges crime. . . ."[23] Under barbarian procedure, those whose reputations had been stained by false accusation also had recourse to the purgative of the law. False accusations and calumny were viewed as legal encumbrances that any man careful of his legal status must want to remove. Oath-taking could clear one's name and restore or preserve legal status. The purgative effect of the oath is explicit in one of the earliest Anglo-Saxon law codes, *The Decrees of Wihtred, King of the People of Kent* (6 September 695).[24] Two archbishops were present on this law-making occasion, and "each order of that church of that people spoke with a single mind with the loyal populous."[25] The code was strongly ecclesiastical in focus, stating that "the king is to be prayed for" and setting the bishop's oath as equivalent to that of the king. It also addressed the ways in which churchmen and laymen should approach the altar to give legal oaths. "A priest should clear (*clænsie*) himself with his own truth in his holy vestments before the altar, thus saying: 'I speak truth in Christ, I do not lie': Similarly a deacon should cleanse himself. A cleric should cleanse himself . . . A stranger should cleanse himself . . . similarly a king's thegn. . . . a man of freeman rank (ceorl) . . . and let the oath of all these be incontrovertible."[26] The strong religious influence on this code may be responsible for the use of the verb "to cleanse," perhaps an attempt to render into the vernacular the Latin "purgare."[27] Indeed, the cleansing action of oath-taking had a more painful counterpart in the "clean wound" evidence provided by ordeals of water and fire.

The Eschatological Ordeal

It has been argued that Fursey's encounter with the fiery realms in the afterlife should be viewed through the lens of trial and ordeal by fire.[28] In that vision, the fire is both a location for trial and a means of trial. It is in the fire that the prosecuting demons challenge Fursey by recalling the promises of baptismal vows. The fire's discretion and judgement forms the eschatological ordeal: the successful candidate will walk through the fire, but the reprobate will stay in it. Carozzi argued that baptism and purgation (baptism by fire) were comparable rituals, in that each focused on the notion of examination and trial. Thus Fursey's trial and ordeal finds its analogs in the ancient rituals of the church and the language of spiritual trial, which is found in the New Testament, apocalypses, and the martyr and ascetic literature of the early church. In this seventh-century vision there is no discernable influence of Irish or Germanic law.

The evidence for direct influence of barbarian law on depictions of purgatory is stronger for the ninth century. Carozzi's discussion of *Redaction 6* of the *Vision of Paul* is a convincing study of the way penitential, legal, and conciliar concerns could find expression in a revision of an existing visionary text. Indeed, his analysis of the sins described in the work, issues that were very current in mid-eighth-century councils and penitentials, allowed him to show that at its core, *Redaction 6* was in all probability a work of the second half of the eighth century rather than of the ninth century.[29] *Redaction 6* was possibly also the first to introduce purgatory to the *Vision of Paul* tradition of texts, although that may not have been until the ninth century.[30]

Once depictions of purgatory began to inform the reader on the specific transgressions of individual sinners the door was open for a purgatory that reflected contemporary and topical issues as expressed in penitentials, church councils, and the law. This is precisely what Carozzi found in his analysis of *Redaction 6*. In addition to seeing the influence of contemporary religious concerns in the vision, he was able to detect plausible correspondences between the infractions described in *Redaction 6* and specific references in contemporary barbarian laws.[31] In particular, Carozzi noted some named sins in *Redaction 6* that appear to have an agricultural background (arson; stealing horses, mares, and other quadrupeds; using iron trimmings from agricultural implements), for which parallels may be found in the *Lex Alamannorum*, the *Pactus Alemannorum*, and the *Leges Burgundionum*.[32] Some of these connections are still quite speculative and depend on reconstructions based on penitentials, but on the whole they are convincing. Finding a reference to *ferramenta* in a single law code still leaves us in the dark about what such a connection between the two texts might ultimately mean. But in fact, most infractions in *Redaction 6* remained traditional and religious: giving false testimony; defamation; failing to perform penance (public and private); and clerics who lose their chastity, render bad judgements, and do not relieve widows and the poor; and those who steal. But some newer sinners emerge: conjurors of storms (condemned also in a number of eighth-century penitentials) and those who do not fulfill their vows as godparents (penitentials and Council of Leptines).[33]

As it may be supposed, judicial images that had long been associated with depictions of hell began to appear in texts once souls in purgatory were assigned individual tortures. We have seen that there is a certain correspondence between *Redaction 6* and Alamannic law in some very specific but arcane vocabulary. The larger questions still remain: when and how far were images of torture in purgatory drawn from contemporary legal ideology?

The immediate problem confronting such an investigation is the uncertainty about which portions of the earliest texts are positively depictions of purgatory. We have seen (chapter 5) that the *Fragmentary Vision of 757* is the earliest vision of purgatory to propose that souls will experience individualized torment. But because of its fragmentary state and disagreement over interpretation, it is impossible to know whether this is the first to describe purgatorial tortures. I have argued that it is not. In fact, the first case of differentiated tortures in purgatory—*Redaction 6* of the *Vision of Paul*—may have arisen from a mistaken labeling of the earlier text by its ninth-century copyist.[34] The tortures in the text include: fire, being boiled in bitumen and sulphur, and (reserved for bishops and presbyters) being burned inside lead chasubles. The latter torture is reminiscent of Barontus's vision of hell in which sinners sat on lead seats (an infernal *cathedra*) and of the torment of souls in purgatory in the *Vision of Wetti* with which the manuscript of *Redaction 6* is roughly contemporary: Wetti saw a monk in purgatory who, having stored riches in a casket, was now enclosed in a casket of lead until Judgement Day.[35] Even when visions of the afterlife began to describe specific torments awaiting souls in purgatory (or were thought to), they still adhered to the imaginative tortures of earlier visions rather than resorted to tortures that would have been recognizable to those who encountered the secular law. In *Redaction 6*, those who stole iron agricultural implements were punished by having those instruments pierce their eyes, and false witnesses were transfixed by fiery pegs. This was not a recognized penalty under any barbarian law.

For all its savagery from a modern perspective, the pain that could be inflicted under the barbarian legal system seems hardly to have sufficed as an image of eschatological punishment or worked as a deterrent for those inclined to ignore the fate of their souls.

While torments were slow to penetrate purgatory, no quarter was imagined for those who subverted the course of justice: those who failed to administer it, those who perverted its course through corruption, and those who exercised excessive cruelty in carrying it out. Perjury, which derailed the justice offered by secular courts, was consistently decried in penitentials and law codes and was punished in the afterlife. But the worst kinds of torments were reserved for secular law-givers, the counts who, having been cruel and lacking in mercy, could expect no mercy from God in their turn.[36] It is possible to imagine that Count Snoding in the *Fragmentary Vision of 757* was guilty of this kind of sin. The author of the *Vision of Wetti* had no scruples in characterizing those who administered secular law: the counts were "not the avengers of crime but the friends of Satan," selling justice and "putting up their souls for security." He continued: "some of them afflict their people with many perils; despising the law, they condemn the innocent and exonerate the guilty; they ally themselves with thieves and are partners in every crime; preoccupied with bribes, they care nothing for their future recompense."[37] Some of them, the angel declared, were condemned already.

The Judicial Ordeal

"Abbot Sigefrith, dear to God, having passed through the fire and water of the trials of time, was conducted into the paradise of everlasting rest and entered the kingdom of heaven, offering to the Lord in the sacrifice of perpetual praise those vows which he had most carefully promised to God with pure lips," wrote Bede.[38] Hagiographers could be confident that the prayerful saint would pass through his fire and water trial with "pure lips," but the ability of secular law to determine the truth and deliver justice was a more hazardous affair. The Roman use of torture in "putting the question" (the *quaestio*) reflected deeply entrenched assumptions about class and character. Such assumptions did not change with the Christianization of the empire. Christian barbarian law codes were no less concerned about status, except that now, in the role of churchmen in their creation, religious ideology had a more clearly articulated presence in the law. Just as the Christian elite increasingly took over civic and municipal functions in the western provinces, so they also took a more intrusive presence in writing and administering the law. Indeed, God's presence was invoked in the courts, and God's judgement became enshrined in barbarian law and procedure. God's goods and ministers were also protected and compensated by the law. The system of oath-taking was only the most apparent way in which God's name was invoked, and in which status (and therefore legal and religious status) continued to influence legal judgement. However, there were a number of situations in which more direct divine scrutiny was deemed necessary, and in which plaintiffs chose, or were required, to undergo a unilateral or bilateral ordeal. In the ninth century such situations included cases in which oath-taking reached a stalemate—cases of heresy and cases of "hidden crimes" of a sexual nature. The evidence for rationale for the judicial ordeal in the sixth and seventh centuries, however, is far less clear.

While ordeals were to become more diverse in subsequent centuries, the earliest evidence for the judicial ordeal concerned only two types: the ordeal of the cauldron and the ordeal of lot.[39] The ordeal by lot was used primarily for slaves, and if the slave failed the ordeal by choosing the wrong lot, he was flogged and his master (if he had supported his slave) fined.[40] The ordeal of the cauldron was for free men. Its earliest mention as a judicial instrument is in Frankish contexts: the *Lex Salica* (c. 510) and an account of an ordeal between a Catholic priest and an Arian, in a work of Gregory of Tours. The rationale behind the ordeal was that it invoked divine judgement. The ordeal of the cauldron required the accused, or disputants, to recover an iron object (usually a bar, a ring, or a stone) from the bottom of a cauldron filled with hot water. The "proof" of the ordeal was in observing the healing of the hand over a specified number of days. A wound that suppurated was evidence of guilt; a wound that was "clean" indicated God's favour. While not specified in the *Lex Salica*, later evidence informs us that the ordeal was overseen by religious representatives (as were all court procedures) and framed by religious ritual. Also, royal permission was required when one man challenged another to the ordeal.[41] At this early stage, an accused could "redeem his hand" by making payment or finding oath-helpers.[42] Failure at the ordeal of the cauldron usually resulted in a fine.

The ordeal by cauldron is found in barbarian laws directly influenced by Frankish law, including Anglo-Saxon law (*Law of Ine*, c. 690), but it also appears to have developed independently in Irish law from the seventh century on.[43] The ordeal, being one that relies on the interaction of fire and water, is the closest judicial parallel to eschatological depictions in which purgation and punishment of souls took place in association with a river of fire. In visions of the afterlife, the cauldron was a depiction of destruction and damnation. It appears as a motif in one of Gregory of Tours's stories in which King Chilperic was reportedly seen in a vision being broken up and melted in a cauldron.[44] Yet the cauldron motif is not routinely used in visions of the afterlife or in artistic depictions of the afterlife with any regularity before the twelfth century. In Dante's *Inferno*, the poet saw those guilty of fraud being cooked like meat in a pot by devils furnished with pronged forks. The cauldron motif also appears in some other visions of that era in which it is used not for purgatory, but for hell. That is to say, it is viewed as punishment, not a means of establishing innocence and guilt as it was in law. The cauldron has a long and shadowy history as a chthonic image and as an image of food preparation and consumption.[45] There are scriptural sources for consumption in the devouring hell-mouth and the beast of destruction (Leviathan). Curiously, early Christian ascetic literature had imagined cooking bodies as an image of spiritual preparation, and thus of purgation, but this early representation was entirely eclipsed by the biblical image of the mouth of hell. In reducing humans to food, and thus to the status of beasts, the cooking motif of hell's cauldron imaginatively represented the theological view that in hell there were no souls to be saved.

Conclusion

Law codes tell us only part of the story of how Christians thought justice should and could work. The proliferation of stories in monastic, hagiographic, and historical literature in which divine judgment visited the unsuspecting villain with sudden ferocity reveals the way some individuals hoped God would treat their enemies. For themselves, Christians hoped God would show greater mercy for their efforts as they embarked on the long penitential crawl to perfection. While it is possible that the barbarian invasions of the fifth century spurred some Christians on to more introspective and penitential lives, the later Christian barbarian kingdoms contributed very little to visions of purgatory. Indeed, it was not until the ninth-century *Vision of Wetti* and *Redaction 6* that it could be argued (and even then not strongly) that purgatory began to reflect contemporary legal concerns.

In the early middle ages, visions continued to convey images of violence, metaphors of slavery, and the turning inward of pain on the body and on the community. The laws concerning free and unfree status continued to reflect the fear that falling into slavery was tantamount to falling into the pit of hell. Anglo-Saxon law allowed some lucky slaves to be redeemed from the ordeal or from paying for their guilt with their "hyd" if their lord was willing to intervene. But it took a very long time for the instruments of earthly punishment and justice to penetrate depictions of God's justice in purgatory.

Conclusion

It was the Christian's highest hope to be saved for future bliss, preferably without pain and without delay. To be saved "as through fire" was a decidedly inferior option. It was true that this fire offered the Christian the hope of future perfection but it also confronted the Christian with an image of spiritual inadequacy. It is not surprising that early Christians would ask the same questions about this fire that historians now ask: What kind of fire was it? Was it painful? Would it purify the soul, was it punitive, or both? Would it take place immediately after death or at the Final Judgement? Who would go through it and how long would it last? While the answers to these questions varied considerably over time, the very existence of the fire as a means by which some might be saved forced Christians to one common conclusion: that contact with the world had tainted the soul, rendering it unfit for God's immediate society. There would be exceptions: martyrs such as Perpetua, Felicity, and Saturus, "well washed" by the blood they shed, and ascetics such as St. Cuthbert who was "prepared by the fires of internal pain for the joys of everlasting bliss." But most Christians who contemplated this saving fire found their thoughts turned in sorrow to their deficiency. Reflecting soberly on his own fate and that of most Christians, Origen noted that while Aaron and Isaiah had been purified by the fire of the altar, "others who are not of this kind, among whom I reckon myself, shall be cleansed by another fire. I fear it is the one about which it is written 'A river of fire was flowing before him'."[1] Perhaps inevitably, purgatory became a vehicle for reflection on the essential qualities of humanity: its perfectibility, its history, its role in the universe, its susceptibility to pain and emotions and its capacity for mercy, its identity as a community, and its need for the society and help of others.

In spite of the earliest associations of fire with excellence and divinity (one cannot help but think of the flame that cooly licked the hair and forehead of Ascanius Iulus, Aeneas's son), in the hands of Christian theologians the fire turned material, so that pain and suffering became its essential qualities. Purgatorial fire became a way to purify through pain. For those with philosophic training such as Clement, Origen, and the Platonists, it was pain's potential to educate and purify that was fascinating, and it appeared logical that all could be saved by it. Fourth-century theologians, however, who worked so hard to dispel the notion that death posed any barrier for the community of the faithful, found death a fixed barrier when it came to paying for one's sins. In life pain could purify, but after death, punishment must accompany pain as appropriate restitution to God for humanity's infraction. Much ink was spilled devising ways to make purgatory's fires more intense and thus less appealing as an option for salvation. Penance, rather than purgatory, was the recommended path to heaven. Yet, as sermon writers never tired of pointing out, procrastination was a fatal weakness. Since any day could be one's last, the stakes for sinners were plainly high. Would God be merciful? Or would God's condemnation be visited upon them? Somehow, the present life never seemed to offer quite enough time to get it right. It must have seemed that earthly life had become too short for the soul to achieve its potential divinity. The afterlife, by contrast, offered more time for correction. Perhaps salvation could be achieved if time was truly sufficient for it.

Here was Origen's appeal. Origen did not doubt that humankind was tainted and that perfection was only to be found in God, but he was also convinced that the cosmos was a divine engine for salvation and that it continued to be such after the soul had taken off the "garment" of the body. He wondered, "whether after this world there will be a course of healing and improvement, very severe no doubt and full of pain to those who have refused to obey the word of God, yet a process of instruction and rational training through which those who in this present life have devoted themselves to these pursuits and, being made purer in the mind, have attained here and now to a capacity for divine wisdom, may advance to a richer understanding of truth." He even wondered, whether "for the correction and improvement of those who need it there will be yet another world, either similar to the one that now exists, or better than it, or possibly much worse; and how long will the world that comes after this exist, of whatever sort it be, or whether it will exist at all; and if there will ever be a time when there will be no world anywhere, or if there ever was a time when there was no world at all; or if there have been, or shall be, many worlds."[2] In reaction to such lively speculations, pragmatic theologians in the Latin West emphatically shut the doors of hell. In the western tradition, salvation has been taken to be something that must be achieved in life, and at birth the soul's course was inexorably set toward a future, but conclusive judgement.

Bede's triumph was to set aside those elements in Origen's eschatology that were so repugnant to the theology of the Latin West while using his own works to expand the ranks of those who might be eligible to be saved. Grave sinners now found that they had a "very long time," as once promised by Origen, to achieve salvation; not through successive embodiments of the soul, but in a single journey to a heavenly destination. The truly wicked—the devil and his satellites—would still go to hell, and hell would seal them in for eternity. But after all, how many Christians in a Christian society, availed of the Church's salvific rituals, would now join them in perdition?

Bede's explicit if fleeting reference to Origen's error allows us to glimpse him grappling with Origen, and perhaps to a greater extent with Origenism, as the "backstory" to a compassionate afterlife. We do not know if Bede was aware of Origen's *First Principles*, the principal text in which Origen outlined his all-inclusive notions of guaranteed salvation, or whether he knew of Origen only through his commentaries, the fourth-century debates and anathematizing councils of the fourth and sixth centuries. In some respects this does not matter. For Bede, as for western churchmen generally, Origen was the one who left the door to hell open, and the task of the orthodox Christian was to keep it closed. Repeatedly, Bede showed his intellectual and theological alliance with Jerome, Augustine, and Gregory the Great. Jerome and Augustine had also grappled with Origen's legacy, although by that time the nature of fourth-century debates had already reduced Origen's thoughts to a few key issues. Bede was well aware of those historical debates and he knew the exact nature of Origen's eschatological transgression: that the wicked might be saved. This was the position that Bede was so careful to avoid: the "impious" would be condemned to hell but the "scelerous" would be saved. Thus on the most overt level, Bede's attitude toward Origen, as toward any other heretic, was complete repudiation. Origen was not acceptable to western orthodoxy. Yet Origen's was the "beautiful mind" of early Christian exegesis. His was "a genius so powerful, so profound, so acute, so elegant, that there was hardly anyone whom he did not very far surpass," as Vincent of Lérins expressed it, a generation after Origen's first official condemnation. Yet Origen was a great "trial of the Church"; his crime was intellectual hubris, whereby he "wantonly abused the grace of God."[3] That is why Bede took the grace of God as his theme when he wrote on purgatory in his *Homily for Advent*.

It is tempting to hypothesize that Bede knowingly entertained some sympathy for Origen's humanism while he set about rejecting its error. Consummate intellectual that he was, Bede, like Origen, could not imagine that the delights of inquiry would cease in paradise. Where Origen had imagined a *schola animarum*, with lessons in the meaning of the tribes of Israel, feast days and jubilees, herbs and plants, and the judgement of divine providence (on every individual matter!), Bede imagined lectures on the Trinity. It is not clear to what extent Bede's confidence in the powers of extended purgation was influenced by England's contacts with eastern thought in the seventh century. Such contacts are better documented from the ninth century onward, and in the writings of John Scottus Eriugena, a transformed Origenism once again entered the afterlife debate and continued to do so throughout the middle ages. Less appreciated is the extent to which Origen's legacy continued to influence debate about the afterlife between the fourth century and the ninth century, at a time that was crucial in purgatory's formation.

While placing Bede at a critical juncture in the gradual formation of purgatory, I have also challenged some theories that have sought to account for purgatory's rising importance in these centuries. I have tried to show why it is problematic to suggest that the barbarian invasions; the barbarian law codes; tariffed penitential practice; Celtic, Irish, Germanic, and Northumbrian culture; or papal imperialism can, as a singular explanation, account for the emergence of purgatory. It is true that communities changed and that conceptual images of the afterlife also changed in this period, but it is also incontrovertible that purgation and purgatorial processes had long had a place in Christian theological thinking. Yet, in the absence of strong scriptural guidance, discussions of purgatory often arose in large part from the desire of Western Christians to explain *other* things: how Christians could be "saved by fire"; how the dead could be helped through prayer and works of others; how sin could be removed from the soul, and how the soul could be prepared to meet God; how divine justice would ultimately prevail; or why mortality and pain could be reconciled with the actions of a merciful God. While many great thinkers, whether Christian or not, had grappled with such weighty issues in the third and fourth centuries, the principle authority on such matters for medieval theologians was Augustine—a received, or even a perceived version of Augustine—whose authority could be cited in support of a purgatory whose precise definition he had always been at pains to avoid.

In later centuries, visionary descriptions of purgatory became lengthier and more detailed, and differentiated tortures that were not limited to fire became commonplace. The idea that souls in purgatory were undergoing a form of penance did indeed eventually arise as a way of understanding the redemptive nature of suffering and encouraging devotional and penitential practices among the living. Indeed, in artistic images of purgatory of a later age, souls in the fire of purgatory could be distinguished from souls in the fire of hell by the convention of having their hands brought together in a gesture of prayer. This was the result of later theological developments, however, and was not the way purgatory was thought to operate in earlier centuries.

Purgatory was successful as an idea in these early centuries because it accomplished a number of important things: it impressed upon lukewarm Christians the need for ongoing penance; it suggested coherence at the point at which the scriptures and religious practice converged, as in the prayers for the dead; and it drew ordinary Christians within the eschatological net of salvation. Yet, I think we come closest to understanding purgatory's success and longevity when we ask, not when did purgatory achieve doctrinal status, but when did purgatory achieve theological viability? The answer, I have suggested, is the point at which Origen's univeralism was repudiated in favour of an expanded access to salvation as was endorsed in the work of Bede. Purgatory's future was assured once it was supposed that a broad segment of the Christian population could be saved by means of exposure to purgatory's fires, even if they repented only at the very moment of death, and even if they were compelled to rely on the piety and resources of their "friends."

Notes

INTRODUCTION

1. Julianus, *De vita contemplativa* 1. 2; trans. Suelzer, 19; Augustine, *Enchiridion,* 69; trans. Arand, 70.

2. Treatments of violence in the early middle ages often focus on specific acts of violence or the social and legal systems of violence and reparation and often ignore mental attitudes to justice and violence as would have been nurtured in education and in other authoritative contexts. An exception is the collection of papers on violence in late antiquity edited by Harold Drake in which numerous articles examine the intellectual and educational milieu of violence: *Violence in Late Antiquity.*

3. On the First Council of Lyons, see Denziger and Schönmetzer, *Enchiridion symbolorum, 446.* On the Second Council of Lyons, see Le Goff, *Birth of Purgatory,* 284–86. Purgatory's status as Catholic doctrine was pronounced at the Council of Florence in 1439 and the Council of Trent in 1563.

4. Medieval clerics integrated tales of ghostly apparitions into Christian religious culture. Schmitt, *Ghosts in the Middle Ages,* 128, relates that in his *Dialogus miraculorum,* Caesarius of Heisterbach (twelfth century) "corrected" apparitions of the dead who stated that they were in hell. Early Protestants rejected the idea that the dead returned to the living as ghosts; although by the seventeenth century such ideas began to resurface in Protestant publications in England and were even brought to public discussion by one Anglican divine: see Marshall, *Mother Leakey and the Bishop,* 184, 217ff.

5. See Gurevich, "Popular and Scholarly Medieval Cultural Traditions."

6. Biblical translations are from the Revised Standard Version of the Bible (RSV) unless the citation is quoted in a Latin source, in which case I have translated from the Latin in the source.

7. Du Moulin, *Waters of Siloe*. The work has been digitized and is usefully available online on the EEBO website. See Marshall, *Beliefs and the Dead*, 44.

8. For example, Audisio notes that in an era in which they tried to evade detection, some Waldensian communities in Provence between 1530 and 1560 requested the customary thirteen masses up to the first anniversary of death, but not the thirty masses (Trental) that most other wills requested. See his "How to Detect a Clandestine Minority." This suggests that while this grouping of Waldensians was willing to stomach a limited regimen of masses, the Trental, with its supposed papal association, was viewed as particularly objectionable by them and particularly tied to a papal definition of purgatory.

9. See Marshall on Reformation views of purgatory in *Beliefs and the Dead*, especially pp. 143–44.

10. Du Moulin, *Waters of Siloe*.

11. Eire, *From Madrid to Purgatory*, delves deep into the Spanish culture of purgatory as revealed in Madrilense wills and in particular in Philip II's construction of the Escorial, a royal necropolis dedicated to purgatorial ideas.

12. Le Goff, *Your Money or Your Life*. Penitentials and law codes are important for understanding the cultural milieu of visions of the afterlife. Claude Carozzi uses them successfully alongside church councils to suggest dates and contexts for the texts he discusses, for example in *Le voyage de l'âme*, 275ff. He does not attribute the inception of purgatory directly to them.

13. Brown, "Decline of the Empire of God," "End of the Ancient Other World," and "Vers la naissance du Purgatoire."

14. Le Goff, *Birth of Purgatory*, 130–32. Other dates have also been suggested depending on the medium being examined. Wills do not refer to purgatory explicitly until the fourteenth century (Le Goff, "Time of Purgatory"). From an art history perspective, purgatory does not make its popular appearance until the "explosion" of images in the fifteenth century when depictions of souls springing from purgatory began to appear in a wide variety of media: altarpieces, breviaries, frescoes, and engravings. Some isolated fourteenth-century examples circulated among the elite, for example in the so-called Breviary of Charles V, dated somewhere between 1347 and 1380. On this, see Vovelle, *Les âmes du purgatoire*, 17ff.

15. Reviews and response articles include Bredero, "Le Moyen Age et le purgatoire"; Gurevich, "Popular and Scholarly Medieval Cultural Traditions"; Bernstein, "Jacques Le Goff, *La naissance du purgatoire*," ; Southern, "Between Heaven and Hell"; Edwards, "Purgatory: 'Birth' or Evolution?"; McGuire, "Purgatory, the Communion of Saints."

16. Various alternative frameworks have been suggested. Bredero favoured a span of the ninth to the twelfth centuries to explain the birth of purgatory (in "Le Moyen Age et le purgatoire," 132). Gurevich's articles pointed to purification motifs in the visionary literature of the early Middle Ages. Peter Brown's thesis centres on the seventh century as the crucial moment of change.

17. Le Goff's *Birth of Purgatory* (*La naissance du purgatoire* [1981]) has been challenged on a number of grounds but remains an exceptionally useful overview of purgatory's significance to intellectual and religious meaning in the middle ages. Le Goff located purgatory's "birth" in the decade 1170–80.

18. Carozzi, *Le voyage de l'âme*. See also Carozzi, "La géographie de l'au-delà," and Le Goff's response in the same volume, 483–88.

19. In recent literature concerned with the development of western notions about the afterlife, there is agreement among a wide group of scholars that the seventh century is a demarcation in the history of the afterlife. In his widely acclaimed study of visionary literature, *Le voyage de l'âme*, Carozzi notes (pp. 5, 635) that despite occasional anticipation of otherworldly journeying earlier, the true starting point for medieval accounts is the production of the *Vision of Fursey* and the *Vision of Barontus* in the seventh century. Jocelyn N. Hillgarth also sees the rise of Christian visionary literature as largely a product of the seventh-century West ("Eschatological and Political Concepts").

20. Building largely on themes arising from French historiography of the 1970s.

21. The importance of visionary literature was already signposted by Le Goff in *Birth of Purgatory* and by Gurevich in "Au moyen age."

22. Brown, "End of the Ancient Other World"; see also Brown, "Decline of the Empire of God" and "Vers la naissance du Purgatoire."

23. Brown, "End of the Ancient Other World," 24–25.

24. Dunn, "Origins of Purgatory."

25. Ibid.

26. Bernstein, *Formation of Hell*; Trumbower, *Rescue for the Dead*.

27. Ciccarese, "Le più antiche rappresentazioni del purgatorio,"; Carozzi, *Eschatologie et l'au-delà*; Jiroušková, *Die Visio Pauli*.

28. Rebillard, *In Hora Mortis*.

29. Effros, *Caring for Body and Soul*.

30. Angenendt, "Theologie und Liturgie," and its expanded form in Angenendt, *Geschichte der Religiosität*. Sicard, *La liturgie de la mort*, 260–79. Paxton, *Christianizing Death*, 52–55.

31. Landgraf opined that there was no exegetical development in the early middle ages between Gregory the Great and Alcuin, in "1 Cor. 3, 10–17." He does not mention Bede.

32. Noted by Carroll, "An Eighth-Century Exegete on Purgatory," 261–63, but unnoted by subsequent writers.

33. Fulke, *Two treatises written against the papistes*, 194. Fulke exculpated Bede on one account: "for albeit I acknowledge, that he reporteth many fables for true miracles, yet this reuerence I professe to haue of him, that I thinke, he fained not one of them him selfe, but had them as hee confesseth by relation of other." *A defense of the sincere and true translations of the holie Scriptures into the English tong*, 44.

34. Wright, *St. Patrick's Purgatory*, 7, 18, 23: "In Bede's time . . . it seems to have been a matter of speculation whether there existed such an expiatory place or not, but the two visions which the historian has recorded perhaps went further than any reasoning to dispel the doubts that might exist" (p. 23). This was an early and original work of scholarship by the highly respected "antiquarian."

35. For example, Becker, "A Contribution to the Comparative Study of Medieval Visions," 49, identifies the importance of Bede and the Anglo-Saxon contribution although he decries it: "The authority which Bede enjoyed in England throughout the Middle Ages and the unquestioning and reverent credulity which was accorded all his utterances, make his work a most important factor in a study like the present." He further notes of the *Vision of Drythelm* (p. 52): "It is, furthermore, particularly interesting, in that it makes specific mention of purgatory as a place of probation, as distinguished from hell, whence there is no release. Nowhere else throughout Anglo-Saxon literature, outside of Bede, is this doctrine advanced." However, most nineteenth-century Protestant writings on purgatory, or "probationism," appear quite deliberately to have ignored Bede. See, for example, Cochrane's *Future Punishment* which collected various works by "scientists and theologians" on the topic including Dick, "Notes on Probationism and Purgatory."

36. Coleridge, *Prisoners of the King*, who extolled the doctrine as indicative of the "gentleness" of the church did not mention Bede as an authority. Cochrane, *Future Punishment*, also failed to include Bede.

37. Le Goff did not provide an integrated analysis of Bede's writing and examined the *Vision of Drythelm* separately from his other writings. Bede is not generally mentioned in broader studies of the afterlife, for example, in Segal's otherwise detailed *Life After Death*.

CHAPTER 1

1. Le Goff, *Birth of Purgatory*, chaps. 1–3; Merkt, *Das Fegefeuer*; Michel, "Purgatoire."

2. Le Goff, *Birth of Purgatory*, 84.

3. This is not to say that Bede, or indeed Boniface, was always entirely in agreement with contemporary papal policies and decisions, or the way papal councils had sometimes interfered in ecclesiastical matters in England. See Moorhead, "Bede on the Papacy." On Bede as "patriotic Northumbrian," concerned for local reform, see Thacker, "Bede's Ideal of Reform."

4. Bede, *Homilies*; ed. Hurst, *Bedae Venerabilis homiliarum Evangelii Libri II*, 13; trans. Martin and Hurst, *Bede, Homilies of the Gospels*, 17. For Latin text and discussion of its debt to Augustine's *Enchiridion*, see chapter 6 below.

5. Michel, "Purgatoire," lists them: Matthew 12:31–32; Matthew 5, 25–26; Luke 16:9; Matthew 5:22; Luke 23:42; Acts 2:24; 1 Corinthians 15:29; Philippians 2:10; Luke 12:48; 2 Timothy 1:16-18; 1 Corinthians 3:11–15.

6. Malachi 3:2: "For he is like a refiner's fire and like fullers' soap; he will sit as a refiner and purifier of silver, and he will purify the sons of Levi and refine them like gold and silver, till they present right offerings to the Lord." Daniel 3:19–25 on the Hebrews in the fire.

7. Le Goff, *Birth of Purgatory*, 43.

8. Consequently, Gnilka's study that examined 1 Corinthians 3:10–15 as a basis for the study of purgatory, did not include Bede, although he did include pseudo-Bede, *Ist 1 Kor. 3, 10-15*, 83.

9. See Landgraf, "1 Cor. 3, 10–17"; see also, Gnilka, *Ist 1 Kor. 3, 10–15*; Michel, "Purgatoire," 1174–79.

10. I examine the penitential context for discussions of purgatory in chapter 5. The scope of penance's ability to expunge sin was much debated in the third and fourth centuries as pastors confronted the problem of the lapsed. The link between penance in the present life and satisfaction of debt in the afterlife was an early and continuing arena for discussions of postmortem salvation and purgatory.

11. Thus Origen, see von Balthasar, *Origen: Spirit and Fire*, 326.

12. Landgraf, "1 Cor. 3, 10–17," 146. The fire of God was more commonly referenced in writings on Pentecost, for example in Gregory the Great, *Homily 30*, in the *Homilies on the Gospels*, who linked that fire with Hebrews 12:29, to note that "God is called a fire because he consumes the rust of sin" (Trans. Hurst, 240).

13. Marshall, *Beliefs and the Dead*, examines the difficulty in extricating prayer for the dead from belief in purgatory in Reformation England. One might say that prayer for the dead and the idea of purgatory go so well together that they seem unavoidably linked, and indeed, catholic theology cited one as evidence for the other.

14. Second Maccabees was a proof text for purgatory for sixteenth-century Catholics. Reformers, including Luther, claimed that it was not canonical. Le Goff, *Birth of Purgatory*, 42, notes that "medieval Christians looked upon this text as confirming two things: that sins can be redeemed after death and that the prayers of the living are an effective way of accomplishing this."

15. Second Maccabees is a deuterocanonical text, that is, accepted as scripture by the Roman Catholic, Greek, and Russian Orthodox churches, even though it does not have a place in the Hebrew Canon. On the complexity of early canonical lists, see Sundberg, "The Old Testament of the Early Church (A Study in Canon)." Unless otherwise indicated, all citations from the Bible are from the Revised Standard Version.

16. Trumbower, *Rescue*, 26–29.

17. Ibid., 27.

18. Ibid., 29.

19. Ibid., 26–30. On the complex fusion of Jewish and Hellenistic values in the text, see Himmelfarb, "Judaism and Hellenism in 2 Maccabees."

20. This fact was noted by O'Brien who attributed the absence of its early use to variant readings available to the early church fathers ("Scriptural Proof for the Existence of Purgatory from 2 Machabees"). Augustine cited it in the context of prayer for the dead in his *De natura et origine animae*, 1.13.

21. The account of the Maccabean mother (later given the name Salomona) and seven martyrs is found in 2 Maccabees 7 and 4 Maccabees 8ff. The cult of the Maccabean "martyrs" was known in southern Gaul, with feast days observed in August, and the cult was the subject of sermons in some fifth-century communities: see Prévot, "Le modèle des Maccabées dans la pastorale gauloise au Ve siècle." Prévot makes the interesting suggestion that the fifth-century emphasis on the Maccabean mother may be connected to the rise of the cult of the Virgin as "theotokos" (Mother of God) in the wake of the council of Ephesus in 431.

22. *Carmina* 10.15.

23. Robert McGrath, "Martyrdom of the Maccabees," argues that a scene on the Brescia casket (fifth century) represents the Maccabean brothers among flames against its traditional identification as the three Hebrews. By the time of Gregory the Great, *Homilies on the Gospels*, Homily 1, the martyr Felicity was said to have had seven sons who preceded her in martyrdom—perhaps a Christian double for the Maccabean mother?

24. Augustine, *De cura pro mortuis gerenda* 1. 3 only alludes vaguely to 2 Maccabees; Julian of Toledo, *Prognosticum*, appears to be the first to comment on this passage to discuss the value of prayer for the differentiated dead, but when he discusses purgation elsewhere in the work (1. 18) he does not allude to 2 Maccabees. The discourses remained distinct, as they were for Augustine.

25. Bede, *On Tobias*, 4, mentions the ordeals of the Maccabees in relation to the sanctity of the synagogue. Antiochus's conquests and the Maccabean revolt furnished Carolingian illustrators with imperial and military themes; see Gaehde, "Pictorial Sources of the Illustrations to the Books of Kings, Proverbs, Judith and Maccabees," especially 384–89.

26. For this overview, see Trumbower, *Rescue*, 34–41.

27. Gounelle, *La descente du Christ aux Enfers*, examines the *descensus* in various sources including creeds up to the early sixth century.

28. For example, Clement of Alexandria, *Stromateis*, 2. 7. 34; 3. 27. 5; Lactantius, *Divine Institutes*, 7. 21. 7; Origen, *Homilies on Jeremiah*, 2. 3. 2.

29. Daniel 3:19–25.

30. See Hill, *Regnum Caelorum*, 17, 121 n. 199.

31. *Stromata*, 4. 24. Clement owed this perspective largely to Platonic thought. However, Clement's writings on this subject are open to multiple interpretations. See below.

32. *Stromata*, 8. 6.

33. Lactantius, Divinae Institutiones, 7. 21. 7; trans. Bowen and Garnsey, *Lactantius: Divine Institutes*, 431.

34. *Christian Sibylline Oracles*; trans. Treu, NTA vol. 2, 1. 212–13. See an analogous passage in 8. 41-12, of the *Christian Sibylline*: "and thou shalt have light eternal and life unfading, when I bring all men to proof by fire. For I shall smelt all things, and separate them into purity" (Trans. Treu, 670). In the *Latin Sibyl*, it is faith that will purge crime.

35. Bremmer, *Rise and Fall of the Afterlife*, 65.

36. Daley, *Hope of the Early Church*, 34.

37. Tertullian, *Against Marcion* 4.34; trans. Evans, *Adversus Marcionem*, vol. 2, 45–57.

38. Tertullian, *De anima*, 55–58.

39. Tertullian, *De spectaculis*, 30.

40. The alternative view was expressed by Lactantius, *Divinae Institutiones*, 7. 21.7: "No one should think that souls are judged immediately upon dying, however; all are kept under one common guard until the moment comes when their merits are tested by the supreme judge." Trans. Bowen and Garnsey, *Lactantius: Divine Institutes*, 431.

41. Trans. Evans, *Adversus Marcionem*, 4. 34. The Elysian Fields are thus not to be equated with the kingdom of God, which was generally viewed as a celestial city and which was reportedly seen for forty days in the morning hovering over Judea during the era of persecution (*Adversus Marcionem*, 3.24). By relegating the pagan paradise to the interim period, Christians could reconcile traditional tales of paradise with Christian eschatology without diminishing the significance of the Last Judgement and the eternal heavenly residence.

42. *Passio Perpetuae*; trans. Shewring, *Passion of SS. Perpetua and Felicity*. Perpetua's visions of Dinocrates are examined in Trumbower, *Rescue*, 76–90; Amat, *Songes et Visions*, 128–31; Cox-Miller, *Dreams in Late Antiquity*, 158–61, which briefly summarizes scholarly views.

43. *Poena* can be translated as "pain" or "punishment." The distinction largely rests on individual interpretation of the text and the extent to which it is thought to convey pagan or Christian attitudes to death.

44. Trumbower, *Rescue*.

45. Augustine argued that Dinocrates was a Christian; on the significance of this stance, see Trumbower, *Rescue*, 135–36.

46. Ibid., 83.

47. Klawiter, "Priestly Authority of Women in Early Christianity." Klawiter claims that in the New Prophecy movement released confessors continued to hold martyr status when they returned to their communities and continued to claim the power of the keys. This claim distinguished them from, and was ultimately perceived as threatening to, the Catholic Church. See also Butler, *New Prophecy and "New Visions,"* 41.

48. Klawiter, "Priestly Authority of Women in Early Christianity," 258. Amat, *Songes et Visions*, 130, also concludes that while the water fountain imagery is not entirely orthodox, the symbolism is clearly that of baptism, a baptism for Dinocrates effected through his sister's blood in martyrdom.

49. Merkt, *Das Fegefeuer*.

50. Ibid., 23–26; Dölger, "Antike Parallelen zum leidenden Dinokrates in der Passio Perpetuae"; Von Franz, "Die Passio Perpetuae"; Dronke, *Women Writers of the Middle Ages*, 1–17.

51. For example, Pettersen, "Perpetua—Prisoner of Conscience"; Salisbury, *Perpetua's Passion*, 104–6, who focuses briefly and exclusively on Perpetua's assumption of a maternal role through these visions.

52. Bremmer, *Rise and Fall of the Afterlife*, 66.

53. Merkt, *Das Fegefeuer*, 49: "Obwohl man redlicherweise nicht behaupten kann, dass schon in der Passio Perpetuae die Vorstellung vom Purgatorium zutage tritt, finden sich in ihr doch unbestreitbar einzelne Anschauungen (endliches Leiden Verstorbener, Fürbitte, Leidensüberwindung), die in späterer Zeit zum Purgatorium zusammengedacht wurden."

54. Augustine wrote four sermons to celebrate the feast of saints Perpetua and Felicity; see Shewring's translation. Sermon 1 praises not her ability to pray for the dead while living but her ability to pray for Christians now that she is dead. Brent Shaw examines Augustine's sermons on the feast of saints Perpetua and Felicity as "control pieces" ("Passion of Perpetua," see 36ff).

55. Osborn, *Philosophy of Clement of Alexandria*, 80.

56. Daley, *Hope of the Early Church*, 47.

57. Clement, *Paidagogos*, 1. 8 (68): "The punishments that are inflicted on those who sin aim at their salvation." Trans. Wood, *Clement of Alexandri: Christ the Educator*, 60.

58. Origen, *On First Principles*; see Henri De Lubac's introduction to Butterworth's translation. On Origen's eschatology, see Daley, *Hope of the Early Church*, 47–64; Trumbower, *Rescue*, 113–19. On Origen's views of purification, see Michel, "Purgatoire," *DTC*, 13.1, 1193–96.

59. Origen, *Homilies on Jeremiah*, 16. 5.

60. Ibid., 16. 6.

61. Origen, *First Principles*, 2. 10. 4.

62. Ibid., 1. 6. 2 (Latin): "each becomes the cause of his own lapse or fall." Trans. Butterworth, 53.

63. Ibid., 3. 6. 6: "gradually and by degrees, during the lapse of infinite and immeasurable ages."

64. Ibid., 2. 10. 3 (Greek); trans. Butterworth, 146.

65. Ibid., 2. 10. 3.

66. Modern, wistful apologists for Origen abound. Richardson, "Condemnation of Origen," p. 50, commented that in 553, "all that was fine and liberal and mature in the faith and thought of Origen had been condemned."

67. Trumbower, *Rescue*, 114; Rabinowitz, "Personal and Cosmic Salvation."

68. Origen's view that purification of sinners occurred for a time beyond Judgement Day was peculiar to him. See Origen, *Homilies on Leviticus 1-16*, Homily 8. 4, where sinners receive two extra weeks of purification (understood metaphorically). Michel, "Purgatoire," column 1195, discusses this allegory. Bede shows he was aware of this distinctive view in his *Commentary on Proverbs* 2. 11. 7.

69. Lactantius was an exception, believing there was no immediate judgement after death (*Divine Institutes* 7. 21.7).

70. As for example in Saturus's vision of Perpetua and in the play of the newly refreshed Dinocrates. Origen believed the receptacles of the just would be a paradise.

71. Plotinus, *Enneads*, 3.6.5; trans. Mackenna, 193.

72. Augustine, *De civitate Dei*, 10.23, 24 (hereafter *Civ. Dei*).

73. Ambrosiaster, *Commentary on the Pauline Letters*; trans. Migne, *Commentaria in epistolam b. Pauli ad Corinthios*, 200.

74. Ambrose, *Expositio psalmi cxviii*, 20.12. Ambrose continues to assure Christians that the fiery sword will not be feared by Christians who have the fire of love.

75. Ambrose, *De bono mortis*, 10. 44ff.

76. Ibid., 11. 48; trans. McHugh, *St. Ambrose: Seven Exegetical Works*, 104.

77. Ambrose, *Expositio psalmi cxviii*, 20. 24.

78. Du Moulin, *Waters of Siloe*, 345 (*EEBO* image 196): "St. Ambrose hath written an excellent treatise of the benefit of death which is no other but a refutation of Purgatory of the Romish Church." Ambrose's rejection of the "fables of the poets" would have been regarded as an implicit rejection of terrifying visions of hell and purgatory.

79. Clark, "Jerome's Commentary on Ephesians in the Origenist Controversy," is illuminating on the way Origenist thought was in turn defended and repudiated in the intellectual wrangling of Rufinus and Jerome. See also, O'Connell, *Eschatology of Saint Jerome*. For an account of the debate, see Kelly, *Jerome: His Life, Writings and Controversies*, 309–23.

80. Augustine, *Civ. Dei*, 21.13: *sed illis sunt purgatoriae, qui eis coherciti corriguntur*. CCSL 48, 779. On purgatory in Augustine's thought, see Ntedika, *L'Évolution*; Le Goff, *Birth of Purgatory*, 61–85, who terms Augustine the true "Father of Purgatory"; and Trumbower, *Rescue*, 126–40, who examines auxiliary issues.

81. Augustine, *Civ. Dei*, 21. 2. The context is Augustine's refutation of the Platonic idea that all punishments are purificatory. Augustine writes: "this life has been made a life of punishment for us" (*Civ. Dei*, 21. 15). Atwell examines purgation and prayer in "Aspects in St. Augustine of Hippo's Thought and Spirituality," 3–13, although Atwell maintains (p. 7) that Augustine believed the penitential process "if not already begun this side of death, must surely occur after it." No citation accompanies this comment.

82. Augustine, *Civ. Dei*, 20. 26.

83. Ibid., 21. 16.

84. Ibid., 21. 26.

85. Augustine, *Enchiridion*, 18.

86. Augustine, *De Genesi ad litteram*, 12. 33. See Kotila, *Memoria mortuorum*, 124–30, for a lucid discussion of Augustine's eschatological perspective and his interconnection of the present with the future life.

87. *Civ. Dei*, 21. 26.

88. Ntedika, *L'évolution*, 16ff. Ntedika suggested three stages in Augustine's thought in the matter: the first up to 413 when Augustine relied on earlier patristic writings on the fire of judgement; then the second stage, 413–26, during which he was occupied with the *misericordes* and emphasized that tribulations related to the present life; and finally in his third stage, in his *De fide et operibus*, *Enchiridion*, and *City of God*, Augustine conceded that such a fire did exist after death although he never developed the idea beyond a hypothesis. Ntedika also notes that it was in the second stage of Augustine's involvement with the issue that the apocryphal apocalypses like the *Vision of Paul* began to circulate widely.

89. Augustine, *De gestis Pelagiis*, 3. 9-11 where Pelagius was forced to distance himself from Origen's theology of *apocatastasis*. See also Clark, *The Origenist Controversy*, 194–244.

90. *Civ. Dei*, 21. 16.

91. Augustine, *Enchiridion*, 29 [109-10]:

Tempus autem quod inter hominis mortem et ultimam resurrectionem interpositum est, animas abditis receptaculis continet, sicut unaquaeque digna est vel requie vel aerumna pro eo quod sortita est in carne dum viveret. Neque negandum est defunctorum animas pietate suorum viventium relevari, cum pro illis sacrificium mediatoris offertur vel eleemosynae in ecclesia fiunt. Sed eis haec prosunt qui cum viverent haec ut sibi postea possent prodesse meruerunt. Est enim quidam vivendi modus, nec tam bonus ut non requirat ista post mortem, nec tam malus ut ei non prosint ista post mortem; est vero talis in bono ut ista non requirat, et est rursus talis in malo ut nec his valeat cum ex hac vita transierit adiuvari. Quocirca hic omne meritum comparatur quo possit post hanc vitam relevari quispiam vel gravari. Nemo autem se speret quod hic neglexerit, cum obierit apud dominum promereri (Latin ed. Evans, *CCSL* 46, 108; trans. Peebles, *Saint Augustine*, 461–62).

92. The verb *relevo* can be rendered into English in numerous ways, referring to relief, consolation, alleviation, lightning, diminution, deliverance, comfort, or refreshment.

93. Augustine, *De cura pro mortuis gerenda*.

94. Trans. Peebles, *Saint Augustine*, 462–63.

95. Augustine, *Sermons on the Liturgical Seasons*, Sermon 172. While this sermon is commonly cited as Augustine's, doubts have been raised concerning Augustine's authorship of Sermon 172. Its date is not known. See Dekkers, *Clavis Patrum Latinorum*, p. 140 where it is listed under spurious sermons.

96. Ntedika, *L'évolution*.

97. Needless to say, there is significant disagreement on this issue. Kotila summarizes it well; see *Memoria mortuorum*, 124–25. However, I disagree with Kotila's affirmative assessment that these components in Augustine's thought *must* be "intrinsically related."

CHAPTER 2

1. Origen, *Commentary on the Epistle to the Romans* 2. 2. 2; trans. Schreck, vol. 1, 105.

2. Origen, *Homilies on Jeremiah*, 12. 5.

3. Ibid., 2. 3. 2; trans. Smith, *Origen*, 26.

4. See Hill, *Regnum Caelorum*, 17, 121 n. 199.

5. Clement of Alexandria, *Stromateis*, 4. 24. Clement owed this perspective largely to Platonic thought..

6. Ibid., 8. 6.

7. Origen, *First Principles*, 3. 10. *Homilies on Jeremiah*, 2. 3. 2. In *Homilies on Leviticus 1–6*, 11. 7, Origen makes a distinction between penance in this life and punishment in the next: "vengeance is reserved for us in the future." Trans. Barkley, 215.

8. *Bigotian Penitential*, 25; Bieler, *Irish Penitentials*, 203.

9. Augustine, *Civ. Dei*, 19.15, compares sin to slavery.

10. Ibid., 21.13: *sed illis sunt purgatoriae, qui eis coherciti corriguntur*. *CCSL* 48, 779.

11. Augustine, *Civ. Dei*, 21.2.

12. Origen, *Homilies on Jeremiah*, 11.5.2: "For everything that is in generation has need of purification from fire; everything which is in generation has need of punishment." Trans. Smith, *Origen*, 107.

13. *Vision of Paul*. Latin text in *Apocalypse of Paul*, ed. Silverstein and Hilhorst, 160: *Sanguis meus propter vos effusus est, et nec penituistis. Propter vos coronam de spinis in capite portavi manusque meas confixerunt clavis et nec condoluistis. Aquam petivi pendens: dederunt mihi acetum cum felle mixtum. Lancea apaeruerunt latus meum dextrum propter nomen hominum.* Unless otherwise noted, I use the Latin text and English translation of the *Vision of Paul* in Silverstein and Hilhorst, eds. *Apocalypse of Paul*. For additional bibliographic information on this text, see n.53 below.

14. This imaginative perspective was evidently compelling for preachers. See, for example, Caesarius of Arles, *Sermons,* Sermon 57; Eligius of Noyon (drawing on Caesarius), *De supremo iudicio*, 11; ed. Krusch, 256–57.

15. Augustine, *Civ. Dei*, 21.13.

16. *Life of Pachomius* (SBo), 82; trans. Veilleux, *Life of Saint Pachomius and His Disciples*, p. 109.

17. Ibid. p. 109. The examples given are St. Stephen, all the martyrs, Job, and David.

18. Gregory the Great, *Dialogues*, 4. 24; trans. Zimmerman, *Saint Gregory the Great: Dialogues*, 216.

19. Gregory the Great, *Dialogues*, 4. 11; trans. Zimmerman, *Saint Gregory the Great: Dialogues*, 202.

20. Gregory the Great, *Dialogues* 4.11; trans. Zimmerman, *Saint Gregory the Great: Dialogues*, 202.

21. Glancy, *Slavery in Early Christianity,* takes a sober view of what this would have entailed for Christian slaves in practice and argues that most slaves would not have had sufficient control over their own bodies to be able to keep the moral codes, especially chastity, required for membership in the Pauline Christian community.

22. For example, when Melania the Younger decided to sell all her goods, she freed 8,000 slaves, although some of them chose the protection of her brother-in-law, Severus. *Life of Saint Melania the Younger*; ed. Gorce, *Vie de Sainte Mélanie*, 145–57 and n. 6.

23. See Garnsey, *Ideas of Slavery from Aristotle to Augustine*; Kyrtatas, "Slavery as Progress" Bradley, "Animalizing the Slave," which examines the figure of Lucius the Ass in Apuleius's *Metamorphoses* as a foil for understanding the "animalization" of the slave and the process of enslavement.

24. Harrill, "Paul and the Slave Self," views Paul's use of the slave *persona* as critical for understanding Paul's meaning and emphasizes the importance of applying the Roman and Gentile understanding of the slave as having both body and reason (as distinct from the Greek emphasis on body alone) to Paul's comments. He suggests that "using stereotypes about slaves familiar from wider 'pagan' culture, Paul aims to help his encoded Gentile readers move into a dialogic relation with their old, preconverted selves."

25. The conjunction of the slavery metaphor in Paul with eschatological themes relates to Pauline anthropology, not to afterlife expectations, which at this point were not fully developed. Harrill, for example, states, "the eschatological hope of salvation is not release of the soul from the body but redemption of the self ... from the 'law of sin and death' for enslavement to God, where it belongs" (Harrill, "Paul and the Slave Self," 61).

26. Galatians 4:1ff.

27. Glancy discusses this passage and its slave-trade metaphor as it relates to Paul's concerns about Corinthian men using prostitutes. Glancy's work brings stark attention to slavery's acceptance by Paul and others in the early Christian community.

28. Romans 6:22; emphasis added.

29. Romans 6:16.

30. Hebrews 12:5–11.

31. Romans 21.

32. Matthew 25:30.

33. Lactantius, *Divine Institutes*, 4. 4. 2; trans. Bowen and Garnsey, *Lactantius: Divine Institutes*, 230.

34. For this and what follows, see Saller, "The Hierarchical Household," 112–29.

35. On the symbolic significance of the whip as punishment, see Saller, "Whips and Words," in which he writes (p. 127) that these views were "based on a fundamental polarity in Roman civic values between *libertas*, represented as freedom from the whip, and *servitus*, especially subjection to the whip."

36. De Bruyne, "Flogging a Son." Saller also comments ("The Hierarchical Household," 127–28): "the strong endorsement of the whipping of children came only in the Christian literature and was related to an important shift of ideology. With a new emphasis on humility before God, the old hierarchy of status, with its distinction between honourable children and honourless slaves, was downplayed, as all members of the household owed an obedience to God which was to be enforced by the whip in the interest of salvation."

37. Augustine, *Civ. Dei*, 19.15.

38. Augustine was under the impression that the Latin word for slave, *servus*, meant "saved" and had its origin in war captives who were "saved" from death and thus became preserved individuals or slaves.

39. Augustine, *Civ. Dei*, 19. 16.

40. There was a contemporary legal counterpart to this idea in the *Theodosian Code* (hereafter *CT*): 16, 5, 41: Law of Arcadius and Honorius to the proconsul of Africa 407 states: *Licet crimina soleat poena purgare*. (It is customary for crimes to be expiated (purged) by punishment). In this case (heretics), the emperors recommended repentance and promised that if they embraced the true faith they would be absolved from guilt. Trans. Pharr, *Theodosian Code*, 457. Latin in Godefroy, *Codex Theodosianus*, 179.

41. Council of Orleans (511) canon 8. Slaves who were cured at the shrines of the saints sometimes parlayed their cure into a change of status. Gregory of Tours, *De virtutibus sancti Martini* (hereafter *Virt. Mart.*), 2. 4, tells of a priest who promised that if his slave was cured, he would release him and have him tonsured. Another slave master who did not free his slave after a cure was punished by his slave becoming sick again. He got the message (*Virt. Mart.* 1. 22).

42. See Pelteret, *Slavery in Early Mediaeval England*, 77–79, and Pelteret's discussion of the late tenth-century hagiographies of St. Swithun and St. Wulfstan of Worcester (57–60). Slavery continued in Christian kingdoms although there were sporadic attempts to halt the transportation of Christians, especially

when they were bound for Muslim territories. See, McCormick, *Origins of the Medieval Economy.*

43. Gregory the Great, *Dialogues,* 4.19.

44. Glancy, *Slavery in Early Christianity,* 10. See Glancy's compelling discussion of the slave as body in Greek and Roman culture. She notes that while philosophers such as Epictetus (a former slave) argued that the slave still possessed control over his will, leaving only the body to the discretionary treatment of his or her master, the psychological impact of slavery was omitted. Bradley notes that another Greek term for slave, *andrapodon,* "man-footed creature," was built on the foundation of a common term for cattle, namely, *tetrapodon,* "four-footed creature" ("Animalizing the Slave," 110).

45. First Corinthians 15:49: "Just as we have borne the image of the man of dust, we shall also bear the image of the man of heaven." First Corinthians 15:42ff.: "What is sown is perishable, what is raised is imperishable." Although Paul also stated (1 Cor. 15:44), "It is sown a physical body, it is raised a spiritual body." Second Corinthians 5:10: "For we must all appear before the judgment seat of Christ, so that each one may receive good or evil, *according to what he has done in the body.*" Emphasis added.

46. Augustine, *Civ. Dei.*

47. For example, Perpetua was seen speaking to fellow Christians in Saturus's vision, *Passion of SS. Perpetua and Felicity,* 13. A tortured soul was hurled at Fursey during his otherworld visit, burning his flesh. *Vision of Fursey,* 16; ed. Ciccarese, "Le Visioni di S. Fursa," 300–301.

48. For example, the monks who wanted the lights in their church to be kept lit, and the monk who wanted his tomb swept, both in the *Vision of Barontus,* 11, 14.

49. *Vision of Paul,* 19. *Non solum nomina eorum, sed et vultus eorum.* Silverstein and Hilhorst, eds. *Apocalypse of Paul.*

50. Glancy, *Slavery in Early Christianity,* 15–16.

51. First Corinthians 6:19–20. Emphasis added.

52. These are only the most prominent; most apocalypses contained this sort of information. See the *Apocalypse of Peter,* Ethiopic version and Akhmim fragment edited by J. K. Elliott, *Apocryphal New Testament,* 599–612. Unless otherwise noted, I refer to the Ethiopic version, which is the earliest and most complete. *Christian Sibylline Oracles, NTA,* 2:652–85. On the Greek epitome of the *Vision of Paul,* see note 54.

53. For the date of composition debate, see Bremmer, "Christian Hell," esp. 307.

54. Bremmer suggests an Egyptian monastic milieu for the work, "Christian Hell," 306–7. The textual history of the *Vision of Paul* (also known as the *Apocalypse of Paul*) is complex and contested. Versions of the text appear in many languages including a Greek epitome of what is supposed to be a Greek original, no longer extant, a Coptic version, a Syriac version, and a few Latin versions. Numerous vernacular versions were produced throughout the middle ages. The date of the "Long Latin version" used here is disputed. It may have been produced as early as the 420s (see Theodore Silverstein and Anthony Hilhorst, eds., *Apocalypse of Paul: A New Critical Edition,* 11 n.3) or as late as the end of the fifth century (Bremmer, "Christian Hell," 298–325). It is known from two manuscripts: P (Paris, Bibliothèque nationale, nouv. acq. Lat 1631—also known as the Fleury

manuscript), now published in Silverstein and Hilhorst, *Apocalypse of Paul*, and in *St G* (St. Gall Codex 317) published by Silverstein, *Visio Sancti Pauli*. Unless otherwise indicated, I refer to the Long Latin version in Silverstein and Hilhorst, *Apocalypse of Paul*. Claude Carozzi, *Eschatologie et au-delà*, combined the Fleury manuscript with the St. Gall to provide a synthetic text, to which he provides a French translation. An English translation of James's edition of the *P* manuscript is provided by Elliott, *Apocryphal New Testament*, 616–44. The Greek epitome is found in von Tischendorf, *Apocalypses Apocryphae*, 34–69. The literature on the later redactions that circulated in the West throughout the middle ages is enormous. See Silverstein, *Visio Sancti Pauli* for the texts, and also Jiroušková, *Die Visio Pauli*.

55. *Apocalypse of Peter*, 4: "And he shall command hell to open its bars of adamant and give up all that is therein." Elliott, *Apocryphal New Testament*, 602. Adamant was a hard stone.

56. *Vision of Paul*, 18.

57. Ibid., 32. Revelation.

58. *Vision of Paul*, 34, 40 (strangulation), 36 (razor), 40 (blindness), 39 (hands and feet cut), 39 (thirst and hunger), 39 (suspended by eyebrows and hair), 34 (three-pronged iron), 40 (wild animals).

59. Bremmer, "Christian Hell," 309, notes that "new" crimes being punished in hell related specifically to Christian and ecclesiastical infractions.

60. While slaves were probably most at risk of bodily torture by their owners, they were also subject to state penalties when their actions were criminal. See Bradley, *Slaves and Masters*. On the biblical, apocalyptic, and cult images, which informed early apocalyptic depictions of torture, see Himmelfarb, *Tours of Hell*.

61. As related by Bradley, *Slaves and Masters*, 121.

62. As noted by Harries, *Law and Empire*, 137. Interestingly this particular penalty may have become traditional by the middle ages, or conversely, a penalty suggested by reference to visionary texts such as the *Vision of Paul*. Henry I of England had moneyers' hands cut off. Feet were rarely cut off in practice since it limited a slave's ability to work.

63. Latin *Vision of Paul*, 39. Not in the Greek.

64. Bradley, *Slaves and Masters*, 121.

65. In the many western redactions of the *Vision of Paul* the trend was to abbreviate or omit Paul's journey to heaven, while the tortures of hell were preserved and embellished.

66. *Vision of Paul*, 40.

67. For example, suspending individuals from body parts is one of the atrocities of which the Franks accused the Thuringians before the battle of Unstrutt (Gregory of Tours, *History of the Franks*, 3. 7). Pope Gregory I related that when Lombards entered a monastery in Valeria, they had seized two monks and killed them by hanging them from a branch of a tree (Gregory the Great, *Dialogues*, 4. 22. See also Himmelfarb, *Tours of Hell*, 82–92 on hanging as a feature of the earliest apocalypses.

68. The Vienna Cod. 3881 chap. 4; ed. Silverstein, *Visio Sancti Pauli*, 156. Silverstein demonstrates antecedents for this image, but for a northern European audience the image

may have struck a different chord: Tacitus, *Germania*, 12, notes suspension from trees as a form of execution. Sacrifices to Wodan were hung on trees, and the Thuringians (see note above) were also accused of this practice. In the later redaction of the *Vision of Paul*, the trees were described as burning, as would be appropriate to hell. A legal dimension was added when the term *furca*, or forked tree, was exchanged for *crux* in Justinian's *Digest*. See Franchi de' Cavalieri "Della furca et della sua sostituzione alla croce."

69. Revelation 20:14–15; 21: 8, etc. cites a lake of fire. See Himmelfarb, *Tours of Hell*, 106–22, on the category of "environmental punishments."

70. *Apocalypse of Peter*, trans. Müller, 625, notes that the river of fire imagery ultimately derives from ancient Egypt.

71. For example, the Cathedral of Notre Dame, Paris, West Tympanum. For an ancient depiction of slaves chained together and being led away, see the relief on the Amphipolis stone, Thompson, *The Archaeology of Greek and Roman Slavery*.

72. *Apocalypse of Peter*, 10; trans. Elliott, *Apocryphal New Testament*, 607. This is not the fate of the darkly clothed maidens as it is in the *Vision of Paul*.

73. *Christian Sibylline Oracles*, 2, ll.287–90; trans. Treu, NTA, 2:662.

74. *Vision of Paul*, 39: *vidit viros et mulieres cum cathenas ignis*. Introducing greater realism, Redaction 6 of the *Vision of Paul*, Rome Pal. 216, changes this to *cadenas ferreas* (iron chains).

75. A riveting overview including clear photographs of slave chains from ancient times is provided in Thompson, *Archaeology of Greek and Roman Slavery*. Discussion of the early medieval slave trade and pictures of new discoveries of chains in Eastern Europe is found in McCormick, *Origins of the European Economy*, 733–77 (pictures, 742–43), who notes that a shortage of iron and expense made such chains rare. Most slaves for transportation would have been restrained with wooden yokes or rope, which generally leave no archaeological record. See Henning, "Gefangenfesseln in slawischen Siedlungsraum," who also provides a catalogue of Eastern European iron chain finds mostly from the central Middle Ages, and including a Bulgarian find from Bilka, dated to the sixth- through seventh-century, in the Museum at Burgas.

76. Gregory of Tours, *Virt. Mart.*, 3.4, has a slave girl miraculously freed from her neck chains. See also Thompson, *Archaeology of Greek and Roman Slavery*, 238–40.

77. Thompson, *Archaeology of Greek and Roman Slavery*, 238.

78. Ibid., 224, fig. 88, and Iron Age neck shackles, figs. 89, 90

79. Thompson, *Archaeology of Greek and Roman Slavery*, figs. 99, 100. According to Thompson, 238, "manacles seem intended for temporary captivity, for instance after a successful military campaign." Yet, they also served the transportation motif for sinners in hell. See note 80 below.

80. Dated 1163–1250. Medieval depictions of sinners led by demons into hell sometimes show ropes rather than iron restraints. This reflected contemporary practice of restraint. Rope restraints may also have furnished a mixed metaphor of slavery with the biblical bundling of tares, which are to be thrown into the fire.

81. Incarceration was viewed as a torment, and as "a fate which is considered pitiable for the innocent but not severe enough for the guilty." CT, 9. 3. 1. trans. Pharr, 228.

82. The *Theodosian Code* is illuminating on this issue. Under the Christian emperors, judges were to inspect prisons each Sunday, provide food for those without, and make

sure that prisoners are conducted to the baths "in consideration of religion" (*CT*, 9.3.7; trans. Pharr, 230). Those in custody who had not yet been convicted of a crime were not to be restrained with iron manacles but with looser chains (*CT*, 9. 3.1; trans. Pharr, 228).

83. *CT*, 9.2.1 (Emperor Julian) states "the rights of senators and the authority of that order in which We number Ourselves also must be defended from all outrages" and that accused senators must remain free until the judicial investigation began (Trans. Pharr, 227).

84. *Passion of Perpetua*. Perpetua's family posted surety for her good behaviour, which she surely broke in her desire for imprisonment and martyrdom.

85. *CT*, 9. 3.1; trans. Pharr, 228.

86. Lemos, "Shame and Mutilation of Enemies in the Hebrew Bible."

87. Jones, "Stigma: Tattooing and Branding."

88. Jones, "Stigma: Tattooing and Branding," notes that one Christian sect, the Carpocratians, branded the earlobes of their converts with a needle. This was sufficiently bizarre to draw comment from contemporary writers.

89. 1. Aeschylus, *Prometheus Bound*.

90. *Voyage of Brendan*, 25. On Sundays, Judas sat on a rock in the ocean resting from his tortures.

91. *Vision of Paul*, 40.

92. Ibid., 39.

93. Bradley, *Slaves and Masters*, 127 n.78, citing Justininian's *Digest*.

94. See Glancy, *Slavery in Early Christianity*, 25–26: "Symbolically, no slave had a phallus."

95. Brent Shaw examines the symbolic meaning of the nakedness forced on female martyrs in the arena; see "The Passion of Perpetua."

96. Glancy, *Slavery in Early Christianity*, 54.

97. Ibid., 54–55.

98. Augustine, *Civ. Dei*, 19, 15.

99. Harries, *Law and Empire*, 136. Coleman, "Fatal Charades," summarizes the major penal aims of Roman justice as retribution, humiliation, correction, prevention, and deterrence.

100. Shaw, "Passion of Perpetua," 9. The extract Shaw cites is from the novel of Achilles Tatius, *Leukippê and Kleitophon*.

101. Bradley, *Slaves and Masters*, 122.

102. The additional tortures in the Latin *Vision of Paul* may be the embellishments of the Latin translator, and thus representative of the religious and literary taste of the turn of the fifth century rather than of the third.

103. Bremmer, "Christian Hell," 307.

104. MacMullen, "Judicial Savagery in the Roman Empire."

105. Harries, *Law and Empire*, 119. Harries's discussion of judicial violence in late antiquity illuminates this issue; I draw heavily on chapters 6 and 7 for this discussion.

106. Harries, *Law and Empire*, 148, citing Ambrose, Letter 25. 8.

107. Harries, *Law and Empire*, 148. She also notes (p. 121) that by the fifth century, bishops "were formally involved in the supervision of prison conditions."

108. Ibid., 151.

109. *CT*, 12.1.39; 12.1.47; 12.1.80: "The entire order of decurions shall be held immune from those tortures which are due to criminals and from the blows of lashes with lead tips."; 12.1.85; 12.1.126; 12.1.128; 12.1.190. Conversely, certain military ranks and professions were to be expressly liable to torture: military accountants, for example, were to be of ignoble status so that if they were found to be fraudulent in their accounting they could be tortured by means of horses and lacerations. *CT*, 8.3; 8, 4; 8.7, etc.

110. Bradley, *Slaves and Masters*, 129–30.

111. Harries, *Law and Empire*, 124.

112. Bradley, *Slaves and Masters*, 133.

113. Harries, *Law and Empire*, 137 and n. 14. Coleman, "Fatal Charades."

114. Torture was rarely used as a penalty under Roman law: it was a means of extracting confessions from the lower classes, although when death resulted, torture become a penalty.

115. Harries, *Law and Empire*, 124.

116. Glancy, *Slavery in Early Christianity*, 98.

117. Bede, *Ecclesiastical History*, 3. 29.

118. The enormous geographic and demographic scope of the slave trade is presented by McCormick in his discussion of "people on the move" (*Origins of the European Economy*). There are clearly issues of interpretation in discovering evidence for slavery and the slave trade from some of the sources he presents. Nevertheless, it is clear that slave trading was a very important part of the European economy seen as a whole. Wickham, *Framing the Early Middle Ages*, offers a land-based view of labour (particularly, agrarian labour) in early medieval Europe, analyzing the way servile, free, and semi-servile labour functioned and was supported by administrative and social structures. His work makes clear that classical and "plantation" slavery was not common after the ancient world; the picture of labour, and servitude, was much more complex thereafter. Nevertheless, the image of the slave in biblical texts, and as an "ideal" type in classical literature, must still have provided an interpretive context for the conditions of those in dire circumstances. Pelteret's *Slavery in Early Mediaeval England* is especially illuminating on the intersection of Anglo-Saxon slaveholding with the values of the early medieval church.

119. Pomerius, *De vita contemplativa*, 1. 2 and 3.12. 2, respectively; trans. Suelzer, 19, 130.

120. Caesarius of Arles, *Sermons*, Sermon 158 A.

121. Gregory of Tours, *Liber in gloria confessorum*, 70.

122. Respectively, Boniface, *Letters* 49, 28, 10; ed. Tangl, *Briefe des Heiligen Bonifatius*.

123. Caesarius of Arles, *Sermons*, Sermon 150.

CHAPTER 3

1. Shaw, *Burden of the Flesh*, esp. 161–219. Shaw neatly observes that "in the protological and eschatological arguments underlying ascetic theories, the imitation of the angels and the restoration of paradise are linked" (p. 163). See Bynum, *Resurrection of the Dead*, on bodily integrity and the resurrection. On attitudes to the body more generally, see Brown, *Body and Society*.

2. Discussing pain as related to sickness, Gillian Clarke comments: "Illness could be interpreted as an opportunity to repent, as a share of the suffering of Christ, as a demonstration that bodily pain is insignificant compared to spiritual health, or as a fight against demonic attack. Saints could therefore see it as a means of spiritual growth, but that was no to say that illness is a good in itself. Christians, like non-Christians, regarded illness as alien, to be healed, if possible, by doctors or by prayer" ("Health of the Spiritual Athlete," 228).

3. Frank, *Angelikos Bios*.

4. Such views expressed in the works of Julianus Pomerius, John Cassian, and others.

5. On medical knowledge in Gaul in late antiquity, see Rouselle, "Du sanctuaire," much of which is reprised in her longer study, *Croire et guérir*. Rouselle juxtaposes Oribasius's medical collection—representing the Greek medical knowledge, with its emphasis on anatomy, physiology, and diagnosis—with the "Gallic" compilation of Marcellus "of Bordeaux," which combines medical remedies with amulets and therapeutic rituals.

6. Nussbaum, *Therapy of Desire*, discusses the purging analogies of the Skeptics. Quoting Sextus: "For just as fire, having destroyed fuel, destroys itself as well; and just as purgative drugs, having driven the fluids out of bodies, remove themselves as well; so the argument against proof both abolishes every proof and also inscribes itself together with them" (p. 310). See also Shaw, *Burden of the Flesh*, 27–78.

7. As Clarke notes in "Health of the Spiritual Athlete," Plotinus's circle included physicians: see Porphyry, *Life of Plotinus*, 7. Monasteries, too, usually had some monks dedicated to medical matters. The medical properties of herbs were discussed in this literature and experimented with also. Origen imagined that one of the fields of knowledge that would be revealed in heaven was the properties of plants: "he will learn the reason why certain properties are attached to certain roots and herbs" (*First Principles*, 2. 11 .5). On the convergence of health and the spiritual quest, see Clarke, "Health of the Spiritual Athlete."

8. The words are connected etymologically.

9. Second Timothy 2:20. The purged vessel is a vessel "made unto honour." Origen discusses this passage at some length in *First Principles*, 3,1 in the context of human versus divine will, concluding: "God finds a ground of difference in our will, as it inclines to the better of the worse."

10. It was commonly believed that demons could enter the mouth or ears. Descriptions of exorcism usually depicted the demon being forced out of body orifices, most commonly the anus. However, demons could take advantage of any moment of vulnerability or distraction. Ascetic literature, especially the works of Athanasius, Evagrius, and Cassian, provided much useful information on how to recognize and combat demonic infiltration.

11. Bede, *Life of Cuthbert*, 37; trans. Webb, *Age of Bede*, 89.

12. Rouselle, "Du sanctuaire," 1096; *Croire et guérir*, 111.

13. This was an early incident in Martin's ascetic career while he was living on the island retreat of Gallinara. Sulpicius viewed this poisoning as an accident due to Martin's ascetic diet on roots. Sulpicius Severus, *Vita Martini* 6, 5–6.

14. Martin had served in the army of Caesar Julian (later emperor), whose Greek personal physician, Oribasius—citing ancient sources such as Rufus and Ctesias—recommended hellebore as a purgative. For this information, see Rouselle, "Du sanctuaire," 1095–1100, and *Croire et guérir*, 114–17, in which she makes the connection of Martin's history with that of the Greek physician Oribasius, and the descriptions in Sulpicius's *Vita Martini* in which Martin appears to be stimulating the sick person to vomit. Purging through vomiting could be stimulated by use of a feather in the throat. Martin used his fingers. Oribasius's works are found in the *Medical Collection* (see Book 8. 8–9). The work was a collection of earlier medical opinion, but not a slavish one. The books on hellebore were composed after the time when Martin served in Julian's army, although information they contained was ancient. Information on Oribasius's career and theories of Roman dietetics can be found in Grant, *Dieting for an Emperor*. A personal connection of Martin with Oribasius is not to be supposed: the use of purgatives was common and would have been a remedy familiar to army medics. There are five species of hellebore, but two were specified in the sources. According to Oribasius (citing Rufus) black hellebore was used for intestinal evacuation while white hellebore was used as an emetic (Book 7. 26). The use of the plant was recommended only for those who could vomit easily. It should be noted that hellebore was also used in the treatment of madness and melancholy (see Pigeaud, *Folie et cures de folie*, 206–11). This may provide a clue to the treatment of those supposedly possessed by a demon. Pigeaud also notes that Caelius Aurelianus prescribed hellebore for a wide variety of ailments including epilepsy, asthma, oesophageal illness, disease of the liver and spleen, dropsy, diseases of the colon, arthritis, and gout (p. 206). Due to its extreme toxicity, hellebore is no longer used in human medicine (see Frexinos, *L'art de purger*, 47–48).

15. Harper, "John Cassian and Sulpicius Severus," discusses the difference between the hagiographic model promoted by the Lérinian school, which was sparing in miraculous detail, and the saintly model promoted by Sulpicius Severus's portrayal of St. Martin which viewed miracle working as a personal achievement of the saviour-saint. The triumph of the Martinian model of sanctity in the 460s, at a time when the initial opposition to Martin had subsided, set the stage for the miracle compilations of the later bishops of Tours.

16. Sulpicius Severus recorded the first miracles attributed to the saint. In the third quarter of the fifth century, Bishop Perpetuus of Tours invested in the burgeoning cult by building a new church dedicated to St. Martin ornamented with murals depicting scenes from the *Vita Martini*. He commissioned Paulinus of Périgueux to versify the Martinian corpus and in addition supplied a list of more recent miracles attributed to the saint. Gregory of Tours wrote his own miracle books, expanding on those of Perpetuus and Paulinus, and even envisaged that they might be versified. Martin's healing miracles have been studied in the context of Roman-Gallic shrine culture in Rouselle, *Croire et guérir*, esp. 109–22, and in Van Dam's, *Saints and Their Miracles*.

17. Gregory compiled four books of miracles associated with St. Martin and his shrine, in what was an ongoing project for him over a number of years: *De virtutibus sancti Martini episcopi* (hereafter *Virt. Mart*). This work and other documents relating to

the cult of St. Martin are translated and analyzed by Van Dam in *Saints and Their Miracles,* and unless otherwise noted, his translations are used in this chapter. Although I shall focus on Gregory's collection of Martin's miracles here, all of Gregory's works are replete with miraculous content, including his *Libri Historiarum* or *History of the Franks* (= HF), his *De passione et virtutibus sancti Iuliani martyris* (= VJ), *Liber in gloria martyrum* (= GM), *Liber vitae patrum* (= VP), *Liber in gloria confessorum* (= GC), and his lesser-known works. On Gregory's collection in the context of other Merovingian miracle collections, see Heinzelmann, "Une source de base de la littérature hagiographique latine."

18. In some ways he was the sixth century's answer to Aelius Aristides, a petitioner and reporter of dreams and miracles connected with the great healer Asclepius. Like Asclepius, Gregory suffered psychosomatic ailments and a great fear of abandonment by his patron.

19. Gregory of Tours, *Virt. Mart.,* 2, 60. Blood purges were commonly prescribed but were not considered suitable for all patients, nor for all seasons of the year. Spring and autumn were optimal seasons for purges.

20. For example, at the shrine of St. Hilary where, as Fortunatus relates, two lepers from Cahors were healed by smearing dust from the saint's tomb on their limbs (*Vita Hilarii,* 11). Gregory relates that his brother Peter was healed of fever after he used dust from the tomb of St. Julian of Brioude. Julian's dust was even exported by ship and purged a man of demon possession who attended its arrival in the East (*Vita Juliani* 24 and 33, respectively).

21. As an educated Gallic aristocrat, it may be assumed that Gregory had some household medical knowledge, however limited and rudimentary. As a young boy he had formulated a remedy for his sick father drawn loosely from the Book of Tobit, and it was carried out on his mother's instructions (GC, 39). On the visionary aspect of this account, see my *Dreams, Visions and Spiritual Authority,* 84. As a sick adult, he had recourse to doctors and their remedies although with great ambivalence. Ultimately, Gregory chose to treat his own afflictions through a combination of prayer, amuletic use of relics (he presses the altar cloth on his stomach), and purges (whether natural or induced is not revealed). This combination reflects the kind of "Gallic" medicinal practice observed by Rouselle in the works of Marcellus of Bordeaux and Ausonius the Elder (see "Du sanctuaire," 1089–94).

22. Gregory of Tours, *Virt. Mart.,* 1. 40.

23. Galen, Hippocrates, Rufus, and Oribasius are just some of the medical opinions we have on the subject. Bodily purges included vomiting, evacuation of the bowels, or effluence through the nose or any other orifice. Conditions that warranted purges included vertigo, sudden heaviness or pain in the head, tinitus, difficulty hearing, fatigue, lack of appetite, bitter taste, memory loss, palpitations, troubled dreams, and colic, to mention just a few. (Based on Oribasius, *Medical Collection,* Book 7, 26.15, and also cited and discussed by Rouselle, *Croire et guérir,* 97–99.) Recipes for purgatives (for vomiting or for evacuation) used a wide variety of flora, among which hellebore took prominence for effectiveness. Purges of various kinds are attested in medical literature throughout the middle ages. The existence of an eighth-century manuscript fragment, now lost, with a Latin translation from

Oribasius, attests to the continued copying of this kind of medical literature in early medieval monasteries (see Riou, "Un fragment d'un manuscrit disparu d'Oribase").

24. Gregory of Tours, *VJ*, 48.

25. Ibid., 38.

26. Gregory will end a narrative episode with the petitioner being "cleansed" without further comment that the petitioner was healed: cleansing *is* healing, and healing *is* cleansing. For example, when two men were exorcized of demons he comments: *eiecto daemone, sunt mundati* (*Virt. Mart.*, 3. 23). By contrast, Gregory's contemporary Fortunatus, who included a miracle list in his *Life of Germanus of Paris*, by far preferred to refer to the sick as having been restored to health: *salutus*. For example, he used variants on the term "purge" to describe the restoration of a contracted hand and for the idiom "purged of sleep." He used the term to describe the means of a cure but not to pronounce the cure itself. There is always an additional comment that the person was healed.

27. For example, *Virt. Mart.*, 1. 7. Not all appear to have had the sense of the sick boy from Albi who suffered from vomiting, but who fasted on arriving at the saint's shrine (*Virt. Mart.*, 3. 30).

28. Sitting on the railings was strictly prohibited, and those who did so risked being treated harshly. See the story of the demoniacs in Paulinus of Périgueux's work discussed below.

29. Gregory of Tours, *Virt. Mart.*, 1. 38: *tota die inter altare et sanctum tumulum decubantes*. Patrick Nugent's discussion of twelfth-century healing miracles notes how disruptive such healing miracles were, especially when they disrupted the liturgical activities of the monks ("Bodily Effluvia and Liturgical Interruption"). Gregory of Tours was certainly keen to note that miracles had occurred during the Mass or during the saint's festival and remarks on the amazement of bystanders who must have been distracted thereby, but the shock of interruption is not at the forefront of Gregory's representation of events.

30. Gregory of Tours, *Virt. Mart.*, 1. 37.

31. Ibid., 2. 20: *evomens purulentum nescio quid cum sanguine, daemone eiecto, purgatus est*.

32. Ibid., 2. 37: *sanguinem fetidum per os coepit eicere . . . expulso daemone, purgatus erectus est*. Medical literature warned against the use of strong purgatives for those unused to them, including the infirm, children, menstruating women, and the aged. Intestinal purgatives were sometimes recommended for those who could not tolerate purges of the stomach. Medical procedure, then, was to observe and regulate the violence of the purge.

33. Moorhead, "Thoughts on Some Early Medieval Miracles." The connection of demons with sickness and madness is widely attested in antiquity. On some of the complexity in dealing with the demonic in hagiographic sources, see Grey, "Demoniacs, Dissent, and Disempowerment in the Late Roman West," and the literature cited there. Demoniacs make their appearance in hagiographic literature in a variety of guises, but sickness was probably the most common reflection of demonic power. As Grey notes (p. 47): "in late Roman society demonic interference was a recognized, credible cause for disease, illness, and dementia."

34. Gregory of Tours, *Virt. Mart.*, 3. 59.

35. Ibid., 1. 7. Theodomund's name is somewhat suggestive of his miracle.

36. Ibid., 1. 11.

37. Ibid., 1. 30; 2. 60.

38. Ibid., 2. 13.

39. Ibid., 4. 6. See Van Dam's discussion of Gregory's theology of illness in *Saints and Their Miracles*, 105–15.

40. John Moorhead's comparison of eastern and western miracle accounts ("Thoughts on Some Early Medieval Miracles") revealed a greater concentration of demon possession healings in the eastern corpus than in the western and concluded furthermore, that in the West exorcisms were more "peaceful." While "trading insults" was not unknown in the western context, based on Moorhead's examples of eastern exorcisms, it appears that a major difference was the verbal references to "violence" by those being exorcized. He notes that the demon-possessed boy exorcized by Daniel the Stylite shouted, "Oh, the violence of this false magician," the boy exorcized by Theodore of Sykeon shouted, "Oh, the violence of the Nazarene," and a group of demon-possessed men shouted, "Oh violence! Why have you come here, you iron-eater?" The demon possessed of the West were certainly impelled by violence but were attributed less noisy, less articulate expostulations.

41. Paulinus of Périgueux, *De vita sancti Martini episcopi*. Behind Paulinus's verse and Gregory's prose accounts lay a prose collection of miracles supplied by Bishop Perpetuus of Tours, which has no longer survived. The textual connections between the various later works inspired by Sulpicius Severus's Martinian writings are explored in Chase, "Metrical Lives of St. Martin of Tours," and in Van Dam, "Paulinus of Périgueux and Perpetuus of Tours." See also Roberts, "Last Epic of Antiquity." In the absence of Perpetuus's work, it is not possible to know precisely how Paulinus or Gregory interpreted the earlier document.

42. Van Dam notes, in *Saints and Their Miracles*, 202 n.8, that it is unclear whether the site for this miraculous occurrence was the original church built by Bishop Brictio or the larger church constructed by Bishop Perpetuus. Paulinus terms it a *templum*, whereas Gregory terms it a *basilica*.

43. Van Dam, *Saints and Their Miracles*, 201–2: '*Cum inergumini per cancellos basilicae aereo veherenter volatu et saepe in puteum inpulsu daemonis iactarentur abstracti, exinde inlaesi, populis spectantibus, sunt resumpti.*'—*Idque et nostris temporibus vidimus gestum*. Gregory of Tours, *Virt. Mart.* 1. 2, ed. Krusch, 137.

44. The common root of *puteus* (well), the verb *puteo* (stink), and the verb *puto* (cleanse) is *pu-* in Sanskrit.

45. In Roman times *puticuli* were burial pits for indigents and slaves. They represented an undignified end.

46. Paulinus, *De vita sancti Martini episcopi* 1. 89 (hereafter *Vita s. Mart.*): *et gaudens hominem purgandum cella recepit*. Paulinus specifies that the river in question was the Loire, which separated Martin's tomb (in Tours) from his cell (at Marmoutier). Van Dam suggests the man may have been a Hun.

47. When demonic possession was the ascribed cause of mental illness, as must be the case here, we are presented with a very different system of conflict than that

represented by the tempting demon who exercises power over others and that was with primary focus of ascetic literature. On the cosmologic tradition of demon possession with reference to Martin of Tours and the "potestas" attributed to demons, see Stancliffe, *St. Martin and His Hagiographer*, 233–48 and 209, on the connection of demons with disease. The difficulties in distinguishing mental illness from what contemporaries identified as demon possession are manifold. Medical treatises such as that of Oribasius recognized mental sicknesses such as mania and melancholy without ascribing them to demonic possession, but that is of scant help when an author such as Gregory was inclined to pit St. Martin's power against the evil of infirmity. In short, there was probably a wide spectrum of interpretation. Those unfortunates who congregated around church were possibly viewed as potentially curable and their presence there orchestrated by local care facilities, including monasteries. On the Byzantine context for treatment of the insane and demon possessed, see Horden, "Responses to Possession and Insanity," 191, who notes that the possessed were sometime chained and that "the proximity of the enchained to the tomb of the saint indicates the kind of relief that was, in theory, expected for them."

48. Foucault, *Madness and Civilization*, 166–72, and the anecdote on p. 168, which bears an uncanny resemblance to Gregory's account. See also Rouselle, "Du sanctuaire," on healing sanctuaries and thermal baths. These were numerous in late Roman Gaul, but many were destroyed from the fourth century onward. See map appendices to *Croire et guérir* for geographic distribution and destruction dates. On the treatment of mental illness with water and steam baths, see Pigeaud, *Folie et cures de folie*, 205–6.

49. It was believed that the words *cadaver* and *cadendo* (falling) were linked etymologically. The demoniacs' fall (spiritual death) preceded their cleansing and salvation.

50. This pilgrimage took place in 563. Gregory was only twenty-five at the time of this traumatic event, but already he was a deacon. His companions included the cleric Armentarius, perhaps the same Armentarius identified as his doctor by Gregory in Virt. Mart., 2. 1). See Van Dam, *Saints and Their Miracles*, 223 n.43. Heinzelman, *Gregory of Tours*, 31–32.

51. Gregory of Tours, Virt. Mart., 1. 32. Gregory's description of his panic, and his general fearfulness about his health, suggests profound pyschological trauma. Gregory's father Florentius had died when Gregory was only eight, and Gregory reveals himself to have been sickly and anxious all his life. Encouraged by his mother, Gregory believed he had been instrumental in curing his father by carrying out instructions in a vision. This early success may have heightened Gregory's view of his own responsibility for his family's health, shattered ultimately in his father's subsequent early death. Heinzelman, *Gregory of Tours*, 30, suggests that Gregory may not have been destined for a clerical career but took that path in response to his illnesses. Although Gregory heard family stories of the plague years in his youth, it does not appear that Gregory's health fears were specifically connected with plague, even though Gregory was confronted by a resurgence of plague in the 580s and organized rogations to combat it (*HF*, 10.30). On the plague in Gaul, see Stoclet, "Seeking Succor and Solace in Times of Plague."

52. Gregory of Tours, *Virt. Mart.*, 2. 60: *lura leprae luxoriae*. Gregory is remarkably unhelpful here. What was the exact nature of his sin? In ascetic works, "luxury" was a facet of the sin of avarice. Leprosy was the punishment for Gehazi's avarice in 2 Kings 5:27. In Cassian's works, where the pollution of sin and sickness is a common image, he writes: "These people are known to be leprous in spirit and mind, like Gehazi, who, in his desire for the empty riches of this world, was defiled with the unclean contagion of leprosy. In that respect he left us a clear example of how every soul that is polluted by the stain of covetousness is defiled by the spiritual leprosy of vice and, by reason of a perpetual curse, is considered unclean in the sight of God." *Institutes* 7.26 (on avarice); trans. Ramsey, *John Cassian*,182. This image is clearly behind Gregory's thinking. He continues his prayer, asking that he be purged *a concuspicentiis*. Another patristic trajectory links luxury with sins of the flesh: "For sickness of the body restrains sins, but luxury sets on fire the sin of the flesh." (Ambrose, *On Repentance*, 1. 13. 63). Was this his temptation? Perhaps he was simply extremely aware of the stark difference between the pomp of his episcopal existence, with its banquets and palaces, and that of St. Martin, his unkempt, ascetic forerunner.

53. Gregory of Tours, *Virt. Mart.*, 3 Preface (translation slightly changed): *qui nobis talem medicum tribuere dignatus est, qui infirmitates nostras purgaret, vulnera dilueret ac salubria medicamenta conferret.*

54. The potion's appearance and consistency is not described. What was the nature of this dust or powder (*pulvis*)? Greek physicians prescribed a broth made of barley or soft porridge that was easily digested. This acted as a gentle purge. Was the potion concocted from Martin's dust and water of this sort? Was "dust" encouraged by leaving cereal on the tomb or simply mixed in with it? In sufficient quantity, water is an extremely effective purge.

55. Gregory of Tours, *Virt. Mart.*, 1. 37; 2.1.

56. Ibid., 3. 60. It is unclear in this passage whether the help offered on this occasion was proximity to the shrine or dust; the context strongly suggests that Gregory was referring to the dust potion, and thus I retain Van Dam's translation. Gregory's dental-headache symptoms on this occasion suggest a migraine, which can be caused by clenching or grinding the teeth (see Melis and Secci, "Migraine with Aura and Dental Occlusion"). A dental appliance rather than holy dust was used to treat the patient in the modern study. I would like to thank Dr. Robert Summerfield for this reference.

57. Scammony is a natural purgative made from resin of the root of *convolvulus scammonia*; it dissolves in alcohol not water. Hyssop leaves have a minty flavour; they are used for lung conditions and as an expectorant. Pyrethrum, a natural insecticide of the daisy family (*Tanacetum cinerariaefolium*), was probably used against head lice.

58. Gregory of Tours, *Virt. Mart.*, 3. 60.

59. Gregory may have had Psalm 51:7 in mind when writing this rhapsodic passage linking purges and salvation: "Purge me with hyssop, and I shall be clean; wash me and I shall be whiter than snow." Martin's dust surpasses even this divine cleansing remedy.

60. Gregory of Tours, *Virt. Mart.*, 2. 60. See n.52 above on imagery behind this prayer.

61. Gregory of Tours, *VJ*, 9.

62. Van Dam, *Saints and Their Miracles*, 113.

63. Some prisoners may have been mentally sick or "demon possessed," imprisoned close to church or monastery precincts. See Horden, "Responses to Possession and Insanity." If this were so, it would explain some common and sometimes puzzling features of these accounts, for example, the proximity of the prisoners to relic processions and the attitude of those in authority toward their release. One would not expect civil authorities to countenance the release of criminals before term. The attitude of caregivers in a religious institutional setting would be different. The prisoners' shouts, which were often acclamations of the power of saint, sound very like those described of the demon possessed when exorcized of their demons. Having been released of their demons, and healed, they could be released from their chains.

64. Gregory of Tours, *Virt. Mart.*, 1. 22; 2. 59.

65. Ibid., 1. 40.

66. Ibid., 1. 23.

67. On concerns about church officers living off funds designated for the poor, see Pomerius, *De vita contemplativa*, 2. 10.

68. Pomerius, *De vita contemplativa*, 2. 2: "They especially have received the charge for caring for souls. Ably bearing the responsibility for the people entrusted to them, they untiringly supplicate God for the sins of all as for their own: and like an Aaron offering the sacrifice of a contrite heart and a humble spirit which appeases God, they turn the wrath of future punishment from their people" (trans. Suelzer, 59). Gregory relates a vision of the abbot Sunniulf who saw himself in hell for having failed to correct his monastic flock (*HF*, 4.33). The idea was widespread in ascetic culture (see Basil, *Long Rules*, chap. 25, and Benedict of Nursia, *Benedictine Rule*, chap.2).

69. Of Gregory's self-presentation in the public sphere, Mitchell, "Saints and Public Christianity," 82, observes that "as bishop, Gregory was as much a character in his own book as were Chilperic and the other individuals who appear in the *Historiae*" and that "Gregory the literary character was a bishop *par excellence* who bears a marked resemblance to his predecessor and patron, Martin of Tours." However, Gregory's persona in the miracle accounts displays a different relationship to Martin in the private sphere where, unlike the public, Gregory did not attempt to assimilate his persona to St. Martin, portraying himself rather as a subservient figure, alternately elated and miserable in the face of his healing patron.

70. Pomerius, *De vita contemplativa*, 1. 25. 2.

71. See Bauckham's discussion of the *Apocalypse of Peter* and Augustine's third category of "misericordes," in *Fate of the Dead*, 149–59, esp. 152.

72. Gregory of Tours, *Virt. Mart.*, 2. 60: "Then, when I am to be placed on the left side at the [Final] Judgement, he will deign to separate me from the middle of the goats with his sacred right hand, protect me behind his back, and await the judge's verdict. And when in accordance with the Judge's decision I am to be condemned to the eternal flames, he will protect me with the sacred shroud that shields him from boasting and reprieve me from punishment. The angels will say to the King of heaven what they previously said about the monk who was restored to life: 'This is the man for whom Martin petitions.'"

73. Sulpicius Severus, *Vita Martini*, 7.

74. Martin's rescue is purposefully associated with *descensus Christi* narratives. See my essay in *Hell and Its Afterlife*, ed. Moreira and Toscano (forthcoming).

75. Gregory of Tours, *Virt. Mart.*, 4. Preface.

76. The paradox by which the tomb of the saint became the source of life was not confined to Gregory. Venantius Fortunatus commented that the purity of (St. Hilary's) tomb cleansed the blemishes of leprosy and that a woman's hand that had come forth "dead" from her mother's womb returned from the tomb "alive" (*Vita Hilarii*, 13 and 16).

77. Gregory of Tours, *Virt. Mart.*, 2. 60; trans. Van Dam, 259.

78. Gregory of Tours, *Glory of the Martyrs*, 106: "Therefore it is necessary for us to seek the patronage (*patrocinia*) of the martyrs, so that we might be worthy to be helped by their assistance (*suffragiis*)." The use of electoral imagery to describe saintly support and divine election is a reminder of the interconnection of religious and secular vocabulary and of the conceptualization of the divinity occupying a realm analogous to an earthly one

79. Carole Straw examines how the idea of martyrdom was being recast in the work of Augustine and Gregory the Great, "Martyrdom and Christian Identity," 250–66. It is harder to assess how far Gregory of Tours may have been responding to Augustinian thought or to contemporary attitudes, if at all.

80. *Glory of the Martyrs*, 106: "In a trial for a crime the Lord will not condemn (*nec damnet*) to eternity (*in perpetuo*) defendants whom he has redeemed with the price of [the martyrs'] precious blood (*quos pretiosi sanguinis commertio reparavit*)." Trans. Van Dam, 134.

81. As we have seen, it is a false distinction to view punishment as different from purification in post-Augustinian theology. De Nie, *Views from a Many-Windowed Tower*, 206, is correct to reject this passage as denoting purgatory, but for the wrong reason. She writes: "One is tempted to think of the 'light punishment' as something like a purgatory here, but the emphasis seems to be not on purification so much as on retribution."

82. New assessments of Gregory's purposeful theology include Heinzelmann, *Gregory of Tours*, and Van Dam, *Saints and Their Miracles*, especially his section "Body and Theology" 105–15 (not referenced by Heinzelmann).

CHAPTER 4

1. Some of Augustine's works and ideas were slow to penetrate the West. Free Will and the debate about the corporeality of the soul, to give two examples, continued to be debated in Gaul after his death. On Augustinian transmission through known manuscripts, see the ongoing project, *Die handschriftliche Überlieferung der Werke des Heiligen Augustinus*. His work was also transmitted through epitomes and florilegia. See bibliography in Moreira, "St. Augustine's Three Visions and Three Heavens in Some Early Medieval Florilegia."

2. Julian of Toledo, *Prognosticum* 2. 10; ed. Hillgarth, *Prognosticorum futuri saeculi*, 49: *Julianus Pomerius dicit: 'Spiritus illi qui nec tam perfectae sanctitatis hinc exeunt, ut ire in paradisum statim post depositionem suorum corporum possint, nec tam*

criminose ac damnabiliter vivuunt, aut ita in suis criminibus perseverant, ut cum diabolo et angelis eius damnari mereantur, ecclesia pro eis hic efficaciter supplicante, ac poenis medicinalibus expiati, corpora sua cum beata immortalitate recipient, ac regni coelestis facti participes, in eo sine ullo defectu suae beatitudinis permanebunt.' Since the work from which this was supposedly drawn (*The Dialogue on the Nature of the Soul*) has not survived, it is impossible to check the accuracy of this quotation.

3. Augustine, *Enchiridion* 29 [110.], quoting from the end of the chapter where Augustine envisages family solace only in the case of very bad sinners, whereas earlier in the chapter he conceded family solace for souls of all likely conditions.

4. Suelzer, Introduction to Pomerius, *The Contemplative Life*, 4. Klingshirn, *Caesarius of Arles*.

5. Caesarius of Arles, *Opera*; ed. Morin, *S. Caesarii opera omnia*. Unless otherwise noted, translation of Caesarius's sermons are from Mueller's translation.

6. Caesarius of Arles, *Sermons*, Sermon 167. The bulk of this sermon is also found in the sermon collection of Eusebius "Gallicanus," Sermon 6 (*De Epiphania Domini*, 3).

7. Caesarius of Arles, *Sermons*, Sermon 179.

8. Ibid., Sermon 157: "At the Day of Judgement, those on Christ's left hand will be cast into eternal flames, not because they were sinners, but because they had not redeemed their sins through almsgiving."

9. Ibid., Sermon 179: "Souls which have committed either murder or sacrilege or adultery or other sins like these ... if they have not been helped by worthy repentance, will not deserve to reach life by passing through the fire of purgatory, but they will be thrown to death in the eternal fire." This emphasis on only light sins being purged in the afterlife may still have been identified as a consciously anti-Origenist perspective.

10. Ibid., Sermon 179.

11. Ibid., Sermon 167.

12. Ibid., Sermon 179.

13. Ibid., Sermon 19 (*CCSL*, v. 103, 87); Sermon 31 (*CCSL*, v. 103, 135–36); Sermon 14 (*CCSL*, v. 103, 70).

14. Ibid., Sermon 156.

15. Ibid., Sermon 156.

16. Against Jay "La purgatoire," see p. 11, who followed Michel "Purgatoire" col. 1224, in interpreting this passage to mean that souls would undergo individual purgation immediately after death.

17. Caesarius of Arles, *Sermons*, Sermons 179 and 167.

18. Ibid., Sermon 179.

19. Ibid., Sermon 178 and Sermon 157.

20. Sermon 158A. The prayer, *Pio recordationis effectu*, petitioned God *ut concessa venia plenae indulgentiae quicquid in hoc saeculo proprius error adtulit, totum ineffabili pietate ac benignitate sua compenset*. Caesarius's prayers are edited by Sicard, *La liturgie*, 260–79. Also discussed by Paxton, *Christianizing Death*, 52–55.

21. The *Life of Caesarius* comprised two integrated books: *Vita Caesarii*; ed. Morin in CCSL, 103–4, and ed. Krusch, *MGH, SRM*, 3. Translation by Klingshirn, *Caesarius of Arles: Life, Testament, Letters*.

22. It is important not to discount other sources for Gregory's *Dialogues*, including Tertullian's *De anima* and treatises "on the soul" that have not survived. It was a popular topic. Gregory shows some knowledge of Tertullian's ideas in several places in his work, although we cannot be sure how directly. The Augustinian influence is profound, however. On some of the ways that Gregory departed from Augustine's thought, see the important article by Atwell, "From Augustine to Gregory the Great."

23. On Gregory's "eschatological spirituality," see Dagens, *Saint Grégoire le Grand*, 375–400; Gregory the Great, *Dialogues*, 401–29. Dagens presented a subtle and integrated portrait of Gregory as a scholar and spiritual leader, emphasizing the consistencies rather than the disjunctions in Gregory's works and thinking. A summary of Gregory's views on purgatory is also found in an earlier study (Dudden, *Gregory the Great*, vol. 2, 426–30).

24. Commonly, scholars attribute its style to pastoral adaptation, making the *Dialogues* more accessible to ordinary Christians and appeal to popular tastes. Dagens, *Saint Grégoire le Grand*, 404, notes, "Il utilise donc certaines représentations héritées de l'Antiquité païenne pour mieux toucher ses auditeurs."

25. This has led some to doubt Gregory's authorship of the work. In particular, Francis Clark's assessment of the *Dialogues* as pseudo-Gregorian should be noted here since Book Four does appear to be a departure from the stated aims of the work as a whole, which is to provide an account of the miracles of the Italian Fathers, and it presents us with material about purgatory that does not always fit Gregory's more cautious pronouncements elsewhere in his work, *The pseudo-Gregorian Dialogues*. Indeed, the discussion of purgatory in Book Four presents the reader with difficulties that have been recognized even by those who have not doubted Gregory's authorship: de Vogüé, ed. *Grégoire le Grand: Dialogues*. It is indeed possible that the *Dialogues* may not have been published in Gregory's lifetime (see Meyvaert, "Enigma of Gregory the Great's *Dialogues*). See also, Hillgarth, "Eschatological and Political Concepts." However, the issue still attracts attention. Marilyn Dunn has taken Clark's thesis further to suggest that *Dialogues* was a composition with distinctly Anglo-Saxon associations. Dunn accepts Clark's dating of the 670s but rejects the idea that it was composed in Rome (see Dunn, "Origins of Purgatory"). The problem with dating specific ideas through cultural typology (making it fit at a point in time when other documents support those ideas) is that it removes the potential for a document to offer something new.

26. The three stories are those concerning Paschasius, another story about a former proprietor of a bathhouse, and that of the monk Justus. I do not examine the soldier's tale here (*Dialogues* 4.37), because it is not informative on Gregory's theology of purgatory; it is a vision of hell whose central element, the bridge, was appropriated as an image for purgation in the *Vision of the Monk of Wenlock*, discussed in chapter 6.

27. Gregory the Great, *Dialogues*, 4. 26.

28. Ibid., 4.26. These views are also expressed in the Gregory the Great, *Moralia*, Preface, 10, 20, and 35.25; ed. Adriaen. The idea of the white robe is conventional; it appears in Revelation 6:11, and Caesarius states that the damned will be stripped of their garment of faith. In artistic representations of hell, the damned were usually depicted naked while the inhabitants of heaven are clothed. In a later age when

purgatory was depicted in art, souls in purgatory were also naked but would be clothed at the resurrection.

29. Ibid., 28. Unless otherwise noted, translations from Gregory's *Dialogues* are by Zimmerman.

30. Ibid., 4. 28–29. Gregory's answer here echoes his *Moralia*, 9. 95–104; and 15. 35–36.

31. For example, the trial of the just soul and the wicked soul in the *Vision of Paul*; the trial of the visionary himself in the *Vision of the Monk of Wenlock*. Most visions reported some form of trial, whether it be in the form of a judicial court or through a probative ordeal.

32. Gregory the Great, *Dialogues*, 4. 40. Peter's question is answered in 4. 41. The disjunction between Peter's question and Gregory's proof may be due to the hurried or unfinished nature of the work at this point, since the answer that follows possibly derives from an early version of the *Moralia*. See discussion by Clark, *Pseudo-Gregorian Dialogues*, vol. 2, 558–61, and De Vogüé, SC, 251, 73.

33. Psalm 118:1.

34. Gregory the Great, *Dialogues*, 4.41: *Sed tamen de quibusdam levibus culpis esse ante judicium purgatorius ignis credendus est.*

35. A rather more monastic list than that provided by Caesarius, which included sex with one's spouse without procreative intent.

36. Gregory the Great, *Dialogues*, 4.41. Caesarius distinguished between sins that were *capitalia* and *minuta*.

37. *Quia enim non malitia, sed ignorantiae errore peccaverat, purgari post mortem a peccato potuit* (my translation).

38. Gregory the Great, *Dialogues*, 4. 42; ed. Moricca, *Dialogi*, 300; trans. Zimmerman, *Saint Gregory the Great: Dialogues*, 250: "What we are to believe is that through his previous alms deeds he obtained the grace of receiving forgiveness at a time when he was no longer able to do meritorious works."

39. *Qui ingressus easdem thermas, praedictum Pachasium diaconum stantem et obsequentem in caloribus invenit.* That Paschasius was burning is a common misperception derived, no doubt, from the context of the previous conversation between Gregory and Peter. For example, both Atwell "From Augustine to Gregory the Great," 180, and Brown, *Rise of Western Christendom*, 259, suggest that Paschasius was in the fire or that the scalding heat of the baths purged Paschasius in a manner analogous to fire, but this is an unwarranted leap. Heat is not fire. The *exemplum* of Paschasius is simply mismatched with the previous conversation. Nevertheless, scholars have long identified this story as an image purgatory without noting its unusual nature. For example, Dagens, *Saint Grégoire le Grand*, 403.

40. Gregory the Great, *Dialogues*, 4. 42. Romans understood confinement in a prison as punishment. The extent of Paschasius's pain in this place of punishment is, at the very least, unclear.

41. Gregory the Great, *Dialogues*, 4. 42; see chapter 2 on the idea that the sinful dead were like slaves.

42. According to the *Liber Pontificalis*, 53, the schism arose from charges against the incumbent pope Symmachus by two senators, Festus and Probinus. Laurentius, a

rival claimant to the papal throne, became the figurehead for a schism that divided the clergy and the senate. The *Liber Pontificalis* is a sixth-century work that sided with Symmachus. See trans. Davis, *Book of Pontiffs*, 43–46.

43. *Liber Pontificalis*, 54.

44. Benedict saw Germanus's soul being carried to heaven. Gregory the Great, *Dialogues*, 2.35.

45. See Atwell, "From Augustine to Gregory the Great."

46. Gregory the Great, *Dialogues*, 4. 43: *ad aliquantum temporis*.

47. Gregory situated both upper and lower regions underground in his *Moralia*.

48. Gregory the Great, *Dialogues*, 4.57. My translation.

49. Ibid., 4. 57: *si culpae post mortem insolubiles non sunt*. There are shades of Augustine's caution (*Enchiridion*, 110) in this double negative.

50. Gregory the Great, *Dialogues*, 4. 57; trans. Moricca, *Dialogi*, 318. *Cogitare coepi, vel quid ad purgationem morientis facerem*. Justus is a doctor, and now Gregory treats him like a doctor purging a patient. See chapter 3.

51. Gregory the Great, *Dialogues*, 4.48. *Sed plerumque de culpis minimis ipse solus pavor egredientes animas iustorum purgat*.

52. Ibid., 4.57. *Ut saltim in morte de culpa sua mentem illius amaritudo transverberit, adque a peccato quod perpetravit, purget*.

53. Quoting Acts 8:20. *Pecunia tua tecum sit in perditionem*, being Peter's rebuke to Simon Magus. Translated "your silver perish with you," in the Revised Standard Version.

54. Gregory the Great, *Dialogues*, 4. 57. *Ut in illum amaritudo mortis a culpa solubilem faceret*.

55. Ibid., 4.57. *In sua tristitia e corpore exivit*. My translation.

56. Ibid., 4. 57. *Diu est, quod frater ille qui defunctus est in igne cruciatur*. Confrontation with death is an element in spiritual purification (see Straw, "Purity and Death," 16–37).

57. Gregory the Great, *Dialogues*, 4. 57. *Nunc usque male fui, sed iam modo bene sum, quia hodie communionem recepi*.

58. Ibid., 4. 57. *Frater qui defunctus fuerat per salutarem hostiam evasit supplicium*.

59. *Life of Gregory the Great*, 28; ed. Colgrave, 124–27. This work also claimed that Gregory rescued the pagan Emperor Trajan from damnation.

60. Gregory the Great, *Dialogues*, 4.59, both stories. 4.57: "holy sacrifice brings great benefits to souls even after death, provided their sins can be pardoned in the life to come." Ambrose told a similar story (*De excessu fratris*) of the miraculous aid of the host: when his brother Satyrus was about to be shipwrecked, he tied the host around his neck and made it safely to shore.

61. Ibid., 4. 59.

62. Ibid., 4. 46.

63. De Vogüé, *Grégoire le Grand*, vol 3, 161 n. 1

64. Eutychius, Patriarch of Constantinople, argued that the resurrected bodies would be like wind or air, while Gregory's *Dialogues* book 4 affirms the Augustinian insistence on corporeal, material resurrection that Gregory had argued for during his stay in Constantinople. (Eutychius renounced his views before death.)

65. Gregory the Great, *Dialogues*, 4. 46: *Omnipotens Deus, quia pius est, miserorum cruciatu non pascitur*.

66. Ibid., 4.46: *Vis districtionis absorbet*.

67. Atwell, "From Augustine to Gregory the Great," 180. Atwell continues, "[Gregory's] language reflects a new departure in Christian thinking, and there can be no doubt that it gave much stronger impetus to the shift away from the community eucharist to."

68. Gregory the Great, *Moralia*, 15, 29; 15, 66.

69. Gregory the Great, *Dialogues*, 4.52.

70. Ibid., 4.48.

71. Ibid., 4. 25, commenting on 1 Kings 13:20–29.

72. Columbanus, *Sermons*, Sermon 9; ed. and trans. Walker, *Sancti Columbani Opera*, 97–101.

73. Columbanus, *Sermons*, Sermon 10. Columbanus draws on Malachi 4:1: "For behold, the day comes, burning like an oven, when all the arrogant and all evildoers will be stubble; the day that comes shall burn them up, says the Lord of hosts, so that it will leave them neither root nor branch." Columbanus's Latin text differs slightly from the Vulgate, which had not yet reached ascendancy in the West.

74. Meyvaert, "Enigma of Gregory the Great's *Dialogues*," comments pithily on this arch plagiarist. Whereas it may be appropriate to give cultural context to the kind of endemic borrowing practiced by many monastic writers in this era, Taio appears to have been in a league of his own.

75. Hillgarth, "Eschatological and Political Concepts," p. 225. He also notes in the published discussion that followed the article (235) that Isidore may even have cited Gregory's *Dialogues* on one occasion (thus providing an early citation date for the *Dialogues*.)

76. Ntedika, *L'évocation*, 110–12, citing Isidore of Seville, *De ordine creaturarum*, 14, 12, PL, 83, 949–50.

77. Julian of Toledo, *Prognosticum*, 2. 10. See Hillgarth's introduction to his edition and list of 185 surviving manuscripts.

78. The passage attributed to Pomerius states that prayers, together with "medicinal punishments," will allow the body to be received into heaven. These *poenis medicinalibus* are not identified further and may refer only to the painful fire of purgation through which all souls passed before judgement.

79. Ntedika had noted the lack of connection between the discourses in his study of Augustine, *L'évolution*.

80. McLaughlin noted this also. See *Consorting with Saints*, 193.

81. Pseudo-Eligius, *Homily* 8, PL, 87, 618–19. This sermon is partly translated by Le Goff, *Birth of Purgatory*, who incorrectly assigned it to Eligius's authorship and thus to the seventh century. See Dekkers, *CPL*, 2096 and critical literature cited there. Purgation is not discussed either in the sermon attributed to Eligius in his Carolingian *vita altera*, *V. Eligii* 2.16, nor in a direct manner in the *Praedicatio de supremo iudicio*, which may more reasonably reflect the tenor of his teaching as recalled in his diocese. The *Praedicatio de supremo iudicio* does have something to add to the discussion. See the discussion in chapter 5.

82. *Liber de ordine creaturarum*; ed. Diaz y Diaz, *Un anonimo irlandes del siglo VII*. In the middle ages the work was often attributed to Isidore of Seville. It is now considered to have been written by an unknown Irish author between 680 and 700.

83. Ibid., 6 and 7.

84. The author states that hell is an infernal prison, which suggests that it was located below ground (as also per Gregory's *Dialogues*). We are not informed of purgatory's location.

85. Or combined another way, consistent with the possible model of Gregory the Great's *Moralia*, 26. 25. 50–51, there are two routes for the reprobate (to judgement or not) and two routes for the elect (called to judgement or not). Isidore may also have been the source, *Sententiae*, 1: 27.

86. This list of faults is a variant on comparable lists, such as Benedict's *Rule*, chapter 6, Gregory the Great's *Dialogues*, 4. 41, later, the *Vision of the Monk of Wenlock*, and Bede, *On Mark*, 1. A distinction here is that it included those who marry, which in this period may or may not indicate a list more geared to the laity.

87. Gregory's *Moralia*, 26. 27, 50–51, referred only to penance in the present life. Of the two categories of elect, one would furnish the souls of purgatory as understood by later writers: those who are judged but who will reign—those who wipe away the stains of their life with tears and who gave alms. The *Liber de ordine creaturarum* associated these souls with purgatory and cleansing in the afterlife, but with no mention of intercession. Bede used Gregory's fourfold schema, connected it with postmortem purification, and added intercession for the dead in the form of prayer and masses.

88. Marina Smyth posits that a newly acquired knowledge of Egyptian hagiography in the late seventh century, possibly through Adomnán's connections with Wearmouth-Jarrow, prepared Irish scholars for their acceptance of the Anglo-Saxon formulation of purgatory a century later, "Origins of Purgatory," 123, 129. She also notes (on p. 130) that there may have been initial resistance among Irish scholars to the Gregorian emphasis on the use of the Mass for postmortem intercession, although this was apparently resolved by the eighth century when the *Collectio canonum hibernensis* was compiled.

89. See Moreira, *Dreams, Visions and Spiritual Authority*, 136–68, in which only slight reference to purgatory is made, as it was not a developed feature of Merovingian accounts of dreams or otherworld travel.

90. Gurevich put this divergence nicely: "On fait come s'il y avait deux eschatologies la 'petite,' personelle, et la 'grande,' universelle et historique," in "Au moyen age," 264.

91. Bede, *Ecclesiastical History*, 1. 27; Gregory the Great, *Moralia*, 8. 42–43.

92. Osiek, *Shepherd of Hermas*, 4–7. It was also known to Ambrose, Jerome, Augustine, and Cassian. It is also listed as a prohibited book in the Pseudo-Gelasian, *Decretum*; ed. Dobschütz, "Das Decretum Gelasianum."

93. Smyth, "Origins of Purgatory," 113ff.

94. See chapter 6 below. On the influence of earlier writings on the *Vision of the Monk of Wenlock* and its indebtedness to earlier traditions, including the *Vision of Paul*, see Sims-Williams, *Religion and Literature*, 243–72.

95. The recent study of the *Die Visio Pauli* by Lenka Jirouškova has enlarged our knowledge of the complex medieval tradition of this work.

96. Le Goff and Gurevich illuminated visionary literature and other forms of *exempla* in their discussion of medieval views of death and the afterlife. In so doing they distinguished themselves from an earlier generation that had focused instead on material and documentary remains such as epigraphy, architecture, and wills. For a discussion of the debt and divergences of this literature from the studies of Chaunu (*La mort à Paris, XVIe, XVIIe et XVIIIe siècles*) and Ariès (*Western Attitudes Toward Death*), see Gurevich, "Au Moyen Age," 255–75.

97. Gregory the Great, *Dialogues*, 4.43.

98. The convergence of elite and popular folkloric elements in visionary accounts has been discussed by Le Goff, Gurevich, Vovelle, Dinzelbacher, and others.

99. Commenting on the soldier's vision *(Dialogues, 4. 37)*, he remarked that the bricks of gold should not be interpreted literally and that the odours of the vision had basis in scripture. Yet he also suggested that the volcano in Sicily into which King Theodoric was seen to be thrown was a portal to hell, and the clothes of one saintly apparition got wet helping a man in need.

100. Such disputes open the *Vision of Barontus*, *Vision of Fursey*, and *Vision of the Monk of Wenlock*.

101. For example, the soldier's vision in Gregory's *Dialogues*, 4. 47, and the *Vision of the Monk of Wenlock*.

102. Bede's *Vision of Drythelm* depicted purgatorial fires, but Drythelm was not accused of any crime or submitted to trial. He was informed that if he persevered in penance he would return to join the happy people who awaited entry into heaven.

103. Ambrose, *On Repentance*, 1. 8. 36; trans. Schaff and Wace.

104. Prudentius, *Hymn before Fasting(Hymn 8)* in his *Liber Cathemerinon*.

105. See, for example, Origen, *Homilies on Leviticus 1–16*, 8. 5: "if there were nothing in infants that ought to pertain to forgiveness and indulgence, then the grace of baptism would appear superfluous."

106. Bede, *Ecclesiastical History*, 5. 7. (The King in question was Cadwalla).

107. "No one in a state of sin ought to claim a right to or the use of the sacraments" (Ambrose, *On Repentance*, 2. 11.104).

108. Ambrose, *On Repentance*, 1.3.10.

109. The purging metaphor is used by Ambrose, *On Repentance*, 1. 15. 79, who states that the penitent must be separated out or "purged" from the community so that he does not contaminate it like old leaven. On the primacy of the bishop's role in penance, see Uhalde, *Expectations of Justice*; and Rapp, *Holy Bishops in Late Antiquity*, 92–99, who observes, regarding the bishop's imposition of hands, that "this act is called *anadechesthai*, the same word that is used for the baptismal sponsor as he received the newly baptized from the font—further affirmation of the similarity between baptism and penance" (p. 98).

110. Richard Price cautions that scholarly emphasis on canonical penance, which was always to some degree exceptional, has distorted our view of what individual penance and penitential satisfaction entailed for most Christians and especially for monks ("Informal Penance"). I would like to thank Alan Bernstein for bringing this article to my attention.

111. Ambrose, *On Repentance*, 1.2. Ambrose's treatise was written against the Novatians who apparently denied grave sinners the path of penitential reconciliation. Ambrose argued that God was more inclined to mercy than to severity and that even grave sins can be forgiven. He accused the Novatians of hypocrisy in seeking God's mercy for themselves while denying it to others.

112. Ambrose, *On Repentance*, 2. 7. 58.

113. Ibid., 2. 9. 81.

114. Prudentius, *Hymn before Fasting*.

115. Cassian, *Conferences*, 9. 9. 1.

116. Cassian, *Conferences*, 20. 8. 1. Quoting Psalm 6. 7.

117. Ambrose, *On Repentance*, 2. 6. 51.

118. Cassian, *Conferences*, 9. 29. 1; see 9. 28–30 for a discussion of tears.

119. Ibid., 20. 5. 1.

120. Ibid., 20. 8. 5.

121. Ibid., 20. 21. 1.

122. Ambrose, *On Repentance*, 2. 3. 19.

123. Cassian, *Conferences*, 20. 12. 1.

124. Price, "Informal Penance," 32–33.

125. *Shepherd of Hermas*, Vision 2. 5; Venantius Fortunatus, *Carmina*, 10. 1.

126. Cassian, *Conferences*, 24. 26ff.

127. This would change in Bede's writings; see chapter 6.

128. Pomerius, *De vita contemplativa*, 2. 7. 2.

129. Cyprian, *Ad Dem*, 25, quoted by Daley, *Hope of the Early Church*, 42.

130. On the continuation of this debate, see chapter 5 on the respective positions of Fursey and Eligius of Noyon.

131. Cassian, *Conferences*, 9. 13.

132. Ambrose, *On Repentance*, 1. 9. 43. Cassian also notes that "sometimes pardon for sins is also won through the intercession of holy persons" (*Conferences*, 20. 8. 4).

133. "We do not doubt not only that we are worthy to acquire this remission for our sins through their prayers, but also that we are saved from the infernal torments through their intervention" (Gregory of Tours, *Virt. Mart.*, 4. Pref.).

134. Ambose, *On Repentance*, 1. 17. 92.

135. Deurechild won salvation for her rather less pious mother, Jonas, *Vita Columbani* 2.15.

136. *Vision of Wetti*, trans. Traill, *Walahfrid Strabo's Visio Wettini*, p. 55.

137. Ambrose, *On Repentance*, 2. 9. 80.

138. An intercessory offering of a rather different kind is recorded by Bede in his description of a young monk's death from plague at Selsey. The young Saxon monk viewed his imminent death as a kind of sacrificial offering for the continued health of the rest of the members of the community. Bede, *Ecclesiastical History*, 4. 14, explained by an apparition of Saints Peter and Paul.

139. *Vision of Paul*, redaction 2 [Vienna Cod. 3881] in Silverstein, *Visio Sancti Pauli*, 158. It would be interesting to know the work's date. The manuscript is late but it bears many features in common with some of the earliest redactions of the *Vision of Paul*.

140. Effros, *Caring for Body and Soul*, offers a careful analysis of the value of archaeological and liturgical evidence for mortuary customs. See also, Duval and Picard, eds., *L'inhumation privilégiée*.

141. Sicard, *La liturgie*; Angenendt, "Theologie und Liturgie," and its expanded form in *Geschichte der Religiosität*. Palazzo, *A History of Liturgical Books*, gives an overview of liturgical forms and documentation.

142. Anglo-Saxon liturgical works survive in complete form only from the tenth century onward. See Dumville, *Liturgy and the Ecclesiastical History of Late Anglo-Saxon England*; Pfaff, ed. *Liturgical Books of Anglo-Saxon England*; and on sources, especially Isidore, see Jones, "Book of the Liturgy in Anglo-Saxon England." Evidence for the "Celtic" liturgy is examined in Warren, *Liturgy and Ritual of the Celtic Church* (1881), newly edited by Stevenson. See Paxton's comments in *Christianizing Death*, 78–91.

143. Hen, "Unity in Diversity."

144. Brown, *Cult of the Saints*; Angenendt, *Heilige und Reliquien*; McCulloh, "Continuity and Change in Papal Relic Policy." Gregory of Tours, *GM*, 30, indicates that there were still some churches in his time that had no relics.

145. In Roman cities, cemeteries were required to be outside the city walls. Concerns about pollution, hygiene, and the restless dead kept most of the dead far from inhabited areas. In Merovingian Gaul, former Roman cities with urban monasteries maintained such practices. Saint Radegund of Poitiers, for example, was interred in a funerary church outside the city walls. Yet the process of bringing the special dead inside the city precincts had already begun, and as cities expanded later in the middle ages, mausolea, churches, and cemeteries that were once outside cities became incorporated into them. In northern Gaul, Merovingian monasteries were increasingly built on landed estates and were thus outside cities in any case.

146. See chapter 5, n. 35 for discussion.

147. See Effros, *Caring for Body and Soul*, 79–137.

148. Effros discusses interesting examples in Ibid., 92–110.

149. See Ibid., 156–61, on the problems of interpreting moveable objects in graves. For grave objects in Frankish territories, see exhibit catalogue, *Die Franken. Wegbereiter Europas*.

150. Prudentius, Prologue to *Psychomachia*.

151. Augustine, *Civ. Dei*, 20. 9.

152. Ntedika, *L'Évocation*, 34–35.

153. For example, Paxton, *Christianizing Death*, traces the changing perceptions of rituals for the sick and dying. Effros, *Caring for Body and Soul*, 169–204, examines the liturgy and changing views of the afterlife. Sicard's analysis of funerary liturgies is essential on the changing language and perceptions of the afterlife, in *La liturgie*; see especially his conclusion, pp. 399–418.

154. Sicard, *La liturgie*, 137–39.

155. See Paxton, *Christianizing Death*, 90, who notes that in the Spanish *Libri ordinum*, thirty-six psalms were sung over the dying person, concluding with psalm 50 [51]. See also Paxton's comments (on pp. 48–49) on Caesarian influence on the Iberian liturgy and scholarly debates.

156. Sicard, *La liturgie*, 263. Prayers called on those attending the service to remember the dear departed and expressed the hope that: *omnes lubricae temeritatis offensas. Ut concessa venia plenae indulgentiae quicquid in hoc saeculo proprius error adtulit, totum ineffabili pietate ac benignitate sua conpenset* (Sicard, *La liturgie*, 263: Caesarius. See also, Paxton, *Christianizing Death*, 52–55).

157. Sicard, *La liturgie*, 92.

158. *Liber Sacramentorum Gellonensis*; ed. Dumas, # 2895: *et si de regione tibi contraria . . . contaxit . . . tua pietate ablue indulgendo tu, Deus, inoleta bonitate clementer deleas, pietate indulgeas, oblivioni in perpetuum tradas.* See also the *Diri vulneris* prayer in the *Gelasian Sacramentary*, Vatican Reginensis latinus, 316: *et si quas illa ex hac carnali commemoratione contraxit maculas tu deus inoleta bonitate clementer deleas pie indulgeas oblivione in perpetuum tradas.* Edited by Sicard, *La Liturgie*, p. 306.

159. As Paxton remarks of the Roman *ordo defunctorum*, "to die in the bosom of the church was a guarantee of safe passage to heaven. That is why we find little indication of a need for a period of purification or penitential supplication before incorporation into the ranks of the blessed." Paxton and others have observed intensifying penitential concerns expressed in the later Frankish liturgy in response to Irish penitentialism (*Christianizing Death*, 44, 92ff.).

160. Sicard, *La liturgie*, 413. Sicard notes that this is the only eighth-century Gelasian sacramentary to do so. The Book of Cerne prayer reads: *praesta mihi post obitum meum prosperum iter, ad perennis paradisi pervenire suavitatem, ibique cum sanctis animabus mihi requiescere liceat usque ad tempus resurrectionis.*

161. Sicard, *La liturgie*, 280–82, points out that the term *locum paenalem* was used to denote purgatory by Gregory the Great (*Dialogues*, 4, 40–42). There is no clear distinction in the prayer that joins together the place of punishment, the fire of Gehenna, and the flames of Tartarus into a single phrase.

162. Bede knew Isidore's *De ecclesiasticis officiis*; see Lapidge, *Anglo-Saxon Library*, 212.

CHAPTER 5

1. Hillgarth "Eschatological and Political Concepts"; Carozzi, *Le voyage de l'âme;* Brown, "Decline of the Empire of God."

2. Le Goff, *Birth of Purgatory*, 84.

3. Carozzi, *Le voyage de l'âme*, 256.

4. Brown, "End of the Ancient Other World" and "Decline of the Empire of God." These ideas were foreshadowed by Brown in "Vers la naissance du Purgatoire."

5. Brown, "End of the Ancient Other World," 24–25.

6. Dunn, "Origins of Purgatory." Dunn argues that the Gregorian *Dialogues* may have been composed in Northumbria in the 670s. See also Dunn, *Emergence of Monasticism*, 186–90. Clark's thesis in *Pseudo-Gregorian Dialogues* is discussed briefly in chapter 4.

7. Carozzi, *Le voyage de l'âme*, 99; Berschin, *Biographie und Epochenstil*, 104–9, on visions in western literature. It is possible that the visions of Sunniulf of Randan and Salvius (later Bishop of Albi) may have circulated as independent texts, but they

are known only in Gregory of Tours's *History of the Franks*. Salvius's vision in particular shares features in common with Fursey's first vision, including a return to the world because future responsibilities in the church awaited, although it does not include a tour of hell.

8. The *Visio Baronti* (A. D. 678/79) drew explicitly on Gregory's *Dialogues*.

9. Bede, *Ecclesiastical History*, 3. 19. The *Life of Fursey* was known also to Felix, the author of the *Life of Guthlac*, written before 749. See Colgrave's edition, pp. 9, 17, 179–80.

10. Reference in this chapter to the *Life of Fursey* throughout refers to the seventh-century *Vita prima* edited by Johannes Bollandus, and by Bruno Krusch, whose edition does not include the visions. For Fursey's vision I use Ciccarese's detailed study, "Le Visioni di S. Fursa," which includes an edition of the text pages 279–303. Carozzi, *Le voyage de l'âme*, Appendix, 677–92, also provides the Latin text. There is now also a transcription and translation of the damaged text from BL, Harley MS 5041ff., 79–98, by Rackham, *Transitus Beati Fursei*, which is useful for comparison. On Fursey's circle, see Dierkens, "Prolégomènes à une histoire," esp. 385ff., and his *Abbayes et Chapitres*, 71 n. 7; 304 n. 147. Also useful is Ó Riain, "Les Vies de Saint Fursey," and discussion by Dierkens and Rouche that follows, pp, 412–13.

11. See discussion of Erchinoald in Fouracre and Gerberding, *Late Merovingian France*, 99–106. Erchinoald's support for certain Irish monks over others was determined by his political ambitions and Merovingian land-based politics. Fursey's move to Lagny was a move within the same political orbit.

12. On the monastery of Péronne (*Peronna Scottorum*) see Prinz, *Frühes Mönchtum*, 128–29.

13. The debate over whether the *Life of Fursey* is primarily a continental text or one that speaks to Irish sources and concerns is over a century old. See Ó Riain, "Les Vies de Saint Fursey," 406; Ó Riain presents arguments for Irish sources and concerns in the *vita prima* and the *vita secunda* (c. 1100).

14. "Irish" (*scotti*) referred to natives of Ireland but also to those regions of Scotland and northern England where "Celtic Christianity" held sway. Fursey was from Ireland. Brown, rightly in my view, is cautious about positing a context for the vision that is too local or "exotic" ("End of the Ancient Other World," 33–34). By contrast Carozzi commented: "Fursy et ses compagnons font partie d'un peuple non romanisé et converti récemment" (*Le voyage de l'âme*, 138).

15. See Prinz, *Frühes Mönchtum* 128–29. Schäferdiek, "Irish Mission," points out that Columbanus's monasteries such as Luxeuil and Bobbio were not very Irish.

16. Prinz, *Frühes Mönchtum*, 129.

17. Fursey went to Lagny, Foillan, and Ultan (who left Anglia after Fursey's death) to Péronne. Foillan was also involved in the foundation of Fosses after his expulsion from Péronne.

18. Fouracre and Gerberding, *Late Medieval France*, 102.

19. Schäferdiek, "Irish Mission."

20. Ian Wood, "Columbanus," disputes that there was a monolithic Irish culture on the continent. The Irish monks who came with Columbanus were of a different Irish generation than those who came with Fursey etc. We have already noted above

(note 11) that political figures like Erchinoald were selective about the Irish monks they supported.

21. *Life of Fursey*, 3. Beoanus and Meldanus were said to be from Fursey's *provincia*; but between Fursey's purported view of them in his vision in Ireland and their appearance as revered figures at Péronne, there is no mention of either of them as having been Fursey's companion. It is possible that their relics were brought to Lagny by Fursey and later deposited at Péronne with Fursey's own remains. Mostly their inclusion as named clerics in the text is testimony to the intrusion of editorial interests emanating from cult interests at Péronne.

22. The word used here, *paenitentia*, means "penance" or "penitence." The full meaning of "penance" includes repentance, confession, and satisfaction. So while *paenitentia* is often used in sources to refer explicitly to penitential activities, or satisfaction, it was also be used to describe the inner state of repentance (contrition). The verb *paenitio* also meant "to repent." *Paenitentia* used in *Vision of Fursey* harbours ambivalent meaning.

23. My translation from Ciccarese's edition. The choice of *delicta* over *peccata* is significant. *Delicta* were omissions, small things perhaps easily forgotten. The suggestion is that Fursey was not guilty of a grave sin, which would have had a more serious consequence. Omissions due to faulty memory were a persistent worry in monastic and visionary literature. Transparency of all faults to divine (and demonic) scrutiny was a spur to full confession.

24. Brown, "End of the Ancient Other World," 71.

25. Dunn, "Origins of Purgatory," 249.

26. See pp. 101–6 on penance.

27. Dunn, "Origins of Purgatory," 252.

28. Sulpicius Severus, *Vita Martini*, 22.3. A demon upbraided Martin for accepting monks who had lost the grace of baptism, listing their *crimina*. Martin responded that old omissions (*delicta*) were purged by leading a better life and that the sins of those who ceased to sin should be forgiven.

29. *Visio Baronti*. In his edition, Levinson dated the vision to AD 678/79. Hillgarth, *Christianity and Paganism*, 195–204, provides an English translation. Recent discussions of this work include Ciccarese, "La *Visio Baronti*"; Carozzi, "La géographie de l'au-delà," esp. 440–45, and *Le voyage de l'âme*, 139–86; Hen, "Structure and Aims of the 'Visio Baronti'"; Zaleski, *Otherworld Journeys*, esp. 45–52, 70–72; and Moreira, *Dreams, Visions and Spiritual Authority*, 158–67.

30. The passage in Deuteronomy concerns appointing judges and continues (16: 20): "Justice and only justice you shall follow, that you may live an inherit the land which the Lord your God gives you."

31. The walls of fire held back on either side are reminiscent of the waters of the Dead Sea held apart so that Moses and his people might pass through unharmed to the promised land.

32. Scars received in spiritual battle were prized tokens. Augustine believed martyrs in heaven would keep their scars even in their perfected bodies. Prudentius imagined Job, fresh from the battle of virtues against vices, escorting Patience, smiling as he thought of his healed sores and "the scars he shows as his glory" (*Psychomachia*,

162–64; trans. Isbell, *Last Poets*, 133). For Origen, by contrast, spiritualized scars of the soul served as a permanent marker and reminder of the wound of sin (*Homilies on Leviticus*, 8, 4ff.

33. *Life of Fursey*, 16: *nec corpus eius in sancto sepeliendum est loco.*

34. Liturgical prayers were prohibited for unreconciled penitents, although private prayer for such individuals was possible. Ntedika, *L'Évocation*, 34–35, cites the Council of Braga (563), the *Penitential attributed to Theodore of Canterbury*, Book 2. 5, 8, 9: "Dionysius the Areopagite says that he who offers masses for a bad man commits blasphemy against God. Augustine says that masses are to be performed for all Christians, since it either profits them or consoles those who offer or those who seek," and the seventh-century *Canons of the Alleged Second Synod of St. Patrick* # 12 states: "For he who did not in his life deserve to receive the sacrifice, how shall it be able to help him after death?" (Trans. John T. McNeill and Helena M. Gamer, *Medieval Handbooks of Penance*, 82).

35. The practice of burial close to the relics of a saint, within the church precincts, or even within the church, increased in seventh-century Gaul. While this privilege was generally reserved for those who had converted to the monastic life, such burial was sought after by the secular elite also. This did not always sit well with religious communities. Gregory's *Dialogues*, 4.55 tells of Valentine, a defender of the Church at Milan who was dissolute but who was given a church burial in the Church of St. Syrus nevertheless. That night two demons bound Valentine's feet and dragged his body from his grave. The next day his body was found lying in another grave, feet still bound. Gregory commented: "If one dies in the state of mortal sin and arranges to have himself buried in church, he is sure to be condemned for his presumption. The holy place will not win him forgiveness, but will add to his guilt the sin of rashness." On Merovingian burial practices, see Bonnie Effros, *Caring for Body and Soul*, 151–56 contributions to Duval and Picard, eds., *L'inhumation privilégiée*. This is the background for raised anxieties about maintaining the purity of church space, hence the emphasis in Fursey's vision on completion of penance. Burial *ad sanctos* was an issue for the seventh-century Merovingian church: it is not clear how far this was an issue for the church in mid-seventh-century England or Ireland. It appears that the push to enshrine relics (and thus regulate access) began in Ireland in the seventh century when the relics of Brigit and her bishop Conleth were sought out and enshrined. See Cogitosus, *Life of St. Brigit*, chapter 32, which describes the tombs of Brigit and Conleth on either side of the altar in the church at Kildare, and the creation of a distinct monastic boundary around the monastic community. Rollason suggests this may have been an isolated case and notes that whereas the Anglo-Saxon practice of enshrining saints was probably closely linked with Merovingian practices, the connections between Ireland and Gaul did not produce a comparable tradition of elevating and translating holy relics (*Saints and Relics in Anglo-Saxon England*, 50–51). Christian burial within church precincts (cemeteries) is only identifiable in the archaeological record from the late seventh century. Before that time, burial in Ireland and England associated with ancestral property appears to have prevailed among the elite. See, O'Brien, "Pagan and Christian Burial in Ireland," esp. 136, who notes that by contrast with the disinterest of the previous century, in the seventh century "the clergy

was now seeking to establish burial in Christian cemeteries as the norm. In the late seventh century, possibly as a result of the recent series of plagues, Christian religious observances assumed added importance." See also Blair, *Church in Anglo-Saxon Society*, 228–45, who emphasizes that lay burial in churches or church cemeteries was still exceptional in the seventh century, and even the Christian elite often still chose barrow burial at ancestral sites.

36. *Vita Fursei*, 15. The text advises that the property of the saints should be used for those "poor in spirit" or those who have corrected their vices, presumably penitents.

37. In fact, some earlier prohibitions were more exclusive: the mid-fifth-century *Canons of Patrick, Auxilius and Iserninus*, canon 12, states: "If a Christian has been excommunicated, not even his alms are to be accepted." Trans. Bieler, *Works of St. Patrick*, 51.

38. *Vita Fursei*, 16. Bede's synopsis glossed over this discussion: "And he said much more and taught some healthy lessons which need to be taken for the salvation of those who repent at their deaths" (*HE*, 3.19).

39. On almsgiving in the *Visio Baronti*, see Contreni, "Building Mansions in Heaven"; Hen, "Structure and Aims of the 'Visio Baronti.'" Almsgiving was a consistent theme in the sermons of Fursey's contemporary, Eligius of Noyon (discussed further below). It was customary that alms be distributed to the poor at the time of the donor's funeral and sometimes on the anniversary of death or interment. Churches kept lists of deserving poor, considerably facilitating this process. For the need for rituals to make secular donations "pure" (Eastern Mediterranean), see Caner, "Towards a Miraculous Economy."

40. The demon quotes from a passage that begins: "If one sacrifices from what has been wrongfully obtained, the offering is blemished; the gifts of the lawless are not acceptable," and concludes: "The bread of the needy is the life of the poor; whoever deprives them of it is a man of blood. To take away a neighbour's living is to murder him; to deprive an employee of his wages is to shed blood." Ecclesiasticus (Sirach) 34: 18–22. The passage is relevant to the demons' accusation against Fursey, that he did not love his neighbour as himself.

41. *In illo secreto receptacolo ubi iam non est locus penetencie* (*Bobbio Missal*, 534; ed. Lowe).

42. *Vision of Paul*, 43.

43. Eligius, *De supremo iudicio*; ed. Krusch, 760: *Erit quidem et in inferno penetentia, sed omnino infructuusa, et erit ibi penetentia dolorem habens, sed medicinam iam non habens*. The date and authenticity of Eligius's long sermon reproduced in the *Life of Eligius* is much debated. It is widely recognized that the *Vita Eligii* as we have it is a Carolingian production, which altered and edited its earlier source components. The full sermon is found in Migne, *Vita S. Eligii*, 2.15. Krusch produced only the Caesarian part of the long sermon in his edition of the *Vita S. Eligii*, 2.16, and published separately as an appendix to his edition of the Life, another part of the long sermon, the *de supremo iudicio*, for which he found two early manuscripts, one of which he dated to the late eighth century, and therefore earlier than the Carolingian *vita* that incorporated it. Krusch viewed this sermon (*de supremo iudicio*) as having

some claim for authenticity. Hen questions the linguistic rationale behind a recent attempt to date the entire *vita* to the seventh century (*Culture and Religion*, 196–97). Nevertheless, Eligius's long sermon (in fact a compilation of numerous sermons) may have incorporated some earlier, perhaps even authentically Eligian, material. Carozzi accepted them as being contemporaneous with Fursey; see *Le voyage de l'âme*, 121 n. 107. While noting the debate, James McCune's recent work on Eligius does not challenge the attribution, "Rethinking the Pseudo-Eligius Sermon Collection," 446 n. 4.

44. See Fouracre and Gerberding, *Late Merovingian France*, 104 n. 50. Fursey is not the only prominent figure to be "purged" of sins in the seventh century. Another example is Hector of Marseilles, in what is probably the first example of an attempt at political rehabilitation through an imagined purgation of sins, see the *Passion of Leudegar*, chapter 11.

45. Le Goff, *Birth of Purgatory*, 113: "The idea of Purgatory in this story is vague. No details are given about the nature of the fire, and the character of Fursey's burn is ambiguous: does it represent an ordeal, a punishment for sins, or a purification?" The answer is, of course, it represents all three: punishment is not divisible from purgation after Augustine, and the ordeal (probative) aspect of the fire is scriptural.

46. Hagiography was a well-developed genre by the mid-seventh century when the first Irish Saints' *vitae* were composed: Cogitosus's *Life of St. Brigit*, Tírechán's *Life of St. Patrick*, Muirchú's *Life of St. Patrick*, and Adomnán's *Life of St. Columba of Iona*. Sulpicius Severus's *Life of St. Martin* was particularly important; see Stancliffe, "Miracle Stories"; Wood, "Marvellous in Irish and Continental Saints' Lives." Irish hagiographers sought to connect their saints with the universal church. Bitel, "Ekphrasis at Kildare," 609–11, notes that beyond some structural features, Cogitosus's *Vita* "created in Brigit a distinctively Irish holy woman," while "he built for her, by his words, a church of marvelously romanizing pretension, thus putting Kildare and its saint on the Christian map."

47. Brown, "End of the Ancient Other World," 35.

48. See Stancliffe's comments, "Miracle Stories," on demonology as a facet of post-Augustinian pessimism contrasted with Iro-British Pelagian optimism expressed in Irish and Northumbrian hagiography. The exception is Adomnán's *Life of Columba*. Stancliffe comments (p.108): "Here, then we find demons functioning much as they do in continental Lives, and I think that it is no fluke that they appear in the work of the Irish hagiographer who was most European in outlook, and the best read in non-Irish hagiography."

49. Stancliffe, "Miracle Stories," 109.

50. Agilbert is an oft-cited example of this kind of professional mobility in the seventh century. Agilbert was a Frank from Neustria who studied in Ireland, was briefly appointed as bishop to the West Saxons, and ended his days as bishop of Paris. See Bede, *Ecclesiastical History*, 3. 7.

51. Hughes, "Celtic Church," notes the very different ecclesiastical organization of the "Celtic" Church in Wales and Ireland. Sims-Williams, "Visionary Celt," traces the Celts as a largely nineteenth- and twentieth-century literary and scholarly construct (although it existed in medieval times also) based on artificial antithesis of Anglo-Saxon and Celt, and Roman and Celt, a perspective that could propagate the

view that "the Celtic Church was decentralized, shamanistic, and simple: the Church of Rome was centralized, hierarchical, complex and worldly." Quoted by Sims-Williams, "Visionary Celt," 75, from a paper in *The Celtic Consciousness*, ed. Robert O'Driscoll.

52. While debated in the early church, reconciliation before death was assured to penitents by the Council of Nicaea (325) canon 13, and was repeated in later councils, for example, in the Council of Arles II (442–506) canons 28 and 29; Council of Agde (506) canon 15., ed C. Munier, *Conc. Gal.*, A. 314-A. 506, CCSL, 147; and in penitentials, for example, *Penitential of Finnian*, 34; ed. Bieler, 86–87. On death and the penitent see Paxton, *Christianizing Death*, 35–37, 51–52, and the evolution of such provisions in eighth-century sacramentaries, 115, 125–26.

53. Rebillard, *In Hora Mortis*.

54. *Penitential of Finnian*, 35.

55. Concern about payment for intercession arises in the *Vision of Wetti*, which stipulated that the prayers of intercession must be free.

56. Cassian, *Conferences*, 5. 10.1–3. "Each vice, then, since it is begotten by an increase in the one that comes before it, is purged away when the one before it is diminished." Trans. Ramsey, *John Cassian: Conferences*, 190.

57. Carozzi, *Le voyage de l'âme*. Carozzi also made a focused study of the *Vision of Paul* in *Eschatologie et au-delà*. Carozzi's work thus corrects the view that saw no influence of earlier apocalypses on the text; see Berschin, *Biographie und Epochenstil*, 106–7.

58. Flint, *Rise of Magic*, 53, 120, on pyromancy, a divinatory practice based on animal sacrifice and observing grains in fire, as condemned by Isidore of Seville, and Burchard of Worms. However, "niedfyr" is first mention in an eighth-century list of superstitions, the *Indiculus superstitionum et paganarum*, in a manuscript that also contained the canons of the council of 742. Prohibitions 15 reads: "Of fire made by friction from wood, that is, the "nodfyr." See McNeill and Gamer, eds., *Medieval Handbooks of Penance*, 420 and n. 11.

59. The context of Germanic law is discussed in chapter 8. Carozzi's argument for the influence of the Germanic Council on later visions is convincing, and it should also be noted that penitential and conciliar advice often formed part of the same document.

60. Carozzi, *Le voyage de l'âme*, 115-16, who notes that while it is unlikely that the Irish treatise was known to the *Vision's* author, he "bathed" in the same moral milieu.

61. Bede, *HE*, 3.19.

62. Carozzi states the connection differently: he supposes that Bede had a different text available to him, from which both the Péronne scribes and Bede drew (*Le voyage de l'âme*, 100 n. 7, 101. This complication is not necessary to explain Bede's account.

63. Bede, *HE*, 3. 19; trans. Colgrave and Mynors, *Bede's Ecclesiastical History*, 273.

64. Bede, *HE*, 3. 19; Bede's version is slightly changed: the fourth fire is not *ignis immisericordiae* but *ignis impietatis*.

65. Isaiah 50:11. The image of the fire kindled by sin was explained by Origen, *First Principles*, 10.4.

66. Schäferdiek, "Irish Mission," 13–54, esp. 150–52 on Fursey.

67. *Fragmentary Vision of 757*; ed. Tangl, *Die Briefe des Heiligen Bonifatius*, 247–50. The translation in Emerton, *Letters of St. Boniface*, 167–69, must be used with caution. See note 72 below.

68. Emerton, *Letters of St. Boniface*, 167.

69. Bede's *HE* was widely disseminated, and Boniface requested that works by Bede be sent to him.

70. Perhaps even *The Shepherd of Hermas*? Like Hermas, the vision recipient turned his attention to his family: "He also imposed a fast of 40 days for the general offences of his whole family according to the order of the same judge." Carozzi, taking the position that the visionary was a monk, suggests that he imposed the fast on his monastic *familia*. The interpretation depends on the visionary's status at the time of the vision. Drythelm was a layman when he had his vision and entered the monastery as a result. This anonymous monk is instructed to go to a monastery to confess his sins, which may suggest a similar path to Drythelm's.

71. Carozzi, *Le voyage de l'âme*, 264, suggests the rainbow image may derive from Germanic mythology. Bright pathways to heaven were common also in Mediterranean literature: the Abbot Eugendus had a vision of a celestial path like a ladder with crystal steps, and in another a ray of light steaming towards him from the East. See the *Life of Eugendus*, chapters 123 and 137, ed. Martine in *Vie des pères du Jura*, SC 142 (1968). A white rainbow was reportedly seen over Wilfrid of Ripon's tomb on the first anniversary of his death, Eddius Stephanus, *Life of Wilfrid*, 68. Brigit was said to have hung her cloak on a sunbeam, Cogitosus, *Life of St Brigit*, 6. 3.

72. *Ad penalia loca parare tormenta vidit*. Emerton's translation of these places as "places of penance" is inaccurate and misleading since it suggests something other than what the text warrants. Although *penalia* can refer to the "satisfaction" that a penalty on the criminal can provide, its most common meaning is simple punishment. Furthermore, it is clear from the end of this passage that these souls are being taken directly by demons from their bodies *ad tormenta*. Furthermore, Emerton translated *poenalibus puteis* as "penitential pits," misrepresenting what were simply understood as pits of punishment. These misleading translations fundamentally misrepresent the meaning of the text.

73. Lewis and Short, *A Latin Dictionary*, p. 1929, notes that in classical use the *uncus* was the hook by which a condemned criminal was dragged to the Tiber. Not an image suggesting last minute reprieve.

74. In view of Aethelbert's reputation for fornication, the queens may have been royal concubines: queens as they would have been understood by the Anglo-Saxons, but adulterers as understood by religious authorities. Alan Bernstein notes that according to the *Anglo-Saxon Chronicle*, a Cuthburh was married to King Aldfrith of Northumbria, "Named Others and Named Places." We do not know how common a name this was.

75. Ed. Tangl, *Bonifatius Briefe*, notes to Letter 115. The date of King Aethelbald's death gives the text a likely terminus post quem; "likely," because it was not unknown for visionaries to report seeing prominent individuals in hell before they were dead. In this text the visionary claimed to be able to see the merits of the both the living and the

dead—an ability attributed to St. Aldegund of Maubeuge also. Carozzi, *Le voyage de l'âme*, 263, suggests a comparison with the *Vision of Paul*, thereby making the children Aethelbald's bastards, unbaptized in Daniel's time. If the tortured queens were his royal concubines, it would make the vision a very close family affair.

76. While the tortures described in this section are in hell, not purgatory, Carozzi's assessment of the vision as introducing the novel feature of purgatorial torture still holds; at the beginning of the text where purgatory is quite clearly introduced, the author informs us that souls were being tortured there. This vision is thus indeed the first instance of the "infernalization" of purgatory according to his definition—that is to say, the first time a visionary text ascribed to purgatory the differentiated torture of individual sins in the manner that sins were customarily tortured in hell. The individuals in purgatory and their specific tortures are not named, however.

77. St Gallen, Stiftsbibliothek, Cod. Sang. 682; Silverstein, *Visio Sancti Pauli*, 214–18. See also his discussion on the text on pp. 58–61 and 82–90. The fragment is Vatican Library, Codex Palatinus Latinus, 126.

78. Silverstein, *Visio Sancti Pauli*, 89.

79. Ibid., 214.

80. Carozzi discovered plausible correspondence between the sins punished in *Redaction 6* and contemporary concerns as expressed in mid-eighth-century church councils and a barbarian law code. See the discussion in chapter 8. The manuscript is dated to the first quarter of the ninth century in the Library of Switzerland's virtual manuscript catalogue.

81. Carozzi, *Le voyage de l'âme*, 269–70.

82. *Incipit castigatio sanctae paule de hominis peccatoris. Qui peccant et emendant.* The title introduced the idea of correction, and thus it seems fairly certain that the vision was understood as purgatory by at least this one ninth-century copyist. The only other witness to this redaction is a fragment that does not include this title, Rome Pal. 216, f.126v. Its simple title is: *In Christo nomene incipit vita sancti pauli.*

83. *Sanctus paulus ductus est in regnum dei ut videret opera iustorum et poenas peccatorum.*

84. On Carozzi's reading of *usuruntur* as a corruption for *uruntur*, see *Le voyage de l'âme*, 267.

85. *Et interrogavit sanctus paulus; Isti sunt qui castitatem propeccant quomodo hoc enim dant. Respondit ei angelus. Agat paenitentiam dum advixerit parcet ei dominus peccatum suum; Et interrogavit sanctus paulus; Dum tinuisti presbyter. Aut diaconus. Aut subdiaconus. Aut virginis. Aut sponsa christi qui posita peccatum facere. Quomodo hoc enim dant. Respondit ei angelus. Annos quatuor iaceas a terra pura duas super lapide et ipsos annos iniusto paciant famem apud panem et sale et aqua et parcet ei dominus peccatum suum.*The words *enim dant* are clearly viewed as two words in the manuscript, p. 199. See E-Codices: Virtual Manuscript Library of Switzerland.

86. Silverstein, *Visio Sancti Pauli*, 60.

87. Dunn, "Origins of Purgatory," 247–48.

88. For an overview on these issues, especially relating to private, repeatable penance, see Dooley, "From Penance to Confession."

89. Price, "Informal Penance," 32–33.

90. The practice of repeatable private penance administered by a priest was already in place by the Third Council of Toledo (589), canons 8 and 11; see Dooley, "From Penance to Confession."

91. Ibid., 250.

92. Take the *Bigotian Penitential*, for example. In the introduction we encounter the view that Christians will be "saved after punishments." *Salvandos esse post penas.* Prologue, *Poenitentiale Bigotianum*; ed. Wasserschleben, *Die Bussordnungen*, 441–60. Also see ed. Bieler, *Irish Penitentials*, 202/3.

93. *The Penitential of Finnian*, 47 and 29 respectively.

94. Ibid., 21: "after seven years of penance he who fell can be called 'just' and in the eighth year evil shall not lay hold of him." The idea that the penitent became "just" is seen in Paschasius of Dumium, *Questions and Answers of the Greek Fathers*, chapter 23. An angel informed a un-named bishop that God's mercy to the penitent was such that "He soon dissolves their sins and even allows them the rewards of the just." Translation by Barlow, *Iberian Fathers*, p. 145.

95. Bede's *Vision of Drythelm* was the first to change the model of purgation for "light sins" only to one in which more serious *scelera* could be expiated. See chapter 6.

96. Reviewing the *Vision of the Monk of Wenlock*, the *Vision of Drythelm*, and the *Fragmentary Vision of 757*, it is clear that the punishments of souls in purgatory was still, at this stage, extremely general; they owed a great deal to earlier visions and nothing to penitential methods. Purgatorial punishments were not tariffed according to the model provided in penitential lists, but were rather an issue of duration of penalty.

97. Salvian of Marseilles, *Four Books of Timothy*, 1.12; trans. O'Sullivan, *Writings of Salvian*, 290–92.

98. Trans. O'Sullivan, *Writings of Salvian*, 5.

99. *Penitential of Cummean* Prologue. Perhaps from Augustine on opposite remedies and like remedies; see *De doctrina christiana* 14.

100. The image of personified sins as witnesses draws on biblical texts and is found also in early apocalypses, such as the *Apocalypse of Peter*. Bauckham, *Fate of the Dead*, 202–3, notes that "in Jewish judicial practice the witnesses were the accusers" and that this was a powerful image in an eschatological context in which sinners were accused by their own sins since they receive justice and condemnation, which, being unaffected by external forces, is "indisputable."

101. Barontus saw thousands of men bound up by demons and taken to the torment of leaden seats. The categorization proceeded by analysis of the type of sin committed so that murderers would be grouped with murderers and the prideful with the prideful, and so on. The purpose of this categorization was not to assign different penalties, but to put like sin with like so that sinners could be thrown into the fires in discrete bunches. The connection of bundles and the pit of hell derives from Isaiah 24:31–33. The image of the bundles is also used by Gregory in the *Dialogues*. On this richly commented metaphor, especially as it related to sin and heresy, see Savigni, "La parabola della zizzania."

102. Pomerius, *De vita contemplativa*, 2.7.2. (Speaking here primarily about priests who have sinned and who approach the altar for Communion or for their duties.)

103. *Poenitentiale Bigotianum*; ed. Wasserschleben, *Die Bussordnungen*, 441–60. Latin and translation by Bieler, *Irish Penitentials*, 198–239 nn. 255–57. Bieler notes (p. 10) that the work is related to the *Old-Irish Penitential* and the *Penitential of Cummean*, although other works informed it: "Apparently this Penitential had come to the Continent before it took the form in which we now read it." Frantzen states that the penitential is of Breton origin, "Penitentials attributed to Bede," p. 593. McNeill and Gamer, *Medieval Handbooks of Penance*, date the work 700–725, but Vogel, *Les "libri paenitentiales,"* 72, and others have suggested it may be substantially later (late eighth/early ninth century). The earliest manuscript, Cambrai 625 (576) is ninth century. Bieler's edition is used here.

104. Bieler notes that the penitential's citation to Jerome does not correspond to any known writings by him (*Irish Penitentials*, 255). The attribution to Jerome is interesting, however, in that the penitential is quite anti-Origenist in places ("the devil and all his satellites and all wicked men and transgressors shall perish for ever") while at the same time echoing Origen's *Homilies on Leviticus*, Homily 8.

105. Bieler, *Irish Penitentials*, 200–1.

106. Ibid., 201.

107. Ibid.

108. Origen, *Homilies on Leviticus*, Homily 8 reads in part: "Here, as long as we are placed in the flesh, we cannot be pure liquid unless the eighth day should come; that is, unless the time of the future age should come." Trans. Barkley, p. 159.

109. Bieler, *Irish Penitentials*, 203.

110. Ibid., 203.

111. Ibid., 203–4.

112. *Tripartite St. Gall Penitential* (c. 800). McNeil and Gamer, *Medieval Handbooks of Penance*, 283, point out that the instruction cited above, "On how penitents ought to be received," was a feature of a number of late eighth- and ninth-century penitentials.

113. Brown, "End of the Ancient Other World"; "Decline of the Empire of God"; and "Vers la naissance du Purgatoire."

114. Brown, "Decline of the Empire of God," 46.

115. Ibid., 55.

116. Brown, "Decline of the Empire of God," 52; "End of the Ancient Other World," 67, 69.

117. It would be hard to ascribe this mentality to one culture more than another. Tertullian made frequent allusion to the hell "prison" (Matt 5:25–26), from which "you will never get out until you have paid the last penny." Caesarius of Arles also referenced this passage in his sermons. Furthermore, as noted above, Brown recognized that in Fursey's vision God's mercy might actually be seen to prevail over rigorous application of penance. The dialogue has been interpreted in different ways; see discussion above. Brown saw in the demons' retributive demands counterarguments in early medieval culture to a new leniency—the change from single to multiple penances for a particular sin.

118. Brown, "Decline of the Empire of God," 58.

119. See Bauckham, *Fate of the Dead*, 149–59.

120. Indeed, as Bauckham points out, the *Apocalypse of Peter*, which could be read to support the idea of universal salvation, never shared the *Vision of Paul*'s enduring popularity in the Latin West for this very reason.

121. Augustine, *Civ. Dei*, 21. 17.

122. But in the conversion of adults in missionary locales the purificatory benefits of baptism were clearly expressed: Bede about Anglo-Saxon kings dying in baptismal robes, and Cramer, *Baptism and Change in the Early Middle Ages*, on infant baptism. However, according to conciliar legislation, infant baptism was not common in Spain before the Islamic conquests; see McCarthy, "Sacraments of Cleansing."

123. According to Rebillard, *In Hora Mortis*, 226, after 430, penance was no longer a way to obtain pardon, but a way of living within a state of pardon.

CHAPTER 6

1. Hunter Blair's *World of Bede* is an accessible account of Bede's life and scholarship; more recent is Brown, *A Companion to Bede*. Also helpful is the collection of essays, *Bède le Vénérable entre tradition et postérité*. The Jarrow Lectures from 1958 to 1993 are now usefully published in *Bede and His World*, 2 vols. On Bede and his *Ecclesiastical History*, see Goffart, *Narrators of Barbarian History*. For a narrative overview of Boniface's career, see Sladden, *Boniface of Devon*.

2. It is not known whether the Benedictine Rule was used exclusively at Wearmouth and Jarrow. It is considered more likely that, in keeping with the age, a *regula mixta* was in use. Nevertheless, Bede shows intimate knowledge of the Benedictine Rule , as is generally acknowledged in modern scholarship. See Van der Walt, "Reflections of the Benedictine Rule in Bede's Homiliary."

3. In addition to the well-stocked library at Wearmouth-Jarrow, Bede consulted books at Lindisfarne and York and had access to books produced at Canterbury.

4. Bede, *HE*, 5. 23: "As such peace and prosperity prevail in these days, many of the Northumbrians, both noble and simple, together with their children, have laid aside their weapons, preferring to receive the tonsure and take monastic vows rather than study the arts of war. This then is the current state of Britain . . . seven hundred and thirty-one years since our Lord's incarnation. May the world rejoice under his eternal rule, and Britain glory in his Faith! Let the multitude of isles be glad thereof, and give thanks at the remembrance of his holiness." On the problems of Bede's account of Christianization, see Wood "Mission of Augustine of Canterbury."

5. Wood suggests that the rich documentation for Boniface's activities may have inflated the importance of Boniface's role in the missionary endeavour (*Missionary Life*, 57–78).

6. Moorhead, "Bede on the Papacy," offers a refinement of Bede's attitude, noting that Bede emphasized universality of practice rather than strict deference to contemporary papal authority.

7. Latin edited by Tangl, *Die Briefe*, Ep. 10. English translation by Kylie, *English Correspondence of Saint Boniface*, reprinted in Emerton, *Letters of St. Boniface*, as Letter 2.

8. Cosmographic details are also seen in the *Vision of Paul* and the *Vision of Fursey*; also see Carozzi, *Le voyage de l'âme*, 201–5. The vision as a whole is discussed at length by Carozzi, *Le voyage de l'âme*, 195–226. Sims-Williams in *Religion and Literature*, 243–72, examines sources for the vision, but not for the issue of purgation.

9. This is an unusual itinerary; continental visionaries generally saw heavenly realms first before being given a tour of hell. See *Vision of Paul* and the *Vision of Barontus*. But Boniface's account shares this feature with the Northumbrian vision of Drythelm recorded by Bede. It places the visionary's (and soul's) entry point to the otherworld through its centre.

10. *Parvissima haec requies indicat, quia omnipotens Deus in die futuri iudicii his animabus refrigerium supplicii et requiem perpetuam praestaturus est.* The eternal rest these souls will have is release from torment—that is, they will no longer suffer, because they will no longer exist. Annihilation is an unusual feature in Christian visionary literature, which tended rather to emphasize the idea of eternal punishment. On annihilation as the fate of "those who do not belong," see comments on "Pauline" and "Johannine" texts in Bernstein, *Formation of Hell*, 212, 214, and 224 n. 17.

11. This *locus amoenus* has a long history in visions of the afterlife and in Graeco-Roman and Christian literature. The distinction between paradise (literally, a garden) and the city of God was developed in patristic thought.

12. Gregory the Great, *Dialogues*, 4. 36: "he saw a bridge, under which a black and smoky river did run, that had a filthy and intolerable smell."

13. Unlike Gregory's vision of the soldier in which the souls who fall into the pitch find their permanent place there, in the monk of Wenlock's vision, the plunge is followed by a more brilliant surfacing. Gregory accepted that purification happened in the afterlife, but it was not associated with the imagery of the bridge; see supra on *Dialogues*, 4. 39.

14. For example, the soul of an esteemed abbot and teacher was rescued by the souls of those whom he had instructed. Thus the soul once purified continued an existence of action, forming part of the city of Jerusalem's "troop," as if made militant by its own experience of postmortem struggle.

15. Carozzi, *Le voyage de l'âme*, 215.

16. While much scholarly effort has been expended to map out afterlife topographies, the texts often resist this. I tend to agree with Gurevich's perspective, that visions of the afterlife often featured isolated foci without much organization ("Au moyen age," 265).

17. In chapter 20 of the *Vision of Paul*, Paul meets Enoch and Elijah; in chapter 21 he sees the land of promise; in chapter 22 he sees the Acherusian Lake.

18. See views of Clement of Alexandria and Lactantius discussed in chapter 1.

19. Moreira, "Violence, Purification and Mercy."

20. Caesarius of Arles, *Sermons*, Sermon 179.

21. Bede, *HE*, V. 12. Drythelm's vision is discussed in some detail in Gurevich, "Au moyen age," and "Popular and Scholarly Medieval Cultural Traditions," and in Carozzi, *Le voyage de l'âme*. Carozzi dates Drythelm's vision as having taken place before 705, based on the date of King Aldfrid's death, to whom the monk reported it. However, based on where it appears in Bede's narrative, the vision must have taken

place in the 690s and was perhaps reported by the monk many times before it had its desired effect with the king. Sims-Williams agrees on the 690 date (*Religion and Literature*, 250).

22. Bede, *Homilies on the Gospels*, 1.2 (for Advent), see discussion below

23. Revelation 8:7 (fire, hail, and blood); Exodus 9:23–25; Joel 3:3 (fire and blood). Carozzi, *Le voyage de l'âme*, 242 n. 379, points to Jerome, *In Job*, 24, PL, 26, 685D as a source. In fact, ice and snow feature as areas of torment in the *Vision of Paul*, 39 and 42. Bede discusses the image in Luke 13. 28 in his commentary on Luke 4. 13, 28, and also in his *Commentary on Proverbs* 3. 31.21

24. See Origen, *First Principles*, 2. 4, on fever. Jerome, *In Job*, 24, PL, 26: 725D.

25. On Samuel 3, cited Foley and Holder, *Bede: A Biblical Miscellany*, 36.

26. Augustine, *Enchiridion*, 29 [110]: *nec tam bonus ut non requirat ista post mortem, nec tam malus ut ei non prosint ista post mortem.*

27. Ntedika, *L'Évocation*, 110–12, citing Isidore, *De ordine creaturarum* 14, 12, PL, 83: 949–50.

28. There is little known about the Anglo-Saxon liturgy in Bede's era, but the continental Gelasian ritual of the mid-eighth century broadened the spectrum of those for whom the Church prayed. Sicard, *La liturgie*, 416, notes: "Cependant, dans les rituels gélasians, l'aspect le plus nouveau de l'action de l'Église par mode de suffrage en faveur des défunts concerne l'extension de la prière à tous les défunts."

29. *De eo quod ait Isaias*. See discussion of this text below.

30. Interestingly, this fits with the *Book of Cerne*, a Mercian liturgical book of the early ninth century that asks that the soul may go to paradise to rest until Judgement Day: *praesta mihi post obitum meum prosperum iter, ad perennis paradisi pervenire suavitatem, ibique cum sanctis animabus mihi requiescere liceat usque ad tempus resurrectionis*. See Sicard's comments, *La liturgie*, 413, and on a similar passage in the Berlin Sacramentary. These texts conform to the Bedan idea that the just will be purged first, then rest. See Brown, *The Book of Cerne*.

31. This seems to be Bede's suggestion in his *Homily for Advent*; see discussion below.

32. Thus I cannot agree with the statement "on this all-important issue, Drythelm the lay visionary (and not a scholar such as Bede) was the theologian of his district" (Brown, *Rise of Western Christendom*, 375).

33. The four-part otherworld appears intentionally to correspond with the four fates of the soul in the afterlife supposedly delineated by Augustine (Carozzi, *Le voyage de l'âme*; but see Edwards, "Purgatory: 'Birth' or Evolution?" on this misreading of Augustine) and certainly present in Gregory the Great, *Moralia*, 26.27, 50–51, and in texts such as the *De ordine creaturarum* by Isidore, 13 and 14. On the Anglo-Saxon visions, see Kabir, *Paradise, Death and Doomsday*, Sims-Williams, *Religion and Literature*, 243–72, and Gurevich, "Au moyen age."

34. Le Goff, *Birth of Purgatory*, 115.

35. See my article, "Violence, Purification and Mercy."

36. Thus, he states that in this text "il n'est jamais question de purgation." Bede did not used the verb "to purge," but he did use a common synonym when he wrote about purgatory in the *Homilies*: he stated that souls were "cleansed" of the stain of

sins: *a vitiorum sorde mundantur*. Conversely, Pope Gregory, who did not communicate a very formed idea of purgatory as a place or structure, did use *purgare* when he commented that because Paschasius erred through ignorance and not malice, he could be purged after death: *purgari post mortem peccato potuit*. Finally, Bede may in fact have understood purgatory as a noun. See note 44 below.

37. Bede, *HE*, 5. 12: *multos autem preces viventium et elimosynae et ieiunia et maxime celebratio missarum, ut ante diem iudicii liberentur, adiuvant*. Compare: Bede, *Homily for Advent* 2: *vel certe prius amicorum fidelium precibus elemosinis ieiuniis fletibus et hostiae salutaris oblationibus absoluti a poenis et ipsi ad beatorum perveniunt requiem*. Bede, *Commentary on Proverbs*, 2. 11. 7: *vel suorum precibus, elemosinis, missarum celebrationibus absoluti*.

38. Northumbrian copying of the *Liber de ordine creaturarum* discussed above indicates that purgatory was being thought of in spatial terms in some circles in the seventh century, even if that space or location was not really specified. So little is known of the circumstances of its composition that we cannot even speculate on its likely audience.

39. *Relatio* can refer equally to a formal written report or to an oral recital. Bede, *HE*, 5.12.

40. Northumbrian monasteries also functioned as parish churches for the local community and offered hospitality to prominent secular figures and travelers. The audience for a monastic sermon was undoubtedly broader than the monks who inhabited the community.

41. When Le Goff examined the earliest texts of purgation, he addressed Bede's comments as a theologian separately from Bede's activity as a recorder of the visions.

42. Gregory the Great, *Dialogues*, 4.40–41.

43. Trans. Martin and Hurst, *Bede: Homilies on the Gospels*, 17. The Latin text reads: *At vero non nulli propter bona quidem opera ad electorum sortem praeordinati sed propter mala aliqua quibus polluti de corpore exierunt post mortem severe castigandi excipiuntur flammis ignis purgatorii et vel usque ad diem iudicii longa huius examinatione a vitiorum sorde mundantur vel certe prius amicorum fidelium precibus elemosinis ieiuniis fletibus et hostiae salutaris oblationibus absoluti a poenis et ipsi ad beatorum perveniunt requiem*. Ed. Hurst, *Homiliarum Evangelii*, 13. The phrase "seized by the flames" is probably borrowed from Gregory's *Dialogues*.

44. Long before Le Goff's work made it a pressing issue, Henry J. Beck, "A Ninth-Century Canonist on Purgatory," made the argument that in the phrase *flammis ignis purgatorii*, the word *purgatorii* may be an appositional genitive, thus making it a noun. Beck attributed this phrase to Hincmar of Rheims, but Hincmar had it from Bede, as Carroll noted in a note in the next volume of the journal. Lawrence T. Martin and David Hurst translate the phrase as "the flames of the fire of purgatory" in their edition of the Homilies.

45. Weeping was an outward sign of contrition and repentance. Ambrose had written that "he shall be saved in the future who has wept most in this age" (*De paenitentia*, 2. 6. 51). Caesarius of Arles, *Sermons*, Sermon 179, advised the penitent to weep and groan: "Let us mourn for our soul when it is dead in the same way in which we bewail the dead body of another." The Benedictine Rule, chap. 4, also advises that

tears and groans accompany prayer. Gregory the Great, *Moralia*, 26.27, 50–51: "But of the class of the elect, some are judged and reign; these are those who wipe away with their tears the stains of their life." Weeping was favoured as a sign of penitence, but excessive weeping at funerals was condemned; see Effros, *Caring for Body and Soul*, 179–80.

46. Carroll, "An Eighth-Century Exegete on Purgatory," suggests this mistake was rectified by Bede in his *Commentary on Proverbs*, a more formal text, in which he reiterated that some souls with light sins could be absolved by prayers, alms, and the celebration of masses, but added that souls were absolved also by the chastisement of their punishment in the afterlife (*In Proverbia Salomonis*, 2, xi, 7; ed. Hurst, 70.) While the *vel. . . vel* construction of the sentence indicates either /or, the construction is not as emphatically oppositional as *aut . . . aut*.

47. Dating a collection of sermons can be difficult, of course. Sermons often had an oral life before they achieved written form. We do not know if Bede's sermons were preached or whether they were primarily intended for devotional reading. The late date for the sermons' composition is proposed by Bolton, *A History of Anglo-Latin Literature*, 167; Hurst's preface to *Bedae Venerabilis Homeliarum Evangelii* states they are between 730 and 735; and Martin and Hurst's introduction to their translation, *Bede the Venerable: Homilies on the Gospels*, iii, dates them to the 720s.

48. Trans. Martin and Hurst, p. 11. The Revised Standard Version gives 'grace upon grace'. Bede cites from the Vulgate: *Et de plenitudine eius nos omnes accepimus gratiam pro gratia*. Ed. Hurst, CCSL 122 (1955), 8.

49. In the Greek, the term used is αντι, "anti"; thus the phrase reads as "grace *against/instead* of grace." Thus in John 1:16 the law of Moses is set up in strict opposition to Christ's grace and truth. Augustine's interpretation stresses that Christ is the spiritual fulfillment of the law of Moses. Thus, Augustine shifts the meaning from the binary opposition (of law of Moses and Christ's grace and truth) to a more linear, purely Christian register of meaning, in which Christ's grace in the present life provides the grace for the future life: "faith itself is grace, and eternal life is grace for grace." See *Tractates on the Gospel of John*, 3.9.2; trans. Rettig, *St. Augustine, Tractates on the Gospel of John 1–10*, 83; and also Augustine, *Enchiridion* 107, concerning God's gifts, "even man's good deserts are themselves gifts of God. When therefore eternal life is bestowed because of them, what else is this but a return of grace for grace?" I thank Dr. Muriel Schmid for discussing the Greek of John 1:16 with me.

50. Bede was aware of Augustine's anti-Pelagian writings; there is no need to consider his position as a reaction to a more recent expression of Pelagianism in Britain. Pelagius, like Origen, was accused of abusing God's grace (Vincent of Lérins, *A Commonitory*; trans. Heurtley, 144), but in matters of eschatology it was Origen, not Pelagius, who mattered. Indeed, Pelagius's views on salvation were diametrically opposed to those of Origen, denying any form of postmortem purification for the dead. See Clark, *Origenist Controversy*, 212.

51. This is a complicated passage, in which those who are *a carnis corruptione solutis* could be interpreted as those who perfect ascetic practice, but the remainder of the passage makes clear that he is speaking of death and the experience of blessed souls before the Final Judgement.

52. This optimistic view of salvation is a notable departure from Augustine's view, expressed in a work we know to have been available to Bede, the *Enchiridion*, chapter 24 [97]. It seems to be a genuine characteristic of Bede's theology. It comes through strongly in his portrayal of St. Cuthbert as a calm and happy saint, causing him to reflect that "the loving kindness of our Saviour is mighty and abundant. He will give us grace, unworthy though we are, to extinguish the flames of vice in this world, and escape the flames of punishment in the next" (*Life of St. Cuthbert*, 14). This optimism may also have arisen from a response to Origen that was different from Augustine's.

53. As in the *Vision of Paul*, the *Vision of Barontus*, and the *Vision of the Monk of Wenlock*.

54. Like most exegetes of late antiquity, Bede absorbed much of Origen through other more "legitimate" sources that used him, including Jerome and Augustine. Bede's opposition to Origen, like that of Jerome, was selective.

55. Boniface anticipated that Bede's *Commentary on Proverbs* would be helpful to him in his preaching. In fact, Jerome had advised that the Proverbs of Solomon be used in a young girl's education so that she could learn "lessons of life." Jerome, Letter 107. The author's intentions for a work's audience did not always coincide with the way a work was used. Pope Gregory I's *Moralia*, another dense work of scholarship, was used in a variety of ways to aid preachers in search of material. See Meyvaert, "Enigma of Gregory the Great's *Dialogues*," 374–75, on Gregory's anger at discovering that parts of the *Moralia* was being read in church by the bishop of Ravenna, Marinianus.

56. Bede, *De eo quod ait Isaias*, PL, 94, 702–10 (hereafter, *On Isaiah*); trans. Foley and Holder, *Bede: A Biblical Miscellany*, 35–51. Bede dedicated his *Commentary on the Acts of the Apostles* to Acca of Hexham.

57. Isaiah 24:21–23 (Vulgate): *Et erit in die illa visitabit Dominus super militiam cœli in excelso et super reges terræ qui sunt super terram et congregabuntur in congregatione unius fascis in lacum et cludentur ibi in carcerem et post multos dies visitabuntur. Et erubescet luna et confundetur sol cum regnaverit Dominus exercituum in monte Sion et in Hierusalem et in conspectu senum suorum fuerit glorificatus.*

58. Jerome, *In Esaiam* 8; ed. Adriaen, CCSL, 73, 73A.

59. See Kelly, *Jerome: His Life, Writings and Controversies*, 299–304.

60. *On Isaiah*, in *Bede: A Biblical Miscellany*, 41, and as commented on by Foley and Holder in their introduction the text (p. 37). However, unnoticed is the fact that Bede's division of prophesies along these lines was not new. The passage strongly evokes a sermon by Faustus of Riez as it is presented by Caesarius of Arles in his Sermon 58, in which it is stated that "Here he is merciful; there just."

61. This is a distinct echo of the *Vision of Drythelm* and the happy state of souls in the pleasant plain and the advice to Drythelm to be diligent in penance.

62. For Bede's knowledge of Origen, see Lapidge, *Anglo-Saxon Library*, 220–21. Citations from Origen derive from Latin translations by Jerome and Rufinus: they include Commentaries on the Song of Songs, Matthew, and Homilies on the Song of Songs, Exodus, Leviticus, and Kings. Bede gives no indication where his information on Origen's views of purgation came from specifically, although a number of Origen's scriptural commentaries would have provided some aspects of Origen's teaching on

purgation, especially the *Homilies on Leviticus*. However, Bede does not appear to have known, or at any rate does not cite, Origen's *First Principles*, the text most associated with Origen's eschatology. Bede's response may have been in part to the received view of Origen's eschatology in the West.

63. Nor would the wicked receive refreshment or consolation, contra Acca of Hexham: Bede tried to correct the false impression the prelate had formed when reading Bede's interpretation of Isaiah by asserting strongly that those in hell will be "visited," as the verse states, not by some relieving presence, but rather they will be "visited" by punishment. See n. 57 above.

64. "*Mortuo homine impio nulla erit ultra spes.*" *Heu misere hanc sententiam pertransiit Origenes qui post universale extremumque iudicium vitam credidit omnibus impiis et peccatoribus dandam. Notandum autem quod, etsi impiis post mortem spes veniae non est, sunt tamen qui de levioribus peccatis quibus obligati defuncti sunt post mortem possunt absolui vel poenis videlicet castigati vel suorum precibus, elemosinis, missarum celebrationibus absoluti. Sed haec quibuscumque fiunt at ante iudicium et de levioribus fiunt erratis. Qui vero se longo post iudicium tempore liberandos putant falluntur et fortasse ad eos pertinet quod sequitur.* Ed. Hurst, *In Proverbia Salomonis*, 2, xi, 7. CCSL, 119B, 70.

65. Thus Bede had gone further than previous authorities such as Augustine, Caesarius, and Gregory the Great, who had repudiated Origen's noneternal hell simply by affirming its eternity. Bede refutes Origen's noneternal hell, while in the same breath affirming the existence of purgatory. One may speculate that Bede thought this connection had already been made in Gregory' *Dialogues* in which hell's eternity is affirmed, in a book in which postmortem purgation was also discussed, but Gregory nowhere made that connection explicit.

66. See n. 62 above. On Bede's book knowledge more generally, Laistner, "Library of the Venerable Bede," 117–49, has much of value on Bede's patristic sources, although it is also somewhat dated, for example, the *Commentary on Proverbs and Ecclesiastes* once ascribed to the fifth-century Salonius is no longer considered a source for Bede's *Commentary on Proverbs*, because the former is now generally accepted to be a product of the twelfth century. See Flint, "True Author of the *Salonii Commentarii in Parabolas Salomonis.*"

67. This is not because Greek works were not available in Anglo-Saxon England in Bede's time. Bede probably acquired Greek only later in life. See Laistner, *Thought and Letters in Western Europe*, 238–50.

68. *Qui vero se longo post iudicium tempore liberandos putant falluntur et fortasse ad eos pertinet quod sequitur* (*In Proverbia Salomonis*, 2, 11, 7).

69. The notion of cosmic cleansing, more associated with late Christian Platonism in the East, rather than in the West, is not expunged; it appears in the work of Eriugena in the ninth century (*Periphyseon* 5, 935 A, B, C).

70. Not all medieval authors were hesitant to name Origen. Lubac, *Exégèse médiévale*, offers numerous examples of laudatory references to Origen's exegetical corpus.

71. As we have seen in the patristic background to Bede (chapters 1 and 4), attestations to the efficacy of prayer or alms or masses for the dead are readily found. Gregory the Great's *Dialogues* favored masses as a mode of intercession. The

Vision of Fursey does not address postmortem mediation by the living (although Fursey clearly benefits from the intercession of the angels). Fursey was venerated as a saint from the time his *vita* was written, so his intercessory power was assumed. It would be interesting to know whether Fursey's cult was ever associated with intercession for souls in purgatory; if so, our sources do not reveal it. The *Vision of Barontus*, in which purgatory does not yet appear, promotes almsgiving, confession, penance, and lamentation as present remedies for sin. Saint Peter notes that Barontus did some good deeds: he has given alms, confessed to priests, done penance, and been tonsured in St. Peter's monastery to atone for his wrongdoings. In chapter 22 the redactor of the work reminds his audience that they should set their minds to lamentation and make their lives bitter with penance. However, no masses are mentioned.

72. See chapter 4, n. 85.

73. See chapter 4. Bede was familiar with Isidore and knew Julian's *Prognosticon*; see Lapidge, *Anglo-Saxon Library*, 218.

74. Le Goff did not recognize any theological development in the idea of purgatory between the time of Gregory the Great and the twelfth century (*Birth of Purgatory*). Thus he missed Bede's crucial theological contribution.

75. Anxiety about heresy appears often to have shaped discussions about the afterlife. Bremmer argues, for example, that the official acceptance of purgatory by the Catholic Church in the 1140s was a response to Cathar views of the afterlife; see *Rise and Fall of the Afterlife*, 67. The eschatological views of Irenaeus and Hipploytus were responses to Gnosticism.

76. *Homily for Advent*, 2.1: *amicorum fidelium precibus elemosinis ieiuniis fletibus et hostiae salutaris oblationibus.*

77. Cicero, *De amicitia*, and *De officiis*; Seneca, *On Benefits*. These topics had already been much discussed in Greek literature. The degree to which these works reflected contemporary practice and the problems for understanding Roman systems of patronage and gift-exchange is discussed by Griffin, "De Beneficiis and Roman Society." Bede knew some Virgil, and shows some minimal knowledge of Cicero, Pliny, and other classical authors, probably through *florilegia* and the work of grammarians. Brown, "Bede's Neglected Commentary on Samuel," 141, comments of Bede's library: "Its shelves held no works by Cicero . . . and very little of Origen." Nevertheless, Cicero's *De amicitia* was widely read in the Middle Ages; see Hyatte, *Arts of Friendship*.

78. However, the terms by which friendship was expressed, and the meaning behind the vocabulary of friendship, shifted considerably from classical to Christian usage; see Konstan, "Problems in the History of Christian Friendship," 88, in which he notes that "metaphors for Christian ties tended to be derived from the sphere of kinship—paternity or brotherhood—rather than friendship." He notes that Paulinus of Nola and John Cassian rarely use the word *amicitia*, and that in Cassian's case, "where practical advice is offered concerning relationships between ordinary mortals as opposed to those who are perfect in virtue, Cassian predominantly employs the language of brotherhood, *caritas*, and *affectio*" (p. 106).

79. Cicero, *De amicitia*, 2.8.

80. Cassian, *Conferences*, 16. 5 (see also 16. 3 and 28). Similar sentiments are expressed by Ambrose in a work directly influenced by Cicero's treatise: *De officiis* 3. 22. I thank an anonymous reviewer for this citation.

81. This much is acknowledged by Cicero, *De amicitia*, 2.9: "I do not deny that affection is strengthened by the actual receipt of benefits, as well as by the perception of a wish to render service." See also Seneca, *De Beneficiis*.

82. Althoff, "*Amicitiae*."

83. Indeed, the protagonists might not even have much intimate knowledge of those to whom they professed this friendship. This did not preclude some very intimate behaviour thereafter: deadly enemies who became friends through alliance might sleep in the same bed together; see Curta, "Merovingian and Carolingian Gift Giving."

84. Recent studies of the emotions that accompanied friendship and family ties include Rosenwein, *Emotional Communities*; Smith's discussion of friendship and kin (and permutations between) centres on earthly "affinities"; see *Europe after Rome*, 83–114.

85. Bede, *HE*, 1. 32. Gregory writes to King Aethelberht of Kent in 601, opening his letter by extolling God's gifts: "The reason why Almighty God raises good men to govern nations is that through them he may bestow the gifts of his mercy on all whom they rule," and concludes with, "I have sent you some small presents, which will not appear small to you, since you receive them with the blessing of the apostle Peter." See Caner, "Towards a Miraculous Economy," who discusses how the rise of a notion and language of "blessings" facilitated material and spiritual giving, creating a Christian ideal of the "pure" gift approximating that studied by modern anthropologists. Although focused on the eastern monasticism, his study is profitable for considerations of spiritual gifting for the western tradition also.

86. The *Vision of Drythelm* (Bede, *HE*, 5. 12) says that many (*multos*) are helped by prayers of the living (*preces viventium*).

87. McGuire, *Friendship and Community*, xli.

88. It is interesting to note that, whereas the rise of the individual through personal friendship was carefully avoided by monastic communities, this was an age in which scholars have identified a "rise of the individual," especially in light of the literature of sin and penance and of visions of the afterlife.

89. See opening comments of Bede's *Letter to Egbert*.

90. Konstan, "Problems in the History of Christian Friendship."

91. Augustine, *Enchiridion* 29 [110]: "There is no gainsaying that the souls of the dead find solace from the piety of their friends who are alive, when the sacrifice of the mediator is offered for the dead or alms are given in church." Trans. Peebles, *Saint Augustine*, 461. *Neque negandum est defunctorum animas pietate suorum viventium relevari, cum pro illis sacrificium Mediatoris offertur vel eleemosynae in Ecclesia fiunt*. Ed. Evans, CCSL 46, 108. Indeed, in his *Commentary on Proverbs*, Bede used *suorum* as Augustine had.

92. Oliver, *Beginnings of English Law*, 145, discussing Aethelberht's Law 65.1.

93. Saint Odilia prayed for her abusive father; see *Vita s. Odiliae*. Deurechild prayed for her less than pious mother, see Jonas (*Vita Columbani* 2.15). Family

intercession is expected as an expression of filial piety and it also established an economic system dedicated to family masses in proprietary churches. Most popular stories of intercession from the High Middle Ages likewise revolve on family members and especially on spouses.

94. McGuire, *Friendship and Community*, 92.

95. Cassian, *Conferences*, 16. 15. 1.

96. On the textual history of the work, see Dobbie, *Caedmon's Hymn and Bede's Death-Song*; Ker, "Epistola de Obitu Bedae."

97. Looking back at Bede's own words in his *Homily for Advent*, 1.2, we can note that he may have compressed his injunction so that lamentations and prayers could be made by friends and that prayers, alms, and masses could be dispensed by priests, but it is unusual for Bede to be imprecise. Bede's expectation that "friends" would do these services sounds as if he means "arrange to have them done," and if so, this was certainly an expectation that laypeople also might have.

98. Freedman, "Spices."

99. Letter 49: *parva . . . munusculorum . . . turis et piperis et cinnamomi*. Ed. Tangl, *Die Briefe*, 80.

100. Spiritual meaning was attributed to incense (and other spices). Ashbrook Harvey comments extensively on its use in *Scenting Salvation*.

101. Wormald, "Bede and Benedict Biscop," 3–6 and following.

102. Jussen, "Religious Discourses of the Gift," and Curta, "Merovingian and Carolingian Gift Giving," view gift-giving through the lens of political strategy. Arnold Angenendt's very useful article, "*Donationes pro anima*," came to my attention too late to be given attention here.

103. Jussen, "Religious Discourses of the Gift," 186–87. Also Jussen notes that in the field of *munus*, *dominus* is by far the most common term for God in the early middle ages but in patristic writings and in the twelfth century, it is *deus* (p. 178). Cuthbert quoting Bede uses *deus*, perhaps a result of immersion in patristic writing.

104. A *distributor* was an executor of a will. Niermeyer, *Mediae Latinitatis lexicon minus*.

105. A truly reciprocal exchange would require that Bede pray for the priests once he was in heaven. Ilana Silber, "Gift-giving in the Great Traditions," 215, comments that "the otherworldly impulse did not translate, in the case of donations to monasteries, into a denial of reciprocity . . . reciprocity was perceived as fully legitimate, and not at all contradictory to either the other-worldly, spiritual motive or the very idea of giving itself."

106. Bp. Torthelm to Boniface, *Letter 47*, ed. Tangl, *Die Briefe*, p. 76.

107. True altruism was not considered possible for mankind—that model having been set by Christ's sacrifice. Bede would have had a view of friendship as a privilege earned through loyalty (as per Cicero) and service (as per early medieval society). On attempts to create "pure" gifting between hierarchies, see Caner, "Towards a Miraculous Economy."

108. Bede, *HE*, 3. 8: *aureum . . . nomisma*.

109. Bugga to Boniface. *Letter 15* ed. Tangl, *Die Briefe*, 28.

110. Herz, *Sacrum commercium*. God gave his son as a gift and payment for sin.

111. Bede, *Life of Cuthbert*, chap. 37.

112. For example, Cuthwin, the recipient of Cuthbert's letter describing Bede's death, had assured Cuthbert that he (or his community) was regularly offering masses for Bede's soul. Cuthwine is unknown to us from other sources, had not been present at Bede's death, and appears to have been geographically somewhat distant from Wearmouth-Jarrow. His activities on Bede's behalf sound institutional rather than personal, although he craved more personal knowledge of Bede and the story of his death.

113. Eddius Stephanus, *Life of Wilfrid*, chap. 65. Wilfrid died in 709. On issues of the authorship and date of the *Life of Wilfrid*, see Goffart, *Narrators of Barbarian History*, 281ff.

114. Wilfrid had summoned two abbots (Tibba and Ebba) and six of his "most faithful friends" to witness his distribution of his treasure. Some of them are named—a monk, Caelin, a priest, Tatberht, Hathufrith, and a teacher, Alnhfrith. The priest Tatberht was also a kinsman. Thus here Wilfrid's "faithful friends" were monks, priests, and kin who were distinguished by having lower status than the two abbots who were also clearly the bishop's friends [chaps. 63–64].

115. Bede, *Life of Cuthbert*, Preface. trans. Colgrave, *Two Lives of Saint Cuthbert*, 147.

116. Visions of the afterlife in which individuals were called by name to account for their deeds (perhaps especially those that chronicled cases of mistaken identity) must have sharpened this need for bureaucratic precision. On the Anglo-Saxon memorial tradition, see Gerchow, *Die Gedenküberlieferung der Angelsachsen*.

117. In the early church, diptychs recorded the names of the faithful, both living and departed. This memorial tradition for the dead undoubtedly already existed at Wearmouth-Jarrow. While seventh- and eighth-century examples are missing, Bede attests to the existence of earlier lists of the dead, probably in the form of annotations to calendars (*HE*, 4.14 [see n. 2, p. 378, in Colgrave and Mynor's edition]). Bede's request from Lindisfarne gained and maintained connections with his wider community of "friends." No memorial list exists from Lindisfarne or Wearmouth-Jarrow in Bede's time, but Gerchow, *Die Gedenküberlieferung der Angelsachsen*, 121ff., argues the case that the earliest extant Anglo-Saxon example, the ninth-century Durham Book of Life (*Liber Vitae Dunelmensis*) was a Wearmouth-Jarrow production, having accompanied Bede's relics to Durham, rather than from Lindisfarne (accompanying Cuthbert's).

118. "Some of us are purged of evil in this life, some are cured of it through fire in the afterlife . . . the extent of healing will depend on the amount of evil present in each person. The healing of the soul will be purification from evil and this cannot be accomplished without suffering . . . After a long period of time, they will assume again the form which they received from God in the beginning." Gregory of Nyssa, *On the Soul and the Resurrection*; trans. Callahan, *Saint Gregory of Nyssa*, 267, 271.

119. Chapter on "Archbishop Theodore" in Bernhard Bischof and Michael Lapidge, *Biblical Commentaries*, 5–81. Also, Guglielmo Cavallo, "Theodore and the Greek Culture of His Time," in Lapidge, ed., *Archbishop Theodore*, 54–67.

120. As convincingly argued by Bischof and Lapidge, *Biblical Commentaries*, 78–80.

121. Bischoff and Lapidge, chapter "Abbot Hadrian," in *Biblical Commentaries*, 82–132

122. Bischoff and Lapidge, *Biblical Commentaries*, 159–60.

123. Kartsonis, *Anastasis*, 37, with reference particularly to Christology and representations of the death of Christ, writes: "the seventh century witnessed a marked willingness and readiness to provide specific answers to all related questions," and dated the invention of the image of Anastasis to the late seventh century in the wake of clarifications about Christ's nature at the Sixth Ecumenical Council (680–81) and the Council of Trullo (691) (p. 81). Bede was aware of the rulings of the latter council.

124. Lapidge, in Bischof and Lapidge's *Biblical Commentaries*, 141–46, notes that the Synod of Hatfield closely followed the wording of the *acta* of the Lateran Council of 649, a council in which Theodore may have had a personal role. Lapidge thus connects Theodore with Roman orthodox belief in "double procession." On the influence of Roman conciliar procedure on early Anglo-Saxon councils, including the connection of Hatfield with the Lateran Council *acta*, see Cubitt, *Anglo-Saxon Church Councils*, 77–96, who makes the important point that Roman conciliar procedure was nevertheless adapted to native custom.

125. On Augustine's theory of conciliar authority as a feature of his later years, see Vessey, "*Opus Imperfectum*," see 271 and n. 20.

126. Bede, *Lives of the Abbots*, 6, 11. On the importation of books, see Dumville, "Importation of Mediterranean Manuscripts." Also Lapidge, *Anglo-Saxon Library*, furnishes examples of Greek and Latin texts in the library of Wearmouth-Jarrow.

127. Carroll, "An Eighth-Century Exegete on Purgatory."

128. Heito's *Vision of Wetti*; ed. Dümmler, *Heitonis visio Wettini*, 2, 271, and Strabo's *Vision of Wetti*; trans. Traill, *Walahfrid Strabo's Visio Wettini*, 52–53, in which purgation occurs in a fort of smoke and steam, and an abbot suffers on purgatory mountain; *Visio cuiusdam pauperculae mulieris*, possibly also by Heito; see Houben's article and new edition, "*Visio cuiusdam pauperculae mulieris*." I thank Alan Bernstein for this reference.

CHAPTER 7

1. *Life of Gregory the Great*, chapter 6. Trans. Colgrave, *Earliest Life of Gregory the Great*, 83. Colgrave dated the work 704–14. A different story was told of St. Patrick—that he had received the privilege of judging the Irish on Judgement Day.

2. Bede's role in creating this conversion grand narrative in his *Ecclesiastical History* is now widely accepted. See Wood, "Mission of Augustine of Canterbury."

3. This devotion to Rome was notionally powerful. In practice, there was often friction between missionaries and popes, even when, as was the case with Boniface, papal authority and support was an important element in their mission.

4. The letters of Boniface and Lull are published in Tangl, ed., *Die Briefe*. There is an uneven English translation by Emerton, *Letters of St. Boniface*. I follow Tangl's letter numbering. Emerton's numbers are indicated in parentheses when his translation is used.

5. See the discussion in the previous chapter of the *Vision of the Monk of Wenlock* and Boniface's framing attitude.

6. See Prinz's survey of monastic and missionary activity in France and Germany in *Frühes Mönchtum* generally; see pp. 231–62 on Boniface and the Carolingians.

7. When Christian sources indicate that an individual or community was pagan, the reader cannot always distinguish those having had no contact with Christianity from nonexclusive Christians or lapsed Christians or some other combination. The problems of terminology and interpretation are highlighted Ian Wood's article, "Pagan Religions," and in the published discussion that followed, in Ausenda, ed., *After Empire*, 253–68 and 268–79.

8. Wood, "Pagan Religions," 253.

9. A good example of this is the mid-ninth-century "missionary sermon" excerpted and discussed by Levison, *England and the Continent*, appendix X, 302–14. Latin text, 307–12.

10. See Wood's analysis of hagiographic depictions of "missionary" saints in *Missionary Life*.

11. The literature on the missionary movement is enormous. Important overviews include Wood, *Missionary Life*; Fletcher, *Barbarian Conversion*; Brown, *Rise of Western Christendom*; von Padberg, *Mission und Christianisierung*; Schäferdiek, ed., *Kirchengeschichte als Missionsgeschichte*, 2, 1: *Die Kirche des früheren Mittelalters*; and Levison, *England and the Continent*.

12. *Vita Vulframni Episcopi Senonici*, 9. On Radbod, see Wood, *Missionary Life*, 57, 59, 80, 92–93; Lebecq, "Le baptême manqué du roi Radbod"; Geary, "Uses of Archaeology."

13. Radbod died in 719, possibly only a short time after the baptismal fiasco. He made an impression on a succession of missionaries who travelled to Frisia. The toe in the fountain image is found in numerous Belgian depictions of the early modern period when, accustomed to the high fonts in churches, he is depicted straining his leg high over the lip of the font.

14. The story of Radbod's encounter with the new religion is told in two accounts, and they are both late—written about eighty years after the events they describe. Alcuin's *Vita Willibrordi*, written between 785 and 797, relates the early experience of Anglo-Saxon missionaries to Frisian shores and preserves a powerful sermon delivered by Willibrord to the pagan king. The *Life of St. Wulframn of Sens* was written by a monk, Jonas, between 796 and 807 at the monastery of St. Wandrille. It tells the story of Radbod's near baptism. On the date of Alcuin's *Vita Willibrordi* and the *Vita Wulframni*, see Wood, "Saint-Wandrille and Its Historiography," 3, in Wood and Loud, eds., *Church and Chronicle in the Middle Ages*. These texts are discussed further in Wood, *Missionary Life*. Wood observes that Jonas's *Life of St. Wulframn of Sens* arose from the same concerns of Alcuin's work, although in this case seen from a Merovingian, anti-Carolingian perspective. Wood, "Saint-Wandrille," points out also that the chronology of Wulframn's mission is impossible since Wulframn died in 704, and Radbod's ducal reign postdated that time.

15. Lebecq, "Le baptême manqué du roi Radbod."

16. Geary, "Uses of Archaeology," 40, points to the threat of Christianity to Radbod's ethnic identity, for by conversion, Radbod "would have become, in a real sense, a Frank."

17. Russell, *Germanization of Early Medieval Christianity*.

18. Russell accepts the opinion of those who see Germanization occurring in the high middle ages, and this, I think, leads him to overstate the incompatibility issue earlier on—on a social level, Anglo-Saxon Christians, like Bede, were fully enmeshed in relationships of friendship, kinship, and gift-giving that are usually labeled "Germanic."

19. Pearson, "Powerful Dead." His study of Danish sites from the pre-Roman Iron Age to the Early Germanic Iron Age indicates many variations of burial practices and comments (p. 204) that "universal generalizations about the meaning of particular rites, spatial relations and practices involving the dead are unsupportable . . . The meanings of any practice or association can only be recovered by situating it within a changing sequence of traditions."

20. Such as Richard Huntingdon and Peter Metcalf, eds., *Celebrations of the Death*, cited by Williams, "Monuments and the Past." Pearson, "Powerful Dead," cites anthropological studies on "liminality." Both Williams and Pearson are cautious in their use of this literature. H. R. Ellis Davidson (writing under H. R. Ellis), *Road to Hel*, used later Norse literature to illuminate earlier burial practices, with all the problems and caveats that implies.

21. Some Germanic tribes practiced human sacrifice, although it is often difficult to tell whether executions arose from religious, tribal, or judicial contexts or indeed from a combination of these. According to a later source, at Lejre on Sjaelland in the ninth century, ninety-nine men, horses, dogs, and cocks were sacrificed to appease the gods of the underworld. See Wood, *Missionary Life*, 255, based on the account by Thietmar of Merseburg, at the turn of eleventh century regarding Danish practices. Note Parker Pearson's caution, though: "While grave goods do not necessarily indicate belief in an afterlife, the inclusion of eating and drinking sets from the first century BC onwards does imply a need to make some form of provision after death. A lack of such provision in the period before or after may or may not indicate an absence of belief in the afterlife" ("Powerful Dead," 224).

22. See Bonnie Effros, who highlights many of these problems in *Caring for Body and Soul* and its companion volume, *Merovingian Mortuary Archaeology*. Geary, "Uses of Archaeology," 31, questions whether "it is really appropriate to speak of 'Christian' or 'pagan' burials at all."

23. Boniface, *Letter*, 36 [46].

24. McCormick, *Origins of the European Economy*, 731, 739.

25. See Kendall and Wells, eds., *Voyage to the Other World*, in particular the editors' introduction on pp. ix–xix, on which they note that "some belief, strong or weak, in an existence on the Other World apparently activated the burial."

26. Bede, *HE*, 2, 9ff. on the conversion of King Edwin AD 616–32. In many details, including the multiple means of conversion, Bede echoes Gregory of Tours's account of the conversion of the Frankish king Clovis.

27. A distinction should be made here between what Bede relates in his *Ecclesiastical History*—a public programme of Christianity's triumph—and Bede's reflection and acknowledgment of scriptural difficulties when engaged in writing biblical commentaries.

28. See Effros, *Caring for Body and Soul*, and *Merovingian Mortuary Archaeology*, who cautions about ethnic, gender, and status categories for interpreting grave sites. See Wood, "Franks and Sutton Hoo," in Wood and Lund, eds., *People and Places in Northern Europe*, 1–14.

29. Tacitus, *Germania*, 9.

30. Pirmin of Reichenau, *De singulis libris canonicis scarapsus*.

31. Levison argued that this letter, essentially a sermon to the *fratres* surrounding the reader and presbyter Hyglac, was written in the north of England in the mid-eighth century (*England and the Continent*, appendix IX, 295–302. Latin text, 297–300). The description of the course of human misery is a direct quotation from Columbanus, Sermon 9: *Et videte, fratres, ordinem humanae vitae miserae super terram, a terra in ignem, de igne in iudicium, de iudicio aut in gehennam aut in gloriam*, and continues, *in igne probaberis et iudicium intrabis*.

32. *Da, Domine, quia dedimus; miserere, quia misericordiam fecimus; nos implevimus quod iussisti, tu redde quod promisisti. De supremo iudicio*, 7; ed. Krusch, 754. At the conclusion of the sermon Christ's imagined speech on Judgement Day is equally frank.

33. Eligius, *De supremo iudicio*, 8: *post mortem nemo vos redimere potest*. Eligius's views on penance and the afterlife are discussed in chapter 5. A sermon sometimes attributed to Eligius that discusses the transitory fire of purgatory is of a much later date. The Carolingian sermon, Pseudo-Eligius, *Homily* 8, PL, 87, 619, states that only slight sins will be cleansed by almsgiving—perhaps a corrective response to the otherwise insistent emphasis on almsgiving in the genuine preaching of Eligius. The sermon uses 1 Corinthians 3:13 to refer to the fire of purgatory (*de igne purgatorio*). See Vacandard, "Les homélies attribuées à saint Eloi."

34. *Vita Eligii ep. Noviomagensis* 2. 16; ed. Krusch, 705–8.

35. Letter 23, Tangl, ed., *Die Briefe*, 38–41. The letter was written between 723 and 724.

36. The first two, letters 75 and 76, were written between 746 and 747. Letter 91, in which Boniface asks for Bede's *Homilies* and *Commentary*, is c. 747–54. Tangl, ed., *Die Briefe*, 158, 159, 207. Boniface's successor, Lull, received Bede's *Life of Cuthbert* from Gutberct of Wearmouth Jarrow in 764 (Letter 116) and Lull requested more of Bede's works from Archbishop Koaena of York in 767–68 (Letter 125): four books on 1 Samuel to the death of Saul (= *In Samuelem prophetam allegorica expositio*); three books on Esdras and Nehemiah (= *In Ezram et Neemiam prophetas allegorica expositio*); and four books on the Gospel of Mark (= *In Marci evangelium expositio*). See *Die Briefe*, 263.

37. For example, in a sermonizing letter to King Aethelbald of Mercia. Letter 73; ed. Tangl, *Die Briefe*, 146–55. Boniface and his fellow bishops admonished the king and threatened him with hell if he did not change his ways. There is no mention of purgatory—only the mention of purification and correction of penance. It is the fear of

the Final Judgement that is used to threaten the king, not interim suffering. The letter is a clear indication that familiarity with the notion of purgatory does not necessarily mean that it was referred to in other types of writing generated by the same person: context was everything.

38. Carozzi, *Le voyage de l'âme*, 276. I discuss this text in chapters 5 and 8.

39. Letter 115 in Tangl, ed., *Die Briefe*, 247–50. The vision exists only in fragmentary form. See discussion in chapter 5.

40. Origen's views were condemned at the Council of Alexandria in 400. See Augustine, *Civ. Dei*, 21.

41. Letter 59 in Tangl, *Die Briefe*, 108–20. Translated (as Letter 47) by Emerton in *Letters of St. Boniface*. The heretics Aldebert and Clemens are discussed in Laux, "Two Early Medieval Heretics."

42. Sulpicius Severus, *Vita Martini*, 22. After Martin's death, Sulpicius wrote the *Dialogues*, a treatise on ascetics and monastic values. In it he records through the mouthpiece of Postumianus the condemnation of Origen's works at the Council of Alexandria and the turmoil that it caused. See *Dialogues*, 1, 6–7. Sulpicius appears to sympathize with the view that not all of Origen's works deserved condemnation, but it is clear from his description that Origen's views on the salvation of the devil had provoked the strongest negative reaction. Martin held some rather old-fashioned views on the end times; see *Dialogues*, 2.14.

43. Geary, "Uses of Archaeology," 37–39, discusses Frankish cases in which pagan burials were incorporated into Christian burial sites. The case of the royal burials at Jelling at a later age is discussed by Fletcher, *Barbarian Conversion*, 405–6.

44. Effros, "Beyond Cemetery Walls," discusses burial in Christian cemeteries as a contested arena for clerical authority.

45. Trumbower, *Rescue*, 104. The emperor in question was Valentinian II.

46. Effros, "*De partibus Saxoniae* and the Regulation of Mortuary Custom."

CHAPTER 8

1. Salvian, *On the Governance of God*, 7. 12; trans. O'Sullivan, *Writings of Salvian*.

2. Fredericksen, "Apocalypse and Redemption in Early Christianity," 167.

3. Paulinus of Pella, *Eucharisticos*. The downswing in Paulinus's fortunes coincided with the barbarian invasions of 406 and the death of his father. Throughout his long life, Paulinus's hardships were not confined to barbarians; indeed, at one point he lamented that his villa had not received the protection of a resident Goth, and he welcomed a Goth purchaser for his remaining property at the end of his life.

4. Du Moulin, *Waters of Siloe*.

5. Ibid., 392–93. EEBO Image 222. The soul "mufled in a cloke" is presumably taken from Bede's account of the vision of Fursey. The soul that offered to "pull off a man's hose" must be the former bath owner who attended a priest of Tauriana (Gregory the Great, *Dialogues*, 4. 57) and who helped the priest undress.

6. I have been unable to locate the French original to discover whether the English translator changed it.

7. For example, John Dick's contribution to Cochrane, *Future Punishment*, 269, indicated purgatory's prototype was to be found in the "heathenism" of classical works.

8. Le Goff, *Birth of Purgatory*, 87, for what follows.

9. Ibid., 108–10.

10. His comment on the optimism of Celtic and Norse views of the afterlife found its antithesis in Peter Brown's characterization of Mediterranean optimism and Irish preoccupations with sin.

11. Carozzi, *Le voyage de l'âme*, 138.

12. Brown, "End of the Ancient Other World," 45.

13. Visions of Fursey, Drythelm, and the monk of Wenlock.

14. Carozzi's *Le voyage de l'âme* is the most detailed study to date to investigate specific content connections between the texts.

15. Wormald, *Making of English Law*, 38. "In the last two decades, the very concept of 'Germanic' law, so dominant in the nineteenth century, has seemed increasingly marginal." Wormald added the refinement that "what came to matter more than the differences between Roman and 'barbarian' law were the emergent contrasts between that of southern and northern Europe" (p. 44, see also p. 69).

16. Ibid., 72–76, 92, and n. 311. Wood, "Disputes in the Late Fifth- and Sixth-century Gaul," 7, notes that "it has been suggested with reason that the *placitum* developed out of the Roman charter." Fouracre, "'Placita' and the Settlement of Disputes in Later Merovingian Francia."

17. Wormald, *Making of English Law*, 39.

18. Wood, "Disputes," 17–19.

19. Wormald, *Making of English Law*, 29–30, suggests that, in general, Anglo-Saxon law codes were not written in isolation from continental legal examples and developments and that Bede may have intended Aethelberht's initiative "*iuxta exempla Romanorum*" to refer to the legislation of the sub-Roman kingdoms rather than to the legislative legacy of Imperial Rome. On the Merovingian control of Kentish politics, see Wood, *Merovingian North Sea*, and "Mission of Augustine of Canterbury."

20. Kelly, *A Guide to Early Irish Law*.

21. Dooley, "From Penance to Confession," 396.

22. The idea that penitentials arose from barbarian law is expressed by Le Goff, *Your Money or Your Life*, 11: "During the early Middle Ages, a list of penances, which varied according to the nature of the sinful act, was recorded in *penitentials*. Modeled after the laws of the barbarians, these manuals focused upon the acts, not upon the actors. Or rather, the categories to which the actors belonged were judicial ones: clergy or laymen, free men or not free" (author's emphasis,). Also, see Kate Dooley, "From Penance to Confession," 396.

23. *Licet crimina soleat poena purgare*. CT, 16, 5, 41: Law of Arcadius and Honorius to the proconsul of Africa 407. Godefroy, *Codex Theodosianus*, 179.

24. Here I use the edition and translation by Oliver, *Beginnings of English Law*, 147–80.

25. In addition to the king and his nobles, Brihtwold, Archbishop of Britain, and Gefmund, Archbishop of Rochester, attended. Prologue to *Decrees of Wihtred*.

26. *Decrees of Wihtred*, 14ff. Liebermann, *Die Gesetze der Angelsachsen*, Attenborough, *Laws of the Earliest English Kings*, and Whitelock, *English Historical Documents*, 18ff. Whitelock translated "clænse" as "purge," Oliver translated it as "clear," and Liebermann translated it as "reinigen." I have altered Oliver's translation with "cleanse."

27. The term "claensie" does not appear in later Anglo-Saxon law codes, which used "ladian" for "purgatio" instead. See Lieberman, *Die Gesetze der Angelsachsen*, vol.1, 288–89 on 1 Cnut 5, 4.

28. Carozzi, *Le voyage de l'âme*, 126–28.

29. For example, those who fail in their duties as godparents are punished alongside their godchildren. The issue of Christian sponsorship appears in the Council of Leptines (745) and a letter of Pope Zacharias to Pippin c. 747. See Carozzi, *Le voyage de l'âme*, 270. For *Redaction 6*, see Silverstein, *Visio Sancti Pauli*, 214–18, and discussion, 58–61, 82–90. On the early history of Christian sponsorship, see Lynch, *Christianizing Kinship*.

30. See discussion of *Redaction 6* in chapter 5.

31. Only one complete manuscript of *Redaction 6* is extant (St. Gall, Stiftsbibliothek, Codex 682), and it is very corrupt. It is edited by Silverstein, *Visio Sancti Paul, 214-18*. Carozzi's alternative readings for some terms in the text are important and essential to his interpretation. The Germanic Council of 742 is also important to Carozzi's dating of the text. See discussion in chapter 5.

32. Carozzi notes that theft of *ferramenta* is found only in a legal text (*Pactus Alemannorum*) and not in penitentials. See *Le voyage de l'âme*, 272 n. 573.

33. Ibid., 270.

34. The St. Gall Stiftsbibliothek, Codex 682, written in a ninth-century hand, introduces the work with: *Incipit castigatio sanctae paule de hominis peccatoris. Qui peccant et emendant.* This title is not present in the small fragment that is the only other witness to this edition, Rome Pal. 216, f. 126v., also edited by Silverstein, *Visio Sancti Paul*, p. 215.

35. *Vision of Barontus*, chapter 17, ed. Levison, *Visio Baronti*, 391; *Vision of Wetti*, Trans. Traill, *Walahfrid Strabo's Visio Wettini*, 52.

36. See Fouracre, "Disputes in Merovingian Francia," 37–38, who suggests that the negative portrayal of counts in clerical literature may have arisen from their role in carrying out the severe penalties, including execution, that was the legal lot of the unfree.

37. Trans. Traill, *Walahfrid Strabo's Visio Wettini*, 57.

38. Bede, *Lives of the Abbots*, 24.

39. On the history of the ordeal in the middle ages, see Bartlett, *Trial by Fire and Water*. On the use of ordeal in the Frankish legal system see Fisher Drew, *Laws of the Salian Franks*, 32–39.

40. Lex Salica. , 82.

41. Ibid., 120: he who challenges another man to the ordeal must pay a fine if he does not have the king's permission.

42. Ibid., 53.

43. Bartlett, *Trial by Water and Fire*, 4–9.

44. Gregory of Tours, *HF*, 8.5. On the political background to this vision, see Moreira, *Dreams, Visions and Spiritual Authority*, 96–99. The vision is quite evidently one that depicts destruction not regeneration. The image of bodies being broken in the pot was biblical; Ezekiel 24 contains an allegory that describes God's anger:

> Thus says the Lord God: Set on the pot, set it on, pour in water also; put in it the pieces of flesh, all the good pieces, the thigh and the shoulder; fill it with choice bones . . . . Woe to the bloody city, to the pot whose rust is in it, and whose rust has not gone out of it! . . . Heap on the logs, kindle the fire, boil well the flesh, and empty out the broth, and let the bones be burned up. Then set it empty upon the coals, that it may become hot and its copper may burn, that its filthiness may be melted in it, its rust consumed. In vain I have wearied myself, its thick rust does not go out of it by fire. Its rust is your filthy lewdness. Because I would have cleansed you and you were not cleansed from your filthiness, you shall not be cleansed anymore till I have satisfied my fury upon you.

45. Green, "Vessels of Death."

CONCLUSION

1. Origen, *Homilies on Leviticus 1-16*, Homily 9. 7. 8. trans. Barkley, p. 192.
2. Origen, *First Principles*, 2. 3.1.
3. Vincent of Lérins, *A Commonitory*; trans. Heurtley, *Nicene and Post-Nicene Fathers* 11: 143–45.

Abbreviations

AER	*The American Ecclesiastical Review*
ACW	Ancient Christian Writers
Annales E.S.C.	*Annales: Economies, société, civilisations*
AASS	J. Bollandus, *Acta Sanctorum* (Antwerp and Brussels)
BAR	British Archaeological Reports
CCSL	Corpus Christianorum, series latina. (Turnhout: Brepols)
CHR	The Catholic Historical Review
CPL	*Clavis patrum latinorum*, eds. E. Dekkers and A. Gaar. 3rd edition. Brepols, 1995.
CSEL	Corpus scriptorum ecclesiasticorum latinorum (Vienna)
CT	*Codex Theodosianus* (Theodosian Code).
DTC	*Dictionnaire de Théologie Catholique*
EEBO	Early English Books Online
EME	*Early Medieval Europe*
JCS	*Journal of Christian Studies*
JECS	*Journal of Early Christian Studies*
JEH	*Journal of Ecclesiastical History*
JMH	*Journal of Medieval History*
JRS	*The Journal of Roman Studies*
JTS	*Journal of Theological Studies*

MGH AA	Monumenta Germaniae Historica, auctores antiquissimi
MGH, SRM	Monumenta Germaniae Historica, scriptores rerum Merovingicarum (Berlin, Leipzig, Hanover).
NTA	*New Testament Apocrypha.* 2 volumes. Edited by Wilhelm Schneemelcher. English translation by R. Mc L. Wilson. Cambridge: James Clarke & Co., 1991–92.
PL	J. P. Migne, Patrologiae cursus completes, series latina (Paris, 1844–64)
RHE	*Revue d'histoire ecclésiastique*
RSV	The Holy Bible. Revised Standard Version. London: Collins, 1973.
SC	Sources chrétiennes (Paris)
SCJ	*Sixteenth Century Journal*
TTH	Translated Texts for Historians
TU	Texte und Untersuchungen zur Geschichte der altchristlichen Literatur (Berlin)

Bibliography

PRIMARY SOURCES

Aeschylus. *Prometheus Bound*. Translated by Paul Roche. New York: The New American Library, 1964.

Alcuin. *Vita Willibrordi*. Edited by W. Levison, MGH, SRM 7 (1920).

Ambrose. *De bono mortis*. Edited by Carolus Schenkl, CSEL 32 (1896): 701–53. Translated by Michael P. McHugh, *St. Ambrose: Seven Exegetical Works*. Washington, DC: The Catholic University of America Press, 1972.

———. *De excessu fratris*. Edited by Otto Faller, CSEL 73 (1955): 205–325.

———. *De officiis*. Edited by Mauritii Testard, CCSL 15 (2000). Translated by H. de Romestin, *St.Ambrose: Select Works and Letters*. Vol. 10, *Nicene and Post-Nicene Fathers*. Edinburgh: T & T Clark, 1989.

On Repentance (de paenitentia). Edited by Otto Faller, CSEL 73 (1955): 117–206. Translated by Philip Schaff and Henry Wace, *Two Books Concerning Repentance*. Vol. 10, *Nicene and Post-Nicene Fathers*. 2nd series. Edinburgh: T & T Clark, 1989.

———. *Expositio psalmi cxviii*. Edited by M. Petschenig, CSEL 62, no. 5 (1913).

Ambrosiaster. *Commentary on the Pauline Letters*. Edited by Henry Joseph Vogels, *Ambrosiastri qui dicitur commentarius in epistulas Paulinas*, CSEL 81, no. 2 (1968). Also edited by J. P. Migne, *Commentaria in epistolam b. Pauli ad Corinthios*, PL, 17:183–338.

Anonymous. *Whitby Vita Gregorii*. See *Life of Gregory the Great*.

Apocalypse of Peter. Translated by J. K. Elliott, *The Apocryphal New Testament: A Collection of Apocryphal Christian Literature in an English Translation Based on M. R. James*. Oxford: Clarendon, 2007. Also translated by C. Detlef G. Müller, 620–38, in *NTA*, 2 ed. Schneemelcher.

Augustine. *De civitate Dei*. CCSL 47–48 (1955).

———. *De cura pro mortuis gerenda*. Edited by Joseph Zycha, CSEL 41 (1900): 619–420.

———. *De doctrina christiana*. Edited by J. Martin, CCSL 32 (1955).

———. *De Genesi ad litteram*. Edited by Joseph Zycha, CSEL 28 (1894).

———. *De gestis Pelagiis*. Edited by Carolus Urba and Joseph Zycha, CSEL 42 (1902): 49–122. Translated by John A. Mourant and William J. Collinge, introduction and notes by William J. Collinge, *Saint Augustine: Four Anti-Pelagian Writings*. Washington DC: The Catholic University of America Press, 1992.

———. *De natura et origine animae*. Edited by Carolus Urba and Joseph Zycha, CSEL 60 (1913): 301–420.

———. *Enchiridion ad Laurentium de fide, et spe et caritate*. Edited by E. Evans, CCSL 46 (1969). Translated by Louis Arand, ACW, 3. New York: Newman, 1947. Translated by Bernard M. Peebles, *Saint Augustine*. Vol. 4, *The Fathers of the Church*. New York: Fathers of the Church, Inc., 1947.

———. *Tractates on the Gospel of John. In Johannis Evangelium tractatus ccxxiv.* Edited by Radbod Willems, CCSL 36 (1954). Translated by John W. Rettig, *St. Augustine, Tractates on the Gospel of John 1–10*. Vol. 78, *The Fathers of the Church*. Washington, DC: The Catholic University of America Press, 1988.

———. *Sermons on the Liturgical Seasons*. Edited by Sister Mary Sarah Muldowney. Vol. 38, *The Fathers of the Church*. New York: Fathers of the Church Inc., 1959.

Basil, *The Long Rules*. Translated by M. Monica Wagner, *Saint Basil: Ascetical Works*, 223–337. Vol. 9, *The Fathers of the Church*. New York: Fathers of the Church, Inc., 1950.

Bede, the Venerable. *Commentary on the Acts of the Apostles*. Translated by Lawrence T. Martin, *The Venerable Bede: Commentary on the Acts of the Apostles*. Kalamazoo, MI: Cistercian Publications, 1989.

———. *Commentary on Proverbs*. Edited by David Hurst, *In proverbia Salomonis libri iii*, in *Bedae Venerabilis opera, pars ii: Opera exegetica*, CCSL 119B (1983).

———. *Ecclesiastical History*. Edited and translated by Bertram Colgrave and R. A. B. Mynors, *Bede's Ecclesiastical History of the English People*. Oxford: Clarendon, 1969.

———. *Homilies on the Gospels*. Edited by David Hurst, *Bedae Venerabilis homiliarum Evangelii Libri II*, in *Bedae Venerabilis opera, pars iii: Opera homiletica*, CCSL 122 (1955). Translated by Lawrence T. Martin and David Hurst, *Bede the Venerable: Homilies on the Gospels Book One, Advent to Lent*. Vol. 110, Cistercian Studies. Kalamazoo, MI: Cistercian Publications, 1991.

———. *Letter to Egbert*. Edited by C. Plummer, 405–23, *Venerabilis Baedae*. Oxford: Clarendon, 1961.

———. *Life of Saint Cuthbert*. Edited and translated by Bertram Colgrave, *Two Lives of Saint Cuthbert: Text, Translation and Notes*. Cambridge: Cambridge University Press, 1985. Translated by J. F. Webb, 41–102, *The Age of Bede*. Harmondsworth: Penguin, 1988.

———. *Lives of the Abbots (Historiam abbatum Benedicti, Ceolfridi, Eosterwini, Sigfridi at Hwaetberti)*. Edited by C. Plummer, 364–87, *Venerabilis Baedae*. Oxford: Clarendon, 1961.

———. *On Isaiah (De eo quod ait Isaias)*. Edited by J. -P. Migne, PL, 94:702–10. Translated by Arthur G. Holder, in W. Trent Foley and Arthur G. Holder, *Bede: A Biblical Miscellany*, 39–51. Liverpool: Liverpool University Press, 1999.

———. *On Mark (In Marci evangelium expositio)*. Edited by David Hurst, CCSL 120 (1960): 427–648.

———. *On Samuel (In primam partem Samuhelis libri iiii)*. Edited by David Hurst, CCSL 119 (1962).

———. *On Tobias (In Tobiam)*. Edited by David Hurst, CCSL 119B (1983): 1–19. Translated by W. Trent Foley, in W. Trent Foley and Arthur G. Holder, *Bede: A Biblical Miscellany*, 53–79. Liverpool: Liverpool University Press, 1999.

Benedict of Nursia. *Benedictine Rule (Regula Benedicti)*. Edited by Rudolfus Hanslik, CSEL 75. (1960). Also edited by Adalbert de Vogüé and Jean Neufville, *La règle de saint Benoit*. SC, 181–82, with commentaries by de Vogüé, SC 184–86 (1971–77).

Bible. Revised Standard Version: An Ecumenical Edition. London: Collins, 1973. *Biblia Sacra Vulgata*. Edited by Robert Weber. New edition by Roger Gryson. Stuttgart: Deutsche Bibelgesellschaft, 2007.

Bieler, Ludwig. *Irish Penitentials*. Vol. 5, Scriptores Latini Hiberniae. Dublin: Dublin Institute for Advanced Studies, 1975.

Bobbio Missal. A Gallican Mass Book (MS. Paris. Lat. 13246). Edited by E. A. Lowe, with notes and studies by André Wilmart, E. A. Lowe, and H. A. Wilson. Vols. 58 and 61, *The Henry Bradshaw Society*. London: Boydell, 1920, 1924.

Boniface. *Letters*. Edited by M. Tangl, *Die Briefe des Heiligen Bonifatius und Lullus*, MGH, Epistolae selectae, 1. Berlin: Weidmannsche Verlag, 1955. Translated by Ephraim Emerton, *The Letters of St. Boniface*. New York: Columbia University Press, 2000.

Caesarius of Arles. *Sermons*. Translated by Sister Mary Magdeleine Mueller, *Saint Caesarius of Arles: Sermons*. Vols. 31, 47. 66, *The Fathers of the Church*. Washington, DC: The Catholic University of America Press, 1956–73.

———. *Opera*. Edited by G. Morin, *S. Caesarii opera omnia*. 2 vols. Maredsous, 1937–42; Reprinted, G. Morin, *Caesarii Arelatensis Sermones*, CCSL 103, 104 (1953).

Canons of the Alleged Second Synod of Patrick. Translated by John T. McNeill and Helena M. Gamer, 80–86. *Medieval Handbooks of Penance: A Translation of the Principal 'libri poenitentiales.'* New York: Columbia University Press, 1938.

Canons of Patrick, Auxilius and Isernus. Translated by Ludwig Bieler, *The Works of St. Patrick, St. Secundinus, Hymn on St. Patrick*. New York: Paulist, 1953.

Cassian, John. *Conferences (Conlationes)*. Edited by E. Pichéry, *Jean Cassien: Conférences*. SC 42, 54, 64 (1955, 1958, 1959). Translated by Boniface Ramsey, *John Cassian: The Conferences*. Vol. 57, ACW. New York: Newman, 1997.

———. *Institutes (Institutions)*. Edited and translated by Jean-Claude Guy, *Jean Cassien: Institutions cénobitiques*. SC 109 (1965). Translated by Boniface Ramsey, *John Cassian: The Institutes*. Vol. 58, ACW. New York: Newman, 2000.

Christian Sibylline Oracles. Translated by Ursula Treu, NTA, 2:652–85.

Cicero. *De amicitia*. Edited by James S. Reid, *M. Tulli Ciceronis. Laelius de amicitia*. Boston: Allyn and Bacon, 1895.

———. *De officiis*. Edited by M. Winterbottom, *M. Tulli Ciceronis. De officiis*. Oxford: Oxford University Press, 1994.

Claudianus Mamertus. *De statu animae libri tres*. Edited by Augustus Angelbrecht, CSEL 11 (1855): 1–197.

Clement of Alexandria. *Paidagogos*. Translated by Simon P. Wood, *Clement of Alexandria: Christ the Educator*. New York: Fathers of the Church Inc., 1954.

———. *Stromateis*. Translated by John Ferguson, *Stromateis, Books 1–3*. Washington, DC: Catholic University of America Press, 1991.

Cogitosus. *Life of Saint Brigit*. Translated by S. Connolly and J. M. Picard in "Cogitosus's *Life of St Brigit*: Content and Value," *Journal of the Royal Society of Antiquaries of Ireland*, 117 (1987): 5–27.

Columbanus. *Sermons*. Edited and translated by G. S. M. Walker, *Sancti Columbani Opera*. Dublin: The Dublin Institute for Advanced Studies, 1957.

Council of Nicaea. Ed. Henry R. Percival, *The Seven Ecumenical Councils of the Undivided Church*. Vol. 14, Nicene and Post-Nicene Fathers. Edinburgh: T&T Clark, 1991.

Councils (Gallic). Edited by Caroli de Clercq, *Concilia Galliae A. 511–A. 695*, CCSL 148A (1963).

———. Edited by Jean Gaudemet and Brigitte Basdevant, *Les canons des conciles Mérovingiens (VIe–VIIe siècles)*, SC 353, 354 (1989).

Edited by C. Munier, *Concilia Galliae, A. 314–A. 506*, CCSL 148 (1963).

Councils (Papal). Edited by H. Denzinger, *Enchiridion Symbolorum*. Freiburg: Herder, 1955.

Cuthbert. *Letter on the Death of Bede (Epistola de obitu Bedae)*. Edited and translated by Bertram Colgrave and R. A. B. Mynors, 579–87 in *Bede's Ecclesiastical History of the English People*. Oxford: Clarendon, 1969.

Decrees of Wihtred. Edited by Lisi Oliver, *Beginnings of English Law*, 147–80. Also in F. Liebermann, *Die Gesetze der Angelsachsen*. 3 vols. (1903–16; reprint, 1960), and in *The Laws of the Earliest English Kings*. Edited by F. L. Attenborough, 24–31. New York: Russell & Russell, 1963. Translated by Dorothy Whitelock, *English Historical Documents, Volume 1, c. 500–1042*, 362–65. Oxford: Oxford University Press, 1955.

Die handschriftliche Überlieferung der Werke des Heiligen Augustinus. 10 vols. Vienna: Verlag der Österreichischen Akademie der Wissenschaften, 1969–

Du Moulin, P. *The Waters of Siloe: To quench the fire of purgatory and to drowne the traditions, limboes, mans satisfactions and all popish indulgences, against the reasons and allegations of a Portugall frier of the order of St. Frances, supported by three treatises. The one written by the same Franciscan and entituled The fierie torrent, &c. The other two by two doctors of Sorbon. The one intituled The burning furnasse. The other The fire of Helie*. Translated by "I. B." Oxford: Joseph Barnes, 1612.

Eddius Stephanus. *Life of Wilfrid*. Text, translation, and notes by Bertram Colgrave, *The Life of Bishop Wilfrid*. Cambridge: Cambridge University Press, 1985.

Eligius of Noyon. *De supremo iudicio*. Edited by B. Krusch, MGH, SRM 4 (1902): 749–61.

Eriugena. *Periphyseon (De divisione naturae)*. Edited by I. P. Sheldon-Williams, with the collaboration of Ludwig Bieler. Vols. 7 and 9, *Scriptores Latini Hiberniae*. Dublin: Dublin Institute of Advanced Studies, 1968 and 1972.

Eusebius "Gallicanus." *De Epiphania Domini* 2. Edited by J. Leroy and Fr. Glorie, CCSL 101 (1970): 67–73.

Fortunatus. See Venantius Fortunatus.

Fulke, William. *A defense of the sincere and true translations of the holie Scriptures into the English tong*. London: Henrie Bynneman, 1583.

———. *Two treatises written against the papistes the one being an answere of the Christian Protestant to the proud challenge of a popish Catholicke: the other a confutation of the popish churches doctrine touching purgatory & prayers for the dead*. London: Thomas Vautrollier, Blacke friers, 1577.

Gelasian Sacramentary (Vat. Reg. lat. 316) ed. L. C. Mohlberg, *Liber sacramentorum romanae ecclesiae ordinis anni circuli*. Herder: Rome, 1960.

Gregory the Great. *Dialogues*. Edited by Umberto Moricca, *Gregorii Magni Dialogi*. Rome: Istituto Storico Italiano, 1924. Also edited by Adalbert de Vogüé, *Grégoire le Grand. Dialogues*, SC 251, 260, 265 (1978–80). Translated Odo John Zimmerman, *Saint Gregory the Great: Dialogues*. Vol. 39, *The Fathers of the Church*. New York: Fathers of the Church Inc., 1959.

———. *Homilies on the Gospels*. Translated by David Hurst. Kalamazoo, MI: Cistercian Publications, 1990.

———. *Moralia in Job*. Edited in Marc Adriaen, CCSL 143, 143A, 143B (1979–85).

Gregory of Nyssa. *On the Soul and the Resurrection*. Translated by Virginia Woods Callahan, *Saint Gregory of Nyssa: Ascetical Works*. Washington DC: Catholic University of America, 1967.

Gregory of Tours. *Vita Iuliani* (*De passione et virtutibus sancti Iuliani martyris*). Edited by Bruno Krusch, MGH, SRM 1, no. 2 (1885): 112–34. Translated by Van Dam, 162–95, *Saints and Their Miracles*.

———. *De virtutibus sancti Martini episcopi*. Edited by Bruno Krusch, MGH, SRM 1, no. 2 (1885): 134–211. Translated by Van Dam, 199–303, *Saints and Their Miracles*, 199–303.

———. *History of the Franks*. Edited by Bruno Krusch, MGH, SRM 1, no. 1 fasc.1 and 1.1. fasc 2 (1937–42).

———. *Liber in gloria confessorum*. Edited by Bruno Krusch, MGH, SRM 1, no. 2 (1885): 294–370. Translated by Raymond Van Dam, *Gregory of Tours: Glory of the Confessors*, Translated Texts for Historians, Latin Series 4. Liverpool: Liverpool University Press, 1988.

———. *Liber in gloria martyrum*. Edited by Bruno Krusch, MGH, SRM 1, no. 2 (1885): 34–111. Translated by Raymond Van Dam, *Gregory of Tours: Glory of the Martyrs*, Translated Texts for Historians, Latin Series 3. Liverpool: Liverpool University Press, 1988.

———. *Liber vitae patrum*. Edited by Bruno Krusch, MGH, SRM 1, no. 2 (1885): 211–94. Translated by Edward James, *Gregory of Tours: Life of the Fathers*. Translated Texts for Historians, Latin Series 1. Second edition. Liverpool: Liverpool University Press, 1991.

Heito. *Visio cuiusdam pauperculae mulieris*. Edited by Hubert Houben, "*Visio cuiusdam pauperculae mulieris*. Überlieferung und Herkunft eines frühmittelalterlichen Visionstextes (mit Neuedition)," *Zeitschrift für Geschichte des Oberrheins* 124, n.s. 85 (1976): 31–42.

———. *Visio Wettini*. See *Vision of Wetti*.
Indiculus superstitionum et paganarum. MGH, Leges 2, i, 222ff. Translated by John T. McNeill and Helena M. Gamer, 419–21, *Medieval Handbooks of Penance*. New York: Columbia University Press, 1938.
Isidore of Seville. *De ecclesiasticis officiis*. Edited by Christopher M. Lawson, CCSL 113 (1989).
———. *De ordine creaturarum*. PL, 83:913–54.
———. *Sententiae*. Edited by Pierre Cazier, CCSL 111 (1997).
Jerome. *In Esaiam*. Edited by A. Adriaen, CCSL 73, 73A (1963).
———. *Letters*. Edited by F. A. Wright, *Select Letters of St. Jerome*. Cambridge, MA: Harvard University Press, 1980.
———. *In Job. Commentary on Job*. PL 26: 655–850.
Jonas. *Vita Columbani*. Edited by Bruno Krusch, MGH, SRM 4 (1902): 1–152.
———. *Life of Wulframn of Sens*. Edited by W. Levison, 657–73, *Vita Vulframni Episcopi Senonici*, MGH, SRM 5 (1910).
Julian of Toledo. *Prognosticum*. Edited by J. N. Hillgarth, *Prognosticorum futuri saeculi libri tres*, CCSL 115 (1976).
Julianus Pomerius. *De vita contemplativa*. Translated by Mary Josephine Suelzer, *Pomerius: The Contemplative Life*, ACW, 4. New York: Newman, 1947.
Lactantius. *Divinae Institutiones*. Edited by Samuel Brandt, CSEL 19 (1890): 1–672. Translated by Anthony Bowen and Peter Garnsey, *Lactantius: Divine Institutes*, Vol. 40, TTH, Latin Series. Liverpool: Liverpool University Press, 2003.
Lex Salica. Pactus Legis Salicae. Edited by Karl August Eckhardt, MGH, Legum Sectio I, Legum Nationum Germanicarum, 4,1. 1962. Translated by Katherine Fisher Drew, *The Laws of the Salian Franks*. Philadelphia: University of Pennsylvania Press, 1991.
Liber de ordine creaturarum. Edited Manuel C. Diaz y Diaz, *Un anonimo irlandes del siglo VII, estudio y edicion critica*. Santiago de Compostela: Universidad de Santiago de Compostela, 1972.
Liber Pontificalis. Translated and introduction by Raymond Davis, *The Book of Pontiffs (Liber Pontificalis)*. Vol. 5, TTH, Latin Series. Liverpool: Liverpool University Press, 1989.
Liber Sacramentorum Gellonensis. Edited by Antoine Dumas, CCSL 159, 159A (1981).
Life of Caesarius of Arles (Vita Caesarii). Edited by G. Morin, CCSL 103 (1953). Translated by William E. Klingshirn, *Caesarius of Arles: Life, Testament, Letters*. Vol. 19, TTH, Latin series. Liverpool: Liverpool University Press, 1994.
Life of Columbanus. See Jonas.
Life of Eligius. Vita Eligii ep. Noviomagensis. Edited by Bruno Krusch, MGH, SRM 4 (1902): 634–741. Full text, Migne, *Vita S. Eligii*, PL, 87:477–594.
Life of Eugendus, in *Life of the Jura Fathers (Vita Patrum Jurensium)*. Edited by François Martine, *Vie des pères du Jura*, SC 142 (1968).
Life of Fursey. Vita Sancti Fursei. Vita prima. Edited by Johannes Bollandus, AASS, Ian. 2 (January 16, 1643): 35–41; *Vita* also edited by Bruno Krusch, MGH, SRM 4 (1902) 423–49, with visions excised.
Life of Gregory the Great. (Whitby). Text, translation, and notes by Bertram Colgrave, *The Earliest Life of Gregory the Great*. Cambridge: Cambridge University Press, 1968.

Life of Guthlac. Edited and translated by Bertram Colgrave, *Felix's Life of Saint Guthlac.* Cambridge: Cambridge University Press, 1956.

Life of Leudegar. See *Passion of Leudegar.*

Life of Pachomius (Sbo). Translated by Armand Veilleux, *The Life of Saint Pachomius and His Disciples.* Kalamazoo, MI: Cistercian Publications, 1980.

Life of Saint Melania the Younger. Edited by Denys Gorce, *Vie de Sainte Mélanie: Texte Grec, traduction et notes.* SC 90 (1962).

Life of Saint Odilia. Vita s. Odiliae abbatissae Hohenburgensis. Edited by Wilhelm Levison, MGH, SRM 6 (1913) 24–50.

Life of Saint Willibrord. See Alcuin.

Life of Saint Brigit. See Cogitosus.

Life of Wulframn of Sens. See Jonas.

McNeill, John T., and Helena M. Gamer, eds. *Medieval Handbooks of Penance.* New York: Columbia University Press, 1938.

Oribasius. *Medical Collection.* Edited by Charles Daremberg and V. Bussemaker, *Collection médicale.* 6 vols. Paris: A L'imprimerie nationale, 1851–76.

Origen. *Commentary on the Epistle to the Romans.* Translated by Thomas S. Schreck. Vol. 103, *The Fathers of the Church.* Washington DC: Catholic University of America Press, 2001.

———. *Homilies on Jeremiah.* Translated by John Clark Smith, *Origen: Homilies on Jeremiah, Homily on 1 Kings 28.* Vol. 97, *The Fathers of the Church.* Washington DC: The Catholic University of America, 1998.

———. *Homilies on Leviticus 1–16.* Translated by Gary Wayne Barkley. Vol. 83, *The Fathers of the Church.* Washington DC: The Catholic University of America, 1990.

———. *On First Principles.* Translated by G. W. Butterworth, with Introduction by Henri DeLubac. Gloucester, MA: Peter Smith, 1973.

Paschasius of Dumium. *Questions and Answers of the Greek Fathers (Interrogationes et responsiones Graecorum partum).* Translated by Claude W. Barlow, *Iberian Fathers: Martin of Braga, Paschasius of Dumium, Leander of Seville.* Washington DC: Catholic University of America Press, 1969.

Passion of Leudegar. (*Passio Leudegari episcopi Augustodunensis I*). Edited by Bruno Krusch, MGH, SRM 5 (1910) 282–22.

Passion of Perpetua (*Passio Perpetuae*). Text and translation by W. H. Shewring. *The Passion of SS. Perpetua and Felicity MM: A New Edition and Translation of the Latin Text together with the Sermons of S. Augustine upon These Saints.* London: Sheed and Ward, 1931.

Paulinus of Pella. *Thanksgiving (Eucharisticos).* Translated by H. Isbell, *The Last Poets of Imperial Rome.* Harmondsworth: Penguin Classics, 1971.

Paulinus of Périgueux. *De vita sancti Martini episcopi.* Edited by Michael Petschenig, CSEL 16, no. 1 (1888).

Penitentials. Bigotian Penitential. Edited and translated by Ludwig Bieler, *The Irish Penitentials,* 198–239. Vol. 5, Scriptores Latini Hiberniae. Dublin: Dublin Institute for Advanced Studies, 1975. Also, *Poenitentiale Bigotianum.* Edited by F. W. H. Wasserschleben, 441–60, *Die Bussordnungen der abendländischen Kirche nebst einer rechtsgeschichtlichen Einleitung.* Halle: Ch. Graeger, 1851.

Penitential of Cummean. Edited and Translated by Ludwig Bieler, 108–35, *The Irish Penitentials*. Vol. 5, Scriptores Latini Hiberniae. Dublin: Dublin Institute for Advanced Studies, 1975.

Penitential of Finnian. Edited and Translated by Ludwig Bieler, 74–95, *The Irish Penitentials*. Vol. 5, Scriptores Latini Hiberniae. Dublin: Dublin Institute for Advanced Studies, 1975.

Pirmin of Reichenau. *De singulis libris canonicis scarapsus*. PL, 89: 1029–50.

Plotinus. *The Enneads*. Translated by Stephen Mackenna, introduction by John Dillon. Harmondsworth: Penguin Classics, 1991.

Porphyry. *Life of Plotinus*. Translated by Stephen MacKenna, in MacKenna and Dillon trans. *Plotinus: The Enneads*, cii-cxxv. Harmondsworth: Penguin Classics, 1991.

Prudentius. *Liber Cathemerinon*. Edited by Johannes Bergman, CSEL 61 (1926). Translated by H. Isbell, *The Last Poets of Imperial Rome*. Harmondsworth: Penguin Classics, 1971.

———. *Psychomachia*. Edited by Maurice P. Cunningham, CCSL 126 (1966). Translated by H. Isbell, *The Last Poets of Imperial Rome*. Harmondsworth: Penguin Classics, 1971.

Pseudo-Eligius. *Homily 8*. PL 87: 614–27.

Pseudo-Gelasius. *Decretum*. Edited by E. von Dobschütz, "Das Decretum Gelasianum de libris recipiendis et non recipiendis," TU 38, no. 4 (1912).

Redaction 6. (See *Vision of Paul, Redaction 6*).

Salvian of Marseilles. *The Four Books of Timothy to the Church*. Translated by Jeremiah O'Sullivan, 265–371, *The Writings of Salvian, the Presbyter*. New York: Cima Publishing Co., 1947.

———. *On the Governance of God*. Translated by Jeremiah O'Sullivan, 21–232, *The Writings of Salvian, the Presbyter*. New York: Cima Publishing Co., 1947.

Seneca. *On Benefits*. Translated by Aubrey Stewart. London: George Bell and Sons, 1900.

Shepherd of Hermas. Edited and translated by Kirsopp Lake. Vol. 2, *The Apostolic Fathers*. Cambridge, MA: Harvard University Press, 1976. Also, edited by Carolyn Osiek, *A Commentary on the Shepherd of Hermas*. Minneapolis, MN: Augsberg Fortress, 1999.

Sulpicius Severus. *Dialogues*. Edited by Carolus Halm, CSEL 1 (1966).

———. *Vita Martini*. Edited by Jacques Fontaine, *Sulpice Sévère: Vie de Saint Martin*, SC 133–35 (1967–69).

Tacitus. *Germania*. Edited by Rodney Potter Robinson, *The Germania of Tacitus: A Critical Edition*. Middletown, CT: American Philological Association, 1935.

Tertullian, *Against Marcion*. Edited and translated by Ernest Evans, *Tertullian: Adversus Marcionem*. Oxford: Clarendon, 1972.

———. *De anima*. Edited by Jan Hendrik Waszink, CCSL 2 (1954).

———. *De spectaculis*. Edited and translated by T. R. Glover, 230–301, in *Tertullian*. Cambridge, MA: Harvard University Press, 1953.

Theodosian Code. Edited by J. Godefroy, *Codex Theodosianus*. Hildesheim: George Olms, 1975. Translated by Clyde Pharr, *The Theodosian Code and Novels and the Sirmondian Constitutions*. Princeton: Princeton University Press, 1952.

Venantius Fortunatus. Carmina 10: *Ad Armentariam*. Edited by F. Leo, MGH, AA 4, no. 1 (1881): 248–49.
———. *Vita Germani*. Edited by Bruno Krusch, MGH, AA 4, no. 2 (1881): 11–27.
———. *Vita Hilarii*. Edited by Bruno Krusch, MGH, AA 4, no. 2 (1881): 1–11.
———. *Vita s. Martini*. Edited by F. Leo, MGH, AA 4, no. 1 (1881): 293–370.
Vincent of Lérins. *A Commonitory*. Translated by C. A. Heurtley, 123–59. Vol. 11, *Nicene and Post-Nicene Fathers*. Edinburgh: T&T Clark, 1991. *Vision of 757* (Fragmentary) = Boniface, Letter 115. Edited by M. Tangl, 247–50, *Die Briefe des Heiligen Bonifatius und Lullus*, MGH, Epistolae selectae, 1. Berlin: Weidmannsche Verlag, 1955. Translated by Ephraim Emerton, 167–69, *The Letters of St. Boniface*. Columbia University Press, 2000.
Vision of Barontus. Edited by Wilhelm Levinson, *Visio Baronti monachi Longoretensis*, MGH, SRM 5 (1910): 368–94. Translated by *Christianity and Paganism, 350–750: The Conversion of Western Europe*. Edited by Jocelyn N. Hillgarth, 195–204. Philadelphia: University of Pennsylvania Press, 1969.
Vision of Drythelm. In *Bede: Ecclesiastical History of the English People*. Edited and translated by Bertram Colgrave and R. A. B. Mynors, 488–99. Oxford: Clarendon, 1969.
Vision of Fursey. Edited by Maria Pia Ciccarese, "Le Visioni di S. Fursa," *Romanobarbarica* 8 (1984–85): 231–303. The BL, Harley MS 5041ff. 79–98 is edited and translated by Oliver Rackham, *Transitus Beati Fursei: A Translation of the 8th Century Life of Saint Fursey*. Norwich: Fursey Pilgrims, 2007.
Vision of the Monk of Wenlock. Edited by M. Tangl, *Die Briefe des Heiligen Bonifatius und Lullus*. MGH, Epistolae selectae, 1. Berlin: Weidmannsche Verlag, 1955.
Vision of Paul (Apocalypse of Paul). Latin. Edited by Theodore Silverstein and Anthony Hilhorst, *Apocalypse of Paul: A New Critical Edition of Three Long Latin Versions with Fifty-four Plates*. Geneva: Patrick Cramer, 1997. Also edited by Theodore Silverstein, *Visio Sancti Pauli: The History of the Apocalypse in Latin, Together with Nine Texts*. Vol. 4, Studies and Documents. London: Christophers, 1935. Lenka Jiroušková, *Die Visio Pauli: Wege and Wandlungen einer orientalischen Apokryphe im Lateinischen Mittelalter unter Einschluß der alttschechischen und deutschsprachigen Textzeugen*. Leiden: E. J. Brill, 2006. Claude Carozzi, *Eschatologie et au-delà. Recherches sur l'Apocalypse de Paul*. Aix en Provence: Publications de l'Université de Provence, 1994.
Vision of Paul. Greek. Edited by Konstantin von Tischendorf, *Apocalypses Apocryphae*, 1866; repr. Hildesheim: F. Georg Olms, 1966.
Vision of Paul, Redaction 6. (St. Gallen, Stiftsbibliothek, Cod. Sang. 682.) Accessible on E-Codices: Virtual Manuscript Library of Switzerland. Latin text edited by Theodore Silverstein, *Visio Sancti Pauli*, 214–18.
Vision of Wetti. In verse by Heito, Edited by E. Dümmler, *Heitonis visio Wettini*, MGH, Poetae aevi carolini, 2 (1884). In prose by Walahfrid Strabo, Translated by David A. Traill, *Walahfrid Strabo's Visio Wettini: Text, Translation and Commentary*. Bern: Bernard Lang; Frankfurt: Peter Lang, 1974.
Voyage of Brendan. Edited by Carl Selmer, *Navigatio Sancti Brendani Abbatis*. Dublin: Four Courts, 1989.

Walahfrid Strabo, *Visio Wettini*. See under *Vision of Wetti*.

SECONDARY SOURCES

Althoff, Gerd. "*Amicitiae* [Friendships] as Relations between States and People." In *Debating the Middle Ages: Issues and Readings*, edited by Lester K. Little and Barbara H. Rosenwein, 191–210. Maldon, MA: Blackwell, 1988.

Amat, Jacqueline. *Songes et Visions: L'au-delà dans la littérature latine tardive*. Paris: Études Augustiniennes, 1985.

Angenendt, Arnold. "*Donationes pro anima*: Gift and Countergift in the Early Medieval Liturgy." In *The Long Morning of Medieval Europe: New Directions in Early Medieval Studies*, edited by Jennifer R. Davis and Michael McCormick, 131–54. Aldershot: Ashgate, 2008.

———. *Geschichte der Religiosität im Mittelalter*. Darmstadt: Primus Verlag, 1997.

———. *Heilige und Reliquien Die Geschichte ihres Kultes vom frühen Christentum bis zur Gegenwart*. Munich: C. H. Beck, 1994.

———. "Theologie und Liturgie der mittelalterlichen Toten-Memoria." In *Memoria: Der geschichtliche Zeugniswert des liturgischen Gedenkens im Mittelater*, edited by Karl Schmid and Joachim Wollasch, 79–199. Munich: Wilhelm Fink Verlag, 1984.

Ariès, Philippe. *Western Attitudes Toward Death: From the Middle Ages to the Present*. Translated by Patricia Ranum. Baltimore: Johns Hopkins, 1974.

Ashbrook Harvey, Susan. *Scenting Salvation: Ancient Christianity and the Olfactory Imagination*. Berkeley: University of California Press, 2006.

Atwell, Robert R. "Aspects in St. Augustine of Hippo's Thought and Spirituality Concerning the State of the Faithful Departed, 354–430." In *The End of Strife*, edited by David Loades, 3–13. Edinburgh: T & T Clark, 1984.

———. "From Augustine to Gregory the Great: An Evaluation of the Emergence of the Doctrine of Purgatory." *JEH* 38 (1987): 173–86.

Audisio, Gabriel. "How to Detect a Clandestine Minority: The Example of the Waldenses." *SCJ* 21 (1990): 205–16.

Ausenda, G., ed. *After Empire: Towards an Ethnology of Europe's Barbarians*. Woodbridge, Suffolk, and Rochester, NY: Boydell, 1995.

Bartlett, Robert. *Trial by Fire and Water: The Medieval Judicial Ordeal*. Oxford: Clarendon, 1986.

Bauckham, Richard. *The Fate of the Dead: Studies on the Jewish and Christian Apocalypses*. Leiden: E. J. Brill, 1998.

Beck, Henry G. J. "A Ninth-Century Canonist on Purgatory." *AER* 111 (1944): 250–56.

Becker, Ernest J. "A Contribution to the Comparative Study of Medieval Visions of Heaven and Hell, with Special Reference to the Middle English Versions." PhD diss., Johns Hopkins University, 1899. Baltimore: John Murphy Company, 1899.

Bede and His World. 2 vols (= Jarrow Lectures, 1958–93). Aldershot: Variorum, 1994.

Bède le Vénérable entre tradition et postérité. Edited by Stéphane Lebecq, Michel Perrin, and Oliver Szerwiniack. Lille: Ceges—Université de Charles-de-Gaule, 2003.

Bernstein, Alan. E. *The Formation of Hell: Death and Retribution in the Ancient and Early Christian Worlds.* Ithaca, NY: Cornell University Press, 1993.

———. "Named Others and Named Places: Stigmatization in the Early Medieval Afterlife." In *Hell and Its Afterlife: Historical and Contemporary Perspectives*, edited by Isabel Moreira and Margaret Toscano. Aldershot: Ashgate Publishing, forthcoming.

———. Review "Jacques Le Goff, La naissance du purgatoire." *Speculum* 59 (1984): 179–83.

Berschin, Walter. *Biographie und Epochenstil im lateinischen Mittelalter.* 2 vols. Stuttgart: Anton Hiersemann Verlag, 1988.

Bieler, Ludwig, ed. *The Works of St. Patrick: St. Secundinus Hymn on St. Patrick.* New York: Paulist, 1953.

Bischof, Bernhard, and Michael Lapidge. *Biblical Commentaries from the Canterbury School of Theodore and Hadrian.* Cambridge: Cambridge University Press, 1994.

Bitel, Lisa. "Ekphrasis at Kildare: The Imaginative Architecture of a Seventh-Century Hagiographer." *Speculum* 79, no. 3 (2004): 605–27.

Blair, John. *The Church in Anglo-Saxon Society.* Oxford: Oxford University Press, 2005.

Blair, Peter Hunter. *The World of Bede.* Cambridge: Cambridge University Press, 1990.

Bolton, W. F. *A History of Anglo-Latin Literature 597–1066.* Princeton, NJ: Princeton University Press, 1967.

Bradley, Keith R. "Animalizing the Slave: The Truth of Fiction." *JRS* 90 (2000): 110–25.

———. *Slaves and Masters in the Roman Empire: A Study in Social Control.* 2nd ed. Oxford: Oxford University Press, 1987.

Bredero, Adriaan H. "Le Moyen Age et le purgatoire." *RHE* 78 (1983): 429–52.

Bremmer, Jan N. "Christian Hell: From the *Apocalypse of Peter* to the *Apocalypse of Paul*." *Numen* 56 (2009): 298–325.

———. *The Rise and Fall of the Afterlife.* London: Routledge, 2002.

Brown, George Hardin. "Bede's Neglected Commentary on Samuel." In *Innovation and Tradition in the Writings of the Venerable Bede*, edited by Scott deGregorio, 121–42. Morgantown: West Virginia University Press, 2006.

———. *A Companion to Bede.* Woodbridge, Suffolk: Boydell, 2009.

Brown, Michelle P. *The Book of Cerne: Prayer, Patronage and Power in Ninth-Century England.* The British Library Studies in Medieval Culture. Toronto: University of Toronto Press, 1996.

Brown, Peter. *The Body and Society: Men, Women, and Sexual Renunciation in Early Christianity.* New York: Columbia University Press, 1988.

———. *The Cult of the Saints: Its Rise and Function in Late Antiquity.* Chicago: Chicago University Press, 1981.

———. "The Decline of the Empire of God: Amnesty, Penance, and the Afterlife from Late Antiquity to the Middle Ages." In *Last Things: Death and the Apocalypse in the Middle Ages*, edited by Caroline Walker Bynum and Paul Freedman, 41–59. Philadelphia: University of Pennsylvania Press, 2000.

———. "The End of the Ancient Other World: Death and Afterlife Between Late Antiquity and the Early Middle Ages." *The Tanner Lectures on Human Values* 20 (1999): 19–85.

———. *The Rise of Western Christendom: Triumph and Diversity A.D. 200–1000.* Oxford: Blackwell, 2003.

———. "Vers la naissance du Purgatoire: Amnistie et pénitence dans le christianisme occidentale de l'Antiquité tardive au Haut Moyen Âge." *Annales E.S.C.* 52, no. 6 (1997): 1247–61.

Butler, Rex D. *The New Prophecy and "New Visions": Evidence for Montanism in the Passion of Perpetua and Felicity.* Washington, DC: Catholic University of America Press, 2006.

Bynum, Carolyn Walker. *The Resurrection of the Dead in Western Christianity, 200–1336.* New York: Columbia University Press, 1995.

Caner, Daniel. "Towards a Miraculous Economy: Christian Gifts and Material 'Blessings' in Late Antiquity." *JECS* 14, no. 3 (2006): 329–77.

Carozzi, Claude. *Eschatologie et l'au-delà: Recherches sur l'Apocalypse de Paul.* Aix en Provence: Publications de l'Université de Provence, 1994.

———. "La géographie de l'au-delà et sa signification pendant le haut moyen âge," *Settimane di Studio* 19. Popoli et paesi nella cultura altomedievale 1981, vol. 2. Spoleto, 1983: 423–81.

———. *Le voyage de l'âme dans l'au-delà d'après le littérature latine (Ve-XIIIe siècle).* Palais Farnèse: École Français de Rome, 1994.

Carroll, Sister Mary M. Thomas Aquinas. "An Eighth-Century Exegete on Purgatory." *The American Ecclesiastical Review* 112 (1945): 261–63.

Cavallo, Guglielmo. "Theodore and the Greek Culture of His Time." In *Archbishop Theodore*, edited by Michael Lapidge, 54–67. Cambridge: Cambridge University Press, 1995.

Chase, Alston Hurd. "The Metrical Lives of St. Martin of Tours by Paulinus and Fortunatus and the Prose Life by Sulpicius Severus." *Harvard Studies in Classical Philology* 43 (1932): 51–76.

Chaunu, Pierre. *La mort à Paris, XVIe, XVIIe et XVIIIe siècles.* Paris: Fayard, 1978.

Ciccarese, Maria Pia, "Le più antiche rappresentazioni del purgatorio, dalla *Passio Perpetuae* alla fine del IX sec." *Romanobarbarica* 7 (1982–83): 33–76.

———. "La *Visio Baronti* nella tradizione letteraria delle *Visiones* dell'aldilá." *Romanobarbarica* 6 (1982), 25–52.

———. "Le Visioni di S. Fursa," *Romanobarbarica* 8 (1984–45): 231–303.

Clark, Elizabeth A. *The Origenist Controversy: The Cultural Construction of an Early Christian Debate.* Princeton, NJ: Princeton University Press, 1992.

———. "The Place of Jerome's Commentary on Ephesians in the Origenist Controversy: The Apokatastasis and Ascetic Ideals." *Vigiliae Christianae* 41 (1967): 154–71.

Clark, Francis. *The Pseudo-Gregorian Dialogues.* 2 vols. Leiden: E. J. Brill, 1987.

Clarke, Gillian. "The Health of the Spiritual Athlete." In *Health in Antiquity*, edited by Helen King, 216–29. London and New York: Routledge, 2005.

Cochrane, William. *Future Punishment; or Does Death End Probation?* Brantford, ON: Bradley, Garretson & Co., 1886.

Coleman, K. M. "Fatal Charades: Roman Executions Staged as Mythological Enactments." *JRS* 80 (1990): 44–73

Coleridge, H. J. *The Prisoners of the King: Thoughts on the Catholic Doctrine of Purgatory.* London: Burns and Oats, 1884. (First published 1878).

Contreni, John J. "'Building Mansions in Heaven': The *Visio Baronti*, Archangel Raphael, and a Carolingian King." *Speculum* 78, no. 3 (2003): 673–706.

Cox-Miller, Patricia. *Dreams in Late Antiquity: Studies in the Imagination of a Culture*. Princeton, NJ: Princeton University Press, 1994.

Cramer, Peter. *Baptism and Change in the Early Middle Ages, c. 200–c. 1150*. New York: Cambridge University Press, 1993.

Cubitt, Catherine. *Anglo-Saxon Church Councils, c. 650–c. 850*. London: Leicester University Press, 1995.

Curta, Florin. "Merovingian and Carolingian Gift Giving." *Speculum* 81, no. 3 (2006): 671–99.

Dagens, Claude. *Saint Grégoire le Grand: Culture et expérience chrétiennes*. Paris: Études Augustiniennes, 1977.

Daley, Brian E. *The Hope of the Early Church: A Handbook of Patristic Eschatology*. Cambridge: Cambridge University Press, 1991.

De Bruyne, Theodore. "Flogging a Son: The Emergence of the *pater flagellans* in Latin Christian Discourse." *JCS* 7 (1999): 249–90.

DeGregorio, Scott. *Innovation and Tradition in the Writings of the Venerable Bede*. Morgantown: West Virginia University Press, 2006.

Dekkers, Eligius and Aemilius Gaar. *Clavis patrum latinorum*. 3rd edition. CCSL. Brepols: Editores Pontificii, 1995.

De Nie, Giselle. *Views from a Many-Windowed Tower: Studies of Imagination in the Works of Gregory of Tours*. Vol. 7, *Studies in Classical Antiquity*. Amsterdam: Editions Rodopi B. V., 1987.

Denziger, Heinrich and Adolfus Schönmetzer, *Enchiridion symbolorum: definitiun et declarationum de rebus fidei et morum*. Barcinone: Herder, 1973.

De Vogüé, Adalbert, ed. *Grégoire le Grand. Dialogues*, 3 vols., SC 251, 260, 265 (1978–80).

Dick, John. "*Notes on Probationism and Purgatory.*" In *Future Punishment; or Does Death End Probation?* edited by William Cochrane, 268–71. Brantford, ON: Bradley, Garretson & Co., 1886.

Die Franken. Wegbereiter Europas vor 1500 Jahren: Konig Chlodwig und seine Erben. 2 vols. Mainz: Verlag Philipp von Zabern, 1996.

Dierkens, Alain. *Abbayes et Chapitres entre Sambre et Meuse (VIIe-XIe siècles)*. Vol. 14, Beihefte der Francia. 1985.

———. "Prolégomènes à une histoire des relations culturelles entre les îles britanniques et le continent pendant le haut moyen âge." In *La Neustrie*, edited by Harmut Atsma, 2:371–94. Vol. 16, Beihefte der Francia, 1989.

Dinzelbacher, Peter. "The Way to the Other World in Medieval Literature and Art," *Folklore* 97 (1986): 70–87.

Dobbie, Eliott van Kirk. *The Manuscripts of Caedmon's Hymn and Bede's Death-Song: With a Critical Text of the Epistola Cuthberti de obitu Bedae*. New York: Columbia University Press, 1937.

Dolbeau, François. "Bède, lecteur des sermons d'Augustin." *Filologia mediolatina* 3 (1996): 105–33.

Dölger, F. J. "Antike Parallelen zum leidenden Dinokrates in der Passio Perpetuae." *Antike und Christentum* 2 (1930): 1–40.

Dooley, Kate. "From Penance to Confession: The Celtic Contribution." *Bijdragen, tijdschrift voor filosofie en theologie* 43 (1982): 390–411.

Drake, Harold A, ed. *Violence in Late Antiquity: Perceptions and Practices.* Aldershot: Ashgate Publishing, 2006.

Dronke, Peter. *Women Writers of the Middle Ages: A Critical Study of Texts from Perpetua (d. 203) to Marguerite Porete (d. 1310).* Cambridge: Cambridge University Press, 1984.

Dudden, Frederick H. *Gregory the Great: His Place in History and Thought.* New York: Russell & Russell, 1967.

Dumville, David N. "The Importation of Mediterranean Manuscripts into Theodore's England." In *Archbishop Theodore*, edited by Michael Lapidge, 96–119. Cambridge: Cambridge University Press, 1995.

———. *Liturgy and the Ecclesiastical History of Late Anglo-Saxon England: Four Studies.* Woodbridge, Suffolk: Boydell and Brewer, 1992.

Dunn, Marilyn. *The Emergence of Monasticism.* Oxford: Blackwell, 2000.

———. "Gregory the Great, the Vision of Fursey and the Origins of Purgatory." *Peritia* 14 (2000): 238–54.

Duval, Y., and Picard, J. C., eds. *L'inhumation privilégiée du ive au viiie siècle en occident.* Paris: De Boccard, 1986.

Edwards, Graham Robert. "Purgatory: 'Birth' or Evolution?" JEH 36 (1985): 634–46.

Effros, Bonnie. "Beyond Cemetery Walls: Early Medieval Funerary Topography and Christian Salvation." EME 6 (1997): 1–23.

———. *Caring for Body and Soul: Burial and the Afterlife in the Merovingian World.* University Park, PA: Pennsylvania State University Press, 2002.

———. "*De partibus Saxoniae* and the Regulation of Mortuary Custom: A Carolingian Campaign of Christianization or the Suppression of Saxon Identity?" *Revue Belge de philologie de d'histoire* 75 (1977): 269–87.

———. *Merovingian Mortuary Archaeology and the Making of the Early Middle Ages.* Berkeley: University of California Press, 2003.

Eire, Carlos. *From Madrid to Purgatory: The Art and Craft of Dying in Sixteenth Century Spain.* Cambridge: Cambridge University Press, 1995.

Elliott, J. K. *The Apocryphal New Testament: A Collection of Apocryphal Christian Literature in an English Translation Based on M. R. James.* Oxford: Clarendon, 2007.

Ellis Davidson, H. R. (writing under H. R. Ellis). *The Road to Hel: A Study of the Conception of the Dead in Old Norse Literature.* Cambridge: Cambridge University Press, 1943.

Fletcher, Richard. *The Barbarian Conversion from Paganism to Christianity.* New York: Henry Holt and Company, Inc, 1998.

Flint, Valerie I. J. *The Rise of Magic.* Princeton, NJ: Princeton University Press, 1991.

———. "The True Author of the *Salonii Commentarii in Parabolas Salomonis et in Ecclesiasten*." *Recherches de théologie ancienne et médiévale* 37 (1970): 174–86.

Foucault, Michel. *Madness and Civilization: A History of Insanity in the Age of Reason.* New York: Vintage, 1988.

Fouracre, Paul, and Richard Gerberding. *Late Merovingian France: History and Hagiography 640–720.* Manchester: Manchester University Press, 1996.

Fouracre, Paul. "'Placita' and the Settlement of Disputes in Later Merovingian Francia." In *The Settlement of Disputes in Early Medieval Europe*, edited by Wendy Davies and Paul Fouracre, 23–43. Cambridge: Cambridge University Press, 1986.

Franchi de' Cavalieri, Pio. "Della furca et della sua sostituzione alla croce nel diritto penale romano." *Nuovo bulletino di archeologia cristiana* 13 (1907): 63–114.

Frank, P. Suso. *Angelikos Bios. Begriffsanalytische und begriffsgeschichtliche Untersuchungen zum "engelgleichen Leben" im frühen Mönchtum.* Vol. 26, Beiträge zur Geschichte des Alten Mönchtums und des Benediktinerordens. Münster, Westfalen, 1964.

Frantzen, Allen J. "The Penitentials Attributed to Bede," *Speculum* 58 (1983): 573–97.

Fredriksen, Paula. "Apocalypse and Redemption in Early Christianity: From John of Patmos to Augustine of Hippo." *Vigiliae Christianae* 45 (1991): 151–83.

Freedman, Paul. "Spices and Late-Medieval European Ideas of Scarcity and Value." *Speculum* 80, no. 4 (2005): 1209–27.

Frexinos, Jacques. *L'art de purger: Histoire générale et anecdotique des laxatifs.* Paris: La Maison Du Dictionnaire, 1997.

Gaehde, Joachim E. "The Pictorial Sources of the Illustrations to the Books of Kings, Proverbs, Judith and Maccabees in the Carolingian Bible of San Paolo Fuori Le Mura in Rome." *Frühmittelalterlicher Studien* 9 (1975): 359–89.

Garnsey, Peter. *Ideas of Slavery from Aristotle to Augustine.* Cambridge: Cambridge University Press, 1996.

Geary, Patrick. "The Uses of Archaeology Sources for Religious and Cultural History." In *Living with the Dead in the Middle Ages*, edited by Patrick Geary, 30–45. Ithaca, NY: Cornell University Press, 1994.

Gerchow, Jan. *Die Gedenküberlieferung der Angelsachsen, mit einem Katalog der "libri vitae" und Necrologien.* Vol. 20, Arbeiten zur Frühmittelalterforschung. Berlin and New York: Walter de Gruyter, 1988.

Glancy, Jennifer A. *Slavery in Early Christianity.* Oxford: Oxford University Press, 2002.

Gnilka, Joachim. *Ist 1 Kor. 3, 10–15 ein Schriftzeugnis für das Fegfeuer? Eine exegetisch-historische Untersuchung.* Düsseldorf: Michael Triltsch Verlag, 1955.

Goffart, Walter. *The Narrators of Barbarian History (A.D. 550–800): Jordanes, Gregory of Tours, Bede and Paul the Deacon.* Notre Dame, IN: University of Notre Dame, 2005.

Gounelle, Rémi. *La descente du Christ aux Enfers: Institutionnalisation d'une croyance.* Paris: Institut d'Études Augustiniennes, 2000.

Grant, Mark. *Dieting for an Emperor: A Translation of Books 1 and 4 of Oribasius' Medical Compilations with an Introduction and Commentary.* Leiden: E. J. Brill, 1997.

Green, Miranda J. "Vessels of Death: Sacred Cauldrons in Archaeology and Myth." *The Antiquaries Journal* 78 (1998): 63–84.

Grey, Cam. "Demoniacs, Dissent, and Disempowerment in the Late Roman West: Some Case Studies from the Hagiographical Literature." *JECS* 13, no. 1 (2005): 39–69.

Griffin, Miriam. "De Beneficiis and Roman Society." *JRS* 93 (2003): 92–113.

Gurevich, Aaron. "Au Moyen Age: Conscience individuelle et image de l'au-delà." *Annales E.S.C.* 37 (1982): 255–75.

———. "Popular and Scholarly Medieval Cultural Traditions: Notes in the Margins of Jacques Le Goff's Book." *JMH* 9 (1983): 71–90.
Harper, James. "John Cassian and Sulpicius Severus." *Church History* 34, no. 4 (1965): 371–80.
Harries, Jill. *Law and Empire in Late Antiquity*. Cambridge: Cambridge University Press, 1999.
Harrill, J. Albert. "Paul and the Slave Self." In *Religion and the Self in Antiquity*, edited by David Brakke, Michael L. Satlow, and Steven Weitzman, 51–69. Bloomington: Indiana University Press, 2005.
Heinzelmann, Martin. *Gregory of Tours: History and Society in the Sixth Century*. Cambridge: Cambridge University Press, 2001.
———. "Une source de base de la littérature hagiographique latine: le receuil de miracles." In *Hagiographie, cultures et sociétés ive-xiie siècles*, 235–59. Paris: Études Augustiniennes, 1981.
Hen, Yitzak. *Culture and Religion in Merovingian Gaul, AD 481–751*. Leiden: E. J. Brill, 1995.
———. "The Structure and Aims of the 'Visio Baronti.'" *JTS* n.s. 47 (1996): 477–97.
———. "Unity in Diversity: The Liturgy of Frankish Gaul before the Carolingians." In *Unity and Diversity in the Church*, edited by R. N. Swanson, 19–30. Studies in Church History 32 (Oxford: Blackwell, 1996).
Henning, J. "Gefangenfesseln in slawischen Siedlungsraum und der europäische Sklavenhandel im 6. bis 12. Jahrhundert." *Germania* 70, no. 2 (1992): 403–26.
Herz, Martin F. *Sacrum commercium; eine begriffsgeschichtliche Studie zur Theologie der römischen Liturgiesprache*. Münchener Theologische Studien, 15. (Munich: Kommissionsverlag K. Zink, 1958).
Hill, Charles E. *Regnum Caelorum: Patterns of Future Hope in the Early Church*. Oxford: Oxford University Press, 1992.
Hillgarth, Jocelyn N. *Christianity and Paganism, 350–750: The Conversion of Western Europe*. Philadelphia: University of Pennsylvania Press, 1986.
———. "Eschatological and Political Concepts in the Seventh Century." In *The Seventh Century: Change and Continuity*, edited by Jacques Fontaine and J. N. Hillgarth, 212–31. Vol. 42, Studies of the Warburg Institute. London: Warburg Institute, 1992.
Himmelfarb, Martha. "Judaism and Hellenism in 2 Maccabees." *Poetics Today* 19, no. 1, (1998): 19–40.
———. *Tours of Hell: An Apocalyptic Form in Jewish and Christian Literature*. Philadelphia: University of Pennsylvania Press, 1983.
Horden, Peregrine. "Responses to Possession and Insanity in the Earlier Byzantine World." *Social History of Medicine* 6, no. 2 (1993): 177–94.
Hughes, Kathleen. "The Celtic Church: Is This a Valid Concept?" *Cambridge Medieval Celtic Studies* 1 (1981): 1–20.
Huntingdon, Richard, and Peter Metcalf, eds. *Celebrations of the Death: The Anthropology of Mortuary Ritual*. Cambridge: Cambridge University Press, 1991.
Hyatte, Reginald. *The Arts of Friendship: The Idealization of Friendship in Medieval and Early Renaissance Literature*. Leiden: E. J. Brill, 1994.

Jay, P. " La purgatoire dans la prédication de saint Césaire d'Arles." *Recherches de théologie ancienne et médiévale* 24 (1957): 5–14.

Jiroušková, Lenka. *Die Visio Pauli. Wege and Wandlungen einer orientalischen Apokryphe im Lateinischen Mittelalter unter Einschluß der alttschechischen und deutschsprachigen Textzeugen.* Leiden: E. J. Brill, 2006.

Jones, C. P. "Stigma: Tattooing and Branding in Graeco-Roman Antiquity." *JRS* 77 (1987): 139–55.

Jones, Christopher A. "The Book of the Liturgy in Anglo-Saxon England." *Speculum* 73, no. 3 (1998): 659–702.

Jussen, Bernhard. "Religious Discourses of the Gift in the Middle Ages: Semantic Evidences (Second to Twelfth Centuries)." In *Negotiating the Gift: Pre-Modern Figurations of Exchange.* Edited by Gadi Algazi, Valentin Groebner ,and Bernhard Jussen, 173–92. Göttingen: Vandenhoeck & Ruprecht, 2003.

Kabir, Ananya Jahanara. *Paradise, Death and Doomsday in Anglo-Saxon Literature.* Cambridge: Cambridge University Press, 2001.

Kartsonis, Anna. *Anastasis: The Making of an Image.* Princeton, NJ: Princeton University Press, 1986.

Kelly, Fergus. *A Guide to Early Irish Law.* Dublin: Dublin Institute for Advanced Studies, 1988.

Kelly, J. N. D. *Jerome: His Life, Writings and Controversies.* Peabody, MA: Hendrickson Publishers, 1988.

Kendall, Calvin B., and Peter S. Wells, eds. *Voyage to the Other World: The Legacy of Sutton Hoo.* Minneapolis: University of Minnesota Press, 1992.

Ker, N. R. "The *Epistola de Obitu Bedae* with Bede's Song, The Hague Manuscript of." *Medium Aevum* 8 (1939): 40–44.

Klawiter, Frederick C. "The Role of Martyrdom and Persecution in Developing the Priestly Authority of Women in Early Christianity: A Case Study of Montanism." *Church History* 49 (1980): 251–61.

Klingshirn, William E. *Caesarius of Arles: The Making of a Christian Community in Late Antique Gaul.* Cambridge: Cambridge University Press, 1994.

Konstan, David. "Problems in the History of Christian Friendship." *JECS* 4, no. 1 (1996): 87–113.

Kotila, Heikki. *Memoria mortuorum: Commemoration of the Departed in Augustine.* Rome: Institutum Patristicum "Augustinianum," 1992.

Kyrtatas, Dimitris J. "Slavery as Progress: Pagan and Christian Views of Slavery as Moral Training." *International Sociology* 10 (1995): 219–34.

Laistner, M. L. W. "The Library of the Venerable Bede." In *The Intellectual Heritage of the Early Middle Ages.* Edited by M. L. W. Laistner, 117–49. Ithaca, NY: Cornell University Press, 1957.

———. *Thought and Letters in Western Europe A.D. 500 to 900.* London: Methuen and Co Ltd, 1957.

Landgraf, Artur. "1 Cor. 3, 10–17 bei den lateinischen Vätern und in der frühscholastik." *Biblica* 5 (1924): 140–72.

Lapidge, Michael, ed. *Archbishop Theodore.* Cambridge: Cambridge University Press, 1995.

———. *The Anglo-Saxon Library.* Oxford: Oxford University Press, 2006.

——— (with Bernhard Bischof). *Biblical Commentaries from the Canterbury School of Theodore and Hadrian*. Cambridge: Cambridge University Press, 1994.

Laux, John. "Two Early Medieval Heretics: An Episode in the Life of St. Boniface." *CHR* 21, no. 1 (1935): 190–95.

Lebecq, S. "Le baptême manqué du roi Radbod." In *Les assises du pouvoir: temps médiévaux, territoires africains*, edited by Odile Redon and Bernard Rosenberger, 141–50. Saint-Denis: Presses universitaires de Vincennes, 1994.

Le Goff, Jacques. *The Birth of Purgatory*. Chicago: University of Chicago Press, 1984.

———. *Your Money or Your Life: Economy and Religion in the Middle Ages*. Translated by Patricia Ranum. New York: Zone, 1990.

———. "The Time of Purgatory (Third to Thirteenth Century)." In *The Medieval Imagination*, edited by Jacques Le Goff, 67–77. Chicago: University of Chicago Press, 1988.

Lemos, T. M. "Shame and Mutilation of Enemies in the Hebrew Bible." *Journal of Biblical Literature* 125 (2006): 225–41.

Levison, Wilhelm. *England and the Continent in the Eighth Century*. Oxford: Clarendon, 1946.

Lewis, Charleton T. and Charles Short, *A Latin Dictionary*. Oxford: Clarendon, 1987.

Lubac, Henri de. *Exégèse médiévale: les quatre sens de l'Écriture*. 2 vols. Paris: Aubier, 1959–64.

Lund, Niels and Ian N. Wood), eds. *People and Places in Northern Europe 500–1600: Essays in Honour of Peter Hayes Sawyer*. Woodbridge, Suffolk: Boydell, 1991.

Lynch, Joseph. *Christianizing Kinship: Ritual Sponsorship in Anglo-Saxon England*. Ithaca, NY: Cornell University Press, 1998.

MacMullen, Ramsey. "Judicial Savagery in the Roman Empire." In *Changes in the Roman Empire: Essays in the Ordinary*, edited by Ramsey McMullen, 67–77. Princeton, NJ: Princeton University Press, 1990.

Marshall, Peter. *Beliefs and the Dead in Reformation England*. Oxford: Oxford University Press, 2002.

———. *Mother Leakey and the Bishop: A Ghost Story*. Oxford: Oxford University Press, 2007.

McCarthy, Joseph M. "The Pastoral Practice of the Sacraments of Cleansing in the Legislation of the Visigothic Church." *Classical Folia* 24 (1970): 177–86.

McCormick, Michael. *The Origins of the European Economy: Communications and Commerce AD 300–900*. Cambridge: Cambridge University Press, 2001.

McCulloh, John M. "From Antiquity to the Middle Ages: Continuity and Change in Papal Relic Policy from the 6th to the 8th Century." In *Pietas: Festschrift für Bernhard Kötting*, edited by Ernest Dassman and Karl Suso Frank, 313–24. Münster, Westfalen: Aschendorff, 1980.

McCune, James. "Rethinking the Pseudo-Eligius Sermon Collection." *EME* 16, no. 4 (2008): 445–76.

McGrath, Robert. "The Martyrdom of the Maccabees." *The Art Bulletin* 47, no. 2 (1965): 257–61.

McGuire, Brian Patrick. *Friendship and Community: The Monastic Experience 350–1250*. Kalamazoo, MI: Cistercian Publications, 1988.

———, "Purgatory, the Communion of Saints, and Medieval Change," *Viator* 20 (1989): 61–84.
McLaughlin, Megan. *Consorting with Saints: Prayer for the Dead in Early Medieval France*. Ithaca, NY: Cornell University Press, 1994.
Melis, M., and Secci, S. "Migraine with Aura and Dental Occlusion: A Case Report." *Journal of the Massachusetts Dental Society* 54, no. 4 (2006): 28–30.
Merkt, Andreas. *Das Fegefeuer: Entstehung und Funktion einer Idee*. Darmstadt: Wissenschaftliche Buchgesellschaft, 2005.
Meyvaert, Paul. "The Enigma of Gregory the Great's *Dialogues*: A Response to Francis Clark." *JEH* 39 (1988): 335–81.
Michel, A. "Purgatoire." *DTC* 13, no. 1 (1936): 1163–1326.
Mitchell, Kathleen. "Saints and Public Christianity in the *Historiae* of Gregory of Tours." In *Religion, Culture and Society in the Early Middle Ages: Studies in Honor of Richard E. Sullivan*, edited by Thomas F. X. Noble and John J. Contreni, 77–94. Kalamazoo, MI: Medieval Institute Publications, 1987.
Moorhead, John. "Bede on the Papacy." *JEH* 60, no. 2 (2009): 217–32.
———. "Thoughts on Some Early Medieval Miracles." In *Byzantine Papers: Proceedings of the First Australian Byzantine Conference, Canberra, 17–19 May 1978*, edited by Elizabeth Jeffreys, Michael Jeffreys, and Ann Moffatt, 1–11. Canberra: Humanities Research Center, Australian National University, 1981.
Moreira, Isabel. *Dreams, Visions and Spiritual Authority in Merovingian Gaul*. Ithaca, NY: Cornell University Press, 2000.
———. "St. Augustine's Three Visions and Three Heavens in Some Early Medieval Florilegia." *Vivarium* 34, no. 1 (1996): 1–14.
———. "Violence, Purification and Mercy in the Late Antique Afterlife." In *Violence in Late Antiquity: Perceptions and Practices*, edited by Harold A. Drake, 147–56. Aldershot: Ashgate Publishing, 2006.
———, and Margaret Toscano, eds. *Hell and Its Afterlife: Historical and Contemporary Perspectives*. Aldershot: Ashgate Publishing, forthcoming.
Niermeyer, J. F. *Mediae Latinitatis lexicon minus*. Leiden: E. J. Brill, 1977.
Ntedika, Joseph. *L'Évolution de la doctrine du purgatoire chez saint Augustin*. Paris: Études Augustiniennes, 1966.
———. *L'Évocation de l'au-delà dans la prière pour les morts: Étude patristique et de liturgie Latines (IVe-VIIIe S)*. Louvain: Editions Nauwelaerts, 1971.
Nugent, Patrick. "Bodily Effluvia and Liturgical Interruption in Medieval Miracle Stories." *History of Religions* 41 (2001): 49–70.
Nussbaum, Martha. *The Therapy of Desire: Theory and Practice in Hellenistic Ethics*. Princeton, NJ: Princeton University Press, 1994.
O'Brien, Elizabeth. "Pagan and Christian Burial in Ireland During the First Millennium AD: Continuity and Change." In *The Early Church in Wales and the West: Recent Work in Early Christian Archaeology, History and Place-Names*, edited by Nancy Edwards and Alan Lane, 130–37. Oxbow Monograph 16 (Oxford: Oxbow, 1992).
O'Brien, Elmer. "The Scriptural Proof for the Existence of Purgatory from 2 Machabees—12:43–45." *Sciences ecclésiastiques* 2 (1949): 80–108.

O'Connell, John P. *The Eschatology of Saint Jerome*. Mundelein, IL: Seminary of St. Mary of the Lake, 1947.

Oliver, Lisi. *The Beginnings of English Law*. Toronto: University of Toronto Press, 2002.

Ó Riain, Pádraig. "Les Vies de saint Fursey: les sources irlandaises." *Revue du Nord* 68, no. 269 (1986): 405–12.

Osborn, Eric F. *The Philosophy of Clement of Alexandria*. Cambridge: Cambridge University Press, 1957.

Osiek, Carolyn. *Shepherd of Hermas: A Commentary on the Shepherd of Hermas*. Minneapolis, MN: Augsberg Fortress, 1999.

Palazzo, Eric. *A History of Liturgical Books from the Beginning to the Thirteenth Century*. English translation by Madeleine Beaumont. Collegeville, MN: Liturgical, 1998.

Paxton, Frederick, *Christianizing Death: The Creation of a Ritual Process in Early Medieval Europe*. Ithaca, NY: Cornell University Press, 1990.

Pearson, Mike Parker. "The Powerful Dead: Archaeological Relationships Between the Living and the Dead." *Cambridge Archaeological Journal* 3, no. 2 (1993): 203–29.

Pelteret, David A. E. *Slavery in Early Mediaeval England from the Reign of Alfred to the Twelfth Century*. Woodbridge, Suffolk: Boydell, 1995.

Pettersen, Alvyn. "Perpetua—Prisoner of Conscience." *Vigiliae Christianae* 41 (1987): 139–53.

Pfaff, Richard W., ed. *The Liturgical Books of Anglo-Saxon England*. Kalamazoo, MI: Medieval Institute Publications, 1995.

Pigeaud, Jackie. *Folie et cures de folie chez les médecins de l'antiquité gréco-romaine: La manie*. Paris: Société d'édition Les Belles Lettres, 1987.

Prévot, Françoise. "Le modèle des Maccabées dans la pastorale gauloise au Ve siècle." *Revue d'Histoire de l'Église de France* 92 (2006): 319–42.

Price, Richard. "Informal Penance in Early Medieval Christendom." *Studies in Church History* 40 (2004): 29–38.

Prinz, Friedrich. *Frühes Mönchtum im Frankenreich. Kultur und Gesellschaft in Gallien, den Rheinlanden und Bayern am Beispiel der monastichen Entwicklung (4. bis 8. Jahrhundert)*. Darmstadt: Wissenschaftliche Buchgesellschaft, 1988.

Rabinowitz, Celia E. "Personal and Cosmic Salvation in Origen," *Vigiliae Christianae* 38 (1984): 319–29.

Rapp, Claudia. *Holy Bishops in Late Antiquity: The Nature of Christian Leadership in an Age of Transition*. Berkeley: University of California Press, 2005.

Rebillard, Éric. *In Hora Mortis: Évolution de la pastorale chrétienne de la mort au IVe et Ve siècles dans l'occident Latin*. Palais Farnèse: École Français de Rome, 1994.

Richardson, Cyril C. "The Condemnation of Origen." *Church History* 6 (1937): 50–64.

Riou, Yves-Francois. "Un fragment d'un manuscrit disparu d'Oribase, C.L.A. 116 (Vatican, Urb. Lat. 293, F. 95–6, viiie siècle)," *Scriptorium* 33, no. 2 (1979): 235–37.

Roberts, Michael. "The Last Epic of Antiquity: Generic Continuity and Innovation in the *Vita Sancti Martini* of Venantius Fortunatus." *Transactions of the American Philological Association* 131 (2001): 257–85.

Rollason, David. *Saints and Relics in Anglo-Saxon England*. Oxford: Blackwell, 1989.

Rosenwein, Barbara H. *Emotional Communities in the Early Middle Ages*. Ithaca, NY: Cornell University Press, 2006.

Rouselle, Aline. *Croire et guérir: la foi en Gaule dans l'antiquité tardive*. Paris: Librairie Arthème Fayard, 1990.

———. "Du sanctuaire au thaumaturge: la guérison en Gaule au IVe siècle." *Annales E. S. C.* 31, no. 6 (1976): 1085–1107.

Russell, James C. *The Germanization of Early Medieval Christianity: A Sociohistorical Approach to Religious Transformation*. Oxford: Oxford University Press, 1994.

Salisbury, Joyce E. *Perpetua's Passion: The Death and Memory of a Young Roman Woman*. New York: Routledge, 1997.

Saller, Richard P. "The Hierarchical Household in Roman Society: A Study of Domestic Slavery." In *Serfdom and Slavery: Studies in Legal Bondage*, edited by M. L. Bush, 112–29. London: Longman, 1996.

———. "Whips and Words: Discipline and Punishment in the Roman Household." In *Patriarchy, Property and Death in the Roman Family*, edited by Saller, 133–53. Cambridge: Cambridge University Press, 1994.

Savigni, Raffaele. "La parabola della zizzania (Mt 13, 24–30 e 36–43) nei commenti biblici altomedievali (secc. VI–X)," *Christianesimo nella storia* 26, no. 1 (2005): 189–223.

Schäferdiek, Knut, ed. Kirchengeschichte als Missionsgeschchte, 2, 1: *Die Kirche des früheren Mittelalters*. Münster: Kaiser, 1978.

———. "The Irish Mission of the Seventh Century; Historical Fact or Historiographical Fiction?" In *The End of Strife*, edited by David Loades, 139–54. Edinburgh: T & T Clark, 1984.

Schmitt, Jean-Claude. *Ghosts in the Middle Ages: The Living and Dead in Medieval Society*. Chicago: University of Chicago Press, 1998.

Segal, Alan F. *Life After Death: A History of the Afterlife in Western Religion*. New York: Doubleday, 1989.

Shaw, Brent. "The Passion of Perpetua." *Past and Present* 139 (1993): 3–45.

Shaw, Theresa M. *The Burden of the Flesh: Fasting and Sexuality in Early Christianity*. Minneapolis: Fortress, 1998.

Sicard, Damien. *La liturgie de la mort dans l'église latine des origins à la reforme carolingienne*. Münster Westfalen: Aschendorff, 1978.

Silber, Ilana F. "Gift-giving in the Great Traditions: The Case of Donations to Monasteries in the Medieval West." *Archives européennes de sociologie* 36 (1995): 209–43.

Silverstein, Theodore. *Visio Sancti Pauli: The History of the Apocalypse in Latin, Together with Nine Texts*. London: Christophers, 1935.

Sims-Williams, Patrick. *Religion and Literature in Western England, 600–800*. Cambridge: Cambridge University Press, 1990.

———. "The Visionary Celt: The Construction of an Ethnic Preconception." *Cambridge Medieval Celtic Studies* 11 (1986): 71–96.

Sladden, John Cyril. *Boniface of Devon, Apostle of Germany*. Exeter: Paternoster, 1980.

Smith, Julia M. H. *Europe After Rome: A New Cultural History 500–100*. Oxford: Oxford University Press, 2005.

Smyth, Marina. "The Origins of Purgatory Through the Lens of Seventh-Century Irish Eschatology." *Traditio* 58 (2003): 91–132.

Southern, R. W. "Between Heaven and Hell." *Times Literary Supplement* (June 18, 1982): 651–52.

Stancliffe, Clare E. "The Miracle Stories in Seventh-century Irish Saints' Lives." In *The Seventh Century. Change and Continuity*, edited by Jacques Fontaine and J. N. Hillgarth, 87–115. London: Warburg Institute, 1992.

———. *St. Martin and His Hagiographer: History and Miracle in Sulpicius Severus*. Oxford: Clarendon, 1983.

Stoclet, Alain J. "*Consilia humana, ops divina, superstitio*: Seeking Succor and Solace in Times of Plague, with Particular Reference to Gaul in the Early Middle Ages." In *Plague and the End of Antiquity: The Pandemic of 541–750*, edited by Lester K. Little, 135–49. Cambridge: Cambridge University Press, 2007.

Straw, Carole. "Purity and Death." In *Gregory the Great: A Symposium*, edited by John C. Cavadini, 16–37. Notre Dame, IL: University of Notre Dame Press, 1995.

———. "Martyrdom and Christian Identity: Gregory the Great, Augustine, and Tradition." In *The Limits of Ancient Christianity: Essays on Late Antique Thought and Culture in Honor of R. A. Markus*, edited by William E. Klingshirn andMark Vessey, 250–66. Ann Arbor: University of Michigan Press, 1999.

Sundberg, Albert C. "The Old Testament of the Early Church (A Study in Canon)." *The Harvard Theological Review* 51 (1958): 205–26.

Thacker, Alan. "Bede's Ideal of Reform." In *Ideal and Reality in Frankish and Anglo-Saxon Society*, edited by Patrick Wormald, Donald Bullough, and Roger Collins, 130–53. Oxford: Blackwell, 1983.

Thompson, F. Hugh. *The Archaeology of Greek and Roman Slavery*. London: Gerald Duckworth, 2003.

Trumbower, Jeffrey A. *Rescue for the Dead: The Posthumous Salvation of Non-Christians in Early Christianity*. Oxford: Oxford University Press, 2001.

Uhalde, Kevin. *Expectations of Justice in the Age of Augustine*. Philadelphia: University of Pennsylvania Press, 2007.

Vacandard, E. "Les homélies attribuées à saint Eloi." *Revue des questions historiques* 64, no. 2 (1898): 471–80.

Van Dam, Raymond. "Paulinus of Périgueux and Perpetuus of Tours." *Francia* 14 (1986): 567–73.

———. *Saints and Their Miracles in Late Antique Gaul*. Princeton, NJ: Princeton University Press, 1993.

Van der Walt, A. G. P. "Reflections of the Benedictine Rule in Bede's Homiliary." *Journal of Ecclesiastical History* 37 (1986): 367–76.

Vessey, Mark. "*Opus Imperfectum*: Augustine and His Readers, 426–435 A.D." *Vigiliae Christianae* 53, no. 3 (1988): 264–85.

Vogel, Cyril. *Les "libri paenitentiales."* Vol. 27, Typologie des sources. Turnhout: Brepols, 1978.

von Balthasar, Hans Urs. *Origen: Spirit and Fire: A Thematic Anthology of His Writing*. Washington, DC: Catholic University of America Press, 1984.

von Franz, M. L. "Die Passio Perpetuae: Versuch einer psychologischen Deutung." In *Aion: Untersuchungen zur Symbolgeschichte, mit einem Beitrag von Marie-Louise von Franz*, edited by Carl Gustav Jung, 387–496. Zurich: Rascher, 1951.

von Padberg, Lutz E. *Mission und Christianisierung: Formen und Folgen bei Angelsachsen und Franken im 7. und 8. Jahrhundert.* Stuttgart: F. Steiner, 1995.

Vovelle, Michel. *Les âmes du purgatoire ou le travail du deuil.* Paris: Éditions Gallimard, 1996.

Warren, F. E. *The Liturgy and Ritual of the Celtic Church* (1881). Edited by Jane Stevenson. Woodbridge, Suffolk: Boydell, 1987.

Wickham, Chris. *Framing the Early Middle Ages: Europe and the Mediterranean, 400–800.* Oxford: Oxford University Press, 2005.

Williams, Howard. "Monuments and the Past in Early Anglo-Saxon England." *World Archaeology* 30 (1998): 90–108.

Wood, Ian N. "Disputes in the Late Fifth- and Sixth-Century Gaul: Some Problems." In *The Settlement of Disputes in Early Medieval Europe*, edited by Wendy Davies and Paul Fouracre, 7–22. Cambridge: Cambridge University Press, 1986.

———. "The Franks and Sutton Hoo." In *People and Places in Northern Europe 500–1600*, edited by I. N. Wood and N. Lund, 1–14. Woodbridge, Suffolk: Boydell, 1991.

———. "The Marvellous in Irish and Continental Saints' Lives of the Merovingian Period." In *Columbanus and Merovingian Monasticism*, edited by H. B. Clarke and Mary Brennan, 91–103, British Archaeological Reports, International Series 113 (Oxford, British Archaeological Reports, 1981).

———. *The Merovingian North Sea.* Alingsås: Viktoria Bokförlag, 1983.

———. "The Mission of Augustine of Canterbury to the English." *Speculum* 69 (1994): 1–17.

———. *The Missionary Life: Saints and the Evangelisation of Europe 400–1050.* New York: Longman, 2001.

———. "Pagan Religions and Superstitions East of the Rhine from the Fifth to the Ninth Century." In *After Empire: Towards an Ethnology of Europe's Barbarians*, edited by G. Ausenda, 253–68. Woodbridge, Suffolk: Boydell, 1995.

——— (with Neils Lund), ed. *People and Places in Northern Europe 500–1600: Essays in Honour of Peter Hayes Sawyer.* Woodbridge, Suffolk: Boydell, 1991.

———. "Saint-Wandrille and Its Historiography." In *Church and Chronicle in the Middle Ages: Essays Presented to John Taylor*, edited by I. N. Wood and G. A. Loud, 1–14. London: Hambledon, 1991.

Wormald, Patrick. "Bede and Benedict Biscop." In *The Times of Bede: Studies in Early English Christian Society and Its Historian*, edited by Patrick Wormald and Stephen Baxter. Malden, MA: Blackwell, 2006.

———. *The Making of English Law: King Alfred to the Twelfth Century.* Oxford: Blackwell, 1999.

Wright, Thomas. *St. Patrick's Purgatory: An Essay on the Legends of Purgatory, Hell and Paradise Current During the Middle Ages.* London: John Russell Smith, 1844.

Zaleski, Carol. *Otherworld Journeys: Accounts of Near-Death Experience in Medieval and Modern Times.* Oxford: Oxford University Press, 1987.

Index

1 Corinthians 3:11–15, 5, 18–20, 23, 29, 83, 87, 95, 101, 139, 210
2 Maccabees, 18, 20–2
    Maccabean mother and martyrs, 22
Aaron, 76, 207
Abraham, bosom of, 28, 44, 83
Acca of Hexham, 161, 166, 168, 172
Acherusian lake, 150
Aethelbald of Mercia, king, 131, 132, 255 n.75
Alchfrid, anchorite, 186
Alcuin of York, 176
Aldfrid, king, 157
Aldhelm of Malmesbury, 128
almsgiving, 17, 82–3, 87, 103, 107, 122, 159, 166, 189, 191
Althoff, Gerd, 267
Amat, Jacqueline, 219
Ambrose of Milan, 32, 46, 103, 107, 242 n. 60
    On Death as a Good, 32
    On Repentance, 103–5
    on intercession, 106
Ambrosiaster, 31
angels, 120–4, 130, 149, 150
Angenendt, Arnold, 11, 215, 247, 268
annihilation, 260 n. 10
Apocalypse of John, 193
Apocalypse of Peter, 51–3, 57, 76–7
    universalism of, 77

Arianism, 71, 194
Ariès, Philippe, 245
ascetic literature, 136–7, 145
Ashbrook Harvey, Susan, 268
Atwell, Robert R., 93, 221, 240, 241, 242, 243
Audisio, Gabriel, 214
Augustine of Canterbury, 129, 191
Augustine of Hippo, 7, 16–7, 29, 47, 49, 56, 81, 85–6, 93, 95–8, 101, 106, 109, 128, 145, 160, 164, 186, 189, 190, 195, 209
    De cura pro mortuis gerenda, 35
    City of God, 33–4, 60
    Enchiridion, 33–6, 98, 112, 154, 168
    'misericordes,' 33, 143–4, 189
    on prayer for the dead, 35
    on purgatorial fire, 2, 11, 19, 32–37, 124, 151, 154
    original sin, 32, 42, 48, 84
Ausenda, G., 271

Balthild, queen, 117
baptism, 82, 98, 101–2, 126, 180–1, 189–1
barbarian law, 8, 13, 210 (*see also* law, Germanic)
barbarian origin theory, 8, 193–205, 210

Bartlett, Robert, 276, 277
Basil of Caesarea, 135, 195
Bauckham, Richard, 237, 257, 259
Beck, Henry J., 262
Becker, Ernest J., 11, 216
Bede, the Venerable, 3, 5, 8, 11–12, 16–7, 22–3, 28–9, 81, 93, 95, 97, 99, 102, 106, 112, 121, 129–30, 132, 142, 145, 147–9, 152–176, 184–5, 187–8, 195, 203, 209–11
  Commentary on Proverbs, 11, 156–7, 160, 161–6, 168, 187
  Commentary on Samuel, 162
  Ecclesiastical History, 11, 115, 129, 148, 157, 160, 168, 176
  Homilies, 11, 17, 156–7, 159–61, 168, 187, 210
  On Isaiah, 161–6, 168
  Vision of Drythelm, 11, 29, 100, 111–12, 127, 131–2, 147, 152–7, 165–6, 176
  definition of purgatory, 16–8, 159–61
  epitome of *Vision of Fursey*, 129–30
  on eternity of hell, 163–6
  on extended purgation, 112, 154–5, 210
  on intercession, 16–7, 20, 93, 165
  theology of purgatory, 159–66
  on *Vision of Fursey*, 121, 127, 149
Benedict Biscop, 175
Benedict of Nursia, 128
Beoanus, 117–8, 121–2, 124, 130
Bernstein, Alan E., 10, 214, 245, 255, 260
Berschin, Walter, 248, 254
Bieler, Ludwig, 252, 257, 258
Bigotian penitential, see penitentials
Bischoff, Bernhard, 174, 269
Bitel, Lisa, 253
Blair, Peter Hunter, 252, 259
Blandina, martyr, 56
Bobbio Missal, 111, 123
Bollandus, Johannes, 249
Bolton, W. F., 263
Boniface (Wynfrid) of Mainz, 3, 5, 61, 130, 147–52, 157, 171–2, 176, 178, 184, 186–9
  Vision of the Monk of Wenlock (= Boniface, Letter 10), 72, 131, 138, 149–53, 155–8, 178, 187–8
Book of Cerne, 111
books of life, 109, 173, 178, 192
bosom of Abraham, see Abraham, bosom of

Bradley, Keith R., 52, 58, 59, 223, 225, 226, 228, 229
Bredero, Adriaan H., 214
Bremmer, Jan N., 25, 27, 57, 218, 219, 225, 226, 228, 266
bridge imagery, 150–1
  appropriated for purgatory, 151
Brown, George Hardin, 259, 266
Brown, Michelle, 261
Brown, Peter, 9, 10, 12, 113, 114, 119, 125, 129, 136, 142, 143, 196, 214, 215, 229, 241, 247, 249, 250, 253, 258, 261, 271, 275
Bugga, 172
burial practices, 107–9, 121–2, 183–5, 191
  burial *ad sanctos*, 107–8, 122, 247 n. 145, 251 n. 35
  burial with grave goods, 108, 183–5
Butler, Rex D., 219
Bynum, Carolyn Walker, 229

Caesarius of Arles, 61, 81–5, 93, 95, 98, 102, 128, 151, 178, 186, 187, 196
  rule for nuns, 110
Caner, Daniel, 252, 267, 268
Carozzi, Claude, 9, 10, 19, 114, 127, 128, 129, 132, 133, 150, 156, 188, 196, 201, 214, 215, 226, 248, 249, 250, 253, 254, 255, 256, 260, 275, 276
Carroll, Sister Mary M. Thomas Aquinas, 215, 262, 263, 270
cauldron, 204–5
Cavallo, Guglielmo, 269
celestial city of Jerusalem, 150
Cellanus, abbot of Péronne, 128
Ceolla Snoding, count, 131–2, 203
Ceowulf, king, 157, 168
chains, fetters, shackles, 50, 53, 55, 61, 65, 92, 103, 227 n. 75
  neck chains, 53
Charlemagne, 192
Charles Martel, 180, 191
Chase, Alston Hurd, 234
Chaunu, Pierre, 245
Chilperic I, king, 204
Christian Sibylline Oracles, 24, 51–2
Ciccarese, Maria Pia, 10, 215, 225, 249, 250
Cicero, 166
Clark, Elizabeth A., 221, 263
Clark, Francis, 240, 241

Clarke, Gillian, 230
Clemens, priest, 189
Clement of Alexandria, 24, 27–8, 40, 208
Clovis II, king, 117
Cochrane, William, 216
Coifi, high priest, 185
Coleman, K. M., 228, 229
Coleridge, H. J., 216
Colgrave, Bertram, 270
Columbanus, 95, 117, 119
confession, 103
Contreni, John J., 252
correction, corporeal, 41, 48
  through discipline, 40, 41, 45
  through education, 40, 41, 47
  through self-discipline, 41
Council of Ancyra (314), 102
Council of Florence (1439), 213 n.3
Council of Lyons I (1245), 5
Council of Lyons II (1274), 5
Council of Orange (529), 81
Council of Trent (1563), 213 n.3
Cox-Miller, Patricia, 219
Cramer, Peter, 259
criminals, 50–1, 54, 56, 61 (see also slaves)
Cubbitt, Catherine, 270
Cuniberga, abbess, 170
Curta, Florin, 171, 267, 268
Cuthberga, queen, 131
Cuthbert of Lindisfarne, 172
Cuthbert of Wearmouth-Jarrow, *De obitu Bedae*, 169–71
Cyprian, 46, 105, 195

Dagens, Claude, 240, 241
Daley, Brian E., 218, 220
Daniel of Winchester, 131, 187
Dante, 205
De Bruyne, Theodore, 46, 224
Dekkers, Eligius, 222
demoniacs, 65–66
  exorcism as purgation, 72, 233 n. 26
demons, 71–2, 97, 108, 120–4, 128, 130, 132, 149, 234 n. 40, 234 n. 47
  and disease, 237 n. 63
De Nie, Giselle, 238
descensus Christi, 23
Deurechild, nun, 106
Deuteronomy, 121
devil, the, 126, 140

De Vogüé, Adalbert, 92, 240, 241, 242
dialogue, use of, 120–1
Diaz y Diaz, Manuel, 244
Dick, John, 216, 275
Dierkens, Alain, 249
Dinocrates, 25–7
Dinzelbacher, Peter, 245
disease, medical, 66
  spiritual, 66 (see also leprosy)
Dobbie, Eliott van Kirk, 268
Dölger, F. J., 27, 219
Dooley, Kate, 198, 256, 257, 275
Drake, Harold, 213
Dronke, Peter, 27, 219
Du Moulin, P., 195, 214, 220, 274
Dumville, David N., 247, 270
Dunn, Marilyn, 10, 114, 119, 129, 134, 135, 136, 199, 200, 215, 240, 248, 250, 256
Duval, Y., 247, 251

Eadbald of Kent, 171
Eadburga, abbess, 149, 157–58
Earcongota, nun, 171–2
Ecclesiastes, 86
Ecclesiasticus (Sirach), 121, 187
Eddius Stephanus, 172
education
Edwards, Graham Robert, 214, 261
Edwin of Northumbria, 184–5
Effros, Bonnie, 10, 215, 247, 251, 263, 272, 273, 274
Egbert of York, 168
Eire, Carlos, 214
Eligius of Noyon, 123, 127, 186–8
  de supremo iudicio, 188, 243 n. 81
  pseudo-Eligius, 97, 243 n. 81
Elliott, J. K. 225, 226
Ellis Davidson, H. R., 272
Elysian Fields, 25
Emerton, Ephraim, 259. 270, 274
epitaphs, 108
epitomes and florilegia, 95–6
Erchinoald, mayor of Neustria, 116, 123, 127
Exodus, 140

Faremoutiers, 106, 126
fasting, 103, 107, 159, 166
fire, 52, 53
  fiery furnace, 62
  river of, 52, 53, 207

fire (continued)
  valley of, 62
  wall of, 62, 121
Fisher Drew, Katherine, 276
Fletcher, Richard, 271, 274
Flint, Valerie I. J., 254, 265
Foillan, 116
Foley, W. Trent, 261, 264
Foucault, Michel, 235, 237
Fouracre, Paul, 249, 253, 275, 276
Fragmentary Vision of 757, see *Vision of 757*
Franchi de' Cavalieri, Pio, 227
Frank, P. Suso, 230
Frantzen, Allen J., 258
Fredriksen, Paula, 274
Freedman, Paul, 268
Frexinos, Jacques, 230
friends, 'amici fideli,' 159, 161, 166, 168, 172
friendship, 166–73
Fulke, William, 11, 215
funerary liturgy, 107–9
furnace. *See* fire
Fursey, 115, 117, 118

Gaehde, Joachim E., 218
Gamer, Helena M., 251, 254, 258
Garnsey, Peter, 223
Geary, Patrick, 271, 272, 274
Gehenna, 40 (*see also* hell)
Gerberding, Richard, 249, 253
Gerchow, Jan, 269
Germanic Council of 742, 128
Germanic law codes. *See* law, Germanic
Germanus of Capua, 87–8
gifts, accepted from sinners, 118, 121–2, 130
  and gift-giving, 166–73, 192
Glancy, Jennifer A., 49, 50, 223, 224, 225, 228, 229
Gnilka, Joachim, 216, 217
Goffart, Walter, 259, 269
good works, 102, 160–1
Gounelle, Rémi, 218
'grace for grace', 160
Grant, Mark, 231
Green, Miranda J., 277
Gregory II, pope, 187
Gregory III, pope, 61
Gregory of Nyssa, 37, 174

Gregory of Tours, 22, 61, 65–80, 145, 204
  fears for own salvation, 76–9, 106, 237 n. 72
  Martin's miracles, 68–80
  medical crises, 68, 73, 235 n. 51, 236 n. 52
  purges, 67–70
Gregory the Great, 7, 8, 11, 16, 18, 43, 81, 85–97, 129, 148, 164–5, 177, 186, 191, 196, 209
  Dialogues, 10, 17, 85–94, 96, 98, 100, 115, 126, 131, 149–51, 159, 163, 195
  Homilies, 85
  Moralia in Job, 85, 92, 98
Grey, Cam, 233
Griffin, Miriam, 266
Gurevich, Aaron, 213, 214, 215, 244, 245, 260

Hadrian, abbot, 174–5
Haemgils, hermit, 157
Harper, James, 231
Harries, Jill, 56, 58, 60, 226, 228, 229
Harrill, J. Albert, 223
health, 66–7
  and salvation, 74, 79–80
heaven, upper and lower, 149, 153–7, see also paradise, celestial city
Hector of Marseilles, 253 n. 44
Heinzelmann, Martin, 232, 235, 238
hell, eternity of, 163–6, 196 (*see also* torment)
  pits of hell, 72, 131
  torture of sinners in, 49–62
  upper and lower hell, 149–50, 153–6
hellebore, 67, 231 n. 14
hell-fire, 30
Hen, Yitzak, 247, 250, 252, 253
Henning, J., 227
Herefrith, 172
Herz, Martin F., 268
Hildelida, abbess, 149
Hilhorst, Anthony, 223, 225, 226
Hill, Charles E., 218, 222
Hillgarth, Jocelyn N., 10, 96, 215, 240, 243, 248, 250
Himmelfarb, Martha, 217, 226, 227
Hincmar of Rheims, 176
Holder, Arthur G., 261, 264
Horden, Peregrine, 235
Houben, Hubert, 270

Hughes, Kathleen, 253
Huntingdon, Richard, 272
Hurst, David, 262, 263
Hyatte, Reginald, 266
Hygelac, priest, 186

immediate, individual judgement, 86, 155
intercession, 16–7, 20–1, 106–7, 122, 131, 142, 157, 166, 173, 189
  personal, individual, 89, 90, 106
  prayers of, 88, 104, 106, 142
  'quantifiable,' 115
  of saints, 61, 77–9
Irenaeus of Lyons, 25, 40
Irish law, *see* law, Irish
Irish sources for purgatory, 113–145
  'origins,' 135, 142–4
Isaiah, book of, 86, 162
Isaiah, prophet, 119, 207
Isidore of Seville, 81, 95–6, 112, 154, 165
Isis, 185

Jason of Cyrene, 21
Jay, P., 239
Jeremiah, 106
Jerome, 19, 32–3, 106, 139, 162, 164, 209
Jiroušková, Lenka, 10, 215, 226, 245
John Cassian, 104, 105, 128, 139, 141, 166, 169
John Scottus Eriugena, 210
John the Baptist, festival of, 129
Jonas, 180, 183
Jones, C. P., 228
Julian of Brioude, 69, 74
Julian of Toledo, *Prognosticon*, 82, 96, 165
Julianus Pomerius, 3, 61, 76, 81–2, 96, 105, 138
  De anima, 82, 96
  De vita contemplativa, 82
Jussen, Bernhard, 171, 268
just, the, 94, 102, 136
justice, as purgative, 200–5
Justus, 90, 94

Kabir, Ananya Jahanara, 261
Kartsonis, Anna, 270
Kelly, Fergus, 221, 264, 275
Kelly, J. N. D., 221, 264
Kendall, Calvin B., 272
Ker, N. R., 268

Klawiter, Frederick C., 26, 219
Klingshirn, William E., 239
Konstan, David, 266, 267
Kotila, Heikki, 221, 222
Krusch, Bruno, 249, 252, 253
Kyrtatas, Dimitris J., 223

Lactantius, 24, 46
Lagny-sur-Marne, 116
Laistner, M. L. W., 265
Landgraf, Artur, 215, 217
Lapidge, Michael, 174, 248, 264, 266, 269, 270
Laurentius, pope, 87–8.
Laux, John, 274
law, Germanic codes, 129, 197–205
law, Irish, 135–6, 199
law, Roman 137, 197–200
  privilege and status under, 57–60
  legal notions of justice, 57–60
  criticisms of, 58
Le Goff, Jacques, 8, 9, 12, 114, 156, 196, 214, 215, 216, 217, 220, 243, 245, 248, 253, 261, 262, 266, 275
Lebecq, S. 271, 272
Lemos, Tracy M., 55, 228
leprosy, spiritual, 71, 73, 77, 236 n. 52
Lérins, 137, 175
Levison, Wilhelm, 250, 271, 273, 276
Leviticus, 139
Lieberman, Felix, 276
Lindisfarne, 157
Lubac, Henri de, 220, 265
Lull, 61, 130, 170, 186, 188
Lund, Niels, 273
Lynch, Joseph, 276

MacMullen, Ramsey, 228
Malachi, 18
  fiery furnace, 95
  refiner's fire, 139
  purification of priests, 142
Marmoutier, 72
Marshall, Peter, 213, 214, 217
Martin, Lawrence T., 262, 263
Martin of Braga, 71
Martin of Tours, 65, 74, 106, 128, 190
  dust of, 70–71, 73, 236 n. 54, 236 n. 56
  purging at shrines of, 67–80
  tomb of, 70–3

INDEX

martyrs, cult of, 64-5, 79
mass, offering of the, 17, 23, 82, 89, 91-93, 106-7, 159, 165, 169-72, 191
Matthew, 22, 103
McCarthy, Joseph M., 259
McCormick, Michael, 225, 227, 229, 272
McCulloh, John M., 247
McCune, James, 253
McGrath, Robert, 218
McGuire, Brian Patrick, 167-9, 214, 267, 268
McLaughlin, Megan, 243
McNeill, John T., 251, 254, 258
Meldanus, 117-8, 121, 124, 130
Melis, M., 236
Melrose, 157
Merkt, Andreas, 27, 219
Metcalf, Peter, 272
Meyvaert, Paul, 240, 241, 243, 264
Michael, archangel, 123, 150
Michel, A., 216, 217, 220, 239
Migne, J.-P., 252
Mitchell, Kathleen, 237
monastic ethos, 136-7
    literature. See ascetic literature
    rules, 200 (see also rule of)
Moorhead, John, 216, 233, 234, 259
Moreira, Isabel, 232, 238, 244, 250, 260, 261, 277
Moses, 106
mutilation, 55

niedfyr, 128-9, 196
Ntedika, Joseph, 33, 96, 220, 221, 222, 243, 247, 251, 261
Nugent, Patrick, 233
Nussbaum, Martha, 230

Ó Riain, Pádraig, 249
O'Brien, Elizabeth, 251
O'Brien, Elmer, 217
O'Connell, John P., 221
Oliver, Lisi, 267, 275, 276
ordeal, 210-5
ordinary Christians, 64-5, 98
Origen, 27-32, 34, 37, 39-40, 42, 84, 92, 128, 140, 155, 160, 162-5, 174-5, 189, 207-11
    condemnation of, 30, 92, 174-5, 189-90, 209

on universal salvation, 162-5, 189, 211
Origenism, 16, 81, 92, 123, 144, 154, 162-5, 189
    anti-Origenism, 33, 106, 164-5, 174-5
Osborn, Eric F., 28, 220
Osiek, Carolyn, 244
Oswy, king, 61

Pachomius, 42
pain, 40, 196
    absence of, 151
    as purificatory, 63, 151-2, 189, 207-8
Palazzo, Eric, 247
paradise, meadow, 150, 153-7
Paschasius, 87-8, 93
Passion of Perpetua and Felicity, 25, 26, 31, 56, 207
Patrick of Armagh, 137
Paulinus of Pella, 193
Paulinus of Périgueux, 71-2, 77
Paulinus of York and Rochester, 185
Paxton, Frederick, 11, 239, 247, 248, 254
Pearson, Mike Parker, 272
Pelagius, 32-33, 124, 160
    semi-Pelagianism, 81
Pelteret, David A. E., 224, 229
penance, 19, 41, 76, 82, 84, 101-6, 119-21, 125-7, 137-40, 198, 202
    commutation of, 126
    tariffed, 105, 114-5, 119, 134-9, 199-200
    post-mortem penance, debate over, see post-mortem penance
    repeatable, 105, 126
    as remedy, 104-5 see also, repentance
penitentials, 105, 123, 129, 135-42, 145, 197-200, 202
    Bigotian, 124, 139-42
    of Cummean, 124, 137
    of Finnian, 124, 126
Péronne, 115-18, 123, 127-30
    cult of Fursey at, 116
Peter the Deacon, 86, 95
    Sententiae, 95
Peter, Saint, 120, 121
Pettersen, Alvyn, 219
Picard, J. C., 247, 251
Pierre du Moulin, 195
Pigeaud, Jackie, 235
Pippin II, king, 176, 180
Pirmin of Reichenau, 186

placita, 197
Plotinus, 31
post-mortem penance, debate over, 115–125
　unavailability of, 105, 122–5, 129, 132–4, 136, 244 n. 87, 252 n. 43
Porphyry, 31
prayer, four types of, 103–4
prayer for the dead, 17, 35, 96–7, 99, 109–111, 166, 169, 173, 189
Prévot, Françoise, 217
Price, Richard, 105, 135, 245, 246, 257
Prinz, Friedrich, 249, 271
Prudentius, 101, 109
Psalms, 86–87, 106–07
　use in funerary liturgy, 107, 109–11
　psalm 50, 110
　purification in, 107
　pseudo-Eligius. *See* Eligius
punishment, 39–62
　chastisement, 150–1
　and humiliation, 56
　and nudity, 55, 56
　and purification, 23
purgation, metaphors of, 245 n. 109
　as 'baptism of fire,' 128
　cosmic, 23, 95, 164
　through disease, fever, 19, 42
　through exorcism, see demoniacs
　through fire, 19, 83, 108 (*see also* fire)
　through fire and ice, 153, 156
　through martyrdom, 42, 48, 64
　through suffering, 39, 42, 90
purgatory, as cultural metaphor, 13
　definition of, in Bede, 16–8, 159–61
　images of. *See* fire, and purgation, metaphors of.
　Irish sources and origin, see Irish sources
　as lower heaven, 149, 153–7
　as upper hell, 149–50, 153–6
　'proofs,' 18, 24
　use of term in this book, 12
purges, medical, 231 n. 14, 232 n. 19, 232 n. 23, 233 n.32, 236 n. 57
　violence of, 71

Quodvultdeus, 193

Rabinowitz, Celia E., 220
Rackham, Oliver, 249

Radbod of Frisia, 180–81, 183, 189, 191
rainbow, 131–2
Raphael, archangel, 120
Rapp, Claudia, 245
Rebillard, Éric, 10, 215, 254, 259
reformers, Catholic, 8
reformers, Protestant, 6–8, 20, 32, 194
repentance, 86, 102
　on death-bed, 112
resurrection, corporeal, 66, 93, 108
retribution, 43, 60
Richardson, Cyril, 220
Riou, Yves-François, 233
Roberts, Michael, 234
Rollason, David, 251
Roman law, *see* law, Roman
Romanus of Condat, 128
Rosenwein, Barbara H., 267
Rouche, Michel, 249
Rouselle, Aline, 230, 231, 232, 235
Rufinus, 33, 162, 164
Rule of Benedict, 117, 147, 167, 170
Rule of Columbanus, 117
Rule for Nuns. *See* Caesarius
Russell, James C., 182, 272

sacramentaries, 110
Saint-Wandrille, monastery of, 180
Salisbury, Joyce E., 219
Saller, Richard P., 46, 224
Salvian of Marseilles, 137, 193
Salvius of Albi, 124
Satan, see Devil, the
Savigni, Rafaele, 257
Schäferdiek, Knut, 249, 255, 271
Schmitt, Jean-Claude, 213
'schola animarum,' 29, 155, 161, 210
Secci, S., 236
Segal, Alan F., 216
Shaw, Brent, 219, 228
Shaw, Teresa, 229, 230
Shepherd of Hermas, 99, 105
shrines of saints, 67
Sicard, Damien, 11, 110, 111, 239, 247, 248, 261
Silber, Ilana F., 268
Silverstein, Theodore, 133, 134, 223, 226, 227, 256, 276
Sims-Williams, Patrick, 244, 253, 254, 260, 261

sins, classification of, 97, 128, 165
  'light,' 82–4, 93, 105, 150
  'heavy,' 82, 87, 98, 128
  through ignorance not malice, 88
Sladden, John Cyril, 259
slavery as metaphor for sin, 44–5
slave trade, 53–4, 61, 229 n. 118
slaves, 43–4
  analogous to the damned, 50–7
  detention of, prisons, 54
  ordination of, 48
  release and manumission of, 65, 75
  ransoming of, 61
  and shackles, see chains
  as symbols of corporeality, 49–57, 63
  torture of, 50–2, 56–7, 59
Smith, Julia M. H., 267
Smyth, Marina, 10, 244
sons and slaves metaphor, 43–9
  sons as God's slaves, 44–5
Southern, R. W., 214
Spes, abbot, 43
Stancliffe, Clare E., 125, 235, 253
Stapleton, Thomas, 11
Stephanus, deacon, 84
Stoclet, Alain J., 235
Straw, Carole, 238
Suelzer, Mary Josephine, 237, 239
Sulpicius Severus, 77
  Life of St. Martin of Tours, 120
Sundberg, Albert C., 217
Sutton Hoo, 184
Symmachus, pope, 87–8
Synod of Whitby, 147

Tacitus, 181, 185
Taio of Saragossa, 95
Tangl, M., 255, 259, 270, 273, 274
Tartarus, 7, 150
Tertullian, 25, 35, 86
Thacker, Alan, 216
Theodore of Tarsus, 174–5
Theodosian Code, 58
Thompson, F. Hugh, 53, 227
three Hebrews in fiery furnace, 23
torment in hell, eternity of, 149–50, 163–6
  intermittent, 154
Torthelm of Leicester, 171
Toscano, Margaret, 238
Trajan, Emperor, 191

trental, 90
Trumbower, Jeffrey A., 10, 21, 26, 189, 215, 217, 218, 219, 220, 274

Uhalde, Kevin, 245
Ultán, 117, 128

Vacandard, E., 273
Van Dam, Raymond, 72, 231, 234, 235, 238
Van der Walt, A. G. P., 259
Venantius Fortunatus, 22, 105
Vessey, Mark, 270
Vincent of Lérins, 209
Vision of 757, Fragmentary, 114, 130–2, 140, 202–3
Vision of Barontus, 10, 100, 113, 115, 120, 124, 138, 202
Vision of Drythelm. See Bede
Vision of Fursey, 10, 93, 95, 100–1, 106, 111, 113–22, 124–30, 135–6, 142, 145, 149, 152, 155, 158, 201
  see also Fursey
Vision of Paul, 42, 49, 51–5, 57, 60, 81, 95, 99, 101, 115, 123, 128, 131, 134, 149–50, 188, 197
Vision of Paul, Redaction 6, 132–4, 188, 201–2, 205
Vision of the Monk of Wenlock. See Boniface
Vision of Wetti, 100, 106, 145, 202–3, 205
visions of the afterlife, 17, 49–50, 99–101, 106, 112–13, 143, 175, 196–7
  'corporeal' depictions of, 49, 50, 238 n. 1, 242 n. 64
Vitalian, pope, 61
Vogel, Cyril, 258
von Balthasar, Hans Urs, 217
von Franz, M. L., 27, 219
von Padberg, Lutz E., 271
Von Tischendorf, Constantin, 226
Vovelle, Michel, 214, 245

Warren, F. E., 247
Wearmouth–Jarrow, 147, 175
weeping, 17, 103–4, 107, 159, 166, 189
Wells, Peter S., 272
Whitby *Life of Gregory*, 91, 177, 191
Whitelock, Dorothy, 276
Wiala, 131

Wickham, Chris, 229
Wihtred of Kent, Decrees of, 200–1
Wilfrid of Ripon, 172
Williams, Howard, 272
Willibrord, 148, 176

Wood, Ian N., 178, 249, 253, 259, 270, 271, 272, 273, 275
Wormald, Patrick, 170, 197, 198, 268, 275
Wright, Thomas, 215

Zaleski, Carol, 250

www.ingramcontent.com/pod-product-compliance
Ingram Content Group UK Ltd.
Pitfield, Milton Keynes, MK11 3LW, UK
UKHW041959230426
12048UKWH00008B/427